DIVINATION

Divination is any ritual and its associated tradition performed in order to ask a more-than-human intelligence for guidance. A universal human practice, it has received surprisingly little academic attention. This interdisciplinary collection by leading scholars in the field is dedicated to fascinating new insights into divination and oracles arising from recent work in anthropology, religious studies, history and classical studies.

Central importance is given to the practical and theoretical perspectives of diviners as well as scholars of divination; several contributors are both. This book explores philosophical issues such as the nature of divinatory intelligence, the relationship between divinatory and metaphorical truth, the primacy of ontology over epistemology, the importance of reflexivity in scholarly studies of divination, and astrology as the principal Western form of divination. The ethnographic and historical examples range from contemporary Nigeria, urban Cuba, Mayan Guatemala and the shamanic cultures of the circumpolar Arctic to classical Greece and ancient Judea.

Divination
Perspectives for a New Millennium

Edited by

PATRICK CURRY

ASHGATE

Published by
Ashgate Publishing Limited
Wey Court East
Union Road
Farnham
Surrey, GU9 7PT
England

Ashgate Publishing Company
Suite 420
101 Cherry Street
Burlington
VT 05401-4405
USA

www.ashgate.com

British Library Cataloguing in Publication Data
Divination : perspectives for a new millennium.
1. Divination.
I. Curry, Patrick.
203.2-dc22

Library of Congress Cataloging-in-Publication Data
Divination : perspectives for a new millennium / [edited by] Patrick Curry.
    p. cm.
Includes bibliographical references and index.
ISBN 978-1-4094-0555-9 (hardcover : alk. paper) 1. Divination. I. Curry, Patrick.
BF1751.D62 2010
133.3—dc22

2010014655

ISBN 9781409405559 (hbk)
ISBN 9781409405566 (ebk)

Mixed Sources
Product group from well-managed
forests and other controlled sources
www.fsc.org Cert no. SA-COC-1565
© 1996 Forest Stewardship Council

Printed and bound in Great Britain by
MPG Books Group, UK

Contents

Notes on Contributors

Chantal Allison holds an MA in Cultural Astronomy and Astrology and maintains an ongoing interest in the relationship between astrology, divination and the imaginal. She is currently conducting research into divinatory astrology and the historical process in preparation for a Ph.D. Her article on a horoscope by Masha 'alla (tenth century) has been published in *Culture & Cosmos*. She is a founder member of The Imaginals academic peer group.

Geoffrey Cornelius has been a consultant and teacher of divination for many years, with a close interest in the practice and philosophy of astrology. He has taught on programmes in Religious Studies at the University of Kent, and was one of the organizers of the MA in the Cultural Study of Cosmology and Divination. His published writings include 'Verity and the Question of Primary and Secondary Scholarship in Astrology' in Nicholas Campion, Patrick Curry and Michael York (eds), *Astrology and the Academy* (Cinnabar Books, 2004), 'Cardano Incognito: A Review of Antony Grafton Cardano's *Cosmos: The Worlds and Works of a Renaissance Astrologer*' (*Culture & Cosmos*, 2005) and 'From Primitive Mentality to *Haecceity*: The Unique Case in Astrology and Divination' in Patrick Curry and Angela Voss (eds), *Seeing with Different Eyes: Essays in Astrology and Divination* (Cambridge Scholars Press, 2007). Within the specialist study of astrology, his principal writing is *The Moment of Astrology: Origins in Divination* (Penguin, 1994; rev. edn Wessex Astrologer, 2003).

Patrick Curry is an Honorary Research Fellow, Sophia Centre for the Study of Cosmology in Culture, University of Wales, Lampeter. From 2006 to 2009 he lectured in Religious Studies at the University of Kent, Canterbury, where he taught an MA on the Cultural Study of Cosmology and Divination, and from 2002 to 2006 at the Sophia Centre, Bath Spa University. He holds a Ph.D. in the History and Philosophy of Science from University College London. He is the author of several books, most recently *Defending Middle-Earth: Tolkien, Myth & Modernity* (rev. edn Boston: Houghton Mifflin, 2004), *Astrology, Science and Culture: Pulling Down the Moon*, co-authored with Roy Willis (Berg, 2004) and *Ecological Ethics: An Introduction* (Polity, 2006), the last due to appear in a revised edition in 2011. His principal scholarly interests include divination, cultural and political ecology, and enchantment.

Paul Devereux is a research associate at the Royal College of Art, London, and is a founding co-editor of *Time & Mind – The Journal of Archaeology, Consciousness and Culture* (Berg, Oxford). He is a Fellow of the Royal Society of Arts, a Senior

Research Fellow of International Consciousness Research Laboratories (ICRL), Princeton, and a member of the Scientific & Medical Network. Over a period of nearly 30 years he has written or co-written some 26 books for general readerships, primarily on archaeological and anthropological themes, as well as a range of academic papers. His research interests focus especially on archaeoacoustics, the cognitive aspects of archaeology and the anthropology of consciousness. His latest book is Sacred Geography (Gaia Books, 2010).

Dorian Gieseler Greenbaum received her Ph.D. from the Warburg Institute in 2009, with a dissertation entitled 'The *Daimon* in Hellenistic Astrology: Origins and Influence'. She is the author of a number of articles on the history and philosophy of astrology and divination, including 'Rising to the Occasion: Appearance, Emergence, Light and Divination in Hellenistic Astrology', in Angela Voss and Jean Hinson Lall (eds), *The Imaginal Cosmos: Astrology, Divination and the Sacred* (University of Kent, 2007), 'From Lilly to Steiner and Jung: Temperament in Astrology and Psychology, Seventeenth and Twentieth Centuries', in Anna Akasoy, Charles Burnett and Ronit Yoeli-Tlalim (eds), *Astro-Medicine: Astrology and Medicine, East and West*, Micrologus' Library 25 (Florence, 2008) and (with Micah Ross) 'The Role of Egypt in the Development of the Horoscope', in *Proceedings of the Conference 'Social and Religious Development of Egypt in the First Millennium BCE'* (Prague, 2010). She has contributed seven entries to the new *Encyclopedia of Ancient History*, to be published by Blackwell in 2010. She is also a translator and annotator of ancient astrological texts.

Laura S. Grillo holds a Ph.D. in history of religions from the University of Chicago, an M.Div. from Union Theological Seminary and an A.B. in religious studies from Brown University. She teaches at Pacifica Graduate Institute. Her fieldwork on West African divination was sponsored by the National Endowment for the Humanities, the American Academy of Religions and the West Africa Research Association. Her memoir won her six Writer's Residency Fellowships for creative non-fiction from Ragdale and The Virginia Center for the Creative Arts. Recent publications include '"When You Make Sacrifice, No One is a Stranger": Divination, Sacrifice and Identity among Translocals in the West African Urban Diaspora', in A. Adogame and J. Spickard (eds), *Religion Crossing Boundaries* (E.J. Brill, forthcoming) and 'Divination: Epistemology, Agency and the Construction of Identity in Contemporary West Africa' (*Religion Compass*, 2009).

Stuart R. Harrop is the Director of the Durrell Institute of Conservation and Ecology within the School of Anthropology and Conservation in the University of Kent. As an academic he is particularly interested in the relationship between traditional/cultural practices and nature conservation, especially as these are addressed in international law and policy. He also advises the United Nations Food and Agriculture Organization on policy issues relating to traditional agriculture and conservation. He has won and currently holds a number of grants. The most salient of these in the context of this book is a UK Government Darwin Initiative award in excess of £200,000, funding research into the relationship between religion and rainforest conservation in Sumatra. Relevant publications include 'Human Diversity and the Diversity of Life: International Regulation of the Role of Indigenous and Rural Human Communities in Conservation' (*Malayan Law Journal*, 2003), 'Indigenous Peoples, Traditional Ecological Knowledge and the Perceived Threat of the Intellectual Property Rights Regime' (*Law, Science and Policy*, 2004), 'Globally Important Agricultural Heritage System: An Examination of their Context in Existing Multilateral Instruments Dealing with Conservation and Protected Areas' (*Journal of International Wildlife Law and Policy*, 2009) and 'Shamanism, Nature Conservation and International Law' (*Journal of Shamanic Practice*, 2009).

Evan Heimlich lectures widely on performance and discourse, religious and secular metaphysics, as well as cultural history and theory. He has taught Western Civilization at Haskell Indian Nations University, and for a decade taught Intercultural Studies at Kobe University, a national university of Japan. At the time of this writing he was a Visiting Scholar at the Center for Ideas and Society, University of California at Riverside. His publications include ethnographies of Gypsies, Tibetan exiles and Francophone-Americans, a paper on applied political theory in *Trans/American, Trans/Oceanic, Trans/lation: Issues in International American Studies* and a political analysis of cinema in *You're History*, the book that answered Bob Geldof's call for an Intellectual Live 8. He is writing a monograph that examines how certain modern forms of reading function as divination.

Martin Holbraad works in the Anthropology Department of University College London. He has conducted fieldwork on Afro-Cuban religion in Havana since 1998. His research focuses on the relationship between myth and action, the consecration of objects and, more broadly, the logic of cosmological thought in the field of religion as well as in politics. His is co-editor of *Thinking Through Things: Theorising Artefacts Ethnographically* (Routledge, 2007) and 'Technologies of the Imagination' (*Ethnos*, 2009). His monograph on Cuban divination and anthropological truth is in preparation.

Philip M. Peek began African Studies as a Peace Corps teacher in Nigeria, 1964–66. At UC/Berkeley he converted from Comparative Literature to Folklore (MA, 1968). After fieldwork among the Isoko of the Niger Delta, he received a Ph.D. in Folklore from Indiana University in 1976. He recently retired from Drew University where he taught in the Anthropology Department for thirty-seven years. Connections with Africa increased over the years with further research, student programmes and travel to ten different African countries. In addition to numerous articles on African arts and expressive behaviour, especially verbal arts, his publications include *African Divination Systems: Ways of Knowing* (Indiana University Press, 1991), *Ways of the River: Arts and Environment in the Niger Delta* (co-edited with Martha Anderson) (UCLA Fowler Museum, 2002), *African*

Folklore: An Encyclopedia (co-edited with Kwesi Yankah) (Routledge, 2004) and *Divination and Healing: Potent Vision* (co-edited with Michael Winkelman) (University of Arizona Press, 2004). Current projects focus on twins in Africa and divination.

Juha Pentikäinen has been Research Professor of Northern Ethnography, University of Lapland, since 2008. He was founding professor of comparative religion, University of Helsinki, 1970–2008, Research Director of Northern Ecology and Religions, Norwegian Academy, 1997–98 and has held guest professor positions at UC Berkeley, UC Santa Barbara, UCLA, the University of Texas, the University of Indiana and the University of Minnesota. His principal subjects include Northern ethnography, comparative religion, folkloristics and Finno-Ugric mythologies. He is the author of approximately thirty books, 400 scientific articles and ten films on ethnography, comparative religion and folklore; for a bibliography up to 2000, see the *Festschrift: Ethnography is a Heavy Rite: Studies of Comparative Religion in Honor of Juha Pentikäinen* (Åbo Academy Press, 2000). The results of his field work from the 1950s until the present were donated to the University of Lapland in 2007 as the basis of the Northern Ethnography Museum and Digital Archive to be built in the 2010s. Recent publications include *Golden King of the Forest: The Lore of the Northern Bear* (Etnika, 2007), *Shamanhood: An Endangered Language*, ed. with Péter Simoncsics (Novus, 2006), *Shamanhood: Symbolism and Epic* (Akadémiai Kiadó, 2001), *Shamans* (Tampere Museum Publications, 1998), S*hamanism and Culture* (Etnika, 1998) and *Shamanism and Northern Ecology*, ed. (Mouton de Gruyter, 1996).

Petra Stapp currently works in the field of environmental compliance in a national waste management company, having previous experience as a police officer and as an animal health officer within DEFRA. She completed the MA in Cultural Astronomy and Astrology at Bath Spa University in 2006 and is researching a Ph.D. into the phenomenological aspects of human–animal relationships at the University of Wales, Lampeter. She is a founder member of The Imaginals peer group.

Barbara Tedlock is Distinguished Professor of Anthropology at the State University of New York at Buffalo and Research Associate of the Museum of International Folk Art in Santa Fe, New Mexico. Her research and writing has been funded by the National Endowment for the Humanities, National Institutes of Health, the Institute for Advanced Study at Princeton, the Center for the Study of World Religions at Harvard, American Council of Learned Societies, Mellon Foundation, the American Philosophical Society and other foundations. She has published more than a hundred essays and articles together with five books. These include *Teachings: From the American Earth: Indian Religion and Philosophy* (Norton, 1992), *Time and the Highland Maya* (University of New Mexico, 1992), *Dreaming: Anthropological and Psychological Interpretations* (Cambridge

University Press, 1987), *The Beautiful and the Dangerous: Encounters with the Zuni* (Viking, 2001) and *The Woman in the Shaman's Body: Reclaiming the Feminine in Religion and Medicine* (Random House Bantam, 2005).

Anthony Thorley is a retired consultant psychiatrist and medical policy administrator who has been researching landscape energies, myths and historical traditions for over twenty years. In 2006 he graduated with an MA in Cultural Astronomy and Astrology at Bath Spa University and published 'Perceptions of Divination in the Astrological Consultation: A Pilot Study' (*Correlation*, 2006). Currently he is completing a book, *Sacred City, Secret City*, on the Masonic vision of the development of eighteenth-century Bath. In 2009 he published his first novel, *Well Below Average* (Archive). Since 2009 he has been pursuing postgraduate research for a Ph.D. on the conceptual basis of landscape zodiacs as sacred space and acting as part-time tutor in sacred geography at the University of Wales, Lampeter. He is a founder member of The Imaginals peer group.

Angela Voss is an associate lecturer in Religious Studies at the University of Kent, Canterbury, where she pioneered both undergraduate and postgraduate programmes in the cultural study of cosmology and divination. She is also a faculty member for the MA in Western Esotericism at the University of Exeter. Her research background is in music and Renaissance esotericism, and she has published extensively on the astrology of Marsilio Ficino, most recently in *Marsilio Ficino* (North Atlantic Books, 2006). She is also the co-editor (with Patrick Curry) of *Seeing with Different Eyes: Essays on Astrology and Divination* (Cambridge Scholars Press, 2007) and co-editor (with Jean Hinson Lall) of *The Imaginal Cosmos: Astrology, Divination and the Sacred* (University of Kent, 2007). She is interested in all aspects of the symbolic imagination as a means of spiritual knowledge, from ancient times to the present day.

John Wadsworth is a professional astrologer and independent scholar. He holds an MA in Cultural Astronomy & Astrology and is currently preparing a Ph.D. on the imaginal nature of zodiacs. A founder member of The Imaginals peer group, he has been running a twelve-month programme in zodiac mysteries called 'The Alchemical Journey' since 2006.

Preface

The papers in this volume originated in a conference at the University of Kent in October 2007 entitled 'Divination and Dialogue'. I would like wholeheartedly to thank the participants and speakers, and in particular my colleagues there at the time, Angela Voss and Geoffrey Cornelius. Two earlier conferences at Kent on the same general theme are represented by Angela Voss and Patrick Curry (eds), *Seeing with Different Eyes: Essays on Astrology and Divination* (Newcastle: Cambridge Scholars Press, 2008) and Angela Voss and Jean Hinson Lall (eds), *The Imaginal Cosmos: Astrology, Divination and the Sacred* (Canterbury: University of Kent, 2007). I would also like to thank Sarah Lloyd of Ashgate for her help from beginning to end, and Alie Bird for her invaluable assistance with editing. I also gratefully acknowledge a grant assisting with editorial expenses from the Urania Trust.

Patrick Curry

Chapter 1

Introduction

Patrick Curry

Divination is ubiquitous throughout human history and societies. Reflecting that fact, the chapters in this volume are correspondingly singular and diverse. They range in period from ancient Greece to contemporary Britain, and in place from Africa to Siberia. In terms of academic disciplines, too, we find anthropology, classical history and philosophy – sometimes within the same chapter. And such diversity is not only unavoidable but arguably a positive virtue when the subject is so multifaceted (not to say polymorphously perverse).

It would be one-sided, however, to stop with that impression; for there are significant underlying connections, if no complete unity. Let me try briefly to identify those threads. Barbara Tedlock synthesizes the history of dream oracles, the anthropological ethnography of divination and recent breakthroughs in biophysical medicine to demonstrate the continuing coexistence of an 'integrative' divinatory mode with ordinary consciousness. She also breaks valuable new ground in the complex epistemology of that mode.

Philip Peek examines another rich new vein of this subject matter, namely twinning between African diviners and spirit others as well as their clients. This is an instance of the human (natural and cultural) phenomenon of twins, which these diviners have developed in ways that both draw upon and contribute to a cosmology of many worlds and forces. As one comes to expect with divination, it is one with resonances both very old and very new.

Laura Grillo's chapter introduces an autoethnographic memoir of African divination in which she turns the ineliminability of a personal dimension from a problem into an invaluable way to explore the subject more deeply. Again, insofar as all scholarship necessarily includes such a dimension, there are lessons here for us all.

Juha Pentikäinen conducts a valuable overview of Northern European shamanism, a way of life to which divination was and, insofar as it survives, is still central. Given the history of this region, his work of recovery and recording is poignantly ethico-political, but it also has fascinating implications for human consciousness. Despite the considerable differences between 'their' lives and 'ours', the shamans' divinatory cosmos is by no means unrecognizable.

Stuart Harrop, in another exciting new departure, situates divination in relation to natural and human ecology. Human ecological practices have consequences for non-human nature of which we are, perforce, becoming constantly more aware. Those that Harrop considers, which include divination as an integral part, have archaic roots; but to dismiss them on that account would be to lose vital lessons that increase our own chances of survival. One of modernity's most dangerous blind spots is its instinctive contempt for 'superstition'.

My own chapter attempts to negotiate the untenable extremes of both 'established materialism' and 'romantic supernaturalism' by locating (somewhat ambitiously) the human modus vivendi as a middle way which partakes of both matter and spirit/mind but is reducible to neither.[1] Sharpening that understanding, I identify Merleau-Ponty's concept of embodiment as 'chiasmic' with Ricoeur's concept of metaphor as 'tensive'. Divination then becomes a special but characteristically human enterprise, one with implications I begin to explore.

Geoffrey Cornelius gives us that rarity, a relevant new concept. Using the still-seminal ethnography of Evans-Pritchard and theorizing of Lévy-Bruhl, together with his own phenomenological experiments, he brings out the unsettling implications of the chicane, properly understood, for both a reductionistic dismissal and a naïve acceptance of divination. (Within the academy, of course, the former – usually sociological and/or psychological – is much more common.)

Evan Heimlich makes a strikingly original case for mantology, the cultural study of divination, as a new integrated academic discipline. It is one that is as comprehensive and cross-disciplinary as the phenomenon of divination itself. Heimlich comprehensively undermines the view of divination as a primitive, atavistic behavioural relic, pointing to its vital presence in the most modern activities in a way that indicates its potential richness as a field of study, and demonstrates the kind of theoretical sophistication which will be needed to realize that potential.

Dorian Gieseler Greenbaum considers classical Greek astrology in a new light – as a stochastic divinatory art – which relates it integrally with the ancient practice of medicine (something she establishes in considerable detail) as well as navigation and rhetoric. One significant implication is that insofar as challenges remain today that cannot dispense with personal judgement and experience, attempts to meet them require just the same kind of non-algorhythmic strategies. On the same basis it could also be argued that divination, as such a strategy, remains as relevant as ever.

Angela Voss courageously explores the parallels, from tantalizing to striking, between Michael Newton's 'Life between Lives', a therapy/cosmology which could be described as 'New Age' but is in any case certainly new, and the initiatory and divinatory rituals of the ancient world. Once again, we encounter the apparent paradox of an unmistakably 'other' mode of perception and consciousness which nonetheless remains unmistakably present and active in the modern world.

Paul Devereux briefly examines the remarkable survival of archaic necromantic divination as a 'folk belief' which has endured into modernity, partly thanks to the

---

[1]   These terms are Gregory Bateson's, from Gregory and Mary Catherine Bateson, *Angels Fear: An Investigation into the Nature and Meaning of the Sacred* (London: Rider, 1987), p. 64.

counter-modern revival of interest in pre-modern practices and ideas to which his own work has contributed.

Finally, Anthony Thorley, Chantal Allison, Petra Stapp and John Wadsworth ground the more specialized phenomenon of specialized or professional 'practitioner divination' in the more general, not to say universal, human experience of 'essential divination' – itself arguably rooted in the natural world of which we are necessarily a part. They then explore the considerable methodological import of this view.

Divination and the Academy

Bruno Latour has famously pointed out that in fact – that is, in lived practice – 'we have never been modern'.[2] Yet it is also undeniable that wherever and whenever historians may locate its beginnings, modernity is a defensible general term for both a sensibility and (more controversially) a period, a core characteristic of which, to quote Leszek Kolakowski, 'is summed up, of course, in the Weberian *Entzauberung* – disenchantment – or in any similar word roughly covering the same phenomenon'.[3] Another equally apt description might be the apparent triumph of *logos* over *mythos* with 'the myth of mythlessness'.[4] The implication returns us to Latour's point, however; the real triumph is one of official ideological practice over personal quotidian practice, with the schizoid fracturing of experience that that implies.

What is the relevance of this process, both 'subjective' and 'objective', to divination studies or (in Evan Heimlich's excellent term) mantology? There are two crucial considerations. One is that, broadly but undeniably, divination was left firmly stranded on the wrong side of the metaphysical, intellectual and social tracks. Now it would be possible to examine this phenomenon as an instance of the larger debate over the complex relationship between 'magic' and 'modernity'.[5]

---

[2]   Bruno Latour, *We Have Never Been Modern*, trans. Catherine Porter (Hemel Hempstead: Harvester Wheatsheaf, 1993).

[3]   Leszek Kolakowski, *Modernity on Endless Trial* (Chicago: University of Chicago Press, 1990), p. 7. See also Roy Willis and Patrick Curry, *Astrology, Science and Culture* (Oxford: Berg, 2004), ch. 4.

[4]   Robert Jewett and John Shelton Lawrence, quoted in Laurence Coupe, *Myth*, 2nd edn (London: Routledge, 2009), p. 12. For another excellent discussion, see Sean Kane, *Wisdom of the Mythtellers*, 2nd edn (Peterborough: Broadview Press, 1998), as well as Mary Midgley, *Science as Salvation: A Modern Myth and its Meaning* (London: Routledge, 1992) and *The Myths We Live By* (London: Routledge, 2003).

[5]   Of recent literature, see (in anthropology) Birgit Meyer and Peter Pels (eds), *Magic and Modernity: Interfaces of Revelation and Concealment* (Stanford: Stanford University Press, 2003) and (in history) Alex Owen, *The Place of Enchantment: British Occultism and the Culture of the Modern* (Chicago: University of Chicago Press, 2004).

In my view, however, that would be misleading. For one thing, although there are certainly connections, divination cannot seamlessly be accommodated to the category of magic. For another, we should try to retain its distinctiveness at the same time as recognizing its multiplicity and ubiquity.

The other consideration is that relatedly but more specifically, the formation of the modern academy is deeply implicated in that of modernity in ways that have had powerful effects, not just on the methods and concepts that dominate academic life but on its values too. In conjunction with the first, this development has resulted in the established ascendency of an assumption that divination is not really a worthy or fit subject of study and, as a corollary, if it is studied the appropriate way to do so is to treat it as a failed version of something else: usually religion (itself always in danger of receiving the same sort of treatment in turn) or science (proto-, pseudo- or simply ineffective). In anthropology, where divination can be difficult to avoid, the latter variant as a strategy of control and domestication is still very active as evolutionary cognitivism, both social and neurophysiological. Keeping the discussion in the plane of epistemology and therefore solely on questions of belief, representation and so on is very convenient, especially when combined with social functionalism or a functionalist structuralism. It simultaneously invokes the assumed authority of evolutionary theory, allows the observer-theorist to distance him- or herself from the subject matter and its human subjects, and then to inform them what they are 'really' doing. You believe; we know. That effectively prevents the discussion from moving onto ground that reflexively includes, and therefore could radically question, *all* parties: in other words, practice (of which theory is a part; not the reverse) and ontology (of which epistemology is a part; not the reverse). To put it another way, disagreements here are not 'in opinions but in form of life'.[6] If you really want to understand a divinatory form of life, you will have to open up to it in a way that 'allow[s] the material to touch the observer *as truth for the observer*'.[7]

The assumption about divination I have just described, alternately reductive and patronizing, could well be thought of as a *mentalité*: a durable (because largely unconscious) attitude held with considerable emotional animus frequently combined with almost complete ignorance. If I may be permitted a personal anecdote, in my own department at the time of writing (one principally comprising philosophers certainly no less than usually intelligent and no more than usually benighted), I was once semi-publicly interrogated at some length on my research. This culminated in the palpably outraged question, 'Do you *practise* divination?' However unintentionally, this question in its context constitutes a valuable datum, so let us examine it a bit more closely.

---

[6]   Ludwig Wittgenstein, *Philosophical Investigations*, ed. G.E.M. Anscombe (Oxford: Blackwell, 2001), passage 241.

[7]   Geoffrey Cornelius, 'Verity and the Question of Primary and Secondary Scholarship in Astrology', in Nicholas Campion, Patrick Curry and Michael York (eds), *Astrology and the Academy* (Bristol: Cinnabar Books, 2004), pp. 103–13, at p. 108; emphasis in original.

In a more reflective mood, I might have replied by asking whether a historian of art, say, or a philosopher of science would be asked an equivalent question (and in an equivalent way); the obvious negative answer should suffice to show the special treatment reserved for divination. For the question as posed cannot be answered without damage; indeed, that is its very point. Either 'no' or 'yes' only confirms that divination is some special practice requiring special treatment: quarantine, say, followed by decontamination. Furthermore, a 'no', if true, means that the scholar is – perhaps as a consequence – willing to cut her- or himself off from a resource that could have a crucial bearing on her or his scholarship; whereas a 'yes' serves to identify the scholar as a patent irrationalist. (In the event, feeling that I may as well be hung for a sheep as for a lamb, I simply answered, 'Yes, of course!' An astonished silence ensued before the subject was changed.)

I have written extensively elsewhere – critically and, I hope, constructively – on this phenomenon, particularly with reference to astrology as the most durable, widespread and complex form of Western divination.[8] Obviously, it is part of a very long process, at least in historical terms, in which (to quote the eminent philosopher and historian of science Isabelle Stengers) 'objectivity itself has a polemical origin, an origin that cannot be dissociated from the overwhelming concern of silencing story-tellers, quacks, popular customs and creeds, knowledge without credential. They are witnesses for the fact that our history is also that of a process of eradication.' And now, to a significant extent, the academy itself has fallen victim to the same process:

> the multifaceted machine called technoscience is in the process of redefining our own worlds in terms that makes them available for its comparative operations. The relative passivity of the academic world, lending itself to ranking systems of evaluation and productivity comparison which reshape it in a radical manner, is sufficient to demonstrate how easy it is to have people, [even those] who are not naïve or impressed or overpowered, to submit to questions that are not only irrelevant but, as such, sound the death-knell of what matters for them.[9]

---

[8]   Patrick Curry, 'Astrology on Trial, and its Historians: Reflections on the Historiography of "Superstition"', *Culture and Cosmos* 4/2 (2000): 47–56; 'The Historiography of Astrology: A Diagnosis and a Prescription', in K. von Stuckrad, G. Oestmann and D. Rutkin (eds), *Horoscopes and Public Spheres* (Berlin and New York: Walter de Gruyter, 2005), pp. 261–74; 'Introduction', in Angela Voss and Patrick Curry (eds), *Seeing with Different Eyes: Essays on Astrology and Divination* (Newcastle: Cambridge Scholars Press, 2008), pp. ix–xiv. See also Alison Bird, 'Astrology in Education: An Ethnography', D.Phil. thesis (University of Sussex, 2006) and Garry Phillipson, 'Astrology: A Context for Heresy', Ph.D. thesis in progress (University of Wales, Lampeter).

[9]   Isabelle Stengers, 'Comparison as a Matter of Concern', a paper given at the University of Copenhagen on 3 September 2009, forthcoming in *Common Knowledge*.

That point takes us beyond what can be directly addressed here, however. What I want to bring out is simply what emerges from the chapters of this collection: that divination is a very particular kind of human practice with ancient roots that go very deep, yet it is also still very much at work and at play in the contemporary world. It is at once genuinely exotic and common. The challenge to the academy, then, is to recognize and transcend its own formative blind spot by addressing and seriously attempting to theorize it. Anything less would entail betrayal of one of the academy's most fundamental ideals: *Homo sum; humani nil a me alienum puto*. And in the category of 'less' I include any attempts, no matter how ingenious, to accommodate divination without any significant changes in what 'we' already 'know'. Describing and adjusting conditions of native error (regardless of who the natives are) simply will not do. As A.N. Whitehead remarked, 'Philosophy destroys its usefulness when it indulges in brilliant feats of explaining away.'[10]

That observation has only gained force as the pressure increases to explain everything 'scientifically' in a way, and to an extent, that can only be scientistic, not to say imperialistic. It is vitally important that this programme – alternately seductive and coercive, and far from disinterestedly well funded – be resisted. Its imperialism and vacuity alike have been repeatedly exposed (not least by Midgley and Stengers, already mentioned, but also immortally by Paul Feyerabend) but as any 'relativist' worth her salt knows, that in itself settles nothing. But for any prospect of success, it must be resisted intelligently. It is imperative to heed the warning of Eduardo Viveiros de Castro not to engage in 'a simple-minded ontology of mind *versus* matter' by simply counter-asserting the importance or autonomy of the former. I cannot sufficiently emphasize that attempting to contest the reduction of 'representation to reality (cognitivism, sociobiology, evolutionary psychology)' by urging the reduction of 'reality to representation (culturalism, relativism, textualism)' is a fool's errand. In uncritically accepting the fundamental assumptions of the debate itself, such a move covertly legitimizes its opponent, and encourages the whole tedious and fruitless 'tug-of-war' to continue.[11] Rather what is needed is a radical re-theorizing of body, mind and world in ways that contextualize and (so to speak) provincialize all three, that reveal their contingency and their constitutive, not merely external, interrelations. (And may I add that the observation Viveiros de Castro appends to his warning – that 'Even phenomenology … may be a surrender to epistemology' – is also true, but my own chapter seeks to show that it need not, and should not, be so.)

---

[10] A.N. Whitehead, *Process and Reality: An Essay in Cosmology*, ed. David Ray Griffin and Donald W. Sherburne (New York: Free Press, 1979 [1929]), p. 17.

[11] Eduardo Viveiros de Castro, 'Exchanging Perspectives: The Transformation of Objects into Subjects in Amerindian Cosmologies', *Common Knowledge* 10/3 (2004): 463–84, at 484. Quite independently, David Abram, *The Spell of the Sensuous: Perception and Language in a More-Than-Human World* (New York: Vintage Books, 1997), p. 67 sounds exactly the same warning.

In contrast to brilliant feats of explaining away, any such serious theorization of divination will require some fundamental revisions of what 'we know', for reasons and in respects that have been powerfully set out by Martin Holbraad.[12] Indeed, the sine qua non of accepting and working reflexively with ontology – which includes taking divination seriously in its own right – is only the beginning; what follows is the hard work of revising our inappropriate starting concepts accordingly. (In this context, the potential advantages of the observer/theorist also being a practitioner are obvious.)

Promising Paths

In the work presented here, we can already see some of the ways such a project might proceed. At least three related paths, all with paradigm-shifting implications, suggest themselves. One is a post-rationalist concept of truth, no longer universalist and epistemological but rather variously describable as participatory (in the way initiated in anthropology by the brave late work of Lucien Lévy-Bruhl),[13] reflexively performative (rather than descriptive or propositional), pragmatic (in the sense pioneered by William James),[14] pluralist (also sometimes termed 'relativism', although not to be confused with the 'straw herring' of vulgar relativism)[15] and perspectival (especially as developed, through his work with Amerindian culture, by Eduardo Viveiros de Castro).[16] In the present collection, see the contributions of Cornelius, Heimlich and Holbraad for more on this issue.

The second promising path is a post-Cartesian view of bodies no longer as basically inanimate and interchangeable stuff, no matter how complex, but instead as living agents possessed of intelligences, far exceeding our conscious awareness, some of which can be developed by some individuals in very sophisticated ways.

---

[12] Martin Holbraad, 'Definitive Evidence, from Cuban Gods', in Matthew Engelke (ed.), *The Objects of Evidence: Anthropological Approaches to the Production of Knowledge* (Malden and Oxford: Wiley-Blackwell, 2009), pp. 89–104; 'Ontography and Alterity: Defining Anthropological Truth', *Social Analysis* 53/2 (2009): 80–93.

[13] See the discussion in Stanley Jeyaraja Tambiah, *Magic, Science, Religion, and the Scope of Rationality* (Cambridge: Cambridge University Press, 1990), ch. 5. Lévy-Bruhl's late work has been inexcusably ignored and derided.

[14] See Harvey Cormier, *The Truth is What Works: William James, Pragmatism, and the Seed of Death* (Latham, MD: Rowman and Littlefield, 2001). Academic philosophy has paid for its marginalization of philosophers such as James, Michael Polanyi and Stephen Toulmin by abandoning nearly all of the ground where nearly all people live nearly all of their lives.

[15] Barbara Herrnstein Smith's term; see her excellent *Contingencies of Value: Alternative Perspectives for Critical Theory* (Cambridge, MA: Harvard University Press, 1988) and *Belief and Resistance: Dynamics of Contemporary Intellectual Controversy* (Cambridge, MA: Harvard University Press, 1997). See also Latour, *We Have Never Been Modern*.

[16] A good starting point is his 'Exchanging Perspectives'.

Maurice Merleau-Ponty is unmistakably the philosopher who opened our eyes (those who want to see, at least) in this respect. There is a critical point of contact at work here with perspectivism, inasmuch as the body – conceived as 'an assemblage of affects or ways of being that constitute a *habitus*' – is the site of perspectives.[17] Other anthropologists have also moved in this direction. James Fernandez, for example, remarks that 'the best diviners are ones who are exceptionally well tuned in to the primary processes where so many of our problems lie'.[18] And Filip de Boeck and René Devisch – who concur that divination does not mimic or model a world (*pace* Victor Turner) but 'rather makes a world' – also observe that it 'constitutes a space in which cognitive structures are transformed and new *relations* are generated in and between the human body (senses, emotions), the social body and the cosmos'. Accordingly, they argue, 'the cognitive, meaning-centered level in Turner's analysis needs to be balanced by a more praxiological dimension, in which the emphasis is put on agency, enforcement and worldmaking rather than on structure and social engineering ... Attention should be devoted to divination as act rather than fact.'[19] For more on this rich construal of embodiment in this volume, see the contributions of Tedlock, Greenbaum and Curry.[20]

The third way forward is a post-secular recognition and admission of the spiritual or 'metanatural', albeit also in a rigorously non-dualistic sense, as another active participant in determining what happens. Divination may indeed be 'an utterly human art',[21] but if that statement is intended to mean that necessarily only humans are involved, it falls foul of the critique already developed by ignoring or reinterpreting (anachronistically and/or ethnocentrically) the avowals of diviners themselves, highly consistent across both cultures and historical periods, that working with more-than-human spirits is absolutely integral to divination, such that the divinatory outcome is as much a product of their agency as that of the diviner. The non-reality of spirits, like the quasi-machine reality of non-human

[17] Eduardo Viveiros de Castro, unpublished MS, 'Cosmological Perspectivism in Amazonia and Elsewhere', four lectures delivered 17 February–10 March 1998 at the Dept of Social Anthropology, Cambridge, p. 37.

[18] James W. Fernandez, 'Afterword', in Philip M. Peek (ed.), *African Divination Systems: Ways of Knowing* (Bloomington: Indiana University Press, 1991), pp. 213–21, at p. 220.

[19] Filip de Boeck and René Devisch, 'Ndembu, Luunda and Yaka Divination Compared: From Representation and Social Engineering to Embodiment and Worldmaking', *Journal pour Religion African* 24/2 (1994): 98–133; available at http://www.era.anthropology. ac.uk/Era_Resources/Era/Divination/boeck.html (accessed 7 October 2004); emphasis in original. Cf. Barbara Tedlock, 'Sacred Connections between Self, Other and the World: The Emergence of Integrative Medicine', in Curry and Voss, *Seeing*, pp. 311–27.

[20] See also Barbara Tedlock's pioneering *The Woman in the Shaman's Body: Reclaiming the Feminine in Religion and Medicine* (New York: Bantam Books, 2005).

[21] Sarah Iles Johnston, 'Introduction: Divining Divination', in Sarah Iles Johnston and Peter T. Struck (eds), *Mantikê: Studies in Ancient Divination* (Leiden: Brill, 2005), pp. 1–28, at pp. 10–11.

animals and the reservation of subjectivity for humans alone, is not carved in ontological stone, after all; it is merely the latest, strangest and most dangerous outcome of 'the ancient anthropological matrix, the one we have never abandoned'.[22] (And yes, 'we' includes we putative moderns too.) For good reason, reflections on this subject can be found throughout the present book.[23]

These three perspectives – truth, body and spirit – are intimately linked, both substantively and by their mutual distortion under what Latour calls the modern constitution. In their present forms, they are crying out for radical revision, and divination offers just the kind of Archimedean point that is needed for such an enterprise. It is my belief that this volume makes a signal contribution to taking up that challenge, beginning to address it and inviting all interested parties – whether inside or outside the academy – to join the conversation.

---

[22] Latour, *We Have Never Been Modern*, p. 107.

[23] See the recent doctoral thesis from the University of Kent by Geoffrey Cornelius, 'Field of Omens: the Hermeneutics of Inductive Divination' and another in progress there by James Brockbank, 'The Responsive Cosmos: An Inquiry into the Theoretical Foundations of Astrology'.

Chapter 2

Theorizing Divinatory Acts: The Integrative Discourse of Dream Oracles

Barbara Tedlock

All people in all times and places have practised divination as a way of exploring the unknown, making decisions, solving problems and diagnosing ailments. While there have been many attempts to describe diviners and their techniques, what has gone unexamined is the practice of self-knowledge and healing by means of making a pilgrimage to a dream oracle. To accomplish this we need a theory that allows for the experience of the numinous as a central element in the construction of an embodied sacred self. The description and evocation of such a self – consisting of imagination, memory and language – reveals the transformative efficacy of healing by means of a sacred mind–body dialogue within a specific cultural discourse. Here I am posing a theory of divinatory acts based on the practices of diviners who move along a continuum between rational and irrational utterances to arrive at social meaning.

There are hundreds of forms of divination including stargazing, sortilege, reading natural omens and the contemplation of amulets, crystals, mandalas and dreams. Using mediumistic or mantic techniques, readers of signs undergo mental, psychological and spiritual changes, becoming vehicles for numinous energy. In so doing they step aside and allow deities and ancestors to take their seats in their souls and speak ecstatically (*ekstasis* means 'to stand outside oneself') without translating or editing what they have heard, seen or felt kinaesthetically. As the divination proceeds, they may ask rational questions and receive information about the situation at hand. At other times and places animals, objects and events are used mechanically as rational signs sent by external superhuman powers. Temple inscriptions, papyri and the work of historians and hagiographers reveal that in ancient Egypt and Greece the commonest method of divination was through dream oracles. In a Greek papyrus from fifth-century Egypt we read:

> When Apollo enters, ask him about what you wish, about divination, oracle by means of epic poetry, sending of dreams, revelations in dreams, interpretation of dreams, incubation, about all that pertains to the magical experience.[1]

---

[1]   Polymnia Athanassiadi, 'Dreams, Theurgy, and Freelance Divination: The Testimony of Iamblichus', *Journal of Roman Studies* 83 (1993): 115–30.

Here we see that ancient Greeks emphasized the field of mantics and divination about the future by means of non-rational magical forms including dreaming. In late antiquity, mantic dreams had become the norm and by the end of the fifth century the Alexandrians called their dreams, answers or 'oracles'.

Theory, Memory and Manifestation

The English word 'theory' derives from the Greek noun *theoria*, which refers to a sacred pilgrimage to a distant land in order to consult an oracle. Such a visitation involves the observation of material objects together with a heightened form of witnessing or sacramental way of seeing. The Greek verb *theorein*, together with its Latin form *obsevatio*, indicates a journey with a divinatory purpose, combined with attentiveness in caring for sacred objects and places. Persons who undertook such journeys, called *theoros* in Greek, visited shrines where deities revealed themselves. In this ancient world, as in other traditional cultures, religious festivals created a suspension of the world of work, providing an opening for the holy to illuminate the everyday world. The *theoros*, as a festival spectator, found access to meaning as the ultimate support for earthly existence. In time, there was a change in the Greek concept of theory from a festive journey to a work-oriented form of educational travel. Further secularization brings us to our situation today in which a theorist goes to the laboratory, the place of labour, rather than going on a pilgrimage to a shrine, the place of festive manifestation.[2]

The intertwining of spiritual quest, earthly adventure and physical hardship within pilgrimage creates a memorializing event in which people, space, time and movement articulate images of the sacred. Such journeys through an energized landscape help to create social connections, obligations, hierarchy and spirituality. For it is in movement itself that individuals perceive the layout of cosmology.

Pilgrimage shrines have unique qualities derived from their association with a striking natural feature such as a mountaintop, waterfall, cave or glacier. The choice of location depends on the recognition that certain places are different from other places, that they have a special magnetism. Pilgrims travel there seeking connection with healing substances, such as medicinal clay, sand, salt and other minerals, or a charismatic historical or living person, deity, saint, spirit, energy or other numinous power. There they request a favour, offer thanks, fulfil a vow and do penance, in order to gain merit or salvation, or else write themselves into the book of life.

Material evidence for pilgrimage dates from the Upper Palaeolithic when people walked into caves, climbed shafts, crawled into tight passageways and descended into deep wells. There they touched, engraved, pierced, drew and painted on walls, ceilings, floors, stalagmites and stalactites. The custom of leaving clay and

---

[2]   Barbara Tedlock, 'Toward a Theory of Divinatory Practice', *Anthropology of Consciousness* 17/2 (2006): 62–77, at 63.

limestone votive offerings to a deity, in thanks for favours received, goes as far back as the Neolithic.[3]

Languages of Pilgrimage

The ancient Chinese described pilgrimage as a well-organized expedition setting out immediately after the New Year.[4] Buddhist monks carried out personal pilgrimages during which they travelled to every quarter of the country. In the seventeenth century, the Zen poet Basho set out on a wandering quest to experience the ideal of timeless eternity within the natural beauty of northern Japan.[5] A slightly different conceptualization appears in India where the Bengali word for pilgrimage translates as 'journey to the sacred ford'; the expedition involves stopping along the way for self-purification by means of bathing. Like Buddhist and Hindu forms, Greco-Roman, Coptic, Christian and Muslim pilgrimages are journeys in search of healing or another favour, as well as for gaining personal merit.[6]

This emphasis on individuals, rather than groups, is inherent in the English word 'pilgrim', which comes from the Latin *peregrinus* meaning 'foreigner'. It comes down to us by way of Old French *per* 'through' and *ager* 'land', meaning one who journeys through foreign lands. In Old English a pilgrim is a *weyfarere* or 'wayfarer', a lone traveller on foot. Today, in the English-speaking world, a pilgrim is an individual who journeys, preferably on foot, to a shrine in a foreign land in search of healing or other favours.

Pilgrimage is also a sacred journey, the course of life on earth, and by extension the path of the soul to the afterlife. This accounts for the deep symbolic association of pilgrimage with death. Today, Greek and Cypriot Orthodox pilgrims visit Jerusalem in old age to prepare themselves for a good death followed by resurrection. Before leaving for the Holy Land, they confess their sins and when they arrive, they have their feet washed by monks of the Brotherhood of the Holy Sepulchre, change into funeral shrouds and are re-baptized in the River Jordan.[7]

In India, important places of pilgrimage including Benares, Gaya and Hardwar are primarily places for death-related rituals and acts. A pilgrim goes on a journey to submerge the 'flowers', or bone-and-ash remains of a dead relative gathered from the cremation pyre, in the Ganges near Benares. After disposing of the

---

[3]   Paul Cassar, 'Medical Votive Offerings in the Maltese Islands', *Journal of the Royal Anthropological Institute of Great Britain and Ireland* 94/1 (1964): 23–9, at 24.

[4]   Richard Barber, *Pilgrimages* (Woodbridge, Suffolk: Boydell Press, 1991), p. 113.

[5]   Matsuo Basho, *The Narrow Road to the Deep North and Other Travel Sketches* (London: Penguin, 1966).

[6]   David Frankfurter, *Pilgrimage and Holy Space in Late Antique Egypt* (Leiden: Brill, 1998).

[7]   Glenn Bowman, 'Christianities', in John Eade and Michael Sallnow (eds), *Contesting the Sacred* (London: Routledge, 1991), pp. 98–121.

flowers, she dips out a pot of water and takes it home; there her family drinks the water to reincorporate the life-substance of the deceased.[8]

In the Mayan languages spoken in Mexico, Guatemala and Belize the concepts 'pilgrim' and 'pilgrimage' centre on the word for road *b'e* or *b'i*. In K'iche' Maya, there are three terms for pilgrim: *b'inel* 'traveller', *oq'owel* 'one who passes by' and *meb'a b'i'l winaq* 'a poor person walking on the road'. The first two are nearly synonymous and refer to merchants as well as pilgrims. The third, 'poor (or humble) person walking on the road', is used to indicate a male pilgrim who has undergone a long fast including sexual continence, lasting forty days or more, who walks to a distant shrine in order to benefit his community. A journey, for the purpose of either trade or pilgrimage, is called *b'inem*. While we might think of trade as a secular activity and pilgrimage as a religious activity, the fact that they are not linguistically marked in Mayan languages underscores the difference between our value system and theirs.

At one time the Maya site of Chich'en Itza was not only a famous pilgrimage centre but also an important regional market.[9] The main terms for pilgrimage are *numul b'eil* 'an account of the road' and *uximb'al ek'o'b* 'the passage of the stars'. The association of the word for traveller (*ximb'al*) with the course of the stars in the heavens (*ek'o'b*) emphasizes such travel as a cyclical process; pilgrims, like stars, pass through cycles in perpetual journeys through space and time. This linkage of pilgrimage to the stars connects it to divination by the stars, or astrology. Yucatec-speaking Mayans refer to the Milky Way as the celestial *sacb'e* or 'white road'. White Road is also the name of the ancient stone-and-cement pathways connecting villages to central shrines and economic conduits linking rural areas with central marketplaces.

During the Post Classic (beginning after 900 CE) pregnant women and their midwives went on pilgrimages to the island of Cozumel in Yucatan. There they sought a dream oracle from Ix Chel, the Moon goddess, and asked her for help in birthing a healthy baby. They brought with them mould-made clay offerings consisting of body parts – mainly heads, arms and torsos – as well as full figurines of women with babies in their arms.[10]

Today, Mayans make pilgrimages to shrines at archaeological ruins and to communal earth shrines where priest-shamans, who use the ancient calendar in divination and dream interpretation, live. As one Mayan pilgrim to Momostenango, Guatemala, explained to me, 'These shrines are like a book where everything – all dreams, births, marriages, deaths, successes and failures – are written down.

---

[8]   Ann Grodzins Gold, *Fruitful Journeys: The Ways of Rajastani Pilgrims* (Berkeley: University of California Press, 1988), pp. 189–202.

[9]   Jeremy A. Sabloff and William L. Rathje (eds), *A Study of Changing Pre-Columbian Commercial Systems*, Monographs of the Peabody Museum 3 (Cambridge, MA.: Harvard University Press, 1975), p. 319.

[10]   David A. Freidel, 'The Ix Chel Shrine and Other Temples of Talking Idols', in Sabloff and Rathje, *Pre-Columbian Commercial Systems*, pp. 107–13.

We come here once a year to write ourselves into the sacred book of life.' Thus, pilgrimage is a form of writing or discourse, and the shrines are sacred books into which pilgrims write themselves.

Dream Incubation

Pilgrimage is commonly followed by dream incubation for the purpose of diagnosis and healing. In Islamic nations, a key practice engaged in by Sufis and other pilgrims for ensuring visionary healing encounters with prophets or saints is to recite ritual prayers before sleeping at a shrine. There pilgrims meditate upon their life choices and health before sleeping on the tombs.[11] This custom, known as *istikhārah*, reflects, but is not a direct borrowing of, the custom of Greek and Roman dream incubation.

The cult of Asclepius originated at Epidaurus. In time, more than two hundred healing sanctuaries were built in the Hellenic world which attracted many pilgrims. Specific deities were worshipped at individual sanctuaries: Apollo appeared to visitors at Seleucia, Isis at Menuthis and Bes at Abydus. On the island of Delos, at the shrine of Sarapea, many eye-shaped silver and gold votive offerings were found indicating that healing eye ailments was a specialty of the deities who resided there. Since thousands of anatomical votive dedications – including life-sized clay limbs and other body parts such as legs and feet, arms and hands, ears and eyes, torsos, heads, female breasts and reproductive organs as well as male genitalia – were found at Corinth's Asclepions, it is believed it was a general-practice dream incubation site.

The ancient Greeks used dreams as both oracular and diagnostic systems in healing mind–body ailments. Pilgrims visited small temple rooms, known as Abatons, to perform therapeutic dream incubation. There, they might be spontaneously restored to health in their dream by the god, or by one of his totem animals such as a snake or a dog. Alternatively, they received instructions from the deity concerning self-healing. The ancient Greek philosopher Aristotle believed that premonitory dreams of sickness arose when the dreamer's unconscious recognized symptoms that had not yet come to the attention of the waking self. In the Greek tradition of secular medicine, practised by Hippocrates and Galen, it was believed that the internal world of the body contained a cosmological mirror revealing humoral healing forces that could be activated while sleeping at a shrine. Galen trained as a physician because of a dream of his father and he became a staunch believer in the diagnostic and healing powers of dreams.

---

[11]   Nile Green, 'The Religious and Cultural Roles of Dreams and Visions in Islam', *Journal of the Royal Asiatic Society* 13/3 (2003): 187–313, at 307–8.

> There are those who despise both dreams and portents and omens. But we know
> that a prognosis has often come from dreams ... I have saved many other people
> by proceeding from the dream to the cure.[12]

On the Greek island of Cos, where Hippocrates was born, there were many dream
temples where he taught his students to examine their patients' dreams as a way
of looking for symbols alluding to possible cures. He developed the idea that
dreams were windows on illness that reflected the health of the body. Beginning in
the fourth century BCE, in the many temples and hospital buildings, priests, dream
interpreters and healers collected and published accounts of miraculous dream cures.
An important source about the nature of healing at these shrines is a corpus of more
than seventy narratives inscribed as votive offerings on steles. The cures pertained
to specific people who lived during the late Classic. The texts reveal that potential
parents came in the hopes of conception and childbirth. The following narrative,
with its reference to the dreamer in the third person singular, is typical of the corpus.
What is unusual is that it contains a votive text within it.

> Kleo was pregnant for five years. After the fifth year, she came as a suppliant to the
> god and slept in the Abaton. As soon as she had left it, and was outside the sacred
> area, she gave birth to a son who, as soon as he was born, washed himself at the
> fountain and walked about with his mother. Because of these things, the fortunate
> woman inscribed upon an offering: 'The wonder is not the size of the *pinax* [votive
> tablet], but the act of the god. Kleo bore a burden in her womb for five years, until
> she slept here, and he made her healthy.'[13]

With the advent of Christianity the shrine of Asclepius, at the foot of the Acropolis,
was converted into a healing church dedicated to St Andrew. People travelled
there in large numbers to practise dream incubation. During the Middle Ages,
new healing saints and Christian dream incubation shrines emerged. One example
is the church of St Artemios in ninth-century Constantinople where men went
in large numbers to cure their hernias. This interest in dream healing continued
throughout the Byzantine and Ottoman periods. There are many Greek Orthodox
and Roman Catholic Churches today that have incorporated similar ideas about
dream healing and the giving of votive thank offerings after any successful cure. In
many of these shrines pilgrims left jewellery, including gold necklaces, brooches
and rings, as well as surgical and orthopaedic appliances such as canes, crutches,
plaster casts, eye patches, leather corsets and iron splints.

---

[12]   W.V. Harris, 'Roman Opinions about the Truthfulness of Dreams', *Journal of
Roman Studies* 93 (2003): 18–34, at 32.

[13]   Lynn R. LiDonnici, 'Compositional Background of the Epidaurian "Iamata"',
American Journal of Philology 113/1 (1992): 25–41, at 26.

Dream Discourse

Worldwide dreams are considered experiential signals by which sacred or mythic power makes itself known. Many dreamers and healers received these mythic powers from dreams and omens, as well as by means of applications of counter spells and healing plants. Since the structure of the discourse helps to channel the imagination of these dreamers, it is important to pay close attention to the languages of dream healing.

In French, Italian, K'iche' Mayan, Xavante and many other languages the verb stem for dreaming is transitive, indicating that a dreamer acts upon or 'makes' something happen while dreaming. However, in a number of other languages including Egyptian, Greek, English, German, Spanish, Asabano, Kalapalo and Zuni the verb stem describing the process of dreaming is intransitive. This indicates that dreaming is a passive state of being: one either 'has' or 'sees' a dream. While we say in English 'I had a dream last night', indicating that the dream comes from within ourselves, the ancient Greeks said, 'I saw a dream last night',[14] indicating they were passive recipients of a dream image. This difference underscores the variable attention paid to dreaming as an observation by a dreamer and dreaming as an active experience of the dreamer's soul, psyche or self.

Science and Divination

There is another productive way of thinking about the relationship between observation and theory. In recent work in the history of science on the topic of 'observability' it was argued that science was once an extension of the visible, tangible world and that scientists limited themselves to examining how such observables behaved. The result was that observables included both material things seen in the world and unobserved entities imagined by extension from observed phenomena. Observation, thus, was theory-laden.

Today the physical sciences are no longer dependent on sense perception. One of the hallmarks of twenty-first-century science is its refusal to conform to mental images drawn from everyday experience. Instead, scientists imagine parallel universes, quantum non-locality, wormholes in time and space, mass-energy transformations, cosmic strings, gravity-bent light and other strange concepts that defy common-sense reality. Given these remarkable developments within the physical sciences, why should we not approach divination with the same conceptual vigour and openness?

---

[14] Robert Rouselle, 'Women's Dreams in Ancient Greece', *Journal of Psychohistory* 26/2 (1998): 1–26; available at www.geocities.com/kidhistory/ja/womens.htm?20071 (accessed 9 September 2001).

The historian Francesca Rochberg[15] traced the interconnections among the Babylonian scribal traditions of celestial science, including omen divination, horoscopes, dream interpretation and scientific observations of the night sky. She found that many Babylonian omens were problematic and pointed out that scribes indicated eclipses on days when it was impossible to observe a lunar eclipse. If these 'eclipse omens', however, were considered as phenomena of interest to diviners, then they rightfully included unobserved entities that were extensions of observed phenomena. When she examined the meaning of the Babylonian term AN.*KU*, traditionally translated as 'eclipse', she found that it also includes any darkening of the moon by clouds. She argued that science did not emerge from or supersede a magical religious culture but rather the two cultures coexisted for eons.

Divinatory Forms

Today, there are hundreds of forms of divination practised worldwide, including water, crystal and stargazing, the casting of lots or sortilege, the reading of natural omens, the taking of hallucinogenic drugs, dreaming and the contemplation of mystic spirals, amulets, labyrinths, mandalas and thangkas. In some instances the diviner underwent physical or psychological changes so as to be able to serve as a medium, or vehicle, for divinatory power. At other times animals, objects, and events themselves were considered signs of superhuman power. Theorists collapsed these many forms into two main classes of divination: mediumistic – non-rational, inspirational or natural – and inductive – rational, mechanical or artificial. The decision as to which class a particular divinatory act belonged in depended on the degree of rationality the investigator believed the diviner used during the practice of divination. While the early Greeks emphasized the field of mantics, Romans emphasized inductive forms of divination. Many peoples, however, perform mixtures of these two forms of divination.

Mediumistic divination is practised nearly everywhere on earth. In Africa, it occurs among many peoples. Nguni diviners, who are predominantly women, serve as the conduit of psychic information sent by the ancestors. During divination, they proceed through an intuitive 'tuning in' to what their ancestors and other deities communicate to them. Initially they speak ecstatically without editing, translating or censoring what they hear, see or sense kinaesthetically. As the divination proceeds, they ask rational questions and receive specific answers about the situation at hand.[16]

Not only diviners but also clients may shift into altered states of consciousness during divination. Among the Kootenai, a Native American people living in British

---

[15]   Francesca Rochberg, *The Heavenly Writing: Divination, Horoscopy, and Astronomy in Mesopotamian Culture* (Cambridge: Cambridge University Press, 2004).

[16]   W.D. Hammond-Tooke, 'The Uniqueness of Nguni Mediumistic Divination in Southern Africa', *Africa* 72 (2002): 277–92.

Columbia, divination has long been part of their healing system and a key factor in their autonomy as a people.[17] During sweat lodge ceremonies, when it becomes unbearably hot and people within the lodge experience difficulty breathing, they may suddenly receive healing messages. These spiritual signs, which are triggered visually, aurally, kinaesthetically or by intuition, are considered 'strange', 'obscure' and 'symbolic', and thus in need of discussion to understand the content and meaning.

Theories of Divination

Most research to date has cast subordinate populations as performers of 'tribal rites' including divination. This trope of the Other as Diviner draws on and expands the 'antitheatrical prejudice'[18] that is so deeply imbedded within Western culture. The ethnographer Dwight Conquergood pointed out that the trope of the Other as Performer has been used against the Hmong of South East Asia ever since their first encounter with missionaries and the CIA. He noted that the prejudice, which is directly associated with attitudes towards human bodies and emotions, is constructed in opposition to rational thought and scientific reason. As a post-colonialist rhetoric of domination it 'positions performance against, beneath, behind, in opposition to, and as threatening to, progress, order and enlightenment'.[19]

Given this prejudice the practical mastery, or practical knowledge, of diviners has been neglected.[20] When researchers decide in advance that some actions are practical only in the objective realm they themselves define, they exclude from investigation the practical mastery diviners use. A number of investigators who were impressed by the apparent mechanicalness of the divinatory procedure and the orderliness it ascribed to the universe, allowed divination an ancestral or analogical relationship with Western science. This appeared to give diviners a space within the so-called objective domain. However, this is true only to the degree that a diviner's theory or practice is described as resembling those of the investigator and her colonialist society.

Divinatory procedures that actively combine mechanical methods with sudden bursts of intuition present another arena for the investigation of practical mastery. But before I describe these systems, I need to say a few words about intuition.

---

[17]   Bill Brunton, 'Kootenai Divination', *Shaman* 10 (2002): 21–32.

[18]   Jonas Barish, *The Antitheatrical Prejudice* (Berkeley: University of California Press, 1981).

[19]   Dwight Conquergood, 'Performance, Theory, Hmong Shamans, and Culture Politics', in Janelle G. Reinelt and Joseph R. Roach (eds), *Critical Theory and Performance* (Ann Arbor: University of Michigan Press, 2007), pp. 482–505.

[20]   Barbara Tedlock, 'Divination as a Way of Knowing: Embodiment, Visualisation, Narrative, and Interpretation', *Folklore* 112 (2001): 189–97.

The root of the English word 'intuition' comes from the Latin *intuitus* meaning the act of gaining knowledge from direct perception, or from contemplation. The literature on this topic converges around a set of themes that point to intuition as a form of instant interpretation, or 'tuning in', that pushes into and overwhelms conscious knowing or awareness. The source of such intuition may be an apprehension that lies outside sensory channels and analytical thought, existing in subliminal or non-conscious awareness embedded within the unconscious. What appears to be happening is an 'opening up' to inner promptings from mind–body psychodynamic forces.[21]

Wherever diviners have proposed a theory of divination, we find not only inductive or propositional thought, but intuitive or compositional ideas, as well as integrative ways of knowing. These modes of consciousness have neurobiological substrates. In South Africa, Sangoma healers use three main diagnostic methods: through spirits, with bones and with the head. The first type is a form of mediumistic or trance divination in which the diviner communicates with, and becomes possessed by, spirits who are located in the roof. The second type is a form of inductive divination in which the practitioner places bones in medicine within a basket and shakes them, then tosses them out onto a table and examines the way they fall to find out what question the client wants to pose. The third type involves an interpretive approach that is neither a non-rational mediumistic process nor a rational inductive process, but rather a continuum of overlapping cognitive processes and behaviours ranging from trance mediumship to the manipulation of physical objects interrupted by silence filled with deeply embodied insight.[22]

Paul Bohannon described a similar combination of divinatory methods, revealing several underlying cognitive processes, among Tiv diviners. They are called upon at a preconscious level to garner information about feelings as well as events and to do so they toss divining-chains on the ground before them and study the arrangement of the seed shells. This encourages their intuitions to emerge into waking consciousness.[23] This technique is similar to the psychoanalytical practice of free-floating attention. Divining-chain oracles are neither strictly inductive nor strictly intuitive: rather, they operate along a cognitive continuum. Shona divination works in a similar manner.[24] The diviner begins with a seemingly inductive use of a tangible object such as dice, which he casts once or twice until he suddenly 'knows everything'. At this point, he is able to tell his clients where

---

[21] Tedlock, 'Toward a Theory of Divinatory Practice', p. 65.

[22] Axel-Ivar Berglund, *Zulu Thought: Patterns and Symbolism* (Bloomington: Indiana University Press, 1989); Philip M. Peek, 'Recasting Divination Research', in John Pemberton III (ed.), *Insight and Artistry in African Divination* (Washington, DC: Smithsonian Institution Press, 2000), pp. 25–33.

[23] Paul Bohannan, 'Tiv Divination', in J.H.M. Beattie and R.G. Lienhardt (eds), *Studies in Social Anthropology* (Oxford: Clarendon Press, 1975), pp. 149–66, at p. 152.

[24] Michael Gelfand, *Shona Religion with Special Reference to the Makorekore* (Cape Town: Juta Press, 1962), pp. 106–10.

they have come from, the name of the deceased, the type of person the deceased was and the cause of death.

Among the Highland Maya the act of divination combines the inductive use of material objects – tree seeds and quartz crystals – together with narratives centring on the interpretation of the day names within the ancient 260-day calendar. During divination these procedures are combined with a non-rational mediumistic gift called 'the speaking of the blood' in which 'sheet lightning', or *koyopa*, is experienced synaesthetically as racing through the body. Since the human body is a microcosm with its own cardinal directions, mountains, plains, lakes and winds, intuitive embodied sensations are interpreted according to their location, direction and speed. The mapping of the meanings proceeds according to sets of dialectically paired terms, which are in a relationship of interlocking complementarity rather than in the form of dualistic oppositions. It takes a combination of various divinatory methods together with a discussion between a diviner and a client to arrive at the proper 'understanding', or *ch'obonik*.[25] Each of these interlocking embodied systems combines inductive, intuitive and integrative ways of knowing within a multidimensional narrative structure.

Whenever it occurs, divination involves complementary modes of cognition associated with primary process and secondary process thinking.[26] Diviners are specialists who use the idea of moving from a boundless to a bounded realm of existence. They excel in insight, imagination, fluency in language and knowledge of cultural traditions. They construct usable knowledge from oracular messages by combining intuitive-synthetic modes of thinking with logical-analytic modes of thinking. Through a dialogical and interactive mode, they link diverse domains of representational information and symbolism with emotional or presentational experience.[27]

In representational symbolism intentional reference is paramount, the medium of expression is straightforward and inductive reality is dominant. In presentational symbolism meaning emerges directly from experiential immersion in the expressive or emotional patterns of the symbolic medium grasped intuitively.[28] By combining representational with presentational symbolism within a single narrative structure, diviners provide a surplus, or 'superabundance', of understanding for their clients.[29] During the act of divination individual creativity operates: jumbled ideas,

[25] Barbara Tedlock, *Time and the Highland Maya* (Albuquerque: University of New Mexico Press, 1982), pp. 153–71.

[26] James W. Fernandez, 'Afterword', in Philip M. Peek (ed.), *African Divination Systems: Ways of Knowing* (Bloomington: Indiana University Press, 1991), pp. 213–21.

[27] Susanne Langer, *Philosophy in a New Key* (Cambridge, MA.: Harvard University Press, 1942).

[28] Harry T. Hunt, *On the Nature of Consciousness: Cognitive, Phenomenological, and Transpersonal Perspectives* (New Haven: Yale University Press, 1995), pp. 41–2.

[29] R.P. Werbner, 'The Superabundance of Understanding: Kalanga Rhetoric and Domestic Divination', *American Anthropologist* 75 (1973): 1414–40.

metaphors and symbols suggest various possible interpretations, slowly giving
way to an ordered sequencing and a more limited group of possible meanings.
During a dialogue between a diviner and a client, an unambiguous classification of
the history and causes of a situation and what is needed to resolve it emerges.

These types of symbolism are tightly intertwined: referential language is
filled with emotion – intonation and emphasis – while presentational language
is filled with intentional meaning in the form of an incipient portent. Thus, each
of these symbolic modes contains a bit of the other in a subordinate position.
The presentational side of symbolic capacity conveys more about context than
about referential focus. The delay in pragmatic semantic meaning, found in many
systems of divination, allows the time needed for the maximum felt synthesis of
presentational symbolism.

The interactions that take place during divination between these rather different
forms of cognition suggest that we pay attention to biophysical findings in the
area of integral mind–body research. Researchers have discovered that within
the cellular and extracellular areas of the human body there is a protein matrix
composed of liquid crystals and biopolymers that behave as electronic conductors
storing cognitive information. This liquid crystallinity gives us our characteristic
flexibility, sensitivity and responsiveness, allowing for rapid intercommunication
and thus enabling us to function as coherent organized wholes. This form of
consciousness, distributed throughout the entire body, possesses all the hallmarks
of consciousness: sentience, intercommunication and memory. Thus, mind exists
not just in the brain but also throughout the body, especially in the connective
tissues, including the skin, organ linings and membranes, bones, tendons,
ligaments and cartilage. Such tissues are responsible for the rapid communications
that enable the body to function as a coherent whole.[30]

Our entire nervous system, as well as areas of the body where nerves and
capillaries exist, is composed of a special protein matrix consisting of a network
of collagen immersed in water and hydrogen molecules that support rapid jump
conduction of protons. Jump conduction, which is a form of semi-conduction,
is much faster than electrical conduction through nerve fibres. Collagen fibres
in the connective tissues provide channels for communication that are arranged
in accordance with the mechanical stresses to which the tissue is subjected.
Their interlocking lineal alignments provide passageways for electrical
intercommunication resembling acupuncture meridians in traditional Chinese
medicine and the paths that *koyopa*, or 'sheet-lighting', follow in the K'iche'
Mayan bodily divinatory system.[31]

The implications for the study of divination are enormous. The jump conduction
of streams of information within the protein matrix of our bodies is related to

[30]   Mae-Wan Ho, 'Coherent Energy, Liquid Crystallinity, and Acupuncture', talk
given at the British Acupuncture Society, 2 October 1999; available at www.ratical.org/co-
globalize/MaeWanHo/acupunc.htm (accessed 12 September 2007).

[31]   Tedlock, *Time*, pp. 136–7.

the sudden bursts of intuition in the midst of otherwise inductive procedures. For example, the casting of lots, dice or divining chains that has been described in detail within the ethnographic literature.

Conclusions

It is only by directly engaging with diviners and dream interpreters that we can adequately study divination as a meaningful social phenomenon. While it has been categorized as either inductive (rational) or mediumistic (non-rational), divination actually is an integrative form of consciousness. In any one instant of sleeping or waking life, a silent language of signs presents felt realities for reflection and interpretation. If words are involved they are cryptic, poetic and highly allusive, sometimes spoken in a foreign or archaic language. The images these words and signs conjure are paradoxical and evocative: they create a sense of discovery. By paying attention to what people say about their experiences of dreaming and their acts of divination we can develop a theory of practice. Wherever this happens, an integrative way of knowing reveals itself along a cognitive continuum stretching from ratiocination to intuition. The ongoing interactions between these divergent forms of cognition suggest that human consciousness is much more complex than we once thought.

Chapter 3

'Twinning' and 'Perfect Knowledge' in African Systems of Divination[1]

Philip M. Peek

The birth of human twins has never been taken lightly in any society. In fact, the sheer volume of cultural traditions, whether of thanksgiving or horror, that surround such an event signals that far more is involved than simply an additional birth. Beyond the physical presence of multiple births, the idea of twinning seems to be a magnet for much cultural imagination. Many are aware that Elvis Aron Presley was born some 30 minutes after his stillborn twin, Jesse Garon Presley, on 8 January 1935. The rhyming middle names followed a local tradition and anticipated the unusual relationship Elvis maintained with his deceased twin:

> James Ausborn tells of Elvis often taking him to the Priceville Cemetery to visit his twin. Elvis would say to him, 'I want to see my brother.' 'He would go,' says James, 'burdened and low. Elvis would look at the grave and talk a little to Jesse and after the visit, he was always jolly and lifted in spirits.'[2]

This close relationship of Elvis to his deceased brother was 'reinforced by Gladys's [their mother] belief that "when one twin died, the one that lived got all the strength of both"'.[3] Fans and devotees of Elvis Presley are well aware of Jesse and much lore about Elvis and his twins survives today. Greil Marcus's *Dead Elvis: A Chronicle of a Cultural Obsession* (1991) records various manifestations of the public's inability to let go of Elvis's stillborn twin any more than they can let go of 'The King' himself – neither spirit will die! Attributions to this literally unknown

---

[1]   My sincerest appreciation to the Research Unit of the Sainsbury Centre for Visual Arts, University of East Anglia, 2003, for a research fellowship which allowed me to initiate my study of twins and diviners in African cultures. Portions of this paper were presented at a conference at the African Studies Center in Leiden, 'Realities Re-Viewed/Revealed: Divination in Sub-Saharan Africa', 4–5 July 2005, where I benefited greatly from responses by the participants. The version presented here has morphed again and is not quite what was presented at the 'Divination and Dialogue' Conference, University of Kent, Canterbury, 5–7 October 2007. Some alterations are a result of Laura Grillo's apt critical observations following my presentation as well as comments from other participants.

[2]   Elaine Dundy, *Elvis and Gladys* (New York: Macmillan, 1985), p. 128.

[3]   Peter Guralnick, *Last Train to Memphis* (Boston: Little, Brown, 1994), p. 13.

being – from Nick Cohen's novel *King Death* to the Adam Faith Experience's album 'Jess Garon and the Desperados' and Nick Cave's LP 'The First Born is Dead' – demonstrates the power of the twin metaphor. Jesse has imitators just as his (still living?) twin brother does.

These issues may not seem as significant as European traditions about Castor and Pollux, the Gemini Twins, or Romulus and Remus, the founders of ancient Rome, or the twin Catholic saints Cosmos and Damien, but they certainly demonstrate the fascination over time and space, held for centuries among the world's populations, about human twins. These anecdotes about Elvis and Jesse and the nature of their relationship and special communication find parallels all over the world, especially, as we will learn, among African peoples. For example, Elvis and Jesse had special names as twins, one was thought to have absorbed the other in the womb, the closeness of the womb caused a mystical union and they had unique means of communication.

Certainly I do not think that talk about twins is only the stuff of anecdotal stories told in pubs, or of television specials, or even of psychologists' endless tests. Although it is obvious that twins figure prominently in myth and ritual in various cultures in order to help people cope with an enormous variety of issues, I only want to discuss one dimension which helps me understand African systems of divination and the behaviour of many diviners. In this chapter, I will argue that the 'popular culture' or 'folk idea' of the special communication of twins may well be valid. What we do know is that many hold to this assumption and it guides much human behaviour. In my study of African systems of divination, I have continually encountered references to dichotomies, twins, doubles, couples, dualities of all kinds in all aspects of divination. By metaphor, and perhaps by fact, diviners clearly seek twin-like relationships between themselves and spirits as well as between themselves and clients. But even more widespread are dualities expressed in the divinatory apparatus and process. Before investigating this proposition about divination and dialogue in detail among African societies, some other background might be helpful.

Twins and Communication

Although highly debated in the literature, one frequently hears about the special communication between twins. Whatever researchers may determine about the unique relationship between twins, most twins will quickly agree they have such rapport – certainly Elvis behaved that way. Despite dramatic accounts (for example Wallace's *The Silent Twins*[4]), most studies of twins deny the 'myth' of a special language.[5] Some note that the special communication between twins includes non-

---

4   Majorie Wallace, *The Silent Twins* (New York: Prentice Hall, 1986).

5   See, for example, Pamela P. Novotny, *The Joy of Twins* (New York: Three Rivers Press, 1994).

verbal communication as well. In a quick example from Africa, LaGamma reports that in Gabon it is widely believed that 'Even once born, twins continue to prefer dreams as a means of communication.'[6]

One aspect of non-verbal communication that attracts psychologists to the study of twins is the response by a twin to the death of its twin. Just as siblings can invent an esoteric language, so do all siblings lament the death of a brother or sister. But because of assumptions about the special rapport between twins, many assume the loss is that much greater. Indeed, many twins and parents of twins report such and there are numerous support associations to aid these individuals and families.[7] Interestingly, Western psychological discussion and advice focuses on the loss for the living twin, whereas one might argue more attention is paid in African societies to the 'departed' twin. This too raises the link between twins and cross-world communication.

This matter also relates to a phenomenon of the Vanishing Twin which is gaining increased attention. Many singleton births sense they have or had a twin. Recent studies suggest this may be more often than not actually the case. There is even a website devoted to this topic.[8]

A full comparative review of Western and African views on twins cannot be accomplished here, but the fundamental contrast that emerges is that Western psychology clearly focuses on the individual,[9] while African attitudes are far more communally oriented. In the USA, study after study cautions parents of twins about issues of individual identity, whereas in African societies the identity of the pair is intensified, often to the extent that there can be no different treatment whatsoever (for example same foods, same clothes and so on). In fact, to look like or behave like a twin is a common means by which to establish one's closeness to others.

The main point here is that there are an abundance of popular beliefs about twins that demonstrate, in very different ways, their exceptional communication abilities, not only with each other but with outsiders. Not only does the myth of twins' secret languages persist, but the belief in twins' special empathetic abilities continues. Here we have interesting support in popular culture in that two of the most famous advisers in the USA were twins: 'Dear Abby' (Abigail van Buren) and Ann Landers. A more contemporary example is 'The Mystic Twins', Scott

---

[6]   Alisa LaGamma, 'Divination as a Fundamental Organizing Principle in Equatorial Africa', in John Pemberton III (ed.), *Insight and Artistry in African Divination* (Washington, DC and London: Smithsonian Institution Press, 2000), p. 152.

[7]   See Elizabeth M. Bryan, 'The Death of a Twin', *Palliative Medicine* 9 (1995): 187–92; Elizabeth A. Pector, 'Twin Death and Mourning Worldwide: A Review of the Literature', *Twin Research* 5 (2002): 196–205; Neela Banerjee, 'A Singular Pain: When Death Cuts the Bond of Twins', *New York Times*, 1 March 2007, G7.

[8]   http://vanishingtwin.com

[9]   See Novotny, *Joy of Twins* and Dale Ortmeyer, 'The We-Self of Identical Twins', *Contemporary Psychoanalysis* 6 (1970): 125–42.

and Stephen Petullo, who have a very active website.[10] Again, this association is widespread among African cultures.

Twins and the Universe

Before turning fully to African traditions, one other broad area of contemporary research finds parallels in Africa. By far the most fascinating new research involving the phenomenon of identical entities is occurring in physics. In a fascinating article, 'Tangled Twins', starting with reference to the constellation Gemini, Berman notes that there are doubles throughout the galaxy. As well, the behaviour of sub-atomic particles has been observed to occur in pairs. Newly created matter has anti-matter counterparts – 'precise clones with opposite electrical charges'. 'Quantum theory indicates that one particle in a newly created pair appears to respond instantly to what the other is doing, even if the two are far apart.'[11] While Einstein called this 'spooky action at a distance' and doubted its truth, recent experiments have demonstrated the validity of the theory. 'Entangled photons' have been sent in opposite directions. When miles apart, the movement of one will be immediately copied by the other particle – 'spooky action' indeed!

Although they seem farfetched, what is fascinating about such comparisons of 'hard' science and 'soft' myths is that they often coincide. This is the object of Beit-Hallahmi and Paluszny's fascinating article 'Twinship in Mythology and Science: Ambivalence, Differentiation, and the Magical Bond'.[12] Echoing their theme, Lash has observed that 'DNA, the double helix, is perhaps the ultimate twin of our modern mythology'.[13] And yet another example of extraordinary communication.

If I might add one more fascinating correlation of 'fact' and 'myth': the link between rainbows and twins that is encountered in a number of African societies. Normally, rainbows occur in pairs but can only be observed at specific viewing angles with the 'secondary' rainbow's colours being the reverse of the 'primary' rainbow.[14] This information provides a possible explanation for the 'rainbow serpent' present in some cultures and its link to twins, for example as among the Fon and the Tabwa.[15] As well, twins are associated with rain throughout southern Africa.

---

[10]   http://www.MysticTwins.com

[11]   Bob Berman, 'Tangled Twins', *Discover* (July 2001): 31.

[12]   Benjamin Beit-Hallahmi and Maria Paluszny, 'Twinship in Mythology and Science: Ambivalence, Differentiation, and the Magical Bond', *Comprehensive Psychiatry* 15 (1974): 345–53.

[13]   John Lash, *Twins and the Double* (London: Thames and Hudson, 1993), p. 31.

[14]   http://eo.ucar.edu/rainbows

[15]   P. Mercier, 'The Fon of Dahomey', in D. Forde (ed.), *African Worlds* (London; Oxford University Press, 1963), pp. 210–34; Allen F. Roberts, 'Embodied Dilemma: Tabwa Twinship in Thought and Performance', forthcoming in Philip M. Peek (ed.), *Twins*

Now that we have reviewed some of the ways by which twins are noted in Western traditions, we will turn to African cultures. Because my goal is to understand the relationship of twins and divination systems, I would like to trace the line of research that revealed this topic to me. I certainly never started my study of African divination systems with twins in mind, but twins and twinning of all kinds definitely emerged from the data.

Twinning and Divination Apparatus

This is the first area that caught my attention when I started my study of African divination systems. The doubling and pairing of images, objects and actions as well as the literal presence of twins and twinning in the divination systems of African peoples is striking. For a variety of reasons these all seem to be related to enhancing communication between worlds (diviner and spirits and/or ancestors) and within this world (diviners and client). The various forms of doubling that occur in divination systems probably derive from related themes in African cosmologies, epistemologies and theories of personality. We will be reviewing that material momentarily but first we must review the repetitions of elements and processes in the divination systems themselves.

Especially with divination systems utilizing cast items, as with the *Opele* divining chain of the Yoruba (with cognate forms throughout southern Nigeria), the left- and right-hand sides of the chain must be distinguished, often by means of an odd number of cowries on the right and an even number on the left-hand side. The diviner holds the chain in the middle so that four half seed pods (or any objects that provide concave and convex sides) hang on each side; it is cast away from the diviner so that each pod falls with its concave side up or down.[16] Both sides are 'read' and for some groups in southern Nigeria the left and right must fall in reverse/mirror order.[17] During a period of clan wars, an Isoko (an ethnic group in the Niger Delta) diviner cast cassava peelings; unusual perhaps but they provided the critical convex/concave surfaces. Some Isoko diviners from the Niger Delta work in pairs with each casting pairs of *eva* divining chains; then each reads the other's cast in the esoteric *eva* language while the other translates into Isoko. Doubling twice over it seems. Other African peoples whose divination systems require right and left symmetry include the Kaguru of Tanzania: 'In divination … it is said that the signs must appear on both the right and left before the prognostication may

in African & Diaspora Cultures: Double Trouble, Twice Blessed (Bloomington: Indiana University Press).

[16] William R. Bascom, *Ifa Divination: Communication Between Gods and Men in West Africa* (Bloomington: Indiana University Press, 1991), pp. 29–31.

[17] P.A. Talbot, *Peoples of Southern Nigeria*, 2 vols (Oxford: Oxford University Press, 1926), vol. II, p. 188.

be regarded as complete.'[18] It is especially striking to encounter similar practices throughout the African continent. For example, Parrinder reports such among the Sotho and Thonga in southern Africa.[19]

In addition to the distinction of left and right, there are also instances as with Zande rubbing oracles where the halves are considered male and female.[20] Among diviners in Mozambique whom I have observed, several types of pairings are present in their sets of *tinholo*, or divining apparatus. These include objects representing equal numbers of male and females items, bones or other parts of wild and domestic animals, usually with representatives of both land and water, and objects that can fall 'up' or 'down'.[21] The key to all these instances is that a distinction is made of right/left or male/female but each needs the other. The entwinement of these dualities recalls the familiar adage about a coin having to have two sides and the ancient Taoist concept of *yin* and *yang*.

In her comparative study of African divination systems, Laura Grillo has focused on the divination systems of the Dogon of Mali and the Yoruba of Nigeria and those people who neighbour them. Dogon cosmology, sharing many epistemological elements with their neighbours, the Bamana and Maninke, is based on dualities and twinning and forms the basis for Dogon divination. Here, life begins with the Nommo, the primordial twins; but we will return to matters of world view momentarily. As Grillo points out, Ifa divination 'revolves around pairs' – especially the Odu (the configurations produced by the 'casting' of palm nuts or divining chains for which there are numerous verses recounting Yoruba history, prescribing sacrifices and so on).[22] The marks generated by the grasping of palm nuts (or casting of an opele chain) can be understood to occur in pairs; in fact, when the left and right 'arms' of the figure are repeated, it is called a 'twin'.

The careful distinctions of right and left in the divining apparatus, and then the even more careful melding of the two sides/halves (of the whole!) seems to wonderfully reflect the fascinating research being conducted on the so-called split brain.[23] While older characterizations of the types of consciousness associated with either hemisphere (for example the 'dominance' of the left) are no longer

---

[18]   Thomas O. Beidelman, *Moral Imagination in Kaguru Modes of Thought* (Bloomington: Indiana University Press, 1986), p. 32.

[19]   Geoffrey Parrinder, *Religion in Africa* (Harmondsworth: Penguin, 1969), p. 62.

[20]   E.E. Evans-Pritchard, *Witchcraft, Oracles, and Magic Among the Azande* (Oxford: Clarendon Press, 1968), p. 362.

[21]   See also Paulo Granjo, '"It's Just the Starting Engine": The Status of Spirits and Object in South Mozambican Divination', forthcoming in Philip M. Peek and W. van Beek (eds), *Reality Re-viewed: Dynamics of African Divination* (Leiden: Brill).

[22]   Laura Grillo, 'Divination in the Religious Systems of West Africa', Ph.D. dissertation (University of Chicago, 1995), pp. 151ff.

[23]   Philip M. Peek, 'African Divination Systems: Non-Normal Modes of Cognition', in Philip M. Peek (ed.), *African Divination Systems: Ways of Knowing* (Bloomington: Indiana University Press, 1991), p. 205.

so fixed, there is no question that the human brain is highly compartmentalized yet exquisitely integrated for normal human behaviour. It is probable that many diviners have even more carefully synthesized cognitive functioning.

A fascinating combination of points being made here is provided by René Devisch who notes that the Yaka (Congo) diviner considers his slit gong, which already combines male and female symbols, to be his twin.[24] This anticipates the next stage in our discussion which will consider aspects of the diviner's personality.

The Communal Self and Diviners' Spirits

There is no question that diviners are unique human beings. In striking contrast to the commonly expressed negative characterizations, African diviners are usually exceptionally learned and sensitive individuals. They manifest intelligence, compassion and extraordinary perception, which few others in their communities can demonstrate. As observers of social character and moral integrity, they are exemplary citizens ... hardly charlatans duping an unquestioning public. Indeed, most African diviners are exceptionally well-balanced and thoughtful individuals, but not individuals in the sense we usually use the term.

It is they who must manage the most critical forms of communication. They must send, receive then interpret oracular messages from the other (for many the 'real') world. Diviners are, virtually by definition, liminal beings; that is, they are of neither this mundane world nor that of the ancestors and spiritual beings. They must move back and forth in their role as cross-world communicators and thus they cannot be only 'one' being, they must be a composite. Strikingly, they share this feature with divine kings who are also of both worlds. And each culture seems to find its own way to characterize and create that 'communal self'.

The idea of a diviner's communal self is built on a common ground of multiple elements constituting the average citizen, but diviners necessarily combine more elements in a far more intense fashion to accomplish their unique tasks of cross-world communication and aid to their communities. Thus, we find that diviners are not 'individuals' in the broadly Western sense of an isolated singular being, but are better understood as a composite of various forces and entities. In fact, most African peoples portray themselves as combinations of distinct elements, some of which will change during their life time.

The Isoko of the Niger Delta provide a starting point for us. They understand the individual to be composed of, first, *oma*, or spirit double, which guides the individual from the other world; second, *obo*, or skill, ability; and third, *ivri*, tenacity; all of these elements must work in harmony with the individual. Among the Ashanti of Ghana, each individual acquires components from the mother

---

[24] René Devisch, 'Of Divination *Co-naissance* Among the Yaka of Congo', forthcoming in Philip M. Peek and W. van Beek (eds), *Reality Re-viewed: Dynamics of African Divination* (Leiden: Brill).

('blood') and father ('spirit') which combine with a 'life force' to constitute the individual.[25] The concept of a spirit double is found in virtually every African culture. The Bamana of Mali provide another example with their idea of the *Ja*:

> usually translated as 'double', shadow, mirror reflection, but it summarizes more generally what we would render in English as 'identity'. The *ja* of the person is said to mediate between the interior world of the person's soul (*ni*) and the exterior world of the social group.[26]

The Zulu have a wonderful concept of the interrelatedness of the earth and sky and it informs the dialogic, dyadic foundation of thought that I am proposing for epistemologies, including divination. 'The sky and the earth are twins like my two fists are twins or my two feet are twins ... They are both from the beginning ... Being twins they are also husband and wife.'[27]

I would also argue that marriage is often used as means to express an androgynous status of the diviner. The initiation ceremonies for male and female Nyole diviners in Uganda serve to 'settle' the notably androgynous spirit of the new diviner. Many Nyole diviners speak of their having 'married' their divination spirit.[28] Cross-gender elements of diviners' initiation ceremonies are reported as well in Central Africa[29] and throughout southern Africa diviners are possessed by opposed sexed spirits.

In fact, a number of African peoples have cosmologies based on dualities: not simply two deities, as just noted for the Zulu, but often a single entity of two parts. The Fon of Benin have a dual deity of Mawu, the male component, and Lisa, the female component. This entity has been variously recorded as twins or as an androgynous being.[30] Such a duality is encountered elsewhere in West Africa as with the Baule of Côte d'Ivoire and Bamana of Mali who conceive of an indivisible male/female entity as creator. Faro, a water deity who is considered the Bamana creator god, is 'the "double" (*dya* or *ja*) of all that exists'; and, following Dieterlen, 'Faro is depicted as male and female, an androgynous deity which is said to be "neither the beginning nor the end but the center"'.[31] Zahan provides

---

[25]   Kwame Anthony Appiah, *In My Father's House: Africa in the Philosophy of Culture* (New York: Oxford University Press, 1992), p. 98.

[26]   Jean-Paul Colleyn, *Bamana: The Art of Existence in Mali* (New York: Museum for African Art, 2001), p. 243.

[27]   Axel-Ivar Berglund, *Zulu Thought-Patterns and Symbolism* (Bloomington: Indiana University Press, 1989), p. 62.

[28]   Susan Reynolds Whyte, 'Knowledge and Power in Nyole Divination', in Peek, *African Divination Systems*, pp. 153–72.

[29]   Luc de Heusch, *Sacrifice in Africa* (Bloomington: Indiana University Press, 1985), p. 31.

[30]   Mercier, 'Fon', pp. 219–220.

[31]   Colleyn, *Bamana*, p. 243.

a useful summary of the association of twins and androgyny: 'the cultures in which man's original androgyny is considered an ideal state of equilibrium would have a reverential attitude towards twins because, by their ambivalent unity, they represent one of the social manifestations of the original equilibrium of man.'[32]

One of the common explanations for twins is that the mother had had relations with two men and usually one is said to be a deity, as is the case with the Lele of the Congo.[33] Such accounts are also found in ancient Greek tradition. Does this not portray the embodiment of cross-world communication? Is not such an account of the origin of twins exactly what is needed to make twins the key to communication between humans and the spirit world? African cultures may differ in how they conceive of the details but the relationship between twins and divination is a constant in such cases.

The combination of associations – twins, male and female, husband and wife – is striking and is encountered rather often in African cosmologies and epistemologies. As noted earlier, it is also intriguing to recall similar configurations in the classical world. While Castor and Pollux are referred to as the Gemini Twins, in 'reality' they were only brothers; their actual twins were their sisters. Again, there is the combination of male and female twins. And it is this combination that many West African peoples hold as the perfect union of twins.

Mercier writes of the centrality to Fon life, here and in the other world, of twins: 'The ideal type of every group in the divine world is a pair of twins of opposite sex or, more rarely, of the same sex. We have pointed out that among men also the ideal birth is a twin birth and that in the beginning every birth was of that kind.'[34] Not only do male and female twins present the ideal pairing, the absence of a distinction between identical and fraternal twins must be noted. The critical point seems to be the time shared together in the mother's womb, that intense and total proximity is what ensures the identity of twins, not (superficial?) similarity. In fact, it must be stressed that twins are considered to be twins because of their shared experience in the womb and very little attention is paid in African societies to the difference between identical or fraternal twins.

One might also consider the relationship of those diviners who use creatures as agents of the oracular messages as having a twin-like relationship with the creatures. For example, there is mouse divination among the Baule, spider and crab divination in the Cameroons, as well as fox divination among the Dogon.[35]

---

[32]   D. Zahan, *The Religion, Spirituality, and Thought of Traditional Africa* (Chicago: University of Chicago Press, 1979), p. 12.

[33]   Hillel Schwartz, *The Culture of the Copy* (New York: Zone Books, 1996), p. 24.

[34]   Mercier, 'Fon', p. 231.

[35]   Philip M. Peek, 'Recasting Divination Research', in John Pemberton III (ed.), *Insight and Artistry in African Divination* (Washington, DC and London: Smithsonian Institution Press, 2000), pp. 25–33.

Van Beek writes of the close relationship that is developed between the Dogon diviner and the fox.[36]

Again, we might wonder which came first: the phenomena of twin human births or an ideology or theology that ritualized the recognition of twins. We certainly cannot settle such a debate here but we can further illustrate the importance of twins and their links to divination with ethnographic research from West and Central Africa. Previously, we have noted the importance to the Dogon of Mali of twins; these traditions may well have come to the Dogon from neighbouring Bamana and Maninka peoples.

In common with many West African peoples, the Senufo of Côte d'Ivoire inhabit a world begun with a primordial couple who had twins, which is why twins continue to be honoured, especially male and female pairs. Among the ceremonies marking their emergence into this world, a small building is erected next to the family house which is called 'the cottage for twins' and this will then be used by diviners. In addition to the building within which divination occurs, various images of twins fill the diviner's shrine and are worn by diviners in the form of doubled rings and bracelets. These images aid the divinatory enterprise in which twins are sought for cross-world communications on behalf of the diviner's clients. Each diviner's shrine must have tiny twinned baskets or brass replicas. These are so important that even pairs of stones might be used in make-shift shrines.

Clearly the Djimini Senufo, the focus group in Ellen Suthers' excellent research, consider the unique relationship of twins to be the model for divinatory communication: 'Sharing the same womb experience, twins become endowed with, or constituted of, the same perceptions; hence they emerge in the world as congruent images.' 'Because they share perfect knowledge and perception of each other and of the spirit realm, twins do not need speech to communicate with each other or with the host of spiritual entities.' 'The discussion of twins introduces the idea, central to the interpretation of divinatory ritual, that two people can share a perception which does not need to be verbalized to be comprehended. The relationships that twins have with each other in life are similar to the relationships diviners establish with their spirits through ritual.'[37]

Sadly the average Senufo loses the ability to see and hear spirits as they acquire human speech, but twins retain that ability. Further, human talk is thought to obstruct the transfer of knowledge. 'As intermediaries, diviners permit communication that otherwise is impossible between the client, who possesses language, and spiritual entities, who do not.'[38] In further descriptions of the process, Suthers proposes that

---

[36]   Walter van Beek, 'Footprints of the Future: Dogon Fox Divination', *Mande Studies* 7 (2005): 69–88.

[37]   Ellen Suthers, 'Perception, Knowledge, and Divination in Djimini Society, Ivory Coast', Ph.D. dissertation (University of Virginia, Charlottesville, 1987), pp. 11 and 12.

[38]   Ibid., p. 14.

diviners establish a twin-like relationship with the client as well as the spirits and thereby create a means by which to facilitate communication between worlds.[39]

'As pairing makes the client congruent with the diviner and the diviner congruent with the spirits, all come to share a common perception. Through gestures, the diviner transforms his or her body to reflect the image of the client, and thus to reveal the client's problems in concrete terms.'[40] As we will see in a moment, this physical mirroring of the client by the diviner has support from research in psychology. Thus, Dijimini Senufo diviners do everything possible to become like a twin so that they can establish the same immediate and immaculate rapport with the spirit world that the twins have. Space prevents full discussion of the Luba of Central Africa for whom twins and divination are linked in numerous ways, from their historical myths to the daily practice of diviners.[41]

Twinning of Diviner and Client

Although this is a brief survey of a complex topic, I hope there is sufficient evidence to establish the theme of doubling and twinning in terms of the development of the individual as well as the diviner, and the role of these underlying perspectives in the divinatory enterprise in general. Before concluding, I want to quickly touch on the twinning aspects of actual divination sessions. Here again, the ethnographic data I gathered in my initial study of African systems of divination revealed the intimate dynamics between the diviner and the client. Whether or not one sought a local or distant diviner, a striking degree of rapport was soon established between the two individuals. In light of the earlier discussion about ideas about twins and communication, both in the USA and in African societies, the fact that many diviners actively seek a close bond with their client is to be expected.

In addition to the bonding or merging that occurs between diviners and spirit beings, we find that a special relationship is often developed between diviner and client. In fact, in some divination systems, this is absolutely essential and special rituals are enacted to ensure a complete linkage is established. Some scholars, such as Michael Jackson,[42] see this as a crucial element in divination practices in general and he speaks of the transference process that occurs in Kuranko divination between diviner and client. There are also those traditions in which the diviner and client employ a hand-holding form of divination, for example in West Africa among the Batammaliba and Lobi, as well as the sliding divination instruments held by diviner and client as with the Luba. Close and continual physical contact

---

[39] Ibid., p. 16.

[40] Ibid.

[41] See Mary Nooter Roberts and Allen F. Roberts, *Memory: Luba Art and the Making of History* (New York: Museum for African Art; Munich: Prestel, 1996).

[42] Michael Jackson, 'Approaches to Kuranko Divination', *Human Relations* 31 (1978): 117–38.

is also found among the Senufo diviners and clients whose legs rest against each other as they sit side by side during the session. The Lobi acknowledge the shared enterprise of divination by using the same term for both diviner and client.[43]

It is important to recognize that all of these practices are aimed at far more than simply a closeness between diviner and client. Certainly some degree of faith and trust is necessary, but a very special rapport is required for effective divination. One aspect of close human interaction is analysed in William Condon's research[44] on the synching of human interaction wherein, for example, two people in conversation begin to interact with synchronous gestures, to move in harmony with each other. As the conversing pair becomes more engrossed in their exchange, they begin leaning forwards and backwards simultaneously, crossing or uncrossing legs in unison and so on. They virtually become mirror images of each other – twins! This unconscious synchronizing demonstrates more than simply a closeness between the two individuals during a divination session. There is no question that most diviners are very skilled at 'reading' subtle, usually unconscious, body movements of their clients in order to aid them; but the simultaneity of this synching process raises divination to higher level of rapport. This synchronous, harmonious search for answers in the unique divinatory enterprise where questions are asked of those in the other world reveals a critical element which needs further research. Clearly clarity of communication occurs as synching increases.

Conclusions

I have tried to briefly trace an argument that links the pervasive cosmological and epistemological dualities of various sorts in African cultures to the presence of these perspectives in action in divination sessions. Dualities are established and then integrated in the devices and mechanics of divination as well as in the process of interaction between diviner and client. It seems that these practices are embedded within a larger context of dualities and multiplicities related to diviners' personalities, their spiritual companions and each cultures' cosmology. All this discrimination, synthesizing and modelling serves to enhance cross-world communication.

All of the difference-making that characterizes so much of the divinatory enterprise in so many diverse African cultures seems ultimately to be aimed at reconciliation, mediation, synthesis and harmony of discrete contrasted elements. These combinations, often expressed in doubling and twinning, all serve as means to bring people, spirits, ancestors and powers together in order to effect more comprehensive and correct communication. The 'perfect knowledge' that Senufo

---

[43]   Piet Meyer, 'Divination Among the Lobi', in Peek, *African Divination Systems*, pp. 91–100, at p. 94.

[44]   William Condon, 'Communication: Rhythm and Structure', in *Rhythm in Psychological, Linguistic, and Musical Processes* (Springfield, IL: Charles C. Thomas, 1986), pp. 55–78.

twins have of each other stands for the goal of all of these mechanations. While we might speak of replication of the self, the male/female pairing is most desirable and, thus, we are reminded of androgyny – that state which emulates the divinities and permits comprehensive empathy with all humans. This is the ideal state for a diviner.

In a bit of an experiment, let me recall some of our scholarly ancestors. Unavoidably, in the discussion above, we are reminded of Edward Tylor, Sir James Frazer and Carl Jung and the applicability of their insights. It is hardly fashionable to bring forth such names but too often we forget that many of our most effective theoretical contributions were made long ago. One of Tylor's most enduring contributions to the study of culture was his formulation about the foundation of religion based, essentially, on the dream experience and the observation of oneself engaged in often unfamiliar activities: 'the ancient savage philosophers probably made their first step by the obvious inference that every man has two things belonging to him, namely, a life and a phantom'. 'As both belong to the body, should they not also belong to one another, and be manifestations of one and the same soul.'[45] Does this not find support in our summary of the ubiquitous spirit double and the 'communal self', the melding of various independent elements to create the average individual in African societies?

Surely Jung's concept of the anima and animus provides an analytical frame for the cross-gender identification which so many diviners engage in as they seek an androgynous state to enhance their divinatory enterprise. Fundamental to Jung's concept of the individual was that each male psyche had a female component, the anima, while each female psyche had a male component.[46] Such examples of other cultures' concept of the individual are raised not to 'prove' African concepts, but to reflect the similarity of models in different cultures. Although the male/female association is often expressed as the 'marriage' of a man and a woman, I feel this is more a metaphor, not simply a reference to a social institution. 'Marriage' is not an inappropriate designation but it reflects a deeper, more personal, internal harmony of the aspects of the individual diviner.

Much of what we have been describing about the process of divination is based on the fundamental ideas of sympathetic magic long ago set out by Sir James Frazer. The abundance of twins imagery in the divinatory enterprise is essentially based on the ancient premise of 'like produces like'. If twins have 'perfect knowledge' of each other and have immaculate communication with each other, then the more I can approximate that condition, the better my communication, the wiser my knowledge, the better my divination. And, as William Condon's research proves, when two individuals engage in close conversation, their bodies move into synchronous action, thereby deepening their rapport.

---

[45]   Edward Burnett Tylor, *Religion in Primitive Culture* (New York: Harper and Row, 1958), pp. 12–13.

[46]   Carl G. Jung et al., *Man and His Symbols* (Garden City, NY: Doubleday, 1964), pp. 177–95.

For that matter, we can go further back in Western intellectual history to any number of Greek traditions. One might recall Tiresias, the ancient seer who knew life as both a woman and a man, thus providing us with further perspective on the relationship of androgyny and divination. As well, Aristophanes' account of the origin of humans as double beings who were torn apart and now seek their other half to complete themselves can be reviewed in light of new evidence about the Vanished Twin phenomenon. Many of us really did have a twin at the time of conception.[47]

But as fascinating as such ideas may be the prime concern here is the centrality in so many African cultures of dualities, dichotomies, couples and doubles, dyadic structures and dialogic processes. In myriad ways African peoples distinguish two elements only to bring them together to insure the proper order of life.

If any topic was illustrated by the 'chicken and egg' debate, this is it. Did the wonder of twins initiate an appreciation of duality in the world or was a dyadic perspective hard-wired into the human brain? Surely at this point it is more beneficial to simply appreciate the value of the imagery and the associations that permit better understanding of the phenomena of African divination systems.

Another area of study seems to relate to the matter of the depiction of twins but, as yet, links to divination seem slim. Although they are fascinating objects of art, there has yet to be a comprehensive study of the Janus-headed or double-faced masks of Africa.[48] In fact, in many cultures there are multiple faced and multiple featured figures and masks, as well as 'piggy-back' figures (one figure on top of another). With the doubling of eyes, often facing in different directions, these appear to depict enhanced seeing or certainly heightened perception of some kind. Often they are male/female. These images would seem to fall into the areas discussed above but that will have to await another essay.

Diviners must embody the balance of worlds and forces, a tight web of relationships, of sexes and sensibilities, as they act as a fulcrum and a powerful synthesis of abilities. The manufacture and maintenance of the diviner's 'other' is not a sign of weakness – simply a call for supernatural aid – but a widespread practice that ensures the success of this very difficult enterprise. Where we find the correlation of twins and divination, communication seems to be the linking element, the desired goal which is strengthened.

I argue that the ultimate goal, the ideal that guides so many of these instances of duality, is the enhancement of one's understanding of the human predicament, the world we live in and the communication that divination seeks to provide. While oppositions are constantly established, they are not in a dialectical relationship but in one that resolves itself in synthesis, harmony, completion of the self and of the divination process.

---

[47] It is generally accepted that 4 per cent of singleton births are actually twins at conception; then one of the twins absorbs the other. See http://vanishingtwin.com

[48] Philip M. Peek, 'Couples or Doubles? Representations of Twins in the Arts of Africa', *African Arts* 41 (2008): 14–23.

Chapter 4
Memoir as Method, or 'What the Devil Was I up to Anyway?'

Laura S. Grillo

Over the past fifteen years, since completing my dissertation on West African Divination at the University of Chicago, I have written on divination from various angles: divination and identity, divination in the cast of ethics, divination and West African epistemology, divination as a visual canon and divination as an instantiation of Hillman's Archetypal Psychology. Here, I would like to discuss another, riskier way that I have written about African divination: as experience of the uncanny and through *memoir*.[1]

My memoir, entitled 'Ask for the Road',[2] takes place during the summer of 1997 when I returned to Côte d'Ivoire, where I had first lived twenty years before with my former husband, who was a native of the country. By the time I made this trip to conduct post-doctoral fieldwork on contemporary urban divination, it had been ten years since I'd been back, and we'd been divorced for three. I had been ambivalent about returning, unsure how my ex-in-laws would receive me, and reluctant to revisit my past. But Abidjan, the country's economic capital, was the perfect place for my investigation. It is an ethnically heterogeneous city, bustling with immigrants and refugees, where multiple forms of divination are practised and thrive at busy crossroads, in tenement buildings and in quiet courtyards. My aim was to discover how urban divination, without any specific traditional framework to support its practice, manages to remain a compelling practice for Africans.

The family did embrace me anew, lovingly assuring me I was still their sister and daughter, and they helped me find diviners. However, diviners would only interview with me once they had divined for me. How else could they demonstrate their techniques, and more importantly for them, convince me of divination's efficacy? Yet each consultation implicated me more and more as the object of research. The diviners repeatedly referred to my ex-husband and the unfinished issues between us, intensifying the feelings of being haunted that were unleashed by revisiting the places where we'd been together. So, what I

---

[1]   This paper was first given at the 'Divination and Dialogue' conference at the University of Kent in 2007.

[2]   This memoir is currently represented by a literary agent and under review for publication.

thought would be a research expedition that would launch my academic career turned into an intense personal pilgrimage to my past and a negotiation of its significance.

I cast the story as a complex paradox of conflicting identities and moral positions. I was, on one hand, a comfortable insider in my ex-husband's family and their culture, and, on the other, a self-conscious outsider, shamelessly exploiting this intimacy to promote my new identity as an academic. Many of my 'informants', African Christians or Muslims with strong allegiances to their traditions, felt equally torn; their participation in divination presented a crisis of religious identity. As I consulted diviners and realized their uncanny accuracy, I entered more deeply into the world view I was supposedly studying, and I began to lose the emotional and psychic distance I thought necessary for academic pursuit. I struggled with feeling myself to be a voyeur, a sham researcher 'gone native', rather than a professional investigator. I got swept up into a fuller experiential engagement with the seemingly endless cycle of consultation and sacrifice, and tried not to lose my bearings or sense of control. The dilemma plays out at the apex of the story, when, closely caught up in troubling revelations and too personally enmeshed in the research on divination itself, I must decide whether to perform a repeatedly prescribed goat sacrifice, wondering whether it will draw me further off course or help resolve my inner turmoil.

This is the context of the story, one that I hope makes it a good read. However, the deeper issue that drove me to write a memoir in the first place was an academic problem: How to write about experience of the uncanny? As I looked for a way in, I was forced to ask myself, 'what the devil had I really been up to' in undertaking this investigation, anyway, and how could I contend with what it had ultimately stirred up for me? The question, put this way, was inspired by the tongue-in-cheek comment of anthropologist Clifford Geertz that penetrating other people's modes of thought is a complicated business: 'the trick is to figure out what the devil they think they are up to'.[3] What makes the whole enterprise of coming to terms with diviners and their art even trickier is that divination itself engenders a reflexive move that turns the inquirer back on herself; divination is the process of puzzling out one's own meanings and motivations. In investigating divination, I had naturally become the object of my own inquiry. Subject and object were blurred. And so I had to struggle to find a method that would be commensurate with that kind of experience.

I felt that no academic discourse could convey the startling accuracy of the diviners' readings of my past and present situation. Mere assertion of this conclusion without evidence would be dismissed – and me with it, as a dupe of their chicanery or as a naïve victim of my own psychological projections. A fuller

---

[3]   Clifford Geertz, '"From the Native's Point of View": On the Nature of Anthropological Understanding', *Bulletin of the American Academy of Arts and Sciences* 28/1 (1974): 26–45.

illustration inevitably called for disclosure of some of the facts of my life that had become – unexpectedly and uncomfortably – an integral part of the investigation.

A mere academic treatise about the practices of divination could not have done justice to the private and personal grappling that the ritual elicits. My dilemma was not about how to situate African divination as a social phenomenon, nor how to explain it in psychological terms (either in terms of their psychology or mine). Rather, I felt I needed to contend with the unsettling truth that most of the diviners with whom I consulted were inexplicably privy to facts to which they had no empirical means of access. They made me wonder what I believed and made me rethink what I was there to achieve.

The intimacy of the inquiry made me consider writing a novel. Fiction readily offers what postmodern scholarship aspires to deliver. Fiction is vulnerable and self-reflexive: it allows for the musing voice of the narrator to reveal with candor her own predispositions, biases, questions and doubts. Fiction also brings in others as vivid actors, adding a dimension of empathy for the perspective of others and incorporates a multi-vocality that modern scholarship lacks. Finally, a good story is always about a transformation. It demonstrates what postmodern scholars call intersubjectivity: The subject changes as she comes in contact and exchange with the other, the object of the story, and vice versa. In other words, fiction invites the reader to re-experience an experience. Its method is aesthetic, sensational, 'erotic', to use Gregory Shaw's term.[4] On the other hand, a novel or fictionalized account about my encounters with these seers and spiritual guides would have undercut the very thing that made these experiences powerful – they were *true*.

I decided that memoir was the only viable genre for my subject. I took heart in the straightforward acknowledgement by historian of religions Wendy Doniger O'Flaherty that 'all truly creative scholarship in the humanities is autobiographical'.[5] Ultimately, our subjective selves are inextricably bound up in our work. This is not only because who we are shapes our perceptions; a deeply sensed (even if barely acknowledged) yearning, drives it. This is eros at work.

If memoir – or any work – is to rise above mere personal anecdote or solipsism, though, it must have some universal import. The story of my remarkable encounters with West African diviners wrestles with one of the greatest paradoxes of human existence: that each of us harbours a compelling sense of destiny, or struggles to discover one, even as we persist in believing in the integrity of our free will. There is no more classic a preoccupation. This is the yearning at the heart of divination: to lay claim to meaning, to carve our own fate and to negotiate destiny.

---

[4] Gregory Shaw, 'Living Light: Divine Embodiment in Western Philosophy', in Patrick Curry and Angela Voss (eds), *Seeing with Different Eyes: Essays in Astrology and Divination* (Newcastle: Cambridge Scholars Press, 2007), pp. 59–87.

[5] Wendy Doniger O'Flaherty, 'The Uses and Misuses of Other People's Myths', in Russell T. McCutcheon (ed.), *The Insider/Outsider Problem in the Study of Religion: A Reader* (London: Cassell, 1999), pp. 331–49 at p. 336.

What follows is a brief extract from the first chapter of my memoir 'Ask for the Road'. I offer this text as a glimpse into the messy situation of researching divination, the uncanny nature of the experience, and the kind of personal grappling that it elicits. The reader of the fuller version would, at this point in the narrative, already know that 'Hélène' is my former sister-in-law, suffering from a mysterious pain in her jaw, Koné and Amadou are new acquaintances who are helping me find local diviners and interview them in the northern town of Korhogo and 'Simon' is Hélène's brother, my ex-husband.

* * *

Hélène, Koné, Amadou and I cut across the field diagonally, lifting our feet over the rows of mounds and hollows, like hikers in a pristine field of high snows. A distant sound of bells jangled persistently from the isolated hut. Their heavy rhythm impelled me forward. It was strange to hear what sounded like sleigh bells in Africa in August. The incongruity matched my inner disposition. The diviners had been right; my mind was always troubled by the past. How could it be otherwise while I was back in Ivory Coast, haunted by familiar places? Sometimes I felt I was walking through a dream, rehearsing the past so often and everywhere, that I never had to recall it by will. It floated like a spectre casting a pall over my days.

I sat under the lone tree outside the hut and waited for my turn with the diviner. Hélène's face looked tired and drawn, but she didn't sit. She clutched her jaw and paced.

'Aren't you going to come in with me?' I asked.

'No, no, I don't think I want to see him after all. I'll wait out here.' She walked away to be alone with her undiagnosed miseries and her apprehension.

The bells stopped and the hut fell silent. I listened to the stillness of the field. A middle-aged woman emerged from the hut in a stooped posture to clear the low threshold. She straightened up and as she adjusted the fabric of her long wrapped skirt, she noticed us.

'Heh!' she exclaimed, turning to Hélène. 'White also come here now?'

'You've made his reputation,' Hélène said to me, tossing her chin towards the woman as she walked away.

Mr Koné ducked in and out, then gestured me forward. I entered and Amadou followed. In a matter of hours, Amadou had adopted the attitude of a devoted field assistant, curious and proud, ready to play the guide and eager to plunge into discovery. He reached for my tape recorder and made sure that the red recording light was on.

The room was cool and dark, a jarring contrast with the luminous morning that cast no shadows. It smelled of animal hide, sweet and acrid. The diviner, bare-chested and smooth skinned, stood calmly facing us. His drawstring pants, sewn from local hand-woven cotton, were roughly textured and decorated with the undulating shapes of primordial animals painted in brown vegetable dyes. His apprentice, a younger man in a tattered yellow T-shirt, came in and squatted against the opposite wall. The diviner gestured for us to sit. I noticed he was missing the third finger of his left hand. He was barefoot and I saw the toes of his right foot were shorn off. 'Classic,' I thought. 'A wounded healer is always a bridge to the divine.'

'Can you please tell us your names?' Amadou asked on my behalf.

'Nayéréhauo Kolo', the apprentice said, 'and his name is Yéo Gnonfolotian.' He pointed to my thin blue notebook and crooked his finger twice. I passed it to him and he carefully wrote the names out in rounded letters.

'The offering for the spirits is 200 francs CFA,' the apprentice said. It only amounted to about 40 cents, a symbolic token. I put the coins on the ground, and the diviner turned to face the altar. A long scar marred his lower back, as if a burning whip had stretched the skin into a twisted belt.

He lifted a bulky package from the altar and placed it on his head. It was a goatskin sewn to seal its contents. Two tassels dangled from the bundle, weighted with seed-pod bells and small amulets. The diviner pushed a thick coil of dark leather onto his upper arm. Then he picked up two twisted ram's horns with brass bells attached and gave them a shake as if to test them. He shifted from side to side and started to mumble. He was like a pilot checking his instruments, revving the engines.

Two statuettes, blackened by a thickly encrusted patina, were propped against the mud wall and it too was splattered with ribbons of darkened blood. It unsettled me to think of all the sacrifices it had taken to keep the spirits satisfied. Then I noticed that the altar was an overturned mortar. I knew what that meant. Spirits were entrapped there, their invisible energies harnessed to serve the practitioner's ends. Possession was possible.

I had seen this, twenty years before. Simon and I had gone to attend a ritual festival to witness the controlled unleashing of such powers. At the time, I hadn't known what to expect. Then a young man overtaken by possession trance mounted an overturned mortar in the middle of the dirt road. He was one of the initiates who had been dedicated to the genie of the river that morning. He twisted and gyrated, seeming to struggle with an unseen adversary. One after another, other initiates fell into possession. Some seemed drunk and disoriented, stumbling down the road on rubber legs, but the wide fixed eyes betrayed some other, more foreboding force at play. One of them hooted out in bursts like a steam engine about to jerk out of the station. Then he'd stopped, tucked his leg up under him, twisted his head to the side at a curious angle like a nervous chicken and rushed down the road. I'd been shocked by the spectacle. I'd heard about possession-trance, but I hadn't been prepared for the fearful intensity of the transformation, and it had left me shaken. I wondered if I'd be ready to meet it again.

The diviner suddenly stood to attention, snorted and shivered. He breathed uneasily and gave a kind of sneeze. His bells rattled as he began clamouring words in Senoufo. The muscles of his back twitched, and his arms began trembling violently. The sound of the bells broke through with a clatter to herald the coming of the spirits, to proclaim their presence.

I was startled into a wakeful, alert state. It was as if the diviner had become a living altar, as if the potent forces that had lain dormant in their goatskin sheath burst through his body. I was excited by the unexpected jolt and wanted to succumb to the intoxication of this sensational encounter, but I restrained the impulse. This was research. I strained to maintain the disembodied distance of the professional observer. I picked up my notebook and breathed to fix my detached demeanour. I reminded myself that I was there just to observe the technique, yet wasn't sure if what I was doing was anything like an objective science. The truth was, over the previous weeks the more I'd consulted the more I'd come to believe in their gifts. Time after time diviners accurately assessed my past and their readings corroborated one another. I'd begun to take their prescriptions more seriously. I tried to suppress a flush of shame at being a sham researcher 'gone native'. I was glad Hélène had not come in with me. I imagined her flashing an impatient glance at me, the way she used to before she'd grab the pestle from my hand when I was a young wife pounding foufou so incompetently. Here I was now, just as awkward, trying to manage this thing called fieldwork. I was undeniably in need of guidance, but it really wasn't the kind the diviners could give me.

The bells clattered insistently and competed for my attention. The diviner's mumbling became a full throaty bellow sounding a kind of chant. I was surprised and even a little frightened by the force of its vitality. Did I hear more than one voice? As the roaring litany continued, he slowly turned to face his apprentice. His eyes were glazed. They bulged and rolled in an upward gaze. His cheek pinched back in a nervous spasm. Then he put his hands to his lips as if wary of what he was about to say.

'Greetings. The spirits send you greetings,' translated his apprentice. 'We greet you, we welcome you, we know why you have come…'

'She wants a job, they say. She is seeking renown. Her way is cloudy. She wants to get ahead in the world. She wants to make herself known. She presents her candidacy. Others do also and gain the advantage. She will win out.'

My stomach jolted. It was true; I'd quit my tenure-track job to undertake this research. I would need a new post and would have to start looking when I got back. How could I not hope his prediction would come true?

Then began a recitation of sacrifices I should undertake to make it so: 'One cowry shell, unbroken. Put it in cow's milk, then take it out and wash your body in the milk. Replace the cowry in the milk, then, before leaving Korhogo, be sure to place it on a crossroads.' Also, I was to wash in the egg of a quail and leave an offering of shea butter on a tree in the forest where there are ants. This, the apprentice explained, was because 'there is no work without fault, and no piece of butter without a speck of dirt'. The image came as a gentle nudge from the spirit guides who saw the way I could torment myself with perfectionism. I could use a dose of that medicine in my work.

The bells grew louder, and the voice boomed again. 'The spirits know you. They love you! They want to go to work for you so you will get a good job, and so that their name will be known in your country.' The apprentice, folded against the wall, translated calmly, but eyed me for my reaction. 'They say, "it will cost her".'

I shifted my awkward posture on the earthen floor. 'What kind of work are the spirits going to do? What will this involve?' I asked him.

The apprentice explained that for fifty thousand francs, the diviner would make me an amulet, and that this would ensure my success.

The fee was outrageous, but how could I resist this chance? I needed the job and the book I'd write on this work would advance my career. If it could also make his spirits known, why not? I bargained the price for the help he offered, and finally agreed to the small fortune of ten thousand francs, about twenty US dollars.

The bells clattered more loudly, and the diviner announced that 'the spirits' accepted only because I did not know them yet. It was really a kind of credit, I'd see. I would have brilliant success, and then I'd return one day to thank them properly. 'Come back tomorrow and it will be ready.'

The diviner turned and took his leave of the spirits. He lifted the package from his head and returned it to the mortar, then spun and sank to the floor, his back against the wall, one knee up, the other leg outstretched. He looked like a worker just in from the field. He gazed at me blankly as if I were a stranger sharing a train compartment.

'May I interview him now?' I asked. The diviner himself nodded in consent, but he got up to go out to smoke his pipe first. Amadou excitedly checked the tape recorder and put it on pause.

By the time I left the hut, my shame had caught up with me again and my enthusiasm gave way to reason. I resolved not to come back for this amulet. I didn't want to let myself be confused again about the purpose of these consultations. I needed to remain detached, to maintain a modicum of objective distance. This kind of involvement would get me nowhere except deeper into the unfathomable dynamics of the ritual. I didn't want to become coiled into the endless cycle of sacrifice and then indebtedness, which requires more sacrifice … Why had I bartered for the talisman?

I was always struggling, it seemed, getting entangled again in things I thought I was finished with. Why had I come back to Ivory Coast, of all places? I had worked so hard to remake my life, after my husband slashed and burned our marriage here. Why then had I felt compelled to fling myself back into this place, the ground where I had sewn all the desires of my youth, and where all my meanings had finally been felled and left to rot? What had I hoped to retrieve from this pilgrimage? I couldn't remember what I had imagined I'd extract from this wilful confrontation with my past. I couldn't remember what had made me think I could go back and stand again at this crossroad of my fate and make it the point of a fresh departure. Can we negotiate destiny? Or do the spirits guide us all, despite ourselves, inexorably to our fate? Are we the creative fashioners of ourselves, or are we merely led to what we must learn about who we are and how it has to be?

I wondered all this anew the following day when I found myself, to my surprise, back where I'd intended not to return. Koné, Amadou, Hélène and I had hired a car and braved the rugged tracks into the 'bush' to seek out another renowned diviner and healer. But he had gone to tend to his fields and wasn't expected for another week or two. A quiet and dejected group, we rode back to Korhogo, travelling on a road alongside the cassava field and the hut protruding from the mounds like an enormous termite hill.

'Heh! Look where we are,' I exclaimed. 'I guess we should stop and see if the diviner's done the work he promised to do for me.' I heard myself say it. I don't know what made me change my mind. This is the way fate steals upon you, with the sudden reversals of resolve.

We got out of our taxi, and the driver trudged behind us across the field, back to Kolo's place.

'Here,' said the apprentice, holding out to me a fist-sized packet wrapped in twine, like a ball of rubber bands. 'The work he did for you is one without price. You cannot buy anything like this just anywhere. You can't put a market price, for example, on the teeth of a dead man.'

I took the amulet and shuddered as its contents rolled and rattled in my hand. The diviner spoke. 'He says to keep this in your bag, the one where you keep your papers for work. Keep it always in there, and you will win out. You will have a job – one where there are many women and close to the ocean.'

It was a gruesome thing, but here it was. I paid the fee. The diviner looked on as his apprentice folded the dirty bills. 'When you need the spirits' help, hold the amulet in your hands, say what you want, and rattle it three times.'

I wondered if I would do this. At first I'd considered these experiments as an extension of my research. Now they'd begun to burden me. How far afield I'd wandered from my carefully planned academic investigation. Here I was again in the now familiar quandary: beholden yet wary, cautious but tantalized. The reasoned divide between academic and pilgrim had shifted and become blurred. I slipped the talisman into my bag, ready once again to test the fates.

Chapter 5

Central Asian and
Northern European Shamanism

Juha Pentikäinen

Shamanism is a term, originally taken from a Russian word used to describe a phenomenon of the religions of Siberia, that has now become established in international usage. It means a form of culture that revolves around the central position of the shaman, a religious expert who acts as an intermediary between a person in his/her environment and society and the forces and the spirits of the other world. The shaman of the Central Siberian peoples may be either a man or a woman. Among the shamans there probably existed a division of tasks and a hierarchy manifested in a specialization in different shamanistic skills. The respect enjoyed by the shamans was not dependent on their sex but on what they knew and remembered. The Saami *noaidi* (in English *nojd*) is a Northern European equivalent of the Siberian shaman. Among the Saami, shamanism seems to have been a male institution; references to female shamans are found only in the late tradition.

The concept of shamanism became more generally known and its meanings broadened as a result of *Le Chamanisme et les techniques archaïques de l'extase*, written by Mircea Eliade and published in 1951.[1] According to Eliade, shamanism as an archaic technique of ecstasy is the most original form of religion. Because signs of shamanism are found in rock art, it has been considered to represent the religious culture of hunter-gatherer societies of the Palaeolithic Age. A proof of its antiquity is the fact that the phenomenon is found in both the Old and the New Worlds.

The concept of shamanism is not, however, without problems. In the comparative study of religion it is burdened by the scholarly tradition of the nineteenth-century Ur-religion hypothesis with its emphasis on evolution or diffusion. When the word shaman(ism) was translated from Russian into English and German, its meaning took on a nuance reflecting the point of view of the Christian missionaries who defined it. The expression of basic pagan religion was made into an -ism, a primitive belief, in order that the missionary work might receive greater justification. Thus the name of the phenomenon became established as shaman-ism, although this term is not found in earliest documents such as the diary of Avvakum Petrovitch,

---

[1]   Mircea Eliade, *Le Chamanisme et les techniques archaïques de l'extase* (Paris: Librarie Payot, 1951). Translated into English as *Shamanism: Archaic Techniques of Ecstasy*, trans. Willard R. Trask (Princeton: Princeton University Press, 1972).

the Archpriest of the Old Believers, which describes the activities of the shamans he witnessed among the Evenk people in the 1650s.

The concept of shamanism has also proved to be semantically problematic. The one-sided emphasis on trance as a criterion of shamanism has led many scholars to regard it as a universal feature, although this phenomenon is neither global nor similar in all shamanic cultures. Åke Hultkrantz (1920–2006) emphasizes the special features of arctic shamanism,[2] which differs from other forms of shamanism found in southern Asia, the Far East and America. Ecstasy is only one of the characteristics of shamanism. It means the use of various trance-inducing techniques in order to make contact with other worlds or other states of reality. Moreover, the shamanistic view of life emphasizes the existence of more than one soul, of which the free soul can in a state of trance or a dream leave the body and return to it when its spiritual journey is complete. Another central aspect is the view of the universe as existing in three planes, with the shaman acting as an intermediary between the celestial world, our human world and the underworld. In this he has assistant animal spirits; these are manifested in the Saami culture by the supernatural wild reindeer, fish and bird, which are essential for the journey of the shaman's soul, and into which he is believed to be able to metamorphose. The old shaman must initiate his successor into the mysteries before the latter is ordained into the sacral position of reverence among the community. At this stage, the shaman often receives a ritual costume and the insignia and accoutrements of his role, which vary according to culture: a drum or other musical instruments, a mask, belt, shoes, headdress, staff, sleigh, idols, images of the assistant spirits and so on. In many cultures, the decoration of the skin of the shaman's drum constitutes a map for his journey to the other world; among the Saami it varies locally, as does the technical structure of the drum. The use of the drum is not the sole prerogative of the Saami shaman; its use for predicting the future is a practice available to every man.

Shamans commonly used monotone drumming and frenzied dancing in order to attain a state of ecstasy. Among Northern Siberian peoples, they also sometimes used narcotic substances like the fly agaric fungus (*amanita muscaria*). Fasting was also one of their methods of preparation. In addition to dancing accompanied by drumming, the Saami *nojd* chanted shamanistic incantations (*yoiking*); this form of chanting was so important a part of shamanism that it was prohibited, along with the shaman's drum, during the missionary crusade to Lapland in the eighteenth century and in the preaching of the Laestadian revivalist preachers in the nineteenth century.

---

[2]   See Åke Hultkrantz, 'Arctic Religions', in Lindsay Jones (ed.), *Encyclopedia of Religion*, vol. 1 (Detroit: Macmillan Reference, 2005).

The Basic Concepts: *Saman*, Shamanizing, Shamanism, Shamanhood

The concept of shaman comes from Central and Eastern Siberian indigenous peoples, most of whom are speakers of either Mandchu-Tungusic or Nivkh. The word '*saman*' means 'someone who knows'. This 'knowing' is the basic word required to comprehend the whole phenomenon in its ecological cradle in Northern Eurasia. The knowledge is oral, and is described as a painful and responsible capacity, as a duty or vocation that is not easy to accept by someone 'chosen by the spirits' and trained to his/her office by the elder shaman of his/her clan. This process is described here on the basis of Siberian fieldwork that I have conducted since 1988. The concept of shamanhood, instead of shamanism, was suggested in 1994, since the latter term is ism-oriented and thus not accurate in its cultural context. Shamanhood (parallel to the older Russian word *samanstvo*) is a kind of cultural mother-tongue rather than a religion in the languages that lack the concept of 'religion' in the Western meaning of the word (from Latin *religio*).

Shamanizing (Russian *samaniit*) is a word that acknowledges comprehension of the special skills of the *saman*: those of questioning and replying, divining, foreseeing in trance or dreams events, success and fate in life, death and afterlife. It is his/her heavy duty, before and on behalf of his/her clan or people, to remember the great narratives of his/her people, singing, narrating and acting them in the rituals, so healing 'the pains of my people'. The importance of oral and rhythmic memory is emphasized, since almost every one of the sixty Siberian shamans I have met was illiterate. Besides the drum, there are several other instruments used by the shaman in the rituals of healing and divination. Siberia has taught me that the heart of the drum is not its front side, to which previous studies have been limited, but behind its cover: this is where it is possible to find the comprehensive map of the shaman's huge esoteric knowledge and clan symbolism if the researcher has the patience and capacity to listen to 'someone who knows'.

Such reports as *Arctic Languages: An Awakening* and *Endangered Languages*[3] tell of great threats concerning many small languages indigenous to the arctic regions, due to the simultaneous ecological processes in the North.[4] How one language dies while another survives is a question related to ethnic/national processes, which should be carefully studied in comparative research, since there is no comprehensive study on the special role of such native religio-national leaders as shamans in these processes. This kind of approach following the principle 'rather

---

[3]   Dirmid R.F. Collis (ed.), *Arctic Languages: An Awakening* (Paris: UNESCO, 1990); Robert H. Robins and Eugenius M. Uhlenbeck (eds), *Endangered Languages* (Oxford: Berg, 1991).

[4]   For more details, see, for example, Juha Pentikäinen and Péter Simoncsics (eds), *Shamanhood: An Endangered Language*, Instituttet for sammenlignende kulturforskning, Serie B, Skrifter 117 (Oslo: Novus, 2006). See also Juha Pentikäinen (ed.), *Shamanhood: Symbolism and Epic*, Bibliotheca Shamanistica 9 (Budapest: Akadémiai Kiadó, 2001) and Juha Pentikäinen, *Shamanism and Culture* (Helsinki: Etnika, 1998).

deeper than broader', as H. Halpert put it,[5] leads research of shamanic cultures away from the generalizations typical of studies on shamanism following Eliade's classic 1951 work, criticized by Åke Hultkrantz, among others, for speculations regarding shamanism as the 'Ur-religion of mankind' guiding research on shamans and their ecological and cultural milieus. To understand the manifestations of shamanism in different geographical contexts, voices of contemporary female and male shamans must be introduced and studied from original sources in written and oral documents based on unique, so far unpublished field data. During my fieldwork in Siberia since 1988, I have met representatives of the last generation of the persecuted Siberian shamans, who have introduced me to the esoteric secrets of shamanic knowledge. The joint fieldwork related to this project has been carried out mainly among the Khanty and Mansi at the tributaries of the river Ob and the Manchu-Tungusic peoples in Central Siberia and at the Lower Amur region.

How and why has such an archaic phenomenon as shamanism overcome the pressures of the great ideological, religious and ecological changes that have taken place since the nineteenth century in various territories and cultures? This question is an interesting target for research, invoking, for example, the influence of Soviet ideology, the pressures of collectivization and the impact of oil, military and other industries both in Siberia and in America among the indigenous peoples, including ethnic and ecological influences. The fieldwork carried out in these regions will, on the basis of archival and fresh ethnographical data, give evidence of the importance of the role of shamans in the ethnic revival and survival processes of the indigenous peoples. Shamans were persecuted for ideological and religious reasons in their respective countries. Some of those who survived have become remarkable national/ethnic leaders, their traditional authority strengthened by their contribution to the revitalization processes of these peoples.

The conceptual history of shamanism will show how the word 'shamanism' was created under the influence of the Christian world view. Shaman(ism) was identified as the 'old form of paganism', and shamanic peoples (Greek, *ethnos*) as the 'heathens' (*ethnikos*) to be converted by Christian missions. Shamanism as the culture of the circumpolar-subarctic belt from Northern Europe to Central Asia may be characterized by features such as these: it is practised by relatively small and isolated populations; it is oral-unwritten, since it lacks any kind of holy scripts or books; it has a separate class of religious specialists, a scale of the initiated beginning with the simple member of the clan and ending with the shaman of the highest qualifications; contrary to Church (or Party) hierarchy, the shamanic society of practitioners is based on collaboration and partnership rather than subjugation. In its world view, sacred and profane are a correlated pair; sacredness saturates everything – language, society and nature – for someone practising shamanism.

The importance of an ethnolinguistic approach in shamanic research is related to the fact that shamanic peoples today speak languages globally defined as

---

[5]   H. Halpert, 'Folklore: Breath versus Depth', *Journal of American Folklore* 71/280 (1958): 97–103.

endangered. Interestingly enough, the last speakers of many dying languages are the shamans of the northern indigenous peoples. This explains the role shamans are playing in the revival of indigenous cultures worldwide.

Central Siberian Shamanhood in the Process of Cultural Change

Besides languages that include the native concept of *saman*, there are many Siberian indigenous languages that have their own words to classify their religious specialists (including special terms for female shamans), as well as expressions for 'shamanizing', for the drum, for the hammer and for the other shamanic instruments and tools. Even if the native concept of *saman* is lacking, the basic concepts are expressed by shamanic beliefs and behaviours. The simplified assumption is that 'shamanism' is a common term for all kinds of popular belief that preceded the appearance of universal religion in Northern Eurasia (and the rest of the globe as well) during the greater part of the Holocene, that is, in the last ten thousand years and, in all probability, also before.

What is said about popular beliefs, including shamanism, is true, *mutatis mutandis*, also for native languages; the more so when we take into consideration the outstanding role played by poetic (shamanic, sacral) narrative in the ancient Uralic society – as Eugene Helimski has emphasized.[6] Centuries' long harassment and persecutions did not harm shamanism and its followers so much as the recent exploitation of reserves of subsoil wealth, first of all of mineral oil, with devastating consequences to nature, flora and fauna and, consequently, also to the society and the *genre de vie* of natives. The oil industry drew workers in large numbers who needed housing, so modern cities of concrete were built in the middle of the West Siberian marshland (and elsewhere in the region) in the second half of the twentieth century, driving out natives from their ancient settlements, pasture lands, game preserves and fishing areas. In spite of the fact that oil companies today show more restraint, first of all with regard to land rights, and pay relatively generously for the land acquired from natives, the money they offer and the goods the natives can buy with it – the practice of consuming, in short – destroys all that has remained of the traditional way of life – without applying force, and mostly by the natives' own volition.

Shamans are not priests, but ordinary men or women who engage in shamanistic duties when the need arises: when someone is sick or when someone dies, or when an important question concerning the community's livelihood or happiness needs to be answered. The essential point is that the community, which has appointed the shaman, trusts in the shaman's power to act as an intermediary between this

---

[6]   Eugene Helimski, 'Proto-Uralic Gradation: Continuation and Traces', in H. Leskinen et al. (eds), *Congressus Octavus Internationalis Fenno-Ugristarum*, Pars I: *Orationaes plenariae et conspectus quinquennales* (Jyväskylä: Jyväskylä Moderatores, 1995), pp. 17–51, at p. 44.

world and the afterlife. The role of the shamans has been so pivotal in Siberian cultures that several shamanistic people and small communities have fallen into mass psychosis when their shamans have died. Shirokogoroff, among others, has stated that finding a new shaman is a prerequisite for the continuing existence of such communities.[7]

Comparison between Siberian Shamans and Finno-Ugric *Nojds*

In spite of the fact that the majority of Siberian cultures do not know the concept 'shaman', they are shamanic. Some of the circa thirty-five northern peoples who speak Uralic languages, a family of languages that also includes Finns and the Ob Ugrians, call their shamans '*noita*' (Fi.) or '*nait*' (Mansi). There are epic songs (Fi. *runo*, Saami *leudd*) telling about the trips of the souls. Their mythologies include a number of souls or spirits, which all have their own names. It was believed that the 'spirit' of the shaman could depart from the shaman's body to take trips to the kingdom of death, for example. The purpose of these trips was to find solutions to the problems encountered by the community or its members. These trips to the kingdom of death were considered dangerous. The shaman took them on behalf of the community, to retrieve a patient's soul, to seek the knowledge needed for the healing rite or to find solutions to problems. Finnish epic poetry includes examples of shaman trips: shaman travels to meet the people's primitive witch, Antero Vipunen, who had died long ago and was already decomposing with spruces growing from his temples.

Transformation powers are essential for a shaman. It is believed that shamans are able to control different levels of consciousness and are able to fall into a state of ecstasy; they can even change their gender during the rite or transform themselves into different animal forms. Shamans do not operate alone. They have a number of 'auxiliary spirits' to help them. One of these is more important than the others; the Nanais at the Lower Amur, for instance, talk about special 'nuptial spirits' that choose the shaman. The shaman meets these nuptial spirits in dreams, and sometimes the shaman reveals that he or she has had sexual intercourse with a spirit, which may appear in the form of a bear, a tiger or a sea lion, for example.

Shamans possess different gifts and skills. Some of them are inherent and manifest themselves directly after birth; the community is able to determine whether a baby is going to be a shaman from its teeth, fontanel or hair. Later in life other indicators, like dreams that come true, unusual experiences or virtual insanity, show whether the person possesses 'the painful gift of shamanism'. In many cultural traditions, the shaman's role is undesirable, and accepted only under duress. Not all the skills of shamans are hereditary; some are received from the

---

[7]   S.M. Shirokogoroff, *Psychomental Complex of the Tungus* (London: Kegan Paul, 1935).

spirits. The work of shamans is physically hard, because they have to carry the 'weight of the spirits' during the rituals.

Not all Siberian healers or religious men or women are called shamans. Shamans may belong to different levels of the internal hierarchy of the community. Shamanism for the Khants in the Ob region is a mythical clan phenomenon concerning animal and human families. Families made up of parents and their children are not as important in hunting communities as kin consisting of different generations, branches and clans connected matri- or patrilineally. Each clan has its own guardian spirit that reflects the surrounding nature. The bear, the wolf, the reindeer, the swan, the red-throated diver and the otter are important mythical animals for the Khants, who live in the northern tundra and taiga areas. The killer whale, the beluga, the *kita* migratory fish, the tiger and the sable are popular in the Amur region. The essential point is that shamanism thrives within the clan and the family, and that continuation can be found for the ageing shaman from within the clan. It is considered fatal if someone tries to muddle the shamanic paths in the afterlife by, for example, refusing to receive the 'call of the spirits to accept the painful fate of a shaman'. A topical issue in the Amur region during the 1990s was the rehabilitation of a Nanai nurse named Ella, who refused to become a shaman.

The shamanic skills include healing, a knowledge of herbs (herbalism) and mythology. In addition to psychopathologic characteristics, often called insanity, the main criterion in the election of a shaman is the knowledge of shamanistic folklore, myths, songs and incantations. Naturally, the previous shaman has a say in the election: it is, after all, his or her duty to transfer all mythical and other information across to his/her successor. The shaman has to know the name of the family's original shaman and the names of all shaman ancestors; she or he has to know the myths about the clan's or family's genesis and be able to describe the connections to the animal system and what species of animal the clan descends from totemistically. Before the initiation, the shaman mentor informs the new shaman about different ceremonies.

A shaman's oath is known in many cultures. In this oath, the shaman expresses his or her ethical principles and the source and purpose of the mythical information he or she possesses. The oath of the Buryats, who live by Lake Baikal, goes like this: 'After this initiation and after having been blessed as a shaman, I swear I will protect children and be a father to orphans. I shall not withhold the truth about the fate of the ill. May the father in heaven be aware of this oath, and may mother earth be its witness.'[8]

Shaman equipment, such as the drum, clothes, mask, bag, belt, musical instruments and idols, portray the figures that the shaman has learned to control on his transmigratory trips. They describe the shaman's travel route, the 'shaman's road' as it is called, and they may also be a cognitive map of earthly topography.

---

[8]   L. Kuzmina, 'Generic Diversity of the Shamanic Folklore among the Peoples of Siberia', in Ildikó Lehtinen (ed.), *Traces of Central Asian Culture in the North*, Mémoires de la Société Finno-Ougrienne 194 (Helsinki: Suomalais-Ugrilainen Seura, 1986), pp. 71–80.

More importantly, however, the equipment conveys myths that delineate the topography of another, invisible world, for both the shaman and the community.

The traditional shrine of shamans is a hut, '*tshum*', or a *yurt*. The hut is used as an everyday dwelling, and is transformed into a holy place with traditional rituals before the rites. As a matter of fact, the structure of the hut reflects the three-tier world. The fireplace is the centre of the hut; the fire must not die out during the rite and to prevent this it is fed with bellows. The 'holy smoke' that wafts out through a hole in the ceiling symbolizes the connection of the ongoing rite with the powers in heaven, on earth and in the underworld, which maintain the universal balance. When someone is being healed, his or her pain touches the whole cosmos and the healing can happen only if universal harmony can be attained. The rites are performed by the fire. Usually the shaman sits in the northern corner of the hut, on a reindeer or bear skin that has been placed over a sacred piece of wood – birch or spruce twigs. The supporting bulk of the hut is the 'axis mundi', corresponding to the tree of life that supports the cosmos. Thus the hut is a scale model of the celestial universe, concretely consecrated by its complex ritualistic structure. The shaman's stick or crane turns the hut into a holy space by pointing out of the hole through which the shaman takes his or her magical flight between the different layers of the world, sometimes resting on the bottom of the lake or on a crest of a cloud.

What is performed here: is it a religion or something else? When I asked Lindza Beldy, a Nanai shaman, this question in 1992, she answered: 'Religion? That is something the Russians have. We only have our shamans.' Outsiders often focus on the superficial features of shamanism (the drum, the mask, the shaman costume and cap) with which shamanism has been identified and by which it has been condemned. Research into practical shamanism, symbolism, folklore, mythology and terminology has largely been forgotten behind the visible shamanic emblems and elements.

When an ageing shaman leaves on his or her final trip, he or she often tries to drown the drum – the shaman's soul – in a swamp. The purpose of this is to ensure that nothing disturbs the shaman's peace in the afterlife. The death of a shaman is recorded in arctic mythology: 'the departure of a lonely man' to his own river, and to the abode of the dead, to join the other dead members of the family. The decision to publicly announce the intention to set off on this journey of no return means social death for the shaman. If another person joins the shaman and helps him achieve his voluntary death, it is not considered to be a crime comparable to murder.

The kingdom of death is located in the north and underground. The kingdom of death is a 'travel resort' for witches, but for ordinary people it is a final destination. The cemeteries of the Khants are located on a different side of the river to the area inhabited by humans. The '*Buni*' of the Nanais is a shadowy place behind the Amur Mountains: it is both a geographical location and a mythical destination for shamans. It is believed that a bridge, a tensed phallus, crosses the Buni River, beyond which lies the cemetery area. Within the Buni area, all clans have their own Bunis and the shaman escorts the deceased there. In September 1991 and 1994 I recorded this *kasa taori* ritual on video. These were the first – and probably the last – times since Stalin's persecutions of 1937 that these rites had been performed; most of the shamans who performed the ritual were dead by 2007.

Encounters between Shamans and Missionary Religions

In earlier days, it was customary that shamans should not be buried underground like ordinary people. They were buried unattached to the ground, so that the shaman's spirit was free to travel between the layers of the universe. It was the visible elements of this kind that became the target for missionary actions of the new religions invading the Northern Hemisphere, the main alternative being Christianity, with both its Western (Catholic and Protestant) and Eastern branches (Eastern Orthodox and Old Believer groups). In Central Asia there are signs of Islamic influence (Sufism). In Eastern Asia, particularly in the subarctic region, the influence of Buddhism is apparent (Lamaism). Taoism, which is 3,000 years old, has influenced regions near the border with China. The healing rites of Taoism represent Chinese shamanism.

The missionary work of Christians began back in the Middle Ages and was not only religious but also imperialistic in nature. The first churches and chapels in Lapland were built close to the mouths of the fjords and the rivers of the Arctic Ocean. They were the northern landmarks of the conquests of the Occidental and Oriental churches and of the empires supporting these churches. The parallel existence of missionary religion and traditional belief can be seen in Eastern Asia where the shamanism of Manchurian-Tungusian and Yakutian peoples has been affected by Tibetan and Mongolian Buddhism, particularly Lamaism. During my Siberian field trips I noted that Nanais may use red Miao-clothes as their altar, for reasons they cannot explain. In addition to worshipping Nanai spirits, they also worship Miaos. Vladimir Basilov, who has studied Central Asian Islamic shamanism, describes a symbiosis of shamanism and Islamic Sufism.[9] The Central Asian shaman is usually a woman and she travels to the Muslim paradise to enjoy cooling baths.

The religion of the Ob Ugrian Khants is still pre-Christian, although missionary work has been underway in the region for about two hundred years. It is an example of a natural religion that has survived through adaptation. Khants have accepted baptism, they visit Russian churches when away on business trips and they also practise their own shamanistic religion in the taiga and tundra areas. In the 1920s and 1930s, when churches were closed due to the atheistic revolution, the practice of religion was continued in the wilds. Characteristics of Christian belief, brought by the missionaries in the eighteenth century, have integrated with pre-Christian beliefs. In such a mixed mythology, Jesus Christ may be the youngest son of the

---

[9]   Vladimir Basilov, *Schamanentum bei den Völkern Mittelasiens und Kasachstans*, trans. R. Schletzer [from Russian into German], Mittelasiatische Studien 1 (Berlin: Schletzer, 1992).

God of the sky, *Toorum*, as one 90-year-old shaman told me in 1990. In his holy sleigh, this shaman also had an icon of St Nicholas, who was one of the most beloved saints of the Old Ritualists (Raskolniks). He also told me that he knew a man whose father had been baptized. The icon proves that the Khanty culture was in contact with the dissenters from the Russian Orthodox Church in the seventeenth and eighteenth centuries.

The Role of Shamans in the Indigenous Battle for Survival: The Khants

Traditional northern nature religions have been best preserved in the areas of the former Soviet Union. The atheistic revolution of 1917 was a major setback for missionary religions, but did not affect shamanism to any great extent. Although some shamans were killed during Stalin's persecutions, traditional religion survived. It stayed alive in a sort of frozen state; it avoided the ideological developments brought about by Western civilization, the school system and Americanism that changed the nature of religion in the Nordic countries and the New World.

Let's take a closer look at the fate of the Khants. In 1990 I visited a Khanty winter village, where the inhabitants told me about the tragic reasons behind their latest great change of residence, which had taken place about twenty years earlier. Their former winter village was flattened by diggers making way for a railway, their sacrificial grove was replaced by a natural gas tower, their old cemetery was destroyed and tourists who came to fish burned down their summer village. The Khants had to move 50 kilometres further into the forest; they had to build new winter, spring, summer and autumn villages, find new lichen areas for the reindeer, make new trap paths and find new fishing areas. The new areas of the Khants cover approximately 200 square kilometres of forests, tundra and swamp lands. The harmony of the winter village was broken in January 1990, when a Bashkir turned up and suggested that geological exploration should start in the region. 'We will not take anything away from you. We'll just examine what riches we can find under your reindeers' grazing lands. If we find oil, civilisation will change your backward life.' The Khants could not take it anymore. They did not even negotiate, but summoned all the men of the village to a meeting, where they decided on a four-point action plan. Oleg Donskijh, who was part of my expedition, and I were asked to publish the following thesis in a glasnost-spirited Soviet magazine:

1. The old usufruct warrants proprietary rights to the land.
2. Geological explorations of the Khanty lands must be prohibited, because they disturb nature's ecological balance.
3. Indigenous peoples must have the right of self-government within their own regions.
4. Indigenous peoples must have the right to decide which school their children attend. During the first four years, tuition must be given in the pupil's native language.

The old Khanty shaman was present when the Bashkir came to the village. He also carefully kept track of what happened at the meeting, which was chaired by his sons, the shaman disciple and reindeer owner Ivusef and his brother Yeremey from the city of Surgut, our guide and the master builder of the Ob River bridges. When it was time for the rituals, the old shaman took command. In the case of the Khants, shamanism is experiencing a renaissance and it has been linked to the battle for ethnic survival. The old shaman, whom I met in the Khanty winter village, was one of eight shamans captured during Stalin's persecutions of the 1930s. He was the only one to avoid execution; he had told the policemen that he wasn't a real shaman: 'I wouldn't be here, if I were a real shaman.' That was true, he told me; he said he belonged to the category of shamans who never worked their magic to harm anyone. In all the winter villages I visited, every man owned a drum. Shamanism is not going to die with the old shaman. Proof of the continuity is demonstrated by the fact that one of the shaman's sons was involved in the initiation phase of 1990. He should be the next shaman, if, as the saying goes, 'spirits are submissive'.

Shamanism is an integral part of current northern identity. Those arctic peoples who have kept up shamanism seize their shamans like drowning men clutching at straws. It seems that the renaissance of shamanism is clearly an intrinsic part of the ethnic revival of the Siberian peoples. It remains to be seen whether this return to old values will provide a path that leads away from the current stringent conditions. The Ugrians of Ob were, according to the researchers who visited their region at the turn of the century, doomed to extinction within a couple of decades. In 1897, for instance, the number of Ostyaks (Khantys) was only 19,700 and the prominent linguistics experts of the time, Heikki Paasonen and K.F. Karjalainen, believed that extinction was inevitable. The decline of the peoples was both economic and intellectual. The revolution changed the situation for two decades. Lenin's nationality policy supported tuition in native languages and established a basis for the restricted autonomy of the small peoples. According to the principles of Lenin's policies, the Khants and Mansis were entitled to self-government within their own autonomous district, which is called Khanty-Mansiysk. In practice, the autonomy has only been formal and restricted to a 'unit of indigenous peoples' consisting of only a few members and operating only in local administration concerning economic, social and educational issues.

A new feature in the shamanism of the Khants in the 1990s has been the shift from family and clan institutions to wider, even national assemblies. Khanty men convene at shamanistic sessions in March and September. In these sessions, as well as discussing seasonal fluctuations in their livelihoods, they also discuss the current ethnic and national aspirations of the Khanty people. They have declared that their natural religion is their national religion; the Komis, Maris and Udmurts have made similar declarations.

Since the 1990s, Sakha (in the Autonomous Republic of Yakut) has been seeking independence from Russia. The objective of the Sakhas is to revive the Sakha language and its national characteristics. Political attention has been paid to shamanism, which was suppressed during Stalin's persecutions. Shamanism has been on the agenda of conferences arranged with the support of UNESCO and the shaman theatre of Yakutia performs plays that describe shaman culture.

The problem in Yakutia is that the village shamans and healers do not have confidence in a politicized shamanism. They prefer to continue practising their old rituals in the villages rather than participate in folk festivals that have only recently been revived. I have noticed similar attitudes with respect to the revival of the natural religions of the Finno-Ugrian peoples. The recent phenomenon can thus be interpreted as a birth of a shamanistic folklore, portrayed by local dance groups and ensembles, whose members' native language is usually Russian.

The Role of Shamanism and the Changing Map of Arctic Languages

Northern cultures are shaped by arctic nature. The intensity of seasonal changes, scarcity of natural resources and harsh living conditions determine cultural characteristics and affect the economic and social structure. The concept 'arctic' is itself both ecological and mythical. The term comes from the Greek word *arktos*, which means bear. Originally, arctic areas described those areas in the Northern Hemisphere that were located underneath the Great Bear (Big Dipper) constellation.

The climatic southern border of the arctic zone is 10°C in July. Although the Arctic Circle is generally regarded as the geographical southern border of the north, we usually refer to a larger area when we talk about the north. On an ecological basis, we can divide the north into two cultural categories: the arcticum, which includes the northern seas and the tundra areas around them, and the taiga, the subarctic forest area. Short summers and long and cold winters are typical characteristics of both tundra and taiga, and the fauna and flora are basically the same.

The word *circumpolar* emphasizes both the location near the pole and, when used in describing religions, it also reflects the point of view used in the comparative studies of these cultures. The most important factor creating this uniformity is the ecology of the northern areas. Its barren nature and remote location have preserved the cultures in similar forms for thousands of years. Actually, northern biology may be affected by the cold, but it also defies it. There are more species here than you would imagine; the number of species in the arctic zone is approximately 200 while, in subarctic forests, the number of species may be as high as 600. The shaman's role within the culture has been the control of the arctic/subarctic fauna and flora and herbalistic and ethnomedicinal expertise.

Ethnicity is emphasized in the definitions of northern religions. Contrary to some missionary or literary religions that are founded on the supremacy of human beings, the key quality of ethnic religions is the way in which nature, economy, society, language and other cultural factors are comprehensively interconnected. The northern languages do not have exactly equivalent words for 'religion'; the holiness or religiousness of different phenomena is defined by real life and rituals, custom and habits. Religion has been so well integrated into real life that its characteristics and limits are defined naturally, in contrast to the missionary religions that have spread around the northern areas. Cultural identity is the essence of northern religions. Lately a feeling of there being a common northern family of indigenous peoples has been gaining momentum. Northern indigenous peoples call themselves the Fourth World and demand attention and recognition at international assemblies. The concept is political. The First World consists of Europe and the Mediterranean regions, the American continent is the Second, Asian and African developing countries are the Third and now the northern minorities search for their own place, described as the Fourth World.

None of the superficial characteristics, the Arctic Circle, eternal glaciers or temperature levels, are decisive when we try to decide whether a culture is northern or not. For instance, many peoples living on the southern side of the Arctic Circle in Russia consider themselves to be part of the '*narody severa*', a group of twenty-six northern peoples. The Athabascan and Algonkian Indians in subarctic Canada, and the Ainus in Hokkaido, Japan also identify themselves as northern peoples. Northern can thus be understood as being a characteristic of a nation or ethnic group that feels that it belongs to the group of northern peoples.

Hugh Brody believes that the best way to find our true selves is to go to the place where we think the edge of the world is.[10] When we face societies and countries that question our assumptions and prejudices, we may realize the importance of other people and the real truth about ourselves. The northern edge of the world has been an interesting subject matter for researchers since ancient times. Mythical expectations have been attached to the North; for example, witches are said to become stronger the further north they live. For a researcher of religions, northern areas are also interesting since the boundary between myth and history is so blurred.

The North has been defined from a southern point of view. The North has been unfamiliar, 'Terra Hyperborea Incognita', the unknown land of the Hyberboreans. The history of exploration journeys and missionary work has been the conquest of this unknown region. The North has been the edge of the world, its topography characterized by the myths of the afterworld before the southern people started including the northern areas in their maps. At first, maps depicted northern regions as uncontoured grey areas floating in water.

Herodotus (485–425 BCE), a Greek historian, wrote about Hyperboreans who live in the North, in Terra Hyperborea, behind the mountains, who are dignified, peaceful people. Although archaeological findings show that several Viking expeditions travelled through polar areas, the topography of the northern areas was surprisingly obscure in the maps of the early Middle Ages and in the ancient Sagas of the Icelanders. In the ninth century, medieval Icelanders were familiar with a world reaching from Jerusalem to Newfoundland. Undoubtedly they were

---

[10] Hugh Brody, *Living Arctic: Hunters of the Canadian North* (London: Faber and Faber, 1988), p. xiii.

even more familiar with the topography of their own isles and the regions of Scandinavia, Finland, the Baltic and Greenland.

Medieval maps served a different purpose than contemporary maps. They were not used to measure the distance or direction from the northern isles to Jerusalem. Instead, medieval maps were a sum of the historical and geographical knowledge of the time, a mythical travel guide with an added artistic dimension.

Gradually, information on the northern peoples of Tsarist Russia was amassed. Travel reports such as Philip J. von Strahlenberg's *Das nord-und östliche Theil von Europa und Asia[11]* included observations about the arctic religions and particularly shamanism. Von Strahlenberg (1676–1747) was an officer in the Swedish army who was captured by the Russians at the battle of Pultava and imprisoned for thirteen years. He devoted most of his time in prison to the study of folklore and linguistics, and presented the idea of the Finno-Ugrian family of languages in his work. He mentioned nearly all of the languages that are currently included in this set of languages. Von Strahlenberg believed that the speakers of these languages had once been one nation, to which the Huns also belonged.

As knowledge about different peoples was amassed in the nineteenth century, a new branch of science, northern ethnography, was born. Ethnography was nation-oriented historiography, which described the language, way of life and religion of a nation on the basis of the information that the historians themselves had gathered on their journeys.

The old northern cultures were nomadic; home was all of the surrounding area that the eye could see and not a particular place or house. Nomads marked their home areas with trap paths, dams and fish traps. Mobility also manifested itself in their religion. The northern nomads packed their Gods into sledges and worshipped trees and stones along their routes. The religions of these indigenous peoples are ethnic, and different ethnic groups can be identified on the basis of their linguistic characteristics. Language is the most important factor that highlights the uniqueness of an ethnic group. Nowadays, most northern Siberians are multilingual or at least bilingual, and master the official language (Russian) better than their native language. Within the arctic zone, however, shamanistic expressions are prominent, and it seems that shamanism is one of the most original elements of the northern peoples' philosophy of life.

Between about seventy and one hundred ethnic groups live in the northern regions, depending on how you define an 'ethnic group'. The northern language map is changing: about three to five languages die every decade; by the year 2050 probably half of the current languages will have disappeared. The state of native languages is a topical problem, in spite of the revival process of the indigenous cultures. Exploitation of oil and gas resources has initiated an ecological and social process that threatens the existence of many indigenous peoples.

---

[11]   Philip Johann von Strahlenberg, *Das nord- und östliche Theil von Europa und Asia*, intro. J.R. Krueger, Studia Uralo-Altaica 8 (Szeged: Univ. Szegediensis de Attila József Nominata, 1975 [1730]).

In Northern Russia, the most northern languages (Nganasany, Nenets, Khanty, Dolgany, Chukchi, Koryak) seem to have the brightest future. Other languages have been fading away so quickly that their total disappearance within a century seems inevitable. They do not disappear suddenly, however; even when Russian has taken the place of everyday languages, native vocabulary is still used when repairing fishing nets and traps, when tending to reindeer, when picking berries, on traditional hunting trips and, of course, during rituals. The language of shamanism is still part of the culture, even when the native language is otherwise forgotten. Archaic religions may significantly help to maintain and even revive local cultures and languages.

Small nationalities were threatened first and foremost by Nikita Khrushchev, Premier of the USSR between 1958 and 1964. His school reform programme supported Russian and the idea of *'aerogorod'*, rural agricultural cities, killed both the villages and their languages by gathering the rural population into cities and other 'dynamic' population centres, where small languages were swiftly replaced by Russian. Khrushchev also launched a programme called the 'Dream of the Century'. Akademgorodok, the Academic City, was founded close to Novosibirsk and scientific centres started exploring and exploiting natural resources, leading to considerable changes in the living conditions of the indigenous peoples.

The culture and the habits of the northern peoples require a lot of space. Modern technology has put the traditional northern way of life in danger. Oil discoveries in Alaska have revolutionized the history of Alaska – a cheap piece of land at the time when the Russians sold it to the Americans – and its inhabitants: immigrants, Inuits, Aleuts and Indians. The Nenets were expelled from Novaya Zemlya to make way for a strategic nuclear test site. The rich natural gas resources in Ob, Yenisey and Yamal seem to take the wilderness away from the northern indigenous peoples. As the last wilds are being destroyed, most of the total of seventy northern peoples whose lifestyle relies on the wilds are disappearing.

Shamanism in Practice: Animal Ceremonialism of Bear Feasts and Reindeer Offerings

The mythologies of many northern peoples include stories about initial relationships between a primitive man or woman and an animal. According to myths, the progenitor of a tribe is usually an animal with human characteristics. Kai Donner, who has studied Finnish-related peoples, says that the animal progenitor is the most important among the divine beings of the tribe.[12] Killing that particular animal is considered to be cannibalism. In the bear rituals of the Siberian peoples, the interplay between the animal representing masculine power and womanhood is emphasized. In 1990, a Khanty shaman told me the myth of the relationship

---

[12] Kai Donner, *Bland Samojeder i Sibiren: Åren, 1911–1913, 1914* (Helsingfors: Söderström, 1915).

between the Khants' progenitress and the holy bear. A bear is killed and, after it has been dead for a week, a woman, or a male shaman dressed as a woman, wakes the bear up. The bear is then sent away, and it is believed that it rises up to the Great Bear constellation. The Big Dipper/Great Bear is thus the heavenly representative of the mythical progenitor of the Khants. The death of a bear is a wedding spectacle for the Khants, in which the sacred origin of the people is revered.

The myths describing the interaction of Gods, spirits and people are often structurally similar, but the content varies depending on which animal is central in each environment, economy or culture. The rituals follow a certain pattern, irrespective of the particular spirit that is being worshipped. The master brings game home and a welcoming feast is arranged in honour of the animal. At this feast, the animal's meat is eaten, and the guest of honour is then sent on a return journey with rituals, where the bones and other remains of the animal are processed. This type of ritual is typical of the Gilyaks and the Ainus, of the Indians in North America, of the Continental Inuits in North Alaska, of the Mistassini Crees and the Bering Aleuts.

The basic idea of the rituals is to treat the guest in a way that ensures that there is enough game, spirits and actual animals to guarantee a successful hunting and fishing season the following year. The aim is to adjust the behaviour of the hunters and fishermen according to the annual rhythm of the animal world. This means that the hibernation and migration periods of game and fish are taken into account. Northern hunters and fishermen knew the migration routes and times by heart. They were also aware of the hibernation periods of bears and reptiles, and reacted to them in their everyday lives and in their rituals. The basic objective of periodic religious rituals was to ensure the continuing success of hunting trips, that is, the fertility of the animals and finally the happiness and existence of the family, clan or nation. It is the shaman's duty to call to mind this mythical relationship and to portray it in the rituals.

Rituals are arranged at particular times, when a species of animal is expected to appear at a certain place or is expected to wake from its hibernation at the beginning of the hunting season. The Ainus, the Gilyaks and Khants observed the rhythm of the bear, whereas the whalers on the Alaskan coast or Bering Strait followed the movements of whales.

The Amur Nanais arranged their *kasa taori* ritual according to the rhythm of the running of the migratory fish. The aim of this ceremony, which I recorded on video in September 1991 and again in September 1994, was to send the *mugden* spirits of the dead to Buni, the kingdom of death. The dead are sent away so that they cannot threaten the activities of the living or affect success in fishing. A central episode in the ritual is the erection of a tree of life. The shaman climbs up the tree and keeps a lookout for the migratory fish; when he 'sees' them, he symbolically harpoons the fish.

As the economic structure of a community changes, the rituals are adapted to new situations. An important development in the North was the taming of the reindeer to be used as a draft animal and to produce meat and milk. Reindeer nomadism became an expansive culture. The most effective reindeer breeders were probably the Nenets, the Saamis and the Chukchis in northern tundras, and the forest Saamis, Komis, Khants and Evenkis in subarctic forest areas.

Until recently, the Khants have lived in a *tshum*, which is a tepee-type hut with reindeer skin covers. These huts can be carried along, except for the supporting poles. On a windy tundra it is a practical shelter; a Khanty family can set up its hut in five minutes. The area in between the villages and around them is understood as being the common property of the Khanty clan. The area to the north of this Khanty area belongs to the Nenets, and the western and northern neighbouring areas belong to other Khanty clans. Each family marks its hunting territory with eight to ten poles. Fishing equipment, clothes and other effects are kept in unlocked sheds.

The slaughter of the reindeer is a holy event and the balance between nature and society, human happiness and livelihood depends on the proper management of this important event. In a one-day ritual in 1990, carefully led by a shaman, a white male calf was offered to the God of the sky, and a grey female reindeer was offered to the God of the land. The reindeer were lassoed and marked with white clothes and killed by hitting their heads with an axe and stabbing a knife into their hearts. As the reindeer were dying, the shaman prayed: 'See, we offer you a calf. This is a gift, take its soul.' The shaman told me that the soul has to be sent away in this manner; otherwise it would be considered to be murder.

A bloodless slaughter is conducted according to definite rules. The reindeer are positioned sitting on their hindquarters, facing heaven; this set-up has been created based on a mythical model in the sky, namely a constellation the shamans call the 'evening star'. After the skin has been removed without shedding any blood, the meat is cut up and the blood is processed. The Khanty men drink the warm blood of the animal and eat its viscera and genitals; thus the reindeer offering is also seen as a fertility rite that aims to ensure the clan's continuity.

After the slaughter is over, the skin and meat of the reindeer are collected and set in front of the holy sleigh. The men remove their headgear and the shaman prays on behalf of the living and the dead: 'Let things remain good for us, don't let anyone get taken ill.' When a sacrificial feast has been set out on the snow, the Gods are invited: 'Invite your mother, invite anyone you like.' All the members of the clan, the living and the dead, in fact the whole of nature, are present at the sacrificial feast. The Gods of the sky and the land get their share of blood and vodka first, and then it is the turn of the human beings. After drinking, the meat is shared among the participants and families return to their homes and continue the feast there. The ceremony is concluded by pulling the holy sleigh, which has served as an altar, through a holy gate, accompanied by an incantation. Next morning, the head of the white reindeer is hung at the top of the highest birch in the sacrificial grove – for the God of the sky – and the head of the grey reindeer is hung on a branch of a willow tree close to the ground, for the God of the land.

The Khanty way of life protects nature. Marked or fenced areas, like the reindeer pen, trap paths or fish dams, are sacred, separate from nature. Khants do not approve of the ploughing of land; for them it would be the same as ripping open a mother's breasts. A growing forest is also sacred to the Khants, and therefore the subarctic taiga is probably not their natural living environment. Could it be that the Khants are, after all, arctic tundra people, as the archaeological findings in the Barzava Mountains suggest?

Lapp Noaidi, Saami Shaman

Old Norse sagas from the Viking Age (800–1250) locate the home of Lapp Noaidis as the province of Finnmark in northen Norway, whose inhabitants (Finns) were famous for their magical skills. In the Old Norse saga texts, the word 'Finn' might refer to a Finn, a Finnish person, a Saami or a sorcerer (shaman). In the twelfth century, warnings were even issued in the Parliament of the Norwegians against travelling to Lapland for fear of the sorcerers. A history of Norway written in the same century (c.1170) contained a detailed description of how Norwegian Christians experienced the flight of an entranced Saami shaman's soul in order to bring back to life a Lapp woman who had just been pronounced dead. In his difficult journey to the other side, the sorcerer battles with another shaman who had caused the death of the victim, metamorphosing into the shape of a whale before returning to this world and awakening the woman from the dead.

The first work to deal with Saami shamanism on a broader scale was written in Sweden for political reasons and published during the country's period as a major European power in the seventeenth century. As the troops of King Gustav II Adolph swept into Europe, rumours spread there about Lappish sorcerers who had helped them on their invincible path. Therefore the State Chancellor of Sweden, Magnus de la Gardie, initiated a project to obtain and promulgate information about Lapland in order to quash this false rumour. Johannes Schefferus, who was invited from Alsace to be Professor of Rhetoric at the University of Uppsala, was commissioned to undertake this task and his work *Lapponia* appeared in 1673.[13] Schefferus himself never went out into the field; instead he collated the reports of clergymen and officials working in Lapland. With regard to the study of Saami shamanism, the commission itself makes the treatment a cursory one, although there are drawings of the drum and of the rites.

Most information about the Saami pre-Christian view of the world was obtained through the missionary crusade to Lapland, which intensified at the end of the seventeenth century. It was inspired first by orthodox Christian ideals, then by Pietism and finally by the spirit of the Age of Enlightenment. There are considerable problems attached to the reliability of the sources. Since the information concerning the drums and their use was collected as part of the intensive conversion of the Lapps, the shamans and their families (in order to save their lives in the northern wave of witch hunts) were reluctant to give any

---

[13]   Johannes Schefferus, *The History of Lapland*, Suecica rediviva 22 (Stockholm: Rediviva, 1971). Originally published as *Lapponia* (Oxford, 1673).

information; this resulted in a more profane interpretation of the meanings of the drum than was actually the case.

Some shamans' drums have survived from this period, and Ernst Manker has made a careful inventory of them, although one should regard Manker's interpretations of the markings on the skins of the drums critically.[14] The drums come mainly from Swedish Lapland; most of the drums in a collection made under the leadership of Thomas von Westen from the Lapps of Norway, which then belonged to Denmark, were destroyed in a fire in Copenhagen in 1787.

The Age of the Drums ended when missionary work intensified to such an extent in the period from the 1670s to the 1740s that shamanism all but disappeared into the mountains and fells to become the secret religion of the last pagans, with plenty of oral information about the existence of the possessors of the drums. The main duties of the Saami shaman, or noaidi, included effecting cures, ecstatic prophesy (*arpa*) and working magic to ensure success in hunting. In addition, he sometimes played the role of sacrificial priest if the circumstances particularly demanded a sacrifice. The Saami shaman did not act as a psychopomp (a conductor of the soul of a dead person to the next world) which was generally one of the functions of the shaman in Siberia.

The following is an extract from Nicolaus Lundius's description, dating from the 1670s, in which he used the word Lapp to refer to the shaman: when the shaman is summoned to cure a sick person, first a sacrifice is made and

> after the sacrifice he [the shaman] begins to drum. As he drums, he falls to the ground and lies there as if dead, and his body is hard and rigid like a stone. He lies there for an hour, and he has told those present that after an hour they must chant. As they chant, he then rises from the dead, takes hold of the drum, puts it to his ear, strumming on it quietly every so often. When he has played the drum in this way for a while, he sits and meditates again for a moment. Then he begins to recount where he has been: he relates that he has been under the earth; he says that under the earth there lives a people who walk with their feet against out feet, and that this people is very handsome. A magic spirit has taken the soul of the Lapp to these people, and the Lapp says that the underground people have in their possession some object belonging to the sick person, be it his headdress or his boot or his mitten. If the Lapp is now powerful enough to regain the object, the sick person will become well again; if not, then he will continue to suffer from his illness. These underground beings know beforehand that the Lapp is coming to them below the earth, and the Lapp says that they prudently close their doors. Surely, however, the Lapp finds some crack through which he can crawl. When he then journeys back, the magic spirit transports his

---

[14] Ernst Manker, *Die lappische Zaubertrommel* 1, Acta Lapponica I (Stockholm: Nordiska Museet, 1938) and *Die lappische Zaubertrommel* 2, Acta Lapponica VI (Uppsala: Nordiska Museet, 1950).

soul swiftly through mountains and valleys so that stones and sand strike him like rain and hail.[15]

Ecstatic divination meant the use of ecstasy to obtain information about things like the whereabouts of stolen or lost property. It must be distinguished from the aforementioned use of the drum for prophesy. Saami folklore has legends about conflicts between powerful shamans (for example Peaivvas of Kemi Lapland and Akmeeli of Sodankylä) and their clans. These stories usually relate to the shaman's role in working magic to ensure good fortune in hunting; the shaman captured the soul of the prey and led it to the hunting grounds of his people. The shamans sometimes also battled directly with one another in the form of their auxiliary spirits, usually wild reindeer. Like that of shamans elsewhere, the status of the Saami shaman was high and people also sought counsel from him in situations other than those that warranted purely shamanistic expertise. The craze for shamanistic training that raged in various parts of Lapland, for example Karasjok, Inari and Jokkmokk, in the late twentieth century was not rooted in the traditional shamanism of Lapland, nor were the shamans' journeys that were arranged in conjunction with it performed according to the models of Saami shamanistic rituals. Rather it represented a kind of neo-shamanism, which reflected the influence of the Core Shamanism school of the American Professor Michael Harner and J. Horowitz, who led Nordic séances in Copenhagen. Saami author Nils Aslak Valkeapää (1943–2001) found inspiration for his writing and his chants (*jojks*) in the Saami mythology with which he was so deeply familiar. A classic example of Valkeapää's oeuvre is his illustrated anthology of poems, *Beaivi, áhčážan (The Sun, My Father)*,[16] which resounds with the voices of the old shamans of Lapland, albeit couched in the language and metre of modern verse. The eastern Saami word leudd particularly means a special jojk, an epic genre typified by its sacred rhythm and shamanic messages (of which the Finnish equivalent is luote).

Further Reading

Ahlbäck, Tore and Bergman, Jan (eds), The Saami Shaman Drum, based on papers read at the Symposium on the Saami Shaman Drum held at Turku, Finland in August 1988 (Åbo: Scripta Instituti Donneriani Aboensis XIV, 1991).
Bäckman, Louise and Hultkrantz, Åke, Studies in Lapp Shamanism, Studies in Comparative Religion 16 (Stockholm: Almqvist & Wiksell International, 1978).

---

[15]   N. Lundius, 'Descriptio Lapponiae', in K.B. Wiklund (ed.), *Bidrag till kännedomen om de svenska landsmålen ock svenkt folkliv*, XVIII.5 (Uppsala, 1905), pp. 6–7.

[16]   Nils-Aslak Valkeapää, *Beaivi, áhčážan* (Kautokeino: DAT, 1988).

Boyer, Bruce, 'Further Remarks Concerning Shamans and Shamanism', Israel Annals of Psychiatry and Related Disciplines 2/2 (1964): 235–57.

Janhunen, Juha, 'Siberian Shamanistic Terminology', in Ildikó Lehtinen (ed.), Traces of the Central Asian Culture in the North, Mémoires de la Société Finno-Ougrienne 194 (Helsinki: Suomalais-Ugrilainen Seura, 1986), pp. 94–117.

Karjalainen, K.F., Die Religion der Jugra-Völker 1–3, trans. Oskar Hackman and Arno Bussenius [from Finnish into German], FF Communications 41, 44, 63 (Helsinki: Suomalainen tiedeakatemia, 1922).

Kulonen, Ulla-Maija, Seurujärvi-Kari, Irja and Pulkkinen, Risto (eds), Saami: A Cultural Encyclopaedia, Suomalaisen kirjallisuuden seuran toimituksia 925 (Helsinki: Suomalaisen kirjallisuuden seura, 2005).

Pentikäinen, Juha, (ed.), *Shamanism and Northern Ecology* (Berlin: Mouton de Gruyter, 1996).

— *Die Mythologie der Saamen*, Ethnologische Beiträge zur Circumpolarforschung 3 (Berlin: Schletzer, 1997).

— (ed.), *Shamans*, Tampere Museum Publications 45 (Tampere: Tampere Museum Publications, 1998).

— (ed.), *Sami Folkloristics*, NNF Publications 6 (Åbo, 2000).

— *Golden King of the Forest: The Lore of the Northern Bear*, trans. Clive Tolley (Helsinki: Etnika, 2007).

Pika, Alexander (ed.), Anxious Northern Indigenous Peoples in Soviet Union and Post-Soviet Russia: Selected Documents, Letters and Articles, International Work Group for Indigenous Affairs (IWGIA) Document 82 (Copenhagen, 1996).

— (ed.), Neotraditionalism in the Russian North: Indigenous Peoples and the Legacy of Perestroika, Circumpolar Research Series 6 (Seattle and London: Canadian Circumpolar Institute, 1999).

Rydving, Håkan, The End of Drum-Time: Religious Change among the Lule Saami, 1670s–1740s, Acta Universitatis Uppsaliensis, Historia Religionum 12 (Uppsala: Almqvist & Wiksell, 1993).

Siikala, Anna-Leena, The Rite Technique of the Siberian Shaman, FF Communications 220 (Helsinki: Academia Scientiarum Fennica, 1978).

—, 'Shamanistic Themes in Finnish Epic Poetry', in Ildikó Lehtinen (ed.), Traces of the Central Asian Culture in the North, Mémoires de la Société Finno-Ougrienne 194 (Helsinki: Suomalais-Ugrilainen Seura, 1986), pp. 223–33.

Chapter 6

The Carbon Footprint of Oracles:
How Green is Divination?

Stuart R. Harrop

Preamble

Throughout much of human history our ancestors have used, and some of their descendants still use, divinatory practices as a means to relate to the natural world, to work and function within its non-linear complexity and to make key decisions for their survival and well-being. From their eyes they may have been working to propitiate spirits, to acknowledge noumenal forces in their struggle and thus to access the otherwise invisible and inaccessible powers that guide them in their paths through life. In some instances these practices, carried out to secure effective hunting or other use of natural resources, contributed positively to the conservation and creation of the diversity of life on Earth by contributing to what we would now describe as *sustainability*. Many ethnographies, stories and myths depict, within the paradigm of ancient and contemporary divination proponents, why and how this sustainability effect was achieved.[1] Additionally, a number of theories derive from our empirical perspective. These explanations, devised within the constraints of modernity, seek to explain successes and failures from the viewpoint of the very paradigm that supplanted the diviners' world in which spirits were embodied in rock, stone, water, plants and animals. However, understanding the basis for the mechanisms involved remains a difficult task and may require a full alignment with the world of the diviners and thus the relinquishing of many of our current, prevailing concepts that support our contemporary approach to environmental propriety and ethics.

This analysis examines the extent to which divination, as a component of long-evolved tradition, has supported and can continue to support the conservation and maintenance of species, habitats and ecosystems with a particular focus on the pragmatic way in which this role of divination is, or could be, supported within globally applied law and policy relating to natural resource conservation.

Article 8 (j) of the Convention on Biological Diversity (CBD) urges countries

---

[1]   Sean Kane, *Wisdom of the Mythtellers*, 2nd edn (Peterborough: Broadview Press, 1998).

> to respect, preserve and maintain knowledge ... and practices of indigenous and
> local communities embodying traditional lifestyles relevant for the conservation
> and sustainable use of biological diversity.

This is a wide-ranging obligation within an international legal instrument signed by most world leaders at the 1992 Rio Earth Summit. The CBD, and indeed this provision, has many frailties from a legal perspective. However, it is a ground-breaking measure because, *inter alia*, it acknowledges, for the first time and at the highest level of global decision-making, that cultural heritage, embodied in living tradition long neglected and persecuted by the volition of something we may embody within the term 'modernity', has a key part to play in the preservation of our planet. Because of the universal prevalence of oracles, divining and other methods of decision-making deriving from intermediaries who believe they are accessing the numinous, this wealth of cultural tradition necessarily includes a wealth of divination practices.

International diplomacy in the field of environmental protection is often seriously compromised because states are unwilling to relinquish sovereignty in an area that provides no obvious short-term gains (compare this to the universal and devout willingness to enter into multilateral trade agreements that provide the concomitant promise of rapid economic gains). Moreover, couple this reluctance with the suggestion that deposed, colonized or 'conquered' peoples should receive redress for their grievances and be given back the right to exist within their pre-modern territories and cultures, and the reluctance is made far stronger. Consequently, the provisions in environmental or other instruments that might support traditional practices are hedge-bound with qualifications and confusion arising from the multilateral negotiating process, and a number of questions arise that should have been resolved, in an ideal world, prior to the texts being presented for the signature of world leaders. These questions are legion but a number of them are set out herein.

To what extent can this international mandate be used to support aspects of traditional culture that deploy divination? Who are local communities and what are traditional lifestyles? Must the divination itself be executed in a way that is environmentally friendly or must only its consequences have a positive environmental effect in conjunction with other linked practices within the relevant tradition? Can contemporary applications of traditional practices applied in the 'West' be similarly supported?

There is still a vast gulf between the paradigm of traditional practices and the established, predominant paradigm, centred as it still is on concepts of 'development' and 'progress'. These concepts are remnants of modernity and at a political level they are a powerful force affecting conservation diplomacy. They are epitomized in the popular, political – and impossible – concept, bearing in mind the limited and fragile resources carried by our planet, known as *sustainable development*. These two paradigms are often literally, rather than metaphorically, *worlds apart*. And yet, if Article 8 (j) of the CBD is to be taken seriously, we are required not to pick and choose within the context of the prevailing paradigm but to embrace the entirety of relevant traditional cultures in our endeavours to conserve the Earth's natural resources and to embrace new institutional approaches to understanding and transmitting the associated praxes and knowledge. Moreover, we may even be required to jettison modernity for good and accept the epistemological bases of this knowledge on an equivalent basis to our still predominant Newtonian-based world view.

The Ambit of Divination

In this chapter *divination* is intended to comprise a wide range of activities. These activities may include formal divination, such as the turtle carapace oracles of Bronze Age China, the scapula oracles of the Northern Native Americans and many other formal, traditional divination methods. The term also includes the less formal and pervading use of omens within the world surrounding the shaman-diviner. These omens may be delivered through dreams and other means, within the waking world, such as the shapes in clouds, sand, mud and rock and other manifestations of nature, which to the perennially alert mind constitute *reaffirmations from the world around us.*[2] In paraphrase, divination is a term extended herein to encompass its widest possible meaning and thus capture the practices that are common in the lives of many people living within traditional lifestyles who have a relational link with the environment and thus perceive a pervasive subjectivity within the entirety of the organic and inorganic world around them. The concentration herein is on divination and its relationship with the environment and thus the popular culture of urban divination used for the furtherance of trade, family matters and so on, popular in many parts of the world, is excluded from examination.[3]

In traditional contexts reliance on omens and formal divination methods have assisted nomadic peoples to be guided as they travel within their spatial territories and within the temporal changes imposed upon them through the passage of the seasons and the longer-term shifts of climate and hunting and gathering conditions. These decisions may have been made on the basis of omens that had an empirically measurable basis, such as the appearance of migratory birds heralding the onset of winter or spring, or that are otherwise either arbitrary or based on noumenal guidance depending upon the perspective of the observer. Divinatory practices are and have also been components of traditional agricultural practices. Again these are sometimes based on an empirically determinable background of complex signs predicting seasonal changes which determine the best times to plant, reap, bring domesticated animals to winter shelter and to release them to the untamed

---

[2]   See Carlos Castaneda, *The Teachings of Don Juan: A Yaqui way of Knowledge* (Berkeley: University of California Press, 1968).

[3]   See, for example, H.G. Quaritch Wales, *Divination in Thailand: The Hopes and Fears of a Southeast Asian People* (London: Curzon Press, 1983).

lands. Other aspects of the practices are based on the application of non-linear manifestations and the interventions of 'chance' within the natural world. Within current methodologies, these are only explicable in terms of the ethnographies that describe them (as, by example, recording the manifestations as the consequences of the intervention of the spirits) or through the application of mathematical theories imposing probability factors on complex systems which might interpret the practices as enhancing otherwise heavily biased human decision-making.

The relationship between divination and the imposition of random choice mechanisms on human decision-making is particularly evident in oracles applied to hunting decisions. However, it is beyond the scope of this chapter to analyse empirically the extent to which such practices work; to determine the reasons why they may work or why they fail or to compare different techniques in the search for optimum approaches. An enquiry along these lines would require novel methodologies and significant data sources, which are necessarily vanishing with rapidity along with the remaining cultural diversity of traditional peoples. Such an enquiry would also need to draw upon a significant contingent of disciplines to reach any reasonable conclusions. Suffice it to say that there are a number of perspectives. At one extreme the modernist, perhaps existential, approach imposes meaning on the act of divination *ex post facto*. At the other extreme the theurgical, or even thaumaturgical perspective might propose that the act of divination – perhaps the very point of randomization – accesses a manifestation of the divine.

The extreme version of the modernist perspective is expressed in an analysis of divination carried out to assist hunting decisions by Khayyam Moore.[4] He commences with the a priori assumption that 'Magic is, by definition and reputation, a notoriously ineffective method for attaining the specific ends its practitioners hope to achieve through its use.'[5]

Khayyam Moore's focus is on the divination practices of the North American Montagnais-Naskapi who use, among other things, the shoulder blade of a caribou as an instrument within an oracle. The bone is cracked over fire and by using a rigorous set of interpretative rules the Naskapi, following dreams incubated to help them in their hunting decisions, analyse the cracks on the scapular, as they would a newly drawn map of hunting territory that shows optimal hunting directions and locations. Khayyam Moore's expressed purpose is to analyse the quality of this oracle as a problem-solving mechanism. In the circumstances, although he is not able empirically to measure the efficacy of the activities and is relying on a closed class of second-hand observations, he concludes that there is some demonstrable benefit in this divinatory method. He argues that if humans were left to their own devices to decide the direction of the hunt, their natural bias and inability to avoid

---

[4]   O. Khayyam Moore, 'Divination: A New Perspective', in A.P. Vayda (ed.), *Environment and Cultural Behavior: Ecological Studies in Cultural Anthropology* (Garden City, NY: Natural History Press, 1969), pp. 121–8.

[5]   Ibid., p. 121.

an emphasis on hunting in a *preferred* direction would result in an unsustainable harvest of the target-animals in that area.

Thus he proposes that the divinatory tool used in this instance operates as a randomizing mechanism, which ensures that hunting remains sustainable through securing that target species do not become wary of humans or are not over-hunted by repeated emphasis on hunting in particular areas. In conceding this mechanism to support the oracle's success, he also notes how widespread this type of divinatory mechanism has been, and still is to a minor extent, in North American peoples and also notes that it occurs in Asia, India and Europe. Rather than suggesting that these methods derive their effectiveness from the noumenal, accessed through the effect of randomization, Khayam Moore explains their popularity across continents because the system removes bias and imposes impersonal chance on actions crucial to the survival of hunter-gatherers in the harsher latitudes of the world. He uses a similar interpretation to refer to the success and popularity of the Chinese turtle carapace oracle[6] and also insists that the well-known divination of the Azande, observed by Evans-Prichard, may also be explained in this manner.[7]

This is a stark, modernist interpretation of divination, and yet the precise point made by Khayyam Moore leads on to the other extreme that argues that divination has a theurgical, even thaumaturgical basis. Some believe that the *I Ching*'s structure of broken and unbroken lines derives from the cracks in the turtle carapace oracles of the Shang Dynasty. Indeed, the texts of these oracles are, in some instances, reflected in the accompanying texts to the *I Ching*.[8] Thus, there is a lateral comparison between this method of divination and the scapular oracle of the Naskapi. In alluding to the mechanism of change, and echoing the views of C.G. Jung's synchronistic explanation in his seminal forward to the Wilhelm-Baynes translation of the *I Ching*,[9] Karcher describes the very randomness of divination as opening a crack in this mundane world for the numinous to enter to guide us. In a commentary on the *I Ching*'s Hexagram 62, *Xiao Guo*, he also graphically and metaphorically describes this point of change as 'the tiny flying bird ... the microscopic *ji* ... the hardly visible fragment of a place where change occurs'.[10]

---

[6]   See more generally for a description of the history and practice of this method's use, D.N. Keightley, *Sources of Shang History: The Oracle Bone Inscriptions of Bronze Age China* (Berkeley: University of California Press, 1978).

[7]   E.E. Evans-Pritchard, *Witchcraft, Oracles and Magic among the Azande* (Oxford: Clarendon Press, 1937).

[8]   S. Karcher, *Total I Ching: Myths for Change* (London: Time Warner, 2003).

[9]   *I Ching, or Book of Changes*, trans. R. Wilhelm and C.F. Baynes (London: Routledge & Kegan Paul, 1968).

[10]   Karcher, *I Ching*, p. 423.

Origins

The battle is against the speed of change. The relentless pace of development and globalization threatens to homogenize approaches to conservation and eradicate the last memory of key traditional practices and knowledge that hold crucial clues for local and global environmental health. The challenge is embedded in epistemological distinctions and differences. The process or the dynamic commonly captured within the inadequate term *modernity* has been, and still is, crashing through the old world irrevocably. Whether literally or metaphorically, the paradigm continues to burn the witches and the wisdom codices, rape the sacred groves and subjugate knowledge that does not conform to the epistemological perspective of this paradigm. With a volition of its own, it still seeks to dominate and to subdue the Earth. We are only too aware that the tropical rainforests, which as the most bio-diverse ecosystems on the planet epitomize the chaos that (echoing Karcher) creates the space for the spirits to reach to the diviner, are still disappearing at rates that have final and irreversible consequences. This rapid recession of forest boundaries is maintained despite the non-stop advocacy, rhetoric and continuous breaking news concerning the dire need to arrest the destruction.

We are consumers and we live in a world governed by consumption. Polices that support such 'use' are hedged with the need to secure sustainability but we rarely have the data to know what is truly sustainable and the principle of sustainability is so easy to abuse. Biological and cultural diversity are often found together and thus they are relentlessly disappearing hand in hand. Indeed, they are frequently and inextricably linked and in places the human connection to so-called 'wilderness' has been instrumental in creating and nurturing the richness. Necessarily, therefore, cultural and biological diversity have grown and radiated together in some instances. Indeed, these are often the biological and cultural hotspots where the remaining rich traditional practices are found, practices that developed during the long evolving march from the early hominids to contemporary *Homo sapiens*. Even when we try to stem the flow of biological and cultural destruction, our strategies are *modern*, and we embrace the cultural knowledge within a modern framework, be it through capital-driven intellectual property rights regimes milking and corralling the tip of an iceberg of ethnobiological knowledge or modernist curricula restraints leaving little room for the participation of the paradigm of the shaman, the curanderos and the dreamers. We are products of modernity and cannot easily shake off the relentless momentum of this paradigm. The medium of this book, this chapter and this paragraph is steeped in it. I am steeped in it.

We have spent most of our history and preliterate primordial history, indeed 90 per cent of our time as humans on Earth, living as an inextricable component of the natural world within a generalized definition of *hunter-gatherers*. The roots of much of our cultural diversity arose during this time and the earliest myths, dealing with the interaction of humans with the natural forces of the Earth and the cosmos, probably began to evolve within a world without pen and parchment.[11] Perhaps it was in this context of a seamless interrelationship with the natural world that the *shaman*, the first diviner, arose. We do not know when this occurred although some putative evidence suggests the existence of so-called 'shamanism' twenty thousand years ago. However, the origin of this walker between the worlds could be far older. Nevertheless, we do know, from the recent and contemporary ethnographies detailing shamanic divining practices within the remnants of indigenous peoples, that divining was a crucial component of many praxes governing interaction with the natural world and the manner in which it was utilized for the good and persistence of the shamans' communities.

Indigenous Peoples, Rural Communities and the Natural World[12]

Our use of the term 'natural' tends to connote an environment free from the effects of humans. The word may also be used in a manner that suggests that land altered or affected by human activity is unnatural. Thus cultivation of the natural produces the artificial.[13] Nevertheless, the history of the wild remnants of land in the world is often one of alteration and of cultivation, however subtle the means of change. Although both recent and ancient human activity has been responsible for massive habitat degradation and species destruction, many ancient and continuing practices have been responsible for shaping what we conceive today as the *natural world*. Further, the natural world we see around us now may consist of, as a minimum, second generation ecosystems which have gradually, or in some cases relatively quickly, replaced the pre-human ecosystems altered by the activities of our predecessors.[14] All is changing – all is in flux – and we have to assume responsibility for our positive, as well as our negative, roles in this world of change.

Therefore, the concept of *wilderness* as pristine, uncultivated land unsullied by human intervention is based, in many respects, on a failure to recognize the role that early and existing aboriginal peoples have played in forming a significant proportion of wild landscapes. In many instances lands were altered without long-term strategies as species were recklessly hunted to extinction or trees were

---

[11] See Castaneda, *Teachings of Don Juan*.

[12] See, for a general examination of the human influence of the 'natural', I.G. Simmons, *Environmental History: A Concise Introduction* (Oxford: Blackwell, 1993).

[13] 'Natural', according to the *Concise Oxford Dictionary* (9th edn, p. 906), means 'existing in or caused by nature; not artificial, uncultivated: wild (existing in its natural state)'.

[14] By example, even the apparently natural vast plains of grasslands facing the European settlers crossing North America from East to West may have been only partly created by climatic change resulting in a deforestation of the area. The debate is not over on the issue but some argue that the hunting and fire management practices of the original peoples crossing the Asia–America land bridge may have played a major part in this drastic alteration of ecosystems. See Simmons, *Environmental History*.

relentlessly cleared for building and burning. However, more complex, projected and thus sustainable strategies were employed in some cases where humans, who wished to secure sustainable sources of game, food-plants or medicinal and sacred plants, facilitated the formation of unique areas of natural wilderness. Many richly diverse areas of the Amazon rainforest, by example, contain gardens of key plants used and carefully maintained, in accordance with knowledge, by the native peoples who inhabit the land.[15] Superficially, these areas bear no resemblance to the well-ordered English cottage garden; instead they epitomize our concept of the archetypal, rainforest wilderness.[16]

Reliance on a misconception of the origin of wilderness can sometimes lead to erroneous and disastrous environmental strategies. When Aboriginal peoples in Australia were encouraged and partly coerced to leave their nomadic way of life and move to centralized settlements, the desert and scrub wilderness in which they had previously lived quickly converted to a far poorer ecological condition.[17] Unknown to those who had assumed control of the land, the seemingly arbitrary and chaotic burning of the land carried out by the first peoples was a sophisticated system of fire management. This system derived from complex, traditional knowledge deploying radically different approaches to conservation using, inter alia, divinatory dreams and omens to make the decisions that we would make in a linear manner based on our empiricism. The epistemological gulf between those living traditional lifestyles and the incoming modern peoples was so great that wisdom could not be recognized.

There are many examples of remarkably effective and sophisticated practices of both indigenous peoples and rural communities around the world that contribute to creating the natural world and enhancing its ability to support biological diversity. However, not all indigenous and traditional, rural practices are necessarily supportive of conservation goals.

Sophisticated, traditional conservation practices require a detailed understanding of the ecology of the domains of the practitioners. Some involve the wholesale manipulation of the environment such as the aboriginal use of fire, others involve the selected setting aside of animal resources or the deliberate planting and protection of key species useful to a community such as medicinal plants (as with the gardens of the Amazon). These practices are invariably designed, as land management practices, to produce a sustainable yield of resources for a community and are

---

[15]   D.A. Posey, 'Indigenous Peoples: Missing Links and Lost Knowledge in the Conservation of Brazil's Tropical Forests', in R.J. Hoage and K. Moran, *Culture: The Missing Element in Conservation and Development* (Washington, DC and Dubuque, IA: National Zoological Park, Smithsonian Institution and Kendall/Hunt, 1998), pp. 113–24.

[16]   R. Lok, 'A Better Understanding of Traditional Homegardens through the use of Locally Defined Management Zones', *Indigenous Knowledge and Development Monitor* 9/2 (July 2001): 14–19.

[17]   S. Stevens, *Conservation through Cultural Survival: Indigenous Peoples and Protected Areas* (Washington, DC: Island Press, 1997).

very rarely carried out solely to satisfy a deep ecological urge (although reverence for the natural world is often a major but not always a decisive factor). Thus the Tukanoan groups of peoples in South-East Columbia have carefully integrated their land drainage policies and their fisheries conservation initiatives. They avoid clearing flood plain vegetation because it sustains the fish that are a crucial food source. They also prohibit fishing in certain streams in their lands to ensure that there are refuges for fish in order to secure sustainable populations.[18] However, some traditional practices do not conserve natural resources. The Machiguenga in the Peruvian Amazon have a view of an infinitely renewable food source in nature deriving from a time when the Amazon was an apparently endless source of food and provision and the people extremely few and far between. Thus, without any obvious sense of good game management practice, they exploit populations of fish to the extent that they may extinguish whole species within the river tributaries within travelling distance of their homelands.[19]

Divination within Traditional Conservation Practices

Divination is relevant to conservation in two ways. First, there are modes of divination that may contribute to the extinction of species. The oracle described by Castaneda in his first book, *The Teachings of Don Juan*, involved sewing up the mouth of one innominate lizard and the eyes of another using, remarkably or perhaps incredibly, a wooden needle, fibres of Agave and the thorn of a Choya. First, this event challenges even the most basic approach to animal welfare. Second, if it really takes place as a common practice among the Sonoran peoples, with whom Castaneda allegedly worked, more information about the species is required to determine the sustainability of such a practice. I suspect we need not concern ourselves too much with this example, since the credibility of this record has been seriously put in doubt.[20] However, the ethnographical description of the divination that ensues from Castaneda's described trial of this method compares well with parallel descriptions and so, if Castaneda was not simply writing fiction, we might hope that he was simply hiding a true practice by creating a smokescreen of impossibility and thereby saving the relevant source population of lizards from would-be neo-sorcerers. The turtle carapace oracles of the Shang Dynasty in China similarly had a potentially negative conservation impact. Many thousands

---

[18]   B.J. Meggers, *Men and Culture in a Counterfeit Paradise* (Washington, DC: Smithsonian Institution Press, 1996).

[19]   D. Posey and W. Balee, *Resource Management in Amazonia: Indigenous and Folk Strategies*, vol. 7: *Advances in Economic Botany* (Washington, DC and London: Smithsonian Institution Press and The New York Botanical Garden, 1989).

[20]   R. De Mille, *Castaneda's Journey: The Power and the Allegory* (Santa Barbara: Capra Press, 1977).

of oracles were carried out[21] and it is possible that the populations of one or more species of turtle could have been detrimentally affected by what may have been an unsustainable practice. However, we have insufficient records to make any judgement on the diviners of the Shang. In any event, turtles were a food source then, as they are now, and may have been bred in captivity for the purposes of both food and divination. Indeed, Chinese traditional aquaculture, still prevalent today, derives from an ancient tradition of ingenuity.

These two examples serve merely to illustrate how certain oracles that use mechanisms sourced from nature could be in need of carbon footprint management. However, they do not concern the scope of this chapter, beyond a brief reference. Its main concern is the second role of divination in conservation, which has operated for thousands of years: where it is deployed as a component of traditional practices and as a means to regulate and inform choices and key decisions concerning the human relationship with the natural world.

There are a number of instances where divinatory practices within this second category have demonstrated empirically measurable, positive conservation benefits, sometimes out-performing the most supposedly sophisticated scientific strategies. What is more, these are executed voluntarily without constraint, imposition or imposts on the public purse. Examples include the seemingly irrational aboriginal fire management in Australia already mentioned, but other examples will illustrate the manner in which different levels of social complexity may function within these systems.

In one case, the James Bay Cree – when permitted to operate within their cultural paradigm – demonstrated an ability, in a region within subarctic North America, to manage the hunting of moose and other large mammals in a manner that persistently secured remarkably stable populations of animals. Indeed, the official wildlife authorities, relying on contemporary protected area scientific method, have not been able easily to emulate this achievement.[22] The paradigm of the James Bay Cree comprises a multi-naturalist approach whereby animals and humans both possess selfhood and both emanate from a unified matrix of spirit. The Cree believe that they receive omens from the spirits from the natural world around them, thereby preventing overhunting. Thus they work at the very basic level of divination by watching carefully for affirmations from the natural world around them which then dictate the decisions they must take concerning their hunting practices. These divinatory signs are interpreted within the ambit of the norms established, maintained and transmitted within their culture. According to Feit:

> The Cree's cultural system of understanding nature differs fundamentally from
> that of Western science. While Western science links animals, vegetation, and
> inorganic habitats in an 'ecosystem model,' the Cree incorporate all potentially

---

[21]   See Evans-Pritchard, *Witchcraft, Oracles and Magic*.

[22]   H.A. Feit, 'Self-Management and Government Management of Wildlife: Prospects for Coordination in James Bay and Canada', in Hoage and Moran, *Culture*, pp. 95–111.

active spirits and entities that they experience into a unified 'social cosmos,' where standard indicators such as cohort sizes, aggregation sizes, age and sex ratios and frequency of encounters are considered not mere biological phenomena but actual messages from the animals and spirit masters.[23]

Thus, in the widest sense, the Cree approach to sustainable use of their territories involves a complex system of defining their relationship with the spirits as well as the animals around them in order to walk in accordance with the subtle balance dictated within their cosmological paradigm.

J. Stephen Lansing has painstakingly studied the complex structures interlaced with water temples in Bali that are designed to control and manage irrigation in terraced rice fields. These structures ensure a robust and ingenious agricultural system that defies linear understanding and yet solves a remarkable matrix of challenges and problems. In Lansing's own words:

> A system that is either frozen solid or chaotic cannot transmit information or adapt. But a complex network – one that is near the edge of chaos – can do both. As it happens the [Bali system] provides an unusually clear illustration of this point.[24]

These structures blend numerous pragmatic components with the sacred or numinous. Thus the complex response to the challenges and perturbations faced by this integrated system include divination practices and access to what Lansing refers to as a 'collective unconscious', along with a relational view to the challenges faced by the participating communities derived from a perceived relationship between the mastery of the inner self and its reflection in the outer world. This mirror of the microcosm in the macrocosm implies the Hermetic maxim 'As above so below', which necessarily forms the bedrock of Western astrological divination.

Ultimately, this complex system far out-performs the ecologically dangerous 'green revolution' systems that almost destroyed this crucial traditional system, along with delicate, local ecological balances, when they were imposed over what appeared, to those in charge of progress, to be a useless morass of superstition. In a vast and extensive examination of the role of the components of these complex operations going far beyond conventional ethnography, and including structural analysis along with systems ecology techniques to model the structures, Lansing is able to confirm the resilience, the robustness – and indeed the ingeniousness – of the systems. However, he is not able to comprehensively explain why they work,

---

[23]   Ibid.

[24]   J.S. Lansing, *Perfect Order: Recognizing Complexity in Bali* (Princeton: Princeton University Press, 2006), p. 84.

beyond falling back on their complexity and reliance on numerous components that may still only be examined from a phenomenological perspective.[25]

Of course, there are many hypothetical explanations for the functioning of these systems beyond the foundational belief in the persistence of spirit and mind throughout the natural world, a persistence that posits access to guidance from the numinous. Khayyam Moore suggests that the randomization that results from the use of oracles informs an apparently illogical interface with nature that has the effect (for example) of resting hunting areas, thereby contributing to sustainability. The same might be said of the type of activity carried out by the Australian Aboriginal fire-managers and the methods of management used by the James Bay Cree; but there are many other explanations that might determine an approach to the mechanisms at work.

Thus, in one possible, hypothetical scenario, an elder of the Cree may be walking in his ancestral wild lands and subconsciously notice that the tracks of animals are becoming smaller (suggesting that over-hunting is reducing the number of adults) or that the forest is quieter (perhaps because of over-hunting). In the evening he may have a divinatory dream in which he is warned by his spirit guides about the forest and the animals in it and thereby decides to tell his people to cease hunting. Because of his position within the community his decree is adhered to absolutely until he receives another omen that permits hunting to recommence. This apparent spiritual intervention through the medium of dream, from the Cree perspective, may also be explicable as a psychological reaction to the circumstances. The basis of the psychological perspective may then give rise to further analysis in a number of directions depending on the epistemology of the enquirer. Thus a depth psychologist may meet the Cree half-way while a psychologist holding firmly to a bio-medical model may move much further away.

All such enquiries require an a priori assumption that everything is ultimately knowable and thus we cannot rely on description alone. It is always possible, however, that we live in a triple-tiered world where there is the known, the unknown (which may become known) and the truly unknowable (which we are simply not equipped to know through the lack of an appropriate form of consciousness). To access the last mentioned we can only meet its description and, in relation to divination within traditional communities, we may simply have to accept the proponents' paradigm. Eduardo Viveiros de Castro points out that 'there is one virtually universal Amerindian notion, it is that of the original state of non differentiation between humans and animals, as described in mythology'. He goes on to describe the original common condition of humans and animals as 'not animality but, rather, humanity'.[26] Taking this as a description we may find

[25]   Ibid.; see also J.S. Lansing, *Priests and Programmers: Technologies of Power in the Engineered Landscape of Bali* (Princeton: Princeton University Press, 1991).

[26]   E. Viveiros de Castro, 'The Transformation of Objects into Subjects in Amerindian Cosmologies', a paper given at the University of Manchester, 1998 and 'Deixis and Amerindian Perspectives', *Journal of the Royal Anthropological Institute* 4 (1998): 469–88.

that there is a consistency in effect and approach in traditional divination that maintains rather than destroys natural resource sustainability.

If we can accept these traditional practices at face value there are other more easily measurable aspects that must be taken into account. In particular, traditional practices operate within traditional norms and are thus adhered to often without question by members of a community. Thus, if they have a conservation benefit they possess power and do not require additional financial resources for their support. These incidences are easily measurable and thus demonstrable within accepted and well-established methodologies.

One example of a dying tradition that can engender powerful pro-conservation actions in relation to a charismatic species and its crucial rainforest habitats is Tiger Shamanism. In rainforest areas in the Far East, where tiger populations still retain a fragile hold within the diminishing habitat, legends of the Tiger Shaman still persist. In Vietnam, as McNeely and Wachtel recall,[27] one tiger only took women from a particular village as its prey. The Tiger Shaman's divination concluded that there was some marital infidelity in the village. Once this was attended to, the problem tiger, in this case cast as moral avenger, ceased to take human prey. In Kerinci, Sumatra, where the Sumatran tiger (*Panthera tigris sumatrae*) is endemic and retains its tenuous stronghold (numbering no more than 400 individuals), these people are called Pawang Harimau. Their role is to act as intermediaries between the community and the tiger in order to maintain the status quo. When a human–tiger conflict arises, the Pawang Harimau will intermediate with the problem tiger and thereby divine the course of action that the community must take. There are a number of instances where this has resulted in a change in behaviour within a village and thus an assumption of responsibility for the problem rather than all-out persecution of the tiger. Although the dominant religion in Kerinci is Islam, many practices such as that of the Pawang Harimau have been assimilated into the application of the religion and thus there is wide respect for the tiger and such a demonstrably positive attitude may be that species' last chance for survival. In one instance, a mosque in the forest regularly receives the visits of a tiger during prayers. Rather than fearing the visits, those praying have given the tiger the name 'the tiger who wants to convert to Islam'.[28]

Of course, respect for one species may also have wider repercussions. The tiger survives because there are still pockets of rainforest, particularly in montane areas on Sumatra, and respect for the tiger through the divinatory intercessions of the Pawang Harimau may also generate a respect for the forest and contribute to the halting of its decline. Of course, this type of respect for species and the wider natural environment is dependent on the persistence of traditional cultural beliefs. That persistence requires state and international support as the relentless

---

[27] J.A. McNeely and P.S. Wachtel, *Soul of the Tiger: Searching for Nature's Answers in Exotic Southeast Asia* (Garden City, NY: Doubleday, 1988).

[28] This is based on anecdotal evidence passed to the author during field work in Sumatra in 2007.

pace of development and progress wipes away and devalues ancient perspectives. Yet international legal provisions are already in place that, on the face of it, would seek to halt this growing lack of respect for what is becoming an increasingly alien epistemological perspective.

The Convention on Biological Diversity

There are a number of instruments within international law and policy that may be relevant to the issue of supporting divination as a positive conservation practice. Only one is dealt with in any length in this chapter: the Convention on Biological Diversity (CBD). Its importance to this issue has already been summarized but a deeper analysis is required. First, this is an instrument of law and thus its members, who have followed internal procedures to ratify it, are required to implement it in their own law and policies. This is not the case with policy or soft-law, such as Agenda 21, which is not binding on member states. Second, the CBD was a ground-breaking convention because it dealt, for the first time, with whole ecosystems (including the role of inorganic matter integral to the functioning of the biological components of ecosystems) and also ventured to accept and work to support some of the roles of humans in building and maintaining those ecosystems.

Two stipulations are particularly relevant: Article 8 (j) and Article 10 (c). The full text of the relevant part of Article 8 (j) includes the requirement that CBD member-states:

> as far as possible and as appropriate ... subject to its national legislation, respect, preserve and maintain knowledge, innovations and practices of indigenous and local communities embodying traditional lifestyles relevant for the conservation and sustainable use of biological diversity and promote their wider application with the approval and involvement of the holders of such knowledge, innovations and practices.

First, it will be clear that the clause is a tangled web of negotiating compromises typical of many international provisions dealing with the environment. There are numerous ambiguities that require further resolution that are not dealt with in the context of this chapter. We must also be aware that the USA has not agreed to be bound by the CBD, which puts the whole convention in a weaker international position.

Second, the practices must be 'relevant for the conservation and sustainable use of biological diversity'. The spin of sustainable use has also been added. This is a contemporary concept which is pasted on to ancient cultures and, as has been mentioned, not all of them would comply with this requirement where they have developed in low populated areas with a vast abundance of biological diversity. For this reason, and because divination is also used for many purposes, not all traditional divination practices are supported by the CBD; but divinatory practices in traditional societies were necessarily developed through the relationship with the natural world and thus embedded in ways of living that had to secure the survival of the community and thus contribute to a sustainable way of living within the natural world. It is not clear whether the clause seeks to divide practices into those that work and those that do not. However, to take this route would demonstrate the utmost audacity. Where divination or other practices that have the effect of conserving the natural world are embodied within traditional practices, they are likely to be wrapped in an inextricable web of cultural traditions, norms and practices that moves and flows with the transmission of custodianship from generation to generation. The idea of severing what we, with our modernist, mercantile minds, would consider the good from the bad, would not only be morally wrong but also a failure to understand the importance and nature of functioning of traditional knowledge: a condescending intrusion into the right of a people to maintain the entirety of their cultural heritage and a freezing of a practice that is designed to fluidly respond to the changes within the people who carry and transmit it and within the world in which they live and move.

The phrase 'respect, preserve and maintain knowledge, innovations and practices' seeks to secure the preservation of more than a mere archival remnant of practices. Tradition is always dynamic and the reference to maintenance suggests a continuation of the evolution and development of such knowledge and practices. The word 'respect' is both particularly helpful from a policy perspective but difficult to interpret from a legal point of view. Politically, it connotes the perpetuation of traditional culture beyond the dust of museums by actively teaching it and by deploying the knowledge holders as teachers, conservation policy-makers and so on.[29] Indeed, it is understood by the CBD policy-makers to mean that 'Relevant traditional knowledge should thus be accorded a status in national life comparable to that shown to scientific knowledge.'[30]

Thus the implication is that aspects of the practice of divination should be taught not only as ethnography, nor as anthropological/historical snap-shots within curricula, but as a rigorous set of living and essential praxes and procedures. Article 8 (j) must also be read in conjunction with Article 10 (c) which requires CBD Member States to

> as far as possible and as appropriate … protect and encourage customary use of biological resources in accordance with traditional cultural practices that are compatible with conservation or sustainable use requirements.

---

[29]   UNEP/CBD/COP/3/19 Knowledge. Innovations and Practices of Indigenous and Local Communities: Implementation of Article 8 (j) (note by the Executive Secretary), paragraph 65.

[30]   UNEP/CBD/TKBD/1/2 Traditional Knowledge and Biological Diversity (note by the Executive Secretary), paragraph 83.

This places the issue of divination in a wider framework of cultural norms and law and could relate not only to oracles being used to direct hunting and gathering, and to dictate agricultural practices such as when to sow crops, irrigate them, reap, clear land in preparation for cultivation and so on, but also to the use of turtle carapaces, scapula bones, spiders and so forth in oracles themselves. Moreover, it also encourages the preservation of whole cultural structures, of which divination is a mere component, in order to secure the wider conservation benefits that come from adherence to cultural norms in the manner described in the context of the Tiger Shaman.

It is clear, therefore, that lurking within the norms of established international law, hedge-bound as it is by the trappings of modernity, there is the seed of an institutional way back to support for a world in which even the stones and trees may speak to us and guide us into ways in which our planet may be nurtured back to health.

Chapter 7
Embodiment, Alterity and Agency: Negotiating Antinomies in Divination

Patrick Curry

… if intellect does not deserve the crown of crowns, only intellect is able to award it. And if intellect only ranks second in the hierarchy of virtues, intellect alone is able to proclaim that the first place must be given to instinct.

(Marcel Proust)[1]

Our body itself is the palmary instance of the ambiguous.

(William James)[2]

'Self-alienation' (*allotriôthen*) constitutes our very essence.

(Gregory Shaw)[3]

We step and do not step into the same rivers; we are and are not.

(Heraclitus)[4]

A hopeless attempt to see things whole is at least as worthy as the equally hopeless task of isolating fragments for intensive study, and much more interesting.

(Joseph Meeker)[5]

Although most of this chapter is given over to issues that extend well beyond divination, my intention is to thereby offer a fruitful and insightful way of thinking

---

[1]   *Marcel Proust on Art and Literature 1896–1919*, trans. Sylvia Townsend Warner, 2nd edn (New York: Carroll and Graf, 1997), pp. 25–6.

[2]   William James, *Essays in Radical Empiricism* (Mineola, NY: Dover, 2003 [1912]), p. 80.

[3]   Greg Shaw, citing Simplicius (c.490–c.560), 'Living Light: Divine Embodiment in Western Philosophy', in Patrick Curry and Angela Voss (eds), *Seeing with Different Eyes: Essays on Astrology and Divination* (Newcastle: Cambridge Scholars Press, 2007), pp. 59–87, at p. 74.

[4]   T.M. Robinson, *Heraclitus: Fragments* (Toronto: University of Toronto Press, 1987), D-K, Frag. 49a.

[5]   Joseph Meeker, *The Comedy of Survival: Studies in Literary Ecology* (New York: Charles Scribner's Sons, 1974), p. 12.

about it. Of the first two subjects stated in my title, I will mainly explore their interrelationship, suggesting that it is as all-pervasive as it is complex and subtle. I will then introduce the third-named subject. From time to time, vistas will open up which we shall only be able to notice before moving on. Occasionally something else will appear, namely the post-secular implications of the approach I am taking. Finally, anyone averse to theoretical speculation should probably pack extra provisions.

A principal purpose is to try to resolve an impasse between two intellectual positions that grow out of wider and deeper differing orientations to life: in broad terms, a participatory phenomenology and an analytical structuralism. My starting point to this end is a passage in a series of remarkable lectures given by Eduardo Viveiros de Castro in 1998 to anthropologists in Cambridge.[6] However, it in turn refers to an important earlier work by Tim Ingold which must therefore briefly be discussed.[7] Ingold convincingly argued that the claim that nature is 'only' a cultural construction is fatally incoherent. The problems can be summarized like this:

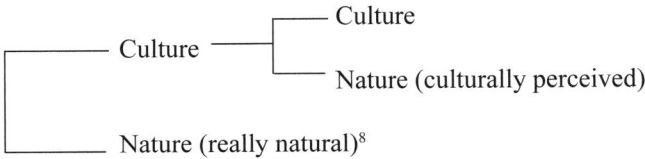

Thus:

1. Cultural constructionism takes as a given – that all human beings culturally construct their natural environments – what ethnographic evidence readily confirms is socio-historically contingent: aboriginal hunter-gatherer societies do not think or live in ways that conform to, or even readily

---

[6]   Eduardo Viveiros de Castro, 'Cosmological Perspectivism in Amazonia and Elsewhere', four lectures delivered 17 February–10 March 1998 at the Department of Social Anthropology, University of Cambridge. See also his paper based on these lectures, 'Exchanging Perspectives: The Transformation of Objects into Subjects in Amerindian Cosmologies', *Common Knowledge* 10/3 (2004): 463–84 and 'Cosmological Deixis and Amerindian Perspectivism', *Journal of the Royal Anthropological Institute* 4/3 (1998): 469–88, reprinted in Michael Lambek (ed.), *A Reader in the Anthropology of Religion* (Oxford: Blackwell, 2002), pp. 306–26.

[7]   Tim Ingold, 'Hunting and Gathering as Ways of Perceiving the Environment', *The Perception of the Environment: Essays in Livelihood, Dwelling and Skill* (London: Routledge, 2000), pp. 40–60. Viveiros de Castro was responding to an earlier version: Tim Ingold, 'Hunting and Gathering as Ways of Perceiving the Environment', in Roy Ellen and Katsuyoshi Fukui (eds), *Redefining Nature* (Oxford: Berg, 1996), pp. 117–55. (In my view, Ingold has here not only deconstructed social/cultural constructionism but destroyed its intellectual credibility.)

[8]   The diagram is from Ingold, *Perception*, p. 41.

comprehend, the paradigmatically 'Western' ontological divide between 'nature' and 'culture'.

2. Nature is thus illegitimately apportioned, in line with this (false) universalist assumption, between '"really natural" nature (the object of study for natural scientists) and "culturally perceived" nature (the object of study for social and cultural anthropologists)'.[9]

3. If the concepts of nature and culture are themselves cultural constructs, then so is the culture that constructs them, and so on. The result is a vicious infinite regress.

Abandoning this wreck of a theoretical programme, Ingold argues instead that for the anthropologist as well as his/her subject, 'apprehending the world is not a matter of construction but of engagement, not of building but of dwelling, not of making a view *of* the world but of taking up a view *in* it'.[10]

> Far from dressing up a plain reality with layers of metaphor, or representing it, map-like, in the imagination, songs, stories and designs serve to conduct the attention of performers *into* the world, deeper and deeper, as one proceeds from outward appearances to an ever more intense poetic involvement. At its most intense, the boundaries between person and place, or between the self and the landscape, dissolve altogether. It is at this point that, as the people say, they become the ancestors, and discover the real meaning of things.[11]

We shall have reason to admire but qualify this eloquent prescription.

For his part, Viveiros de Castro finds that Ingold's 'perspicacious diagnosis of metaphorical projectionism is better than the cure he propounds'. I do not claim that the former has correctly represented the latter's position, but that is not really the point; it is, rather, the intellectual issues at stake.[12] Responding to what he sees as Ingold's remedy, then, Viveiros de Castro says:

> My structuralist reflexes make me wince at the primacy accorded to immediate practical-experiential identification at the expense of difference, taken to be a conditioned, mediate and purely 'intellectual' (that is, theoretical and abstract) moment. There is here the debatable assumption that commonalities prevail upon distinctions, being superior and anterior to the latter; there is the still more debatable assumption that the fundamental or prototypical mode of relation is identity or sameness. At the risk of having deeply misunderstood him, I would

---

[9]   Ibid.

[10]   Ibid., p. 42.

[11]   Ibid., p. 56.

[12]   In fact, in email correspondence with me, Ingold has sharply rejected Viveiros de Castro's version of his (Ingold's) position. I therefore ask his pardon for using this account in order to clarify the issues.

suggest that Ingold is voicing here the recent widespread sentiment against 'difference' – a sentiment 'metaphorically projected' onto what hunter-gatherers or any available 'others' are supposed to experience – which unwarrantably sees it as inimical to immanence, as if all difference were a stigma of transcendence (and a harbinger of oppression). All difference is read as an opposition, and all opposition as the *absence* of a relation: 'to oppose' is taken as synonymous with 'to exclude' – a strange idea. I am not of this mind. As far as Amerindian ontologies are concerned, at least, I do not believe that similarities and differences among humans and animals (for example) can be ranked in terms of experiential immediacy, or that distinctions are more abstract or 'intellectual' than commonalities: both are equally concrete and abstract, practical and theoretical, emotional and intellectual, etc. True to my structuralist *habitus*, however, I persist in thinking that similarity is a type of difference; above all, I regard identity or sameness as the very negation of relatedness.[13]

Now, I agree with the substance of this statement. Nonetheless, Viveiros de Castro's rejection of what he portrays as Ingold's neo-phenomenology leaves us in an unsatisfactory position. It is unsatisfactory for those with an intuition, at the least, that Ingold is not entirely wrong; and for anyone aware of the wall of mutually hostile silence, within and between university departments in the humanities and social sciences, separating broadly structuralist/constructionist adherents (usually predominant) from broadly phenomenologists (usually a minority). Beyond divination studies, then, my goal is to move us on from this unhealthy impasse – not, I hasten to add, through a facile synthesis, but through an uneasy resolution that denies either position complete vindication while showing that neither can be entirely excluded.

'Alterity'

It is time to define and refine the terms of the argument. With some degree of liberty, I am using 'alterity' – otherness – as shorthand for a 'structuralist' formation/sensibility. The essence of alterity is *difference*, and 'the "difference" of alterity initially takes the form of negation'.[14] That is, alterity points 'back' to difference, which marks the inherent and foundational relationality and pluralism of this and all related terms; as Viveiros de Castro remarks, 'You do not "see a difference" — a difference is what makes you see.'[15] (I am reminded of how

[13]   Viveiros de Castro, 'Cosmological Perspectivism'. See also the other works cited in n. 7 above.

[14]   Martin Holbraad, 'Defining Anthropological Truth', a paper given at Cambridge on 24 September 2004, a later version of which was published as 'Ontography and Alterity: Defining Anthropological Truth', *Social Analysis* 53/2 (2009): 80–93.

[15]   Viveiros de Castro, 'Cosmological Perspectivism'.

an earlier anthropologist, Gregory Bateson, characterized 'the world of form and communication', as distinct from force and matter, in terms of 'differences and ideas. A difference which makes a difference is an idea. It is a "bit," a unit of information.')[16]

But note that 'essence', 'inherence' and 'foundation' in this context precisely cannot be thought of as single, stable, universal or any of the other terms classically associated with them; and all the more so since hermeneutics and post-structuralism conjointly deflated the fantasy, hitherto shared by structuralists and scientific positivists, that it is possible to (so to say) stand outside any phenomenon and interpret its meaning from a pre-interpretive/pre-structured point of view (equivalent to Thomas Nagel's famous 'view from nowhere'). Ludwig Wittgenstein's reflections move in just the same critical direction, provided one notices the crucial point that his 'language games' do not float unmoored but are a function of lived life: 'It is what human beings say that is true or false; and they agree in the language they use. That is not agreement in opinions but in form of life.'[17]

But do not both points – the hermeneutic/post-structuralist and Wittgensteinian – impel us towards Ingold's neo-phenomenologist and Heideggerian 'indwelling'? Or do they simply mark the unavoidability of such an exigency in some form, one that is not necessarily dictated by its proponents?

Another useful term in this context is 'discourse'. Borrowing from Laclau and Mouffe, I use it to refer to both practice and theory (that is, theoretical practice).[18] As such, it includes but exceeds the linguistic, and is thus equivalent to Wittgenstein's so-called language games. This existential or pragmatic dimension is what alterity also points 'forward' to, as flagged by Jack Reynolds: 'alterity is best construed as that which literally alters'.[19] That is, in the encounter of one perspective with another, to borrow from Viveiros de Castro again, 'Nothing "happened", but everything has changed.'[20]

---

[16]   Gregory Bateson, *Steps to an Ecology of Mind* (New York: Ballantine Books, 1972), pp. 271–2. Bateson independently discovered many of the points made by others cited in this chapter, and sometimes earlier.

[17]   Ludwig Wittgenstein, *Philosophical Investigations*, trans. G.E.M. Anscombe (Oxford: Blackwell, 2001) 75ᵉ. (As Garry Phillipson has pointed out to me, 'way of living' would arguably be a better translation than 'form of life'.)

[18]   Ernesto Laclau and Chantal Mouffe, *Hegemony and Socialist Strategy: Towards a Radical Democratic Politics*, 2nd edn (London: Verso, 2001).

[19]   Jack Reynolds, *Merleau-Ponty and Derrida: Intertwining Embodiment and Alterity* (Athens: Ohio University Press, 2004), p. 190.

[20]   Viveiros de Castro, 'Cosmological Perspectivism'.

Embodiment

I am not suggesting embodiment is precisely the counter-pole to alterity, but it is close to acting as one for two related reasons: first, insofar as materiality is taken to be the contrary of non-located difference and, second, insofar as it is as central to phenomenology as difference is to structuralist alterity, with those two discourses commonly opposed.

Embodiment obviously has an inalienable connection with the body as not only where but how we indwell. But that connection can be misleading, given the immense weight of our philosophical traditions, impelling a naturalistic meaning of 'body' and the 'nature' with which it is identified. As Ricoeur remarks, 'Certainly Greek man was far less quick than we are to identify *phusis* with some inert "given"'[21] – as should we now be, if we are to take the contingency of such meanings seriously by availing ourselves of the (relative) freedom of interpretation it offers.

In a non-naturalistic and counter-hegemonic vein, then, to quote Thomas Csordas's apt summary, 'our bodies are not originally objects to us. They are instead the ground of perceptual processes that end in objectification.' (He also notes that a concern with embodiment is not identical to the anthropology of the body that, incidentally, elicits Viveiros de Castro's scorn.)[22]

Our principal guide to embodiment, however – and by close association, the phenomenological pole – will be Maurice Merleau-Ponty. But before turning to him, let us briefly review some 'structuralist' criticisms. To a considerable extent, Viveiros de Castro has already registered these: the questionable priority accorded to identity over difference and so on. At the risk of oversimplifying, they could be said to have been summarized by Emmanuel Lévinas when he accused phenomenology of an 'imperialism of the same'.[23] But I can sharpen them further by borrowing from Martin Holbraad, the originality and sophistication of whose theorizing of divination makes his critique worth taking all the more seriously. (I shall return to it later.)

> The basic critical idea is that, despite protestations to the contrary, phenomenological usages in anthropology simply re-inscribe Euro-American preoccupations with mind v. body onto materials which may well contravene such a distinction. Phenomenologists seek to overcome 'dualism' by nesting its terms within a larger 'dualism', namely that of 'experience' v. 'reflection'

[21]   Paul Ricoeur, *The Rule of Metaphor: The Creation of Meaning in Language*, trans. Robert Czerny (London: Routledge, 2003), p. 48.

[22]   Thomas J. Csordas (ed.), *Embodiment and Experience: The Existential Ground of Culture and Self* (Cambridge: Cambridge University Press, 1994), p. 7.

[23]   Emmanuel Lévinas, 'Philosophy and the Idea of Infinity', *Collected Philosophical Papers* (The Hague: Martinus Nijhoff, 1977), pp. 47–60, at p. 55. For a critique of Lévinas's critique of Merleau-Ponty, see Lawrence Hass, *Merleau-Ponty's Philosophy* (Bloomington: Indiana University Press, 2008), pp. 112–22, 132–3.

(e.g. ready-to-hand v. present-at-hand). The main conceptual tool, namely 'intentionality' (from Bentano through Husserl, to Heidegger and then Merleau-Ponty) purports to overcome subject-object distinctions (by saying, roughly, that the two can only be construed as correlates, i.e. as mutually constitutive), but ends up only upholding them as the 'here' one *must* start from.[24]

Merleau-Ponty and Chiasmic Flesh

My interest here is in the philosophy, especially the later philosophy, of Merleau-Ponty – not as a way to rescue phenomenology *en tout*, but in itself. Such a rescue cannot convincingly be effected because he radically altered the Husserlian character of the phenomenology he inherited and with which it is still commonly associated. In Merleau-Ponty's philosophy, there is no transcendental ego, no 'bracketing', and above all no acceptance of an ontological apartheid of lived world (the domain of *Geisteswissenschaften*) and scientifically real world (that of *Naturwissenschaften*). Now it is true that his *Phenomenology of Perception* failed to break entirely with these philosophical origins; but his posthumously published work, such as *The Visible and the Invisible*, clearly moved beyond them in a way that undercuts the objections of both Viveiros de Castro/Lévinas and Holbraad. Still more to the point, it significantly advances the whole debate.[25]

Merleau-Ponty asserted that relations 'internally' between 'body' and 'mind', or rather, in his terms, between 'body-subject' both as perceived object and as perceiving subject, *and* 'externally' between 'self' and 'other', comprise an *écart*: a constitutive divergence or gap which is *chiasmic*: that is, criss-crossed and intersected such that each is unavoidably entwined with, but never reducible to, the other.[26] To quote Reynolds, *écart* 'names a divergence that is nevertheless not adequately characterized as a dualism, because the differences between the two components of an apparent dualism (e.g., mind-body and even self-other)

---

[24] From an email to the author (2 July 2006). For Holbraad's theorizing of divination, see his 'Gauging Necessity: Ifá Oracles and Truth in Havana', *Mana* 9/2 (2003): 39–72 and 'The Power of Powder: Multiplicity and Motion in the Divinatory Cosmology of Cuban Ifá (or *Mana*, Again)', in Amiria Henare, Martin Holbraad and Sari Wastell (eds), *Thinking Through Things: Theorizing Artefacts Ethnographically* (London: Routledge, 2007), pp. 189–225.

[25] On the ill-informed postmodernist dismissal of Merleau-Ponty, based on such assumptions, see M.C. Dillon, 'Merleau-Ponty and Postmodernism', in Thomas W. Busch and Shaun Gallagher (eds), *Merleau-Ponty, Hermeneutics, and Postmodernism* (Albany: State University of New York Press, 1992), pp. 129–38.

[26] I have drawn extensively upon the excellent analysis and discussion in Reynolds, *Merleau-Ponty*. For a very good recent introduction and discussion of Merleau-Ponty's philosophy as a whole, which I only discovered after writing this chapter, see Hass, *Philosophy*.

are revealed as chiasmically intertwined'.[27] Divergence is limited by dependence, and vice versa; neither complete alterity[28] nor complete identity is possible (for us). Thus, as Reynolds also notes, 'the body cannot be considered in any way that makes the linguistic' – or more fundamentally, in keeping with the terminology adopted here, the discursive – 'extrinsic to it', any more than discourse can be considered wholly extrinsic to embodiment.[29] Merleau-Ponty also termed this reversible interdependence of subject/object, mind/body, perception/thought and self/world, 'Flesh'.[30] By the same token, 'inside' and 'outside' are inseparable and mutually constitutive: 'The world is wholly inside, and I am outside, myself.'[31]

It is just this lack of both complete identity and complete difference that makes awareness or consciousness possible at all; in the case, *per impossibile* as a way of life, of either extreme, no relations whatsoever would be possible and therefore nothing to either be aware or be aware of. Contrariwise, to quote Merleau-Ponty, 'what enables us to center our existence is what also prevents us from centering it completely'.[32] As Reynolds puts it, 'the body is that which allows for any form of perspective at all'.[33] As a corollary, the impossibility of self-identity is what makes possible recognition of, interaction with, and alteration by, others.

This ontological understanding was accompanied by a corresponding critique of the mutually hostile philosophical positions associated with the two extremes Merleau-Ponty rejected: *empiricism* (which seizes upon 'the sensible') and *rationalism* (which hypostatizes 'the intelligible'). Neither is ultimately tenable. Certainly there can be no question of encouraging a scientistic reduction of 'mind' to 'body', as in the perennially fashionable efforts of evolutionary psychology (né sociobiology) and cognitive psychology and anthropology. Nor, however, does Merleau-Ponty entertain a phenomenological reductionism of the kind arguably suggested by Ingold, as this striking passage makes clear:

> What we propose here, and oppose to the search for essence, is not the return to the immediate, the coincidence, the effective fusion with the existent, the search for an original integrity, for a secret lost and to be rediscovered, which would nullify our questions and even reprehend language. If coincidence is lost, this

---

[27] Reynolds, *Merleau-Ponty*, p. 58.

[28] Including that of Lévinas and latterly Derrida.

[29] Reynolds, *Merleau-Ponty*, p. 45.

[30] Maurice Merleau-Ponty, *The Visible and the Invisible* (Evanston, IL: Northwestern University Press, 1968).

[31] Maurice Merleau-Ponty, *The Phenomenology of Perception* (London: Routledge, 2002), p. 474. This was just the conclusion Gregory Bateson arrived at quite independently: *Steps*, pp. 315–20.

[32] Quoted in Reynolds, *Merleau-Ponty*, p. 18.

[33] Reynolds, *Merleau-Ponty,* p. 80.

is no accident; if Being is hidden, this is itself a characteristic of Being and no disclosure will make us comprehend it.[34]

Now it could perhaps still be objected that by starting with mind vs. body and so on, Merleau-Ponty unintentionally affirms those contingent antinomies as foundational. Here, however, I will impertinently cite Holbraad against himself, insofar as he has also – rightly, in my opinion – argued that it is not the anthropologist's (and by extension, any scholar's) duty to simply use ethnographic or other data to confirm what 'we' already 'know', even, if necessary, by 'showing' that informants *don't* know what they are doing or talking about. Rather, that duty is to allow insights from the encounter with alterity to create new concepts and theories.[35] Holbraad terms this process 'inventive definition',[36] which, he says, 'constitutes an appropriate transformation of our default and initially inadequate concept of truth … All we have to go by are our misunderstandings of others' views – our initial descriptions of their statements and practices.'[37]

Holbraad also contrasts common-sense causal and representational (epistemological) explanations – which tend, especially among 'Westerners', to be taken as the sole kind of truth – with oracular and ontological ones. In an important discussion, which builds upon but carries forward those of both Lévy-Bruhl and Evans-Pritchard, he analyses the latter in terms of a 'motile logic' which always exceeds or escapes causal chains, no matter how tight.[38] (Crudely put, 'why' questions cannot be reduced to 'how' questions.)

At this point, however, I simply want to note the surely unexceptional point that the *fons et origo* of 'our' default, common-sense and representational views is the Cartesian dispensation, essentially accepted and modified by Hume and Kant in the course of forging modern philosophy, and cemented into place as a cornerstone of 'the modern Constitution',[39] which underwrites just the separation of nature and culture, body and mind, subject and object. In which case, where else could or should Merleau-Ponty – or anyone else who seeks to subvert this tyranny – start?

---

[34] Merleau-Ponty, *Visible*, pp. 121–2.

[35] This view is very close to Giles Deleuze's of the point of philosophy. On the overlaps and differences between Merleau-Ponty and Deleuze, see Hass, *Philosophy*, pp. 136–44.

[36] Which term he borrows from Roy Wagner (specifically *Symbols That Stand for Themselves* (Chicago: University of Chicago, 1986)). In subsequent work, Holbraad abbreviates this to 'infinitions'.

[37] Holbraad, 'Ontography', p. 90.

[38] Holbraad, 'Gauging Necessity'.

[39] Bruno Latour, *We Have Never Been Modern*, trans. Catherine Porter (Hemel Hempstead: Harvester Wheatsheaf, 1993).

More on Embodiment

Let me mention a few more points about embodiment noted by other scholars. Mark Johnson, for example, has discussed 'embodied structures of understanding … [which] emerge in our bodily functioning; they are recurring patterns in our dynamic experience as we move about in our world. They include containers, balance, compulsion, blockage, attraction, paths, links, scales, cycles, center-periphery.' To which we could add: the up/down of verticality, the bilaterality and directions of horizontality, and declivity/acclivity, among others. The apparently most ineffable concepts and values find their footing in such propriocentric metaphors. Whether Heaven or simply the heavens, we experience it/them as up, and up as heavenly; it is good to be upright and upstanding, not disabled, prostrate or *à quatre pas*, or a species of lowlife and so on. There is in fact no 'physical' parameter that cannot be experienced as a quality and even a power, and no quality or power which is unconnected with the so-called physical world.[40] Johnson concludes that 'Understanding is an event – it is not merely a body of beliefs (though it includes our beliefs).'[41]

This point needs careful handling, however, lest it slide into the simple-minded physicalist reductionism – body/nature $\geq$ mind/culture – that characterizes most academic as well as popular programmes of evolutionary and cognitive psychology and anthropology. Such an attitude was perceptively described by Owen Barfield as 'the fallacy of born literalness', who made the vital point that as long as it holds sway, the 'half-truth that many images have a bodily significance will be swallowed without leading, as it should, to the reflection that this is only possible because the body itself has an imaginal significance'.[42]

Similarly, Thomas Csordas has criticized George Lakoff and Mark Johnson's philosophical handbook of embodiment[43] for concentrating on the ways that the body gives rise to mind/culture at the expense of the reverse: 'Following Merleau-Ponty, I would argue that the body is always already cultural, and that rather than asking how metaphors instantiate image schemas it is more apt to begin with the lived [that is, embodied] experience from which we derive image schemas as abstract products of analytic reflection.' In this process, '*metaphor is the critical meeting ground between textuality and embodiment*'.[44] So although there is much more to say on this subject, that is my cue to turn to our second main guide, Paul Ricoeur.

---

[40]   See the wonderful discussion in David Abram, *The Spell of the Sensuous: Perception and Language in a More-Than-Human World* (New York: Vintage Books, 1997).

[41]   Mark Johnson, *The Body in the Mind: The Bodily Basis of Meaning, Imagination, and Reason* (Chicago: University of Chicago Press, 1987), pp. 206, 209.

[42]   Owen Barfield, *The Rediscovery of Meaning, and Other Essays* (Middletown, CT: Wesleyan University Press, 1977), p. 42.

[43]   George Lakoff and Mark Johnson, *Philosophy in the Flesh: The Embodied Mind and its Challenge to Western Thought* (New York: Basic Books, 1999).

[44]   Csordas, *Embodiment*, pp. 20 (n. 2), 16; my emphasis.

Ricoeur and Tensive Truth

Out of Ricoeur's many works I shall draw upon only *The Rule of Metaphor*, but there is more than enough there to keep us occupied. Once again, to summarily summarize, he shows that metaphor, far from being merely one literary 'device' among others, is integral not only to language but to meaning or what I am calling discourse itself (that is, any meaning we can recognize, think about, discuss and so on). Any being is a 'being *as*' and any seeing is a 'seeing *as*', which is the very heart of metaphor.

Ricoeur's theory is of metaphor as *tensive* in three ways: 'the tension between the terms of the statement, the tension between literal interpretation and metaphorical interpretation, and the tension in the reference between is and is not'. Most important is the last: 'the "place" of metaphor, its most intimate and ultimate abode, is neither the name, nor the sentence, nor even discourse, but the copula of the verb *to be*'. The metaphorical 'is' of 'x is y' simultaneously signifies both 'is' (metaphorically) and 'is not' (literally); it preserves the latter within the former *without* cancelling it. Thus, 'we are allowed to speak of metaphorical truth, but in an equally "tensive" sense of the word "truth"'. Furthermore, 'truth' in this context is not epistemological so much as existential or ontological: 'The copula – *being-as* – is not only relational. It implies besides, by means of the predicative relationship, that *what is* is redescribed; it says *that* things really are this way.' Or as Ricoeur also puts it, 'the enigma of metaphorical discourse is that what it creates, it discovers; and what it finds, it invents'. In this way, 'the creative dimension of language is consonant with the creative aspects of reality itself'.[45] Such creativity is dynamic or, to invoke Holbraad, motile: 'To present men "*as acting*" and all things as "*in act*" – such could well be the *ontological* function of metaphorical discourse.'[46] (Similarly, it seems to me that the difference between Ricoeur's 'metaphor' and Holbraad's 'inventive definition' is also vanishingly small.)

Ricoeur argues this view against two opposing alternatives which take extreme and mutually exclusive positions but which, in his view, must be maintained in a non-exclusive albeit tensive relationship that radically qualifies both. The first such position is in direct continuity with (in Alan Tormaid Campbell's words) a 'tradition in our philosophy [which] has for centuries regarded metaphor as a scandal'.[47] It is a scandal because it breaks or ignores (or at least is strongly suspected of doing so) Aristotle's 'law' of the excluded middle: 'the same attribute cannot at the same time belong and not belong to the same subject and in the same

---

[45] Ricoeur, *Rule*, pp. 6, 292, 283, 300.

[46] Ibid., p. 48; emphasis in original. (Please forgive the 'men'; it was written in 1975.)

[47] Alan Tormaid Campbell, *To Square with Genesis: Causal Statements and Shamanic Ideas in Wayapi* (Iowa City: University of Iowa Press, 1989), p. 109.

respect'.[48] But 'Being-as means being *and* not being.'[49] The attempted remedy is to demythologize language by exposing metaphor ('is') as mere simile ('is like') and replacing it with scientifically licit, that is, non-metaphorical, language. The iconoclasm and systematization so dear to modernity thus join with the modern hypostasis of scientific reference as sole truth; let us call it 'reductionist'.

Ricoeur elegantly shows the impossibility of this effort to domesticate, if not eliminate, the metaphorical 'is'. Simply put, because 'We cannot say what reality is, only what it seems like to us', there is no non-metaphorical language.

> In brief, critical consciousness of the distinction between use and abuse leads not to disuse but to re-use of metaphors, in the endless search for other metaphors, namely a metaphor that would be the best one possible ... There is no non-metaphorical standpoint ... The theory of metaphor returns in a circular manner to the metaphor of theory, which determines the truth of being in terms of presence. If this is so, then there can be no principle for delimiting metaphor, no definition in which the defining does not contain the defined; metaphoricity is absolutely uncontrollable.[50]

To a characteristically modernist and scientific sensibility, that is the real scandal of which the logical offence is merely a sign. (I would also remind the reader of Barfield's point that bodily images are already also imaginal, that is, metaphoric.)

The second and opposite view is a 'naïve and uncritical' meta-poetics in which 'the superiority of image over concept, the priority of undivided temporal flux over space, and the disinterestedness of the vision turned towards life's concerns are to be restored together'.[51] Against its counterpart's reductionism and abstraction, this approach is holist and exalts feelings over concepts. Exemplars include Schelling, Coleridge, Bergson, perhaps late Heidegger, and ultimately Philip Wheelwright (and, I believe, Barfield). Let us call it 'romantic'.

Here, the attempt to realize this putative perfection and unity proceeds by trying to ignore, if not eliminate, the literal 'is not' from within the metaphorical 'is'. And as Ricoeur shows, it is equally, if oppositely, unsatisfactory. Its ultimately anti-intellectual character attempts to, but in good conscience cannot, rid metaphorical truth of its discursive dimension. In fact, although Ricoeur does not say so, it seems to me that the two approaches mirror each other in their desire for a post-discursive truth: in the one case, that of 'matter' and in the other, 'spirit' or 'Being'. Proponents of both resent equally being reminded that 'the "truth", factual or otherwise, about

---

[48]   *Metaphysics*, 1005b20.

[49]   Ricoeur, *Rule*, p. 362.

[50]   Ibid., pp. 299, 339. On metaphor in the construction of scientific theories, see Mary Hesse, *Revolutions and Reconstructions in the Philosophy of Science* (Brighton: Harvester Press, 1980).

[51]   Ricoeur, *Rule*, pp. 294, 296.

the being of objects is constituted within a theoretical and discursive context, and the idea of a truth outside all context is simply nonsensical'.[52]

The naïve and the reductionist schools also share other significant common ground: they 'oppose one another on the field of verificationalist concept of truth, itself bound up with a positivist concept of reality'.[53] That is, both accept the non-scandalous epistemological (representationalist) version of truth as exhaustive or definitive; but where the latter accepts it, the former rejects it – and *with it*, since the two are conflated, discursivity *en tout*. Therefore, insofar as the discursive, in Ricoeur's tensive construal, is ontological and vice versa, both in effect also reject ontology, and fail on that account.

I should also mention that there is a closely parallel contemporary analysis of the ground covertly shared by realists and relativists, both accepting 'one world' while disagreeing only as to whether the truth about that world can be had or not. Terms that have been suggested for the position that is critical of both unviable alternatives range from retaining 'relativism' (Herrnstein Smith) to 'relationism' and/or 'relative relativism' (Latour), 'perspectivism' (Viveiros de Castro) and for that matter 'relational pluralism' (Curry).[54] In all these theories, there can be no question of concurring with vulgar relativism's acceptance of simply different apprehensions of supposedly one world. From all of them, an effectively infinite number of worlds – not necessarily absolutely discrete and incommensurable, to be sure, but nonetheless distinct – follow: as many, indeed, as there are perspectives. 'One must, above all, understand perspectivism not as a theory of knowledge ... but as *an alternative to epistemology itself.*'[55]

A Meta-Metaphor

What I now want to suggest is quite simple: Merleau-Ponty's chiasmic *écart* is tensive in precisely Ricoeur's sense, and Ricoeur's tensive *tertium quid* of

---

[52] Ernesto Laclau, *New Reflections on the Revolution of Our Time* (London: Verso, 1991), p. 105.

[53] Ricoeur, *Rule*, p. 362.

[54] Barbara Herrnstein Smith, *Contingencies of Value: Alternative Perspectives for Critical Theory* (Cambridge, MA: Harvard University Press, 1988) and *Belief and Resistance: Dynamics of Contemporary Intellectual Controversy* (Cambridge, MA: Harvard University Press, 1997); Latour, *We Have Never Been Modern*; Viveiros de Castro, 'Exchanging Perspectives'; Patrick Curry, 'Re-Thinking Nature: Towards an Eco-Pluralism', *Environmental Values* 12/3 (2003): 337–60 and 'Nature Post-Nature', *New Formations* 64 (2008): 51–64.

[55] Manuel Maria Carrilho, 'Rhetoric and Perspectivism', *Revue Internationale de Philosophie* 2/196 (1996): 359–73, at 370; emphasis in original.

metaphorical truth is chiasmic in precisely Merleau-Ponty's sense.[56] That is, *in effect*, the one is the other. Both are relational, non-essentialist and ontological in a way that includes but doesn't eliminate the epistemological (perhaps in a way that parallels, significantly, the way the onto-metaphorical 'is' includes but doesn't cancel the epistemo-literal 'is not'). And both are both-and/neither-nor in relation to the classical or traditional dichotomies of Western philosophy, and thus pitched against the corresponding positions on either side. Greatly simplified, the analysis can be represented in this way:

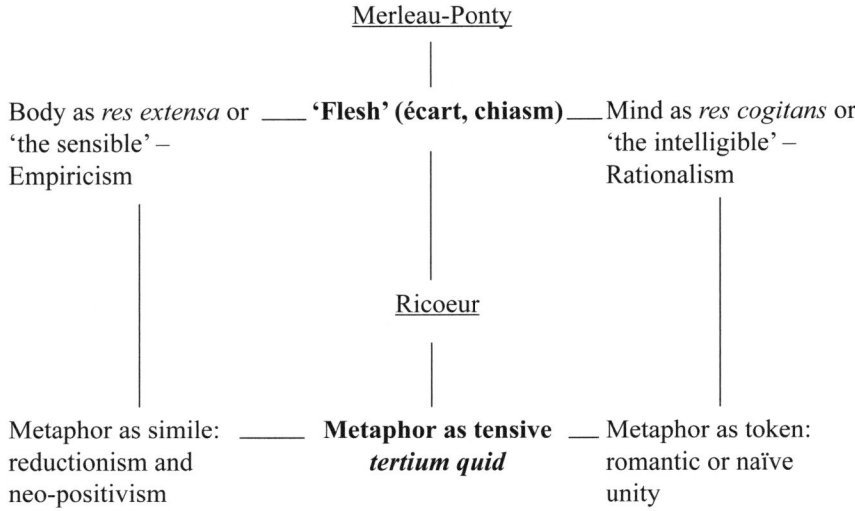

Nor do these commonalities exhaust the mutual elective affinity. Keeping Merleau-Ponty's point in mind that what enables us to 'center our existence' prevents us from doing so completely – and that what prevents us from attaining pure and undivided self-identity is what permits any at all – consider how Ricoeur describes

> the attempt at expression made by a speaker who, wanting to formulate a new experience in words, seeks something capable of carrying his intention in the network of meanings he already finds established. Thanks to the very instability of meaning, a semantic aim can find the path of its utterance … [Thus] the universe of discourse as a universe kept in motion by an interplay of attractions

---

[56] I do not know if this has already been suggested. One cannot read everything (although one should of course try), and there is a constant danger of reinventing some wheel or other. As against that, it is often necessary, in some contexts, to reinvent the wheel. I would also add that Ricoeur has made some critical remarks that betray a poor grasp of Merleau-Ponty's work; see Thomas W. Busch, 'Perception, Finitude, and Transgression: A Note on Merleau-Ponty and Ricoeur', in Busch and Gallagher, *Merleau-Ponty*, pp. 25–35.

and repulsions that ceaselessly promote the interaction and intersection of domains whose organizing nuclei are off-centred in relation to one another; and still this interplay never comes to rest in an absolute knowledge that would subsume the tensions.[57]

I should add here that although I cannot do justice to the subtlety of his case, Ricoeur also argues strongly for the legitimacy and irreducibility (by, for example, poetic discourse) of theoretical speculation. Here too there is a tension that needs to be maintained, and indeed borne: 'the dialectic that reigns between the experience of belonging as a whole and the power of distanciation that opens up the space of speculative thought'.[58]

At this point, we can return to our starting point – the dispiriting disjunction between (neo-)phenomenology and (post-)structuralism – bearing the 'uneasy resolution' I promised. By extension from the equivalence of Merleau-Ponty's chiasm and Ricoeur's tensive truth, embodiment and metaphorical discursivity *are themselves mutually implicated, imbricated, entangled.* In the same spirit, I am not suggesting an identity between embodiment and metaphor; rather, the relationship between them is meta-chiasmic and meta-tensive. That doesn't abolish either of them, nor the distinction between them – only the possibility of their absolute unity or their hyperseparation.[59]

Agency

It is time to introduce the third term of my title. The point of doing so is to enrich the primary metaphorical linkage just made/discovered. The basic idea is that as part of the familiar Platonic-Christian-Cartesian philosophical trajectory, agency – the intention and capacity to act in a relatively autonomous way – has long been associated almost exclusively with subjectivity, the mind, culture and humanity and excluded from their objective, bodily and natural counter-poles. To this list of dualisms should be added male and female respectively, which raises an issue to which we shall return. (To the extent that the subject is embodiment, it can hardly be avoided!)

To a considerable extent, excellent work rescuing agency from this confinement already exists, releasing me from the need to reiterate it in detail here. Much of it has been done by Val Plumwood, who defines agency as 'active intentionality' in order to undercut the usual covertly anthropocentric criterion of agency as

---

[57] Ricoeur, *Rule*, pp. 352, 357.

[58] Ibid., p. 371.

[59] This useful term is from Val Plumwood, *Feminism and the Mastery of Nature* (London: Routledge, 1993).

essentially cognitive.[60] (This move resonates, interestingly enough, with Merleau-Ponty's non-cognitive understanding of wonder, our proper relation to Being, as prior to and generative of consciousness.[61])

Rejecting the same hegemonically driven dualism problematized by both Merleau-Ponty and Ricoeur, Plumwood observes that the 'oppositional formulation of spirit versus matter renders invisible the important concept of a materialist spirituality which does not invoke a separate spirit as an extra, independent individualized ingredient but rather posits a richer, fully intentional non-reductionist concept of the earthly and the material'. Contesting the dominant spiritual-idealist term of the opposition, she emphasizes that 'materiality is already full of form, spirit, story, agency, and glory'.[62] This move is not identical with my assertion of a middle ground, but I believe there is a definite sympathetic resonance. Certainly both encourage 'the reconception of nature in agentic terms as a co-actor and co-participant in the world' which, Plumwood adds, 'is perhaps the most important aspect of moving to an alternative ethical framework'.[63]

Highly congruent is David Abram's influential book *The Spell of the Sensuous*. Of course, congruence with my work here is not surprising, insofar as Abram's primary philosophical move was to think through the implications of the fact that the body-subject (as theorized by Merleau-Ponty) is ultimately inseparable from, as well as utterly dependent on, the Earth in which it is embedded. In other words, significant aspects of the body-subject can equally be recognized in the Earth: in particular, its animacy and agency. 'Intelligence is no longer ours alone but is a property of the earth; we are in it, of it, immersed in its depths ... Each place its own mind, its own psyche.'[64] Hence Abram's invaluable term, the 'more-than-human world'.

This insight confirms paradigmatic aboriginal apprehensions of nature, both ancient and contemporary, for which the term 'animism' has recently been recovered, by Graham Harvey among others, from its patronizing and colonial lineage.[65] By the same token, such apprehensions are mythic, and myth, properly

---

[60]   Val Plumwood, 'The Concept of a Cultural Landscape: Nature, Culture and Agency in the Land', *Ethics and the Environment* 11/2 (2006): 115–50, at 124.

[61]   Patrick Burke, 'Listening at the Abyss', in Galen A. Johnson and Michael B. Smith (eds), *Ontology and Alterity in Merleau-Ponty* (Evanston, IL: Northwestern University Press, 1990), pp. 81–97.

[62]   Val Plumwood, *Environmental Culture: The Ecological Crisis of Reason* (London: Routledge, 2002), pp. 222, 226.

[63]   Plumwood, 'Concept of a Cultural *Landscape*', p. 130.

[64]   Abram, *Spell of the Sensuous*, p. 262.

[65]   Graham Harvey, *Animism: Respecting the Living World* (London: C. Hurst; New York: Columbia University Press, 2006). Cf. Gregory Bateson, *Mind and Nature: A Necessary Unity* (New York: E.P. Dutton, 1979).

understood – as Sean Kane, in both broad sweep and some detail, has shown – entails a living (that is, non-naturalistic) natural world.[66]

Abram too traces the covert alliance between the poles of a dualism consisting of scientistic-materialist discourse (privileging abstract objectivity) and New Age spiritual discourse (privileging subjectivity):

> by prioritizing one or the other, both of these views perpetuate the distinction between human/'subjects' and natural 'objects,' and hence neither threatens the common conception of sensible nature as a purely passive dimension suitable for human manipulation and use. While both of these views are unstable, each bolsters the other; by bouncing from one to the other – from scientific determinism to spiritual idealism and back again – contemporary discourse easily avoids the possibility that both the perceiving being and the perceived being are *of the same stuff*, that the perceiver and the perceived are interdependent and in some sense even reversible aspects of a common animate nature, or Flesh, that is *at once both sensible and sensitive*.[67]

Presumably I don't need to belabour the contiguity of this Flesh (Merleau-Pontian in provenance but now ecophenomenological) with the chiasmic and tensive *tertium quid* I have already discussed. The point of adducing Plumwood's and Abram's work here is simply to ensure recognition that agency, active intentionality, is not an optional add-on but integral, and that it acts in a wild, more-than-human way: a point that resonates, not coincidentally, with Ricoeur's description of metaphoricity, quoted above, as 'absolutely uncontrollable'.

My third witness for a post-Cartesian agency (as well as post-Christian and post-Platonic) is Bruno Latour and Actor Network Theory. Latour's *We Have Never Been Modern* argued brilliantly that the 'modern constitution', keeping society, subjects and humanity absolutely distinct from nature and objects, is literally unliveable. 'We have never been modern in the sense of the Constitution.' Rather, 'the ancient anthropological matrix, the one we have never abandoned', consists of networks which are 'simultaneously real, like nature, narrated, like discourse, and collective, like society'. Insofar as chiasmic Flesh is at once subjective and objective and metaphor entails what is and is not – truths which go unrecognized in our official philosophies – 'We poor subject-objects, we humble societies-natures, we modest locals-globals, are literally quartered among ontological regions that define each other mutually but no longer resemble our practices.'[68]

The network supporting and indeed producing this chapter, for example, includes, without any arbitrarily *a priori* ranking in importance, myself (already a complex micro-network), pieces of paper and books, friends and colleagues, a

---

[66] Sean Kane, *Wisdom of the Mythtellers*, 2nd edn (Peterborough: Broadview Press, 1998).

[67] Abram, *Spell of the Sensuous*, p. 67; emphasis in original.

[68] Latour, *We Have Never Been Modern*, pp. 46–7, 107, 6, 122–3.

computer, a chair and desk, earth, air, food, water and occasionally something stronger, a shared dog and cat, music and so on. The implication is that, as with any network, agency cannot be plausibly restricted to the human actor; because if you took everything else away, this chapter, and even 'I' as I am in this context, would assuredly cease to exist, let alone produce anything. In other words, actors are not sole agents and networks do not to play the role of merely supporting social structure: 'Actor and network ... designates [*sic*] two faces of the same phenomenon.'[69]

Agency is thus a property of the network *as a whole*; and as such, it can manifest anywhere in that network, on the part of any item therein. It does not discriminate between 'subjects' and 'objects', 'persons', 'animals' and 'things'. (Again, this point was anticipated by Bateson: 'mental characteristics are inherent or immanent in the ensemble as a *whole*'.[70])

This point has implications, obvious but nonetheless profound, for divination, in which planets and stars, cards, stones and inky pieces of paper can and do tell people things. And why should we collaborate with modernist and scientistic policing (let alone self-policing) to explain away such common experiences of non-humans, or even officially inanimate things, as agents?[71] Official religion is not the only 'vast moth-eaten musical brocade', to borrow Larkin's fine phrase.[72]

In other words, we may accept that agency is a property of mind or subjectivity, which is inherently relational and therefore discursive; and vice versa. But given that subjectivity is entwined with objectivity in the sense of objectness or materiality, and particularly embodiment, then agency may be said to be equally a property, in practice or in effect, of materiality. And insofar as subjectivity can no longer be restricted to humans, agency too is best described, after Abram, as more-than-human.

In short, agency – active intentionality – is wild. Let me add, though, a vital corollary: that being wild, it is unbiddable.[73] We are not, and no one is, in the position of being subjects who can *make* agency manifest in objects; that would be to retreat to the pathological fantasy, whether individual or collective, of Promethean/Faustian mastery. We are enmeshed and entangled in networks, or Flesh, or tensive worlds – or rather, we *are* such. In that process, certain parts thereof become identified as 'me' and 'us', and these do (as the early humanists realized) have some highly qualified and contingent degree of initiative; but I and we are certainly not 'in control'!

---

    69   Bruno Latour, 'On recalling ANT', in John Law and John Hassard (eds), *Actor Network Theory and After* (Oxford: Blackwell, 1999), pp. 15–25, at pp. 18–19.

    70   Bateson, *Steps*, p. 315.

    71   Cf. Abram, *Spell of the Sensuous*, p. 56: 'to describe the animate life of particular things is simply the most precise and parsimonious way to articulate the things as we spontaneously experience them'.

    72   From Philip Larkin's late poem 'Aubade'.

    73   With thanks to Anthony Thorley for this extremely useful term.

So far I have pointed out and briefly discussed a significant family resemblance, or elective affinity, between certain concepts: Merleau-Ponty's chiasmic Flesh and Ricoeur's tensive metaphoric truth, supplemented by the kind of agency entailed by Plumwood's ecological and materialist spirituality, Abram's more-than-human ecophenomenology and Latour's actor-networks. The motive has been to move on from certain sterile impasses, philosophical and methodological, involving the polarized extremes which each of these closely interrelated concepts problematizes. In what follows, I would like to take up some implications of the argument so far.

Embodiment Again

What about apparently disembodied spirits? On at least two grounds, I am not prepared to rule them out altogether: a great deal of ethnographic and historical evidence, and an awareness of my own metaphysical ignorance. And if there are such, it would seem that not all subjectivity or agency need be embodied, or else we have an unduly restricted understanding of 'body'.[74] That would be consistent with Merleau-Ponty's tensive amalgam, at once sensible and sentient, of 'body', 'mind' and 'world': 'The reversibility that defines the flesh exists in other fields; it is even more incomparably agile there and capable of weaving relations between bodies that this time will not only enlarge, but will pass definitively beyond the circle of the visible.'[75]

In any case, it seems incontestable that for us human beings, subjectivity is necessarily embodied; that is, we are all, *qua* human beings, embodied, and all our experiences – whether 'astral travel', so-called out-of-body or near-death experiences – are only experienced and reported *by* living and embodied human beings. The immediate corollary is that embodiment is a *fundamental* consideration that affects all the worlds we live in (that is, both for and through us), including whatever we know of them.

So, for example, we may have some kind of disembodied existence before birth or after death, but it is not as *humans*, nor anything we, as embodied beings, can really know; so to describe it as 'our' pre- or post-existence is merely a loose manner of speaking. Additionally, so far as we know, the same is true of other animals. The same, however, may not be true of gods, spirits or daimons. But as Jean-Luc Nancy has provocatively remarked, 'all presence' – whether that of a god, a human being or another animal – 'is that of a body'.[76] Certainly that is consistent with what is argued throughout this chapter, that everything discursive (meaningful, mind-like, relational) is also embodied, embedded and emplaced.

---

[74] In the latter case, although this may be a purely personal discomfort, it is somewhat awkward to find oneself returning to occultist discourse of 'subtle bodies' and so on.

[75] Merleau-Ponty, *Visible*, p. 144.

[76] Jean-Luc Nancy, *The Inoperative Community*, trans. P. Connor (Minneapolis: University of Minnesota Press, 1991), p. 146.

In this context, then, it makes sense that if one engages with a spirit – and if that causes discomfort, one could call it a 'more-than-human power' – it has a profound particularity, even if more affective and cognitive than sensually perceptual, location, even if more imaginal than physical, and so on. (Conversely, a truly universal God is surely utterly unknowable *as such*.) Now are these characteristics not also hallmarks of embodiment? So perhaps even with spirits, there is at least a kind of analogue to embodiment. (Another and not necessarily mutually exclusive possibility is that although *daimones* and gods have no physical bodies, human beings involuntarily 'give' them one when interacting with them.)

In cultures less dominated by religions and philosophies of (attempted or putative) disembodiment, the integral place of the body in practices of the sacred is more in evidence. For example, 'The Taoist priestly office primarily involves the learning of ritual forms, the inner truth of which can only be known by and through each person's own body (which is, in fact, the meditative side of the liturgical art). There is no required faith in a collection of intellectual propositions or creedal "secrets".'[77]

I suspect, however, that such liturgical embodiment is a relatively sophisticated and formalized development of something much more primal and (consequently?) even less understood. Let me borrow this from Gregory Shaw:

> Consider the remarkable testimony of Aristides who describes his experience in the presence of Socrates. He says:
>
> By the gods, Socrates, you're not going to believe this, but it's true! I've never learned (*mathein*) anything from you, as you know. But I made progress whenever I was with you, even if I was only in the same house and not in the same room – but more when I was in the same room. And it seemed, to me at least, that when I was in the same room and looked at you when you were speaking, I made much more progress than when I looked away. And I made by far the most and greatest progress when I sat right beside you, and physically held on to you or touched you.
>
> Like the initiates at Eleusis, Aristides does not learn (*mathein*) anything when he enters the presence of Socrates but experiences a transformation that is intensified by gazing, and even more by touching Socrates, as if he were a god. In the West, this is not our usual experience while attending the lecture of a philosopher; it is, however, remarkably similar to the experience of devotees who receive *darshan* in the presence of an enlightened guru.[78]

---

[77] Norman Girardot, 'Foreword', in Kristopher Schipper, *The Taoist Body*, trans. Karen C. Duval (Berkeley: University of California Press, 1993), p. xv.

[78] Shaw, 'Living Light', p. 68, quoting Plato, *Theages* 130d2-e2.

I hardly know what to say about this, except that because we cannot 'explain' something, or find it difficult to imagine how it is even possible, is certainly no reason to reject it out of hand. In this account, something that the keepers of official philosophy (including Socratic) would rather ignore is being pointed out: something important that subverts or ignores the usual apartheid between the 'physical' and the 'spiritual'.

On Sexuality

By 'sexuality', a noun cognate with Luce Irigaray's useful adjective 'sexuate', I mean to include all of 'biological' sex, 'cultural' gender and sexual orientation.[79] Here, thanks to the heavy freight of Platonic-Christian-Cartesian philosophy, another point which should be obvious needs to be stressed: for us, *to be embodied is to be sexuate*. Thus, although not everything or everyone need be sexuate, for us, our sexuality – potentially, at the very least – affects everything.

As testimony to the significance of our subject matter, we find ourselves touching on yet another vast and challenging domain without the time, space or in this case (frankly) knowledge to do it justice. Once again, I shall just make a few points.

Embodiment as construed here suggests, among many other things, that masculine and feminine experiences and worlds, analogously to male and female bodies, neither perfectly coincide nor, insofar as the one implies as much as excludes the other, utterly differ. In other words, human sexuality is also constituted in a chiasmic way – which rules out both pure identity of the sexes (whether 'internally' or between two or more persons) and pure alterity or hyperseparation. Furthermore, contingency, instability and so on is just what enables any sexual relations, and thence experiences, at all. By the same token, it excludes any simple determination of gender, let alone sexual orientation, by biological sex … just as it also means that the last cannot be excluded from those considerations!

There is a fundamental asymmetry between male and female embodiment. That follows (again taking my lead from Irigaray) from the existential fact that while both women and men are embodied, only women can give birth to both women *and* men; women thus birth embodied life itself. We might say that the female makes both itself and the male possible, although that is not what it is 'for'. Similarly – recognizing the deep commonality (theorized by Edward Casey)

---

[79] Irigaray argues (convincingly) that an uncritical use of the sex/gender distinction reproduces an uncritical nature/culture distinction. Margaret Whitford, *Luce Irigaray: Philosophy in the Feminine* (London: Routledge, 1991) and Luce Irigaray, *Key Writings* (London: Continuum, 2004).

between body and place[80] – both women's and men's bodies are places, but only within the sexual disposition of women's bodies is place itself emplaced.

As a result, relations between the sexes are 'reciprocal (but asymmetrical)',[81] just as psychoanalytically both develop in terms of embodiment and sexuality, but not in the same way. The asymmetrical sexuality of embodiment gives rise to different forms of metaphoric truth in relation to the perceived body itself, and by extension 'nature': in the female case, 'I *am* this (even though, since I am minded, I am [also] not)'; in the male, 'I am *not* this (even though, since I am embodied, I [also] am)'. This difference has profound implications for psychosexual and psychosocial developmental, both healthy and pathological.[82] And not to belabour the point, once again the resonances of this kind of embodiment with metaphoricity – the same ones I have already indicated by linking Ricoeur's metaphor with Merleau-Ponty's Flesh – are unmistakable. In any case, there is much more to be said on the subject – not least the erotic, too, as sacred … and vice versa.

'True' Antinomies[83]

On the subject of antinomies, which the approach I advocate reconciles and/or avoids, I want to distinguish between those that are symmetrical – that is, equal and opposite – and those that are not. A mark of the former is that they cannot be reconciled *within* the terms of the contrast between them. These include:

- mind and idealism (and spiritualism) vs. body and materialism: 'two vying "monisms"'[84] constituting a pernicious dualism with which we are all too familiar, and whose resolution lies, I have suggested, in a *relational pluralism*.[85] Correspondingly:

---

[80]   Edward S. Casey, *The Fate of Place: A Philosophical History* (Berkeley: University of California Press, 1997).

[81]   Ibid., p. 328.

[82]   See Muriel Dimen and Virginia Goldner, 'Gender and Sexuality', in Ethel S. Person, Arnold M. Cooper and Glen O. Gabbard (eds), *Textbook of Psychoanalysis* (Washington, DC: American Psychiatric Publications, 2005), pp. 93–114. With thanks to Beate Süss for this source. There is a considerable relevant body of work. In addition to Irigaray and other feminist philosophers, David Tacey's work has taught me much.

[83]   Technically, an antinomy is an irresolvable contradiction. I am, of course, suggesting that the antinomies discussed in this chapter are reconcilable (but without thereby disappearing altogether) from the perspective being urged.

[84]   Hans Jonas, *The Phenomenon of Life: Toward a Philosophical Biology* (Chicago: University of Chicago Press, 1982), p. 16. Cf. Neil Evernden, *The Social Construction of Nature* (Baltimore: Johns Hopkins University Press, 1992), p. 95.

[85]   Curry, 'Re-Thinking Nature'. Cf. Viveiros de Castro, 'Exchanging Perspectives', p. 482: 'multiplicity, not mere duality, is the complement of … monism'. Note also the

- subject(ive) vs. object(ive), as against *the body-subject*, whose activities, as Merleau-Ponty argued, produce the first two as effects (just as Latour also posits in relation to networks).

Here it might be appropriate to enter a word of caution respecting Viveiros de Castro's discussion in his brilliant 'Exchanging Perspectives' to the effect that (despite a disclaimer to the contrary) it might be viewed as arguing for simply a reversal of the usual 'Western' dominance of the objective through an assertion of the counter-truth of an Amerindian metaphysic in which, for example, 'an object is an incompletely interpreted subject'.[86] From various other statements it is evident that this would be a misunderstanding; however, those statements would be even clearer in this respect if strengthened by the approach advocated here. For example, positing 'a universe that is 100 percent relational'[87] would be harder to interpret idealistically if it were clearly understood that such relations are embodied (and that bodies are in turn constituted by relations). Viveiros de Castro suggests as much by pointing out that bodies are the sites of perspectives; however, he contrasts that with spiritual/cultural universalism. While the latter point is undoubtedly true of Amerindian cosmologies, the ontology argued for here radically qualifies *any* putative universalism, whether idealist or materialist, together with any dualism of which a one-sided monism is inevitably a part.

Another such polarity might be:

- the Dionysian (seeking surrender to orgasmic unity and so on) vs. the Apollonian (seeking chaste withdrawal in order to enable self-mastery and so on), as against the *mētic*.

Mētis is 'cunning wisdom', a more-than-human mode exemplified in Hellenic culture by Homer's Odysseus and Penelope and in Chinese by Wu Ch'êng-ên's Monkey.[88] First identified and analysed by (respectively) Marcel Detienne and Jean-Pierre Vernant, and subsequently Lisa Raphals, it deserves more than an encapsulated version here.[89] I just want to make a couple of points. First, it is

---

affinitive resolution, between 'spirit' and 'body', adopted by James Hillman and post-Jungian metaphysics, namely 'soul'.

[86] Viveiros de Castro, 'Exchanging Perspectives', p. 470.

[87] Ibid., p. 473. Tantalizingly, cf. Michel Weber's excellent summary of William James's pluralist ontology: 'relations are fundamentals, *relata* are abstractions'. Michel Weber, 'James's Non-rationality and its Religious Extremum in the Light of the Concept of Pure Experience', in Jeremy Carrette (ed.), *William James and The Varieties of Religious Experience* (London: Routledge, 2005), pp. 203–20, at p. 215.

[88] Suitably chastened by the bodhisattva Kuan-yin, that is; Wu Ch'êng-ên, *Monkey*, trans. Arthur Waley (London: Penguin, 1961).

[89] Marcel Detienne and Jean-Pierre Vernant, *Cunning Intelligence in Greek Culture and Society*, trans. Janet Lloyd (Atlantic Highlands, NJ: Humanities Press, 1978); Lisa

generally highly inadvisable to identify with and take up one end of *any* mutually exclusive polarity. In addition, however, the normative dimension of my argument strongly counsels against adopting either the Dionysian or Apollonian strategies as a way of life (including thought). Indeed, it is not surprising that Nietzsche arguably came to grief by doing just that.

Also, extending slightly the sexual dimension just touched upon, if the orgasmic and the chaste are the respective poles, then their liveable mediation (corresponding to embodiment, tensive truth, pluralism, *mētis* and so on) is *the erotic*.[90]

'False' (Asymmetrical) Antinomies

At this point, I want to qualify the preceding discussion by arguing that both extremes of all the above-mentioned polarities are only possible as (mistaken and destructive) ideals; that is, in contrast to the third term, they cannot be actually lived. So, taken together, they make an asymmetrical counter-pole to the middle way.

We arrive at the same point taking the route of critically examining two more apparent polarities with some intellectual currency. One has been popularized within anthropological and metaphysical discourse by Stanley Tambiah, drawing directly upon Lévy-Bruhl:

- participation – for example 'inside' artistic and/or religious experience, especially of enchantment – 'vs.' causality, for example the putative objectivity from the 'outside' of science, especially the so-called hard sciences.[91]

But, with respect both for Lévy-Bruhl's courageously pioneering work and the considerable heuristic value of Tambiah's synthesis, this contrast is ultimately, and importantly, a fraud. Within the parameters of this discussion and its subject matter, there are only *different forms and degrees of participation*.[92] However, lest this point be misunderstood, let me immediately add that participation is not a matter of a foundational identity or commonality at the expense of difference;

Raphals, *Knowing Words: Wisdom and Cunning in the Classical Traditions of China and Greece* (Ithaca: Cornell University Press, 1992). See also my discussion in Roy Willis and Patrick Curry, *Astrology, Science and Culture* (Oxford: Berg Books, 2004), pp. 104–6.

[90]   This corresponds loosely to Baudrillard's idea of 'seduction'; for a good discussion, see Nicholas Gane, *Max Weber and Postmodern Theory* (Basingstoke: Palgrave Macmillan, 2004).

[91]   Stanley J. Tambiah, *Magic, Science, Religion, and the Scope of Rationality* (Cambridge: Cambridge University Press, 1990).

[92]   This point is expressed in the terms that seem to be replacing the hitherto standard emic/etic contrast in anthropological-sociological discourse: 'distance near' and 'distance far'.

rather it proceeds by just the metaphoric logic articulated by Ricoeur, in which the 'is' of identity preserves rather than cancels out the 'is not' of difference. (Viveiros de Castro's reservations, quoted earlier, are thus accommodated.)

Why are there only different forms and degrees of such participation? Because, simply put, in the case of either absolute identity (such as, arguably, late Heideggerian) *or* absolute alterity (including the onto-ethical kind extolled by Lévinas and latterly adopted by Derrida), nothing whatsoever can be known; or, more properly, nothing can be, or not be. It may still be life of some kind, but it is certainly not our life, including whoever or whatever has any presence in our life.

Another and closely related false polarity is:

• immanence 'vs.' transcendence.

Given immanence as effectively participatory ('within') and transcendence as effectively causal or meta-causal ('outside'), the truth of the matter follows from what has just been said. As Merleau-Ponty put it, 'Transcendence is identity within difference.'[93] On this point I can do no better than to add the words of the late Ronald Hepburn, who argued against despairing of being denied entry to heaven by pointing out that our values and experiences

> are essentially the result of a cooperation of man and non-human nature: the universe would not contain them, were it not for our perceptual-creative efforts, and were it not equally for the contribution of the non-human world that both sustains and sets limits to our lives. To realize that there is this cooperative interdependence of man and his natural environment checks the extreme of pessimism by showing our earth-rootedness even in our aspirations. There is no wholly-other paradise from which we are excluded; *the only transcendence that can be real to us is an 'immanent' one.*[94]

A third misleading polarity is:

• the metaphorical 'vs.' the literal.

Again, by the same reasoning – thoroughly argued by Ricoeur, whom there is no need to repeat here – where the discursive and *a fortiori* the linguistic is concerned, there is *only* the metaphorical. Confining metaphor to a particular linguistic trope alone is the reductionist tactic of proponents of a humanly unrealizable neo-positivism. In practice, no statement can be made whose meaning, in order to be (to use William James's usefully blunt term) cashed in, does not require metaphor.

---

[93]   Merleau-Ponty, *Visible*, p. 225.

[94]   R.W. Hepburn, *'Wonder' and Other Essays* (Edinburgh: Edinburgh University Press, 1984), pp. 181–2; my emphasis.

In Laclau and Mouffe's succinct words, 'literality is, in actual fact, the first of metaphors'.[95]

In this sense, by the same token, there is *only* the liminal (we do not, cannot, live in any absolute place or state, but between them) and the motile (we do not, cannot, live in absolute stasis, but only in more or less dynamic motion). The former term is well known in anthropology, although its original anthropocentric provenance, from the work of Victor Turner, now needs correction in two related ways: first, by Edith Turner's subsequent realization that the ritual objects central to rites of passage are simultaneously and equally material *and* spiritual;[96] and second, by Roy Willis's observation that the *communitas* involved in such rituals is a more-than-human one, comprising animals and nature spirits as well as humans.[97]

The term 'motile' comes from Holbraad's theoretical move, already mentioned, beyond the valuable but purely negative position of Lévy-Bruhl (that is, that *participation mystique* offends or ignores Aristotle's stipulation of the excluded middle).

Both liminal and motile, as construed here, accord well with Merleau-Ponty's own understanding of 'Flesh', which falls into neither of the traditional Western categories of mind-subject/matter-object: 'To designate it, we should need the old term "element," in the sense it was used to speak of water, air, earth, and fire, that is, in the sense of a general thing, midway between the spatio-temporal individual and the idea, a sort of incarnate principle that brings a style of being wherever there is a fragment of being.' And praising Proust, he adduced 'an idea that is not the contrary of the sensible, that is its lining and its depth'.[98]

Post-secularism

Here I cannot resist adding something which the post-secular implications of actually moving beyond modernist Cartesianism – as opposed to stopping halfway, or claiming to do so while stopping well short (as per the late Richard Rorty) – make it legitimate to consider once again.[99] I am referring to the 'spiritual' dimension of liminality and motion, although it is simultaneously and equally 'biological',

---

[95]   Laclau and Mouffe, *Hegemony*, p. 111. Cf. Ricoeur, *Rule*, esp. ch. 7.

[96]   Edith Turner, *Experiencing Ritual: A New Interpretation of African Healing* (Philadelphia: University of Pennsylvania Press, 1992).

[97]   Roy Willis, *Some Spirits Heal, Others Only Dance: A Journey into Human Selfhood in an African Village* (Oxford: Berg, 1999), p. 118.

[98]   Merleau-Ponty, *Visible*, pp. 139, 149. For a good recent discussion, see Louise Westling, 'Heidegger and Merleau-Ponty: Ecopoetics and the Problem of Humanism', in Fiona Becket and Terry Gifford (eds), *Culture, Creativity and Environment: New Environmentalist Criticism* (Amsterdam: Rodopi, 2007), pp. 233–47.

[99]   See my 'Post-Secular Nature: Principles and Politics', *Worldviews: Environment, Culture, Religion* 11 (2007): 284–304.

such that, to quote the Neoplatonist philosopher Porphyry, 'Every threshold is sacred'.[100] Every culture knows this in its bones, especially respecting participation in the three great rites of passage between worlds: birth, sexual intercourse and death. But it also applies to the quotidian mysteries of social intercourse, of food, of sleep, of story. It is not only a 'physical' fact that 'a living thing acquires its energy by means of exchange across a boundary, so that the living thing remains distinct from its environment, yet interacts continuously with it'; in mythopoetic terms too, 'life happens at the boundary between two worlds where energies are transformed'.[101] And reverence has modulations: not only simple respect but courtesy and tact are qualities that are called for, and ideally called forth, by all liminal situations of exchange and transformation.[102]

There is, of course, a 'Western' (Hellenic, but pre-Olympian) deity – one of 'ours' – whose nature and domain is specifically the liminal, and descriptions of whom seem at least as to this point as any secular, let alone scientific observations: Hermes. This leads me to question, with Roberto Calasso, to what extent 'all we have done is invent, for those powers that act upon us' – whether from 'within' or 'without' – 'longer, more numerous, more awkward names, which are less effective'.[103] In this context, it is also tantalizing that Merleau-Ponty's body-subject or body-mind as a chiasmic 'decussation' of crossed and intersecting lines resonates closely with the ancient mythic Indo-European metaphor of three Fates (all feminine) weaving the fabric of our individual and collective fates. I could adduce non-European recognition of how 'the threads of life' are woven, suggesting a pancultural phenomenon.[104]

It is also suggestive that Alphonso Lingis, the translator of Merleau-Ponty's last great unfinished work, eloquently sings the praises of 'that nocturnal, oneiric, erotic, mythogenic second space which shows through the interstices of the daylight world of praktognostic competence', where 'One's vital space is an exteriority whose directions are directives.'[105] But note that this second, vital space does not stand in opposition to the mundane or profane world; it is rather its reversible lining.

Holbraad et al. argue that motile logic amounts to a 'method' rather than an ontology, albeit a method for revealing ontologies.[106] Impelled by such

---

[100] Quoted in Casey, *Fate of* Place, p. 293.

[101] Kane, Wisdom, pp. 103, 111. (Bateson came this way too.)

[102] With thanks to Lindsay Radermacher for this point.

[103] Roberto Calasso, *The Marriage of Cadmus and Harmony* (London: Jonathan Cape, 1993), p. 94.

[104] For example, René Devisch, *Weaving the Threads of Life* (Chicago: University of Chicago Press, 1993).

[105] Alphonso Lingis, 'Phantom Equator', in Busch and Gallagher, *Merleau-Ponty*, pp. 227–39, at pp. 227, 238.

[106] Amiria Henare, Martin Holbraad and Sari Wastell, 'Introduction', in their (eds), *Thinking Through Things: Theorising Artefacts Ethnographically* (Routledge, 2007), pp. 1–31, at p. 23.

considerations, however, I wonder 'method' is so easily separated from methodology, itself an adjunct of the modernist obsession with epistemology – and, inseparably, the impulses to secularize and (thereby) render biddable – which have brought about such 'ontological poverty'.[107] At least equally plausible, it seems to me, is the possibility that 'methods' are better considered rituals. (One example might be, 'You shall not suspend or overrule such major tribal injunctions as the law of the excluded middle unless there are good reasons in a particular case to do so.') But in ritual, *how* you do it is equally if not more important than *what* you do; and that is a function not of method as such but of character, experience, wisdom and other individual embodied traits that methodology tries, *per impossibile*, to replace.

Reflexions

The relational and perspectival ontology I have urged here, when rendered self-referential (in accordance with another hallowed ritual injunction, namely consistency) entails many worlds, and thence ontologies. We are all chiasmically embodied and we all live in tensively true worlds, but not in the same way or the same ones. What we share is our constitution by particular differences and relations.

So this ontology should indeed be apprehended as a method, or ritual, to enable their realization. As such, it is intended to point to the way we live – liminal, motile, tensile – and who we are as such beings, suspended between the polarized antinomies to which that very way of living gives rise. But the middle ways or third things I have identified as the processes of embodied life are precisely not things of any kind (let alone Hegelian syntheses or sublations), because to be just *is* to be between.

Here, of course, 'the noun/verb distinction in our habits of thought allows the proliferation of hypostates – things, categories, abstract entities – which we bestow haphazardly on ourselves and others in the form of names and diagnoses. (What actually makes a thief a thief and a boxer a boxer is that they *do* something.)' In which case, 'Translating actions and qualities into substances (translating doing and having into being)' is to start from the wrong place.[108] How we live will always elude capture by language restricted to putatively propositional reference; it will always be between whatever set of categories is applied to it.[109] The only use of language (not 'kind' of language – this point exists only at a pragmatic level, not at a semantic or syntactic level) to which lived experience will yield is consciously metaphoric, that is, participatory: a 'way of living' (ontological) rather than only an 'opinion' (epistemological), in Wittgenstein's terms.

---

[107] Viverios de Castro, 'Exchanging Perspectives', p. 482.

[108] Campbell, *To Square with Genesis*, pp. 2–3.

[109] 'Set' arising from the term applied and its contrary upon which the meaning of the former depends (whether overtly or covertly).

That applies reflexively to this analysis too. If my middle terms are taken to be representations *of* something (whose adequacy can then be analysed) rather than metaphors pointing *to* something (which they partly create, as per Ricoeur), then the point, and the opportunity, will have been entirely missed. But our language notwithstanding, this need not happen. As Wittgenstein pointed out about rules, syntax and semantics may impel particular kinds of pragmatic usages, but they cannot dictate them. There is thus nothing inevitable or necessary about such misunderstandings (essentializing, reifying and so on). This situation was summarized in typically pithy fashion by Chuang Tzu:

> The fish trap exists because of the fish; once you're gotten the fish, you can forget the trap. The rabbit snare exists because of the rabbit; once you gotten the rabbit, you can forget the snare. Words exist because of the meaning; once you've gotten the meaning, you can forget the words. Where can I find a man who has forgotten words so I can have a word with him?[110]

However, as usual, caution is necessary lest what I have just said be regarded as tacitly re-admitting a 'romantic' lived-unity-beyond-words. Distinctions – albeit contingent and relative ones – are essential to the 'way we live' that I am discussing, for without different entities relations between them (perspectives) are impossible, and without relations that constitute entities, change is impossible. It follows that any attempt to suppress or extinguish distinctions altogether – such as through a willed and therefore pseudo-mystical unity – actively inhibits real transformation, spiritual or otherwise.[111]

Morals (with Methodological Implications)

Briefly, I would counsel colleagues in the humanities and social sciences to eschew both superstitions which Bateson identified as arising from mistaken 'ways of thinking about body-mind', in particular those which attempt to reduce the one to the other: 'These two species of superstition, these rival epistemologies, the supernatural and the mechanical, feed each other ... and both are nonsense.'[112]

Against this unhealthy and damaging scenario, including its academic versions, I have argued that:

---

[110] *Chuang Tzu: Basic Writings*, trans. Burton Watson (New York: Columbia University Press, 1964), p. 140.

[111] See my 'Grizzly Man and the Spiritual Life', forthcoming in the *Journal for Religion, Culture and Nature* (2010).

[112] Gregory Bateson and Mary Catherine Bateson, *Angels Fear: An Investigation into the Nature and Meaning of the Sacred* (London: Rider, 1987), p. 51.

1. There is an integral and irreducible embodied, sexuate and ecological dimension to all human thought, as it is taken to be (for example cognition, recognition, conceptualization and so on).
2. There is an integral and irreducible discursive dimension to all human physicality, as it is taken to be (for example sensation, perception, desires, feelings), as well as when it is more obvious that both are involved (for example emotions and values). And finally, that
3. These two dimensions are themselves tensively intertwined. That they are so does not therefore mean they are unreal or non-existent, or that they are not analytically distinguishable, of course. (To hold that would be to misunderstand chiasm and tensivity.) But that they are relatively real and distinguishable does not mean, in turn, that they are not mutually implicated and interdependent.

More generally still, in our work and what and how we seek to understand, as much as any other part of our lives, we should aspire to being better (fuller, more conscious and so on) versions of the imperfect, conflicted, contradictory beings we already are: neither gods of pure undivided consciousness (inexplicably riven) nor particles of pure discrete matter (inexplicably conscious), but *human*.

But a human scale of values need not be exclusively a scale of human values.[113] It should be clear from what has been said so far that wherever there are genuine relations – that is, in which both or all parties can be altered thereby or, if you will, are vulnerable – there, *ipso facto*, is also ethics. As I have also pointed out, we participate in – we are constituted *by* – unfathomably deep, complex and rich webs, or networks, in which the inhering 'active intentionalities' are by no means solely human (or even necessarily embodied: at least, in the way we are). It follows that ethics cannot exclude humans; nor, however, can it be restricted to them.[114] In short, the appropriate religion for embodied human subjects is that of life itself, with all the limitations, contradictions and so-called imperfections that make it possible at all.

Back to Divination

In closing, let me try to spell out a few implications for the field, which was my original concern. With Chuang Tzu's warning in mind, I shall 'define' divination thus: divination is a ritual (synchronically) and a tradition (diachronically) constituted by, and constituting, an ongoing dialogue with more-than-human

---

[113] Taken, almost verbatim, from David Wiggins's excellent 'Nature, Respect for Nature, and the Human Scale of Values', *Proceedings of the Aristotelian Society* XCX (2000): 1–32, at 8.

[114] See Patrick Curry, *Ecological Ethics: An Introduction* (Cambridge: Polity Press, 2006).

agents. It is enacted in order to ask them for guidance and/or discern their will in the matter at hand, to enable them to respond, and to permit intelligible interpretation of the response. An indefeasible part of the ritual, following from those requirements, is an act of aleatory randomization.[115]

Of this ritual/tradition, then, we may add three points. *First*, there is an irreducible embodied, sexuate and ecological dimension, no matter how 'spiritual' it is. That is, the diviner's body and everything he or she 'physically' performs and experiences is essential to it.[116] Relatedly, the sex/gender of the diviner is consequential; although there will be overlap, so to say – just as there are major biological commonalities between the sexes – we should not expect men and women to divine in the same way, nor with the same 'results'.[117] (Not that we should expect any two individuals to do so either; but that still allows for generic differences at a 'higher' level.) And the animate, enminded, ensouled, non-modern natural world is at the heart of divination. Not only is this evident in the roots of ancient as well as contemporary indigenous divination in the natural metaphors, or metaphoric natural phenomena, of water, stones, wood, rustling leaves, animal behaviour and so on; divinatory spirits, when they are involved, are spirits of place. (Even when those places are imaginal ones, they are particular, not universal or anonymous; see my discussion of dis-/embodied spirits, above.)[118]

Second, correspondingly, there is an irreducible discursive, ideational and spiritual dimension, no matter how 'practical' it is, which is, with the provisos of late Wittgenstein and Chuang Tzu once again in mind, analysable in terms of a 'logic' of divination (or, in specific instances, logics).[119] That is, even the most pragmatic divinations, in sum or in part, cannot be separated from meanings, ideas and perspectives which – *being* differential, relational and perspectival – entail ultimate mystery and the impossibility of instrumental grounding, mastery or manipulation. No analysis of divination can therefore exhaust its meaning(s) in purely epistemological or structuralist-functionalist terms. Like any 'system of objective relations, the acquired ideas are themselves caught up in something like a second life and perception'.[120]

---

[115] See my earlier reflections in Willis and Curry, *Astrology*, ch. 9.

[116] See Dennis Tedlock, 'Mind, Body and Cosmos in Mayan Divination', in Curry and Voss, *Seeing With Different Eyes*, pp. 295–310.

[117] See Barbara Tedlock, *The Woman in the Shaman's Body: Reclaiming the Feminine in Religion and Medicine* (New York: Bantam Books, 2005).

[118] See my discussion in Willis and Curry, *Astrology*, pp. 122–4 and Patrick Curry, 'Divination, Enchantment and Platonism', in Angela Voss and Jean Hinson Lall (eds), *The Imaginal Cosmos: Astrology, Divination and the Sacred* (Canterbury: University of Kent, 2007), pp. 35–46, at pp. 42–4. See also Willis, *Some Spirits Heal*.

[119] See the work of Martin Holbraad cited in note 25.

[120] Merleau-Ponty, *Visible*, p. 153.

Third, divinatory rituals/traditions themselves include an understanding (itself an embodied-and-discursive way-of-life) in which any formal 'contradiction' between the first and second points is rendered inconsequential.

Why does the act of randomizing (throwing coins or pebbles or dice, picking shuffled cards blind, mapping the current sky without foreknowledge of the planets' or stars' position and so on) play such an important part? Here we may refer back to the role of agency as discussed earlier. Such an act uses human will (that is, acts deliberately) to set aside the diviner's or his/her client's own human will, desires and imperatives in order to create a window of opportunity, 'random' or 'meaningless' in human terms, allowing the relevant more-than-human agency – spirit, say – to speak and be heard. (We are so needy, greedy and noisy; and understandably, they cannot always be bothered to shout.)

Here is where we can easily understand the hegemonically interested nature of confining discursive meaning to human language; what an effective way to deprive animate nature of its voice in the war to extend the human empire of 'reason'![121] In this context, that meant a programme to replace the countless voices of divinatory spirits of place with the single vision of the One God's divine revelation. The imperialism was plain in the military, misogynist and sadodispassionate metaphors of Bacon, Descartes and Galileo, but its roots lie much further back; further even than the version of Christianity that provided their basic template. 'I'm a lover of learning', says the Socrates of *Phaedrus*, 'and trees and open country won't teach me anything, whereas men in the town do.'[122] But this became an extremely destructive intervention against the aboriginal (and still surviving, if only just) mode of a divinatory relationship with the natural world.[123] As Leroy Little Bear put it to David Peat, 'Trees talk to you, but you don't expect them to speak in English or Blackfoot.'[124] Or Greek.

I hope the potentially rich relevance of Merleau-Ponty's concept of embodiment is already clear in this context. For an example respecting that of Ricoeur – and this brings in the step of interpretation alluded to in my 'definition' – here is Karen Blixen, reflecting on a spontaneous (and desperate) act of divination which she undertook in May 1931:

> Many people think it an unreasonable thing, to be looking for a sign. This is because of the fact that it takes a particular state of mind to be able to do so, and not many people have ever found themselves in such a state. If in this mood, you

---

[121] See Curry, 'Post-Secular Nature' and 'Nature Post-Nature'.

[122] Plato, *Phaedrus*, trans. Edith Hamilton and Huntington Cairns (Princeton: Princeton University press, 1982), sec. 230d. (Perhaps this is more Plato speaking than Socrates.)

[123] See Abram, *Spell of the Sensuous*, Kane, *Wisdom*, and Curry in Willis and Curry, *Astrology*, ch. 7 and pp. 122–4.

[124] F. David Peat, *Blackfoot Physics: A Journey into the Native American Universe* (London: Fourth Estate, 1995), p. 288. (With thanks to Leslie van Gelder for bringing this book to my attention.)

ask for a sign … it follows as the natural consequence of the demand. In that same way an inspired card-player collects thirteen chance cards on the table, and takes up what is called a hand of cards – a unity. Where others see no call at all, he sees a grand slam staring him in the face. Is there a grand slam in the cards? Yes, to the right player.[125]

I think Blixen errs if, in describing the response as 'natural', she implies it is biddable. The important point here, however, is the question, 'Is there a grand slam in the cards?' – to which the correct answer is, obviously, 'yes and no'. In other words, even without bringing in the process of metaphorical interpretation and thence re-description that is such a major part of the diviner's work, divinatory truth is already metaphorically tensive.[126]

This, incidentally, is a principal and sufficient reason, if not the only one, why empirically 'testing' divinatory claims (including astrological ones) is such a hopeless non-starter, and one that begs to then be redefined by the testers in such a way as to exclude the diviner: a move which in turn guarantees a negative result.[127]

Of course, large and open questions remain. For example, what is the relationship between divination and divinization, that is, becoming divine? In Iamblichean theurgy, the latter is virtually the whole point of the former.[128] But is there even some such process at work among clients of end-of-the-pier palmistry? (Again, I wouldn't rule out the possibility.) And somewhere in between, it is possible to maintain a practice of divination which is integral to developing what Jung called 'a symbolic attitude':[129] an ongoing dialogic way of life in which the more-than-human world and/or its parts can symbolically answer enquiries which arise (consciously or unconsciously) in the course of living. ('Can' is important; such answers can be requested and encouraged, but again, they are not biddable.) In any case, I would suggest that in exploring these issues, the perspectives discussed above – chiasm, tensivity and so on – could fruitfully be borne in mind.

---

[125] Isak Dinesen [Karen Blixen], *Out of Africa* (New York: Random House, 1970), p. 368. For a fuller account and discussion, see Curry, 'Divination, Enchantment and Platonism'.

[126] Cf. Geoffrey Cornelius, *The Moment of Astrology: Origins in Divination*, 2nd edn (Bournemouth: Wessex, 2003), p. 133: 'Since an omen is only an omen if it is recognized as such, it is clear that its significance is dependent on the participation of those for whom it is present.'

[127] See my discussion in Willis and Curry, *Astrology*, ch. 8; and cf. Cornelius, *Moment*, chs 3 and 4. (It never fails to amaze me that so many astrologers are repeatedly so naïve, or deluded, as actually to encourage such 'testing'.)

[128] See Shaw, 'Living Light'.

[129] C.G. Jung, *Psychological Types*, Collected Works, vol. 6 (London: Routledge & Kegan Paul, 1971), ch. 11, paras 814–29, esp. 819.

Chapter 8
Chicane: Double-Thinking and Divination among the Witch-Doctors

Geoffrey Cornelius

Most practices of the people we name as shamans, witch-doctors and medicine-men present our modern rational understanding with an impasse. The logic of much that is done defeats us; it is absurd and often disgusting. Treatments are offered that can have no empirical value, yet the simple primitives seem to believe in them. Primitive healing and divinatory practices are particularly obscure; yet there is in them something elusive and important that the educated modern should seek to accommodate if there is to be any hope of arriving at some understanding of the non-modern and pre-scientific mind and the knowing of divination that is integral to it.

We readily acknowledge an implicit ambiguity in divination when this is treated as an apparently faulty mode of logic. Its trickiness is then interpreted as arising from its mere contingency, and the consequent instability and irregularity of its production. Most participants in its production are presumed not to properly understand these objective facts. Some diviners simply deceive themselves as well as their clients; others who do grasp the empirical facts are presumed to knowingly dissemble to overcome their deficiency. The choice is between divination as ignorance or stupidity and divination as cheating and lying.

Sociological interpretation overcomes this crude reduction by emphasizing the socially cohesive role of divination in traditional cultures; this becomes a logically acceptable account for the function of divination beyond the individual interpretation of any diviner or client. However, the sociological imagination lacks the vantage point from which it might address the specific question of the mode of thought involved in the understanding of divination, its meaning for the participants themselves. I take as a point of reference the prescription of Jean-Pierre Vernant that we must seek to describe not only the sociological parameters of divination, but just as importantly 'divinatory intelligence', the distinctive intellectual process involved.[1] This hermeneutic move is required if we are to take into account the *intentionality* of the diviner who knowingly plays or

---

[1]   Jean-Pierre Vernant, *Mortals and Immortals*, trans. Froma I. Zeitlin (Princeton: Princeton University Press, 1991), p. 303. His essay, originally produced in *Divination et Rationalité* (1974), marks a significant step in modern divination studies, in explicitly posing the question of the intellectual operation involved in divinatory interpretation.

colludes in the game of divination not as the charlatan, lying to cover his or her back, but as negotiator with the spirit world, a mediator between concealed and revealed. The assumption of ignorance or the cynical reduction to charlatanry fail to account for the phenomenon to the extent that the primary goal of divination is resolution, truth-as-unconcealment, and everything that flows from the bounty of good fortune.

I suggest that a defining characteristic of the divinatory form is an artful play of semblances; as good a name as any for this elusive quality is the *chicane*. The inquiry takes its lead from the recognition that the seeming-so of semblance and dissemblance are determinative in securing success in divination for both practitioners and clients. What on the one hand appears as illusion manifests on the other as truth, and this is found to be a universal aspect of divination. This is as true for the twenty-first-century astrologer or Tarot-reader as it is for the *sangoma* with his bones. Before this wide-ranging theoretical conclusion is arrived at, the present task is limited to establishing the viability of this interpretation for non-modern modes of divination, on the basis of ethnographic accounts of traditional African culture. We are fortunate that several pioneering studies in ethnography have coaxed into the light aspects of the phenomenon with a degree of clarity that has not been attained in comparable studies in our own culture. The classic work is that of E.E. Evans-Pritchard on the Azande; taking his perceptive observations of the witch-doctors as a starting point, we discover that these remarkable individuals may have a great deal to teach us about divination and the chicane in all cultures, including our own.[2] Even here the subtle nature of the subject requires an indirect approach through witch-doctor healing, which complements their divination. It is in their healing practice that the chicane stands out unobscured, and I therefore examine this first.

Although the patient work of ethnographers has clarified the relevant phenomena, the original and ground-breaking observations of Lucien Lévy-Bruhl on primitive mentality and the *participation mystique* have been little developed with respect to divination. The related question of witch-doctor healing and magical performance has taken a step into modern debate with the theories of Michael

---

[2]   Edward E. Evans-Pritchard, *Witchcraft, Oracles and Magic among the Azande* (Oxford: Clarendon Press, 1937). Concerning 'witch-doctors', I use this term in this study (rather than the more acceptable shaman, sangoma and so on) in deference to Evans-Pritchard's own usage, to avoid clumsy references to his text. This is regarded as a demeaning naming by most modern anthropologists, in my view mistakenly, since 'witch-doctor' is a straightforward description of one of their principal functions, certainly in Azande culture. The name also connects us with unhappy but directly relevant features of our own culture's past. The word *shaman* properly belongs to a distinct stream of Finno-Ugric culture, although that is not the basis of my reservation. My concern is the way in which it has been adopted, which tends to disguise and romanticize the issues. At stake is the fact that for a variety of reasons most modern anthropologists do not like the stark idea of 'witches' and cannot bring themselves to conceive the possibility of their reality – a reality that is taken for granted as self-evident in many traditional cultures.

Taussig. He argues for a compact between the patient and the 'humbuggery' of the practitioner, where 'the real skill of the practitioner lies not in skilled concealment but in the skilled revelation of skilled concealment'. Taussig's concern is, however, trickery and healing rather than trickery and divination, and while ramifications for 'divinatory intelligence' may be inferred from this discussion, they are not directly addressed.[3]

The chicane has implications for the study of hermeneutics extending beyond traditional culture and beyond the limits of divination. This becomes apparent when it is related to wider categories of symbolic interpretation and to 'double-thinking', a mode of shifting yet discriminating definitions and fluid associations. This mode underlies the possibility of the chicane; it appears in all human dealings beyond the simply literal, and it is difficult to envisage an analysis of, for instance, play, theatre, religion or psychotherapy that did not include double-thinking or an equivalent capacity. It is a stock-in-trade of politics.[4] However, it is in the area of what we may broadly term the mystical, the magical and the paranormal, the realms of faërie, enchantment and the sacred, that double-thinking is fully revealed as foundational.

Double-thinking and the chicane have parallels in related areas of interest, notably in the studies of alchemy, divination and synchronicity of C.G. Jung. Jung recognized the significance of Mercurius and the 'synchronicity trickster', carrying forward a Platonic metaphor from antiquity and the renaissance.[5] Like

---

[3]   Michael Taussig, 'Viscerality, Faith, and Skepticism: Another Theory of Magic', in Birgit Meyer and Peter Pels (eds), *Magic and Modernity: Interfaces of Revelation and Concealment* (Stanford: Stanford University Press, 2003), pp. 272–306. His themes of semblance and viscerality among the witch-doctors deserve more consideration than I can offer here. Although there are significant parallels between Taussig's approach to masking-unmasking and my analysis of double-thinking, I take a different line of interpretation on several counts, not least because his study concerns magical healing and trickery rather than divination and trickery. This continues the habitual tendency for anthropology to conflate the categories, obscuring divination in the high drama of magic and distancing us from divination's more commonplace phenomena. Taussig appears to locate unmasking as skilled and intentional unconcealment of the witch-doctor's semblance, as in the quotation given and in his statement that 'power flows not from masking but from unmasking, which masks more than masking' (p. 273). My focus is the unconcealment of the cultural real (the illness, the witch, the good fortune) achieved through the diviner's chicane.

[4]   Double-thinking serves both wisdom and lies, true statesmanship and fascism. Its negating potential is chillingly portrayed by George Orwell in *1984*.

[5]   Among extensive material in Jung, see his study 'The Spirit Mercurius' in *Alchemical Studies*, trans. R.F.C. Hull, Collected Works 13 (London: Routledge & Kegan Paul, 1967): 'Mercurius, following the tradition of Hermes, is many-sided, changeable, and deceitful.' The trick that Mercurius played on Jung in the middle of his astrological experiment on synchronicity is described by Marie-Louise von Franz in *On Divination and Synchronicity* (Toronto: Inner City, 1980), p. 238. See also Maggie Hyde, *Jung and Astrology* (London: Aquarian Press, 1992), pp. 130, 196–205.

Ficino mixing his pantheons, the alchemist's Hermes in the same breath is the astrologer's Mercury.[6] Mercury is the traditional planet of astrology, alchemy, magic – and thieves.[7] An evocative metaphor is the Greek goddess Mētis, and in this respect Hermes-Mētis present faces of the same phenomenon. Modern commentators have brought forward the essentially metic nature of divination, its cunning intelligence,[8] and Patrick Curry has related *Mētis* to Max Weber's theme of enchantment.[9] Ethnographers have observed a similar characteristic relationship of divination and the trickster.[10] These indications need to be kept in the foreground, against the ready assumption that they are 'only' analogies, as if there is 'in fact' some other more logically satisfying way of talking about divination.

It is therefore suggested that the fluid and unbound associative thinking underlying the chicane is integral to understanding divination, and that knowing diviners are to varying degrees aware of this. This phenomenon is especially apparent in the intermediate realm of interpretation that proceeds through a to-and-fro of negotiation, both in the mind of the diviner and in dialogue with a client.

Metaphors of the Chicane

The chicane is an unsettling notion for anyone, especially a 'believer', seeking a sympathetic reading of divination within a single definition of truth. The idea appears at first to belong to the sceptical inquirer, who at best might allow a sociological rendering of divination into means of social control and adaptation; as such it may fulfil certain social functions but it has no inherent epistemological bite, no truthfulness in-and-of-itself. For our sceptic, since naïve belief is readily manipulated by knowing fraudsters, here is the common English usage of 'chicanery' as deception and trickery. Conversely, practitioners of divination expend much energy in assuring everyone that of course this sort of trickiness has

---

[6]   Ficino was a master of the method I have termed double-thinking, as in his essay on light and the Sun referred to here. This is 'allegorical and, to that extent, a mystical exercise of the wits'. Marsilio Ficino, 'De Sole – the Book of the Sun', trans. Angela Voss et al., in Noel Cobb and Eva Loewe (eds), *Sphinx* (London: Convivium for Archetypal Studies, 1975).

[7]   William Lilly, *Christian Astrology* (London, 1647), pp. 77–8: 'he is author of subtilty, tricks, devices, perjury, &c.'

[8]   John Heaton, *Metis: Divination, Psychotherapy and Cunning Intelligence* (London: Company of Astrologers, 1990); see p. 11 for the relationship of Mētis and Hermes.

[9]   Patrick Curry in Roy Willis and Patrick Curry, *Astrology, Science and Culture: Pulling Down the Moon* (Oxford: Berg, 2004), pp. 104–7.

[10]   Rosalind Shaw, 'Splitting Truths from Darkness: Epistemological Aspects of Temne Divination', in Philip M. Peek (ed.), *African Divination Systems* (Bloomington: Indiana University Press, 1991), pp. 137–52. Shaw sees the trickster myths of divination as a corrective to one-sided positivistic categories which she suggests are characteristic of interpretation in the tradition of Evans-Pritchard.

nothing whatsoever to do with their particular corner of the universe. A curiosity of these stances is that they complement each other, the naïve literalism of some believers mirrored by the reductionism of some theorists. This very polarity becomes a virtue when it lets the diviner pull concealed questions into the open like rabbits out of a hat. Chicane comes to signify both an element within symbolic and divinatory performance, and the game of interpretation for both insider and outsider concerning the mysterious phenomena involved.

'Chicanery' is found in literature as a term for pettifogging legal diversions, designed to deflect the course of justice to the advantage of one of the parties. Chicanes are also practical features in road construction, created for safety or alternatively to enhance racing circuits; here the term designates an artificial bend, intended to force traffic into single file or to slow it down. These usages may derive from military engineering: chicanes are false battlements or obstructions intended to deceive or hinder an advancing enemy. In all of these cases the semblance influences another party's behaviour; it redirects the intention of the other. It does not 'come from' the real, but is employed 'in order to' produce the real. The idea also has a naturalistic and non-dialogical usage in the 'baffle' (French *chicane*) found in fluid dynamics and in acoustics; in the latter case it diverts air and sound-flow in speakers. Although the semantic thread here becomes tenuous, it is retained in the image of diverting a movement away from its predetermined natural course.[11]

Many games involve feints and ploys, and for our purposes an illuminating thread of the metaphor comes from card games, where the term means 'void of trumps'.[12] Chicane is a complement to the *trump* which may override the highest ranking power of an ordinary suit and take the trick; this word in turn derives from *triomphe* or triumph; the art of the chicane dances with the power of the trump, for that is its goal, to rise from negation to triumph. In older conventions of Bridge and some forms of Whist, chicane is a term for a hand holding no cards in the trump suit. Here we find the connotation of the *empty hand*; the hand is void of trumps and therefore lacking all natural capacity, and high skill is required in bidding and playing to a successful conclusion. In partnership games of the Whist family, coded communication is required to confound the enemy and create a successful bid. The no-trump state is the unartful state of nature, the state before the game, where each suit is empty; the game begins with bidding, in the sequence

---

[11]   Among minor usages I have come across the term in the slang of petty criminals as 'chic', meaning having no cash. A hustler starts with an empty hand and ends up in pocket. The French *chic* = elegant has a separate origin in German *schicken* = 'to outfit oneself', which is not without a certain semantic resonance.

[12]   'Chicane: a term from Bridge Whist referring to a hand that is void of trumps. It was scored the same as three honours. In Contract Bridge, the term is obsolete in its original sense, though it is occasionally used to describe a void suit, as "chicane in hearts".' See Ben Cohen and Rhoda Barrow (eds), *The Bridge Player's Encyclopedia* (London: Paul Hamlyn, 1964), p. 63.

bidding-bluffing-playing-tricking-taking. Consider also Poker's duplicitous *bluff*, which is a major part of the art of the game. Here by deception an empty hand may force out rivals and rake in the pot; alternatively a full hand is played as if empty, drawing an opponent into a trap.

Granny's Ring

Chicane depends on a capacity of associative and double-thinking. Its hallmarks are allegory, metonymy and metaphor, paradoxically compounding subtlety and concrete simplicity. It sometimes proceeds by simple and absurd assertion, at other times it moves by hint and innuendo. Its style as well as its significance for divination is exemplified in the following anecdote of Granny's Ring.

I have from time to time experimented with dowsing, which, as with many simple divinatory forms, has an erratic and unpredictable occasional capacity to yield useful results. I am not an especially effective dowser, so on one occasion when I sought an answer to diet problems I asked a thoughtful friend with more talent to help me dowse samples of food hidden by her from my view. The trial was repeated by my hiding the samples for her to dowse, asking the ring to indicate which foods were bad or good for me. Good foods were to be indicated by a strong clockwise circling of the ring; bad foods by a counter-clockwise movement; indifferent foods by little or no movement.

For the experiment my friend used a gold ring on a thread; the ring was precious to her, having belonged to her long-departed grandmother, whom I never knew. The experiment yielded mainly inconsistent results, but that is not what stuck in my mind. What stayed with me is our discussion of the principles involved, which succeeded in articulating the state of mind in which we both approached the divination. We agreed that by using her ring we were *asking Granny to help us*. This goes beyond even *asking the ring to show us*, but we were doing that, too. How can one 'ask' either an inanimate object or someone who is dead to do anything? Therefore from one point of view this is simply a figure of speech; but behind this figure it is a reasonable suggestion that this way of talking gives voice to an affect we acknowledge with that particular ring, and which we have invested in it. By evoking an imaginative and emotional element, the experiment becomes special and charged with significance, which in some way allows a subliminal knowledge to show itself, leading the operator to 'unconsciously' vibrate the thread and tweak the ring to give the right answer. Perhaps my body already knows what is good for it. Put this way, I have described a theory of amplification of subliminal knowledge through physiological responses. This type of explanation is often advanced as a possible 'scientific' theory of dowsing, and it might therefore explain any successes from this and similar experiments.

This seems to be a reasonable theory, yet it is not quite enough, because it does not capture the *sense and meaningfulness* that go with the experience. This 'sense' is difficult to describe, yet is obvious on reflection. It is about an open-handed stance to reality, an unarticulated modus operandi in the face of things. When we question this orientation, within a short stretch of investigation we run into paradox; but it is characteristic of this stance *not* to track back to initial premises or draw out resulting conclusions. It is a simple matter to expose the paradoxes. It does not take the skill of a lawyer to see that the logical conclusion of saying 'let granny help us' is to posit the survival after death of a discarnate entity of – or associated with – granny; this entity has furthermore maintained its or her wits sufficiently over the decades to be with us in the proximity of her ring, and to have the acumen with regard to diet – my diet – to know *how* to help. I do not, and did not at the time, see the need to push through to this particular logical conclusion, but neither did I seek to deny it. In any case there was no reason to suppose that granny, whether incarnate or discarnate, would have had much useful to say about my diet.

If I do not wish to be taken down the road of granny-survival, then there is a different possible interpretation, that we have adopted an animistic approach to granny's ring. This suggests that we must be attributing some power to the ring itself, perhaps passed into it by granny in her lifetime. Then it is the ring that seems to have this wonderful capacity, imbued with some mysterious intelligent power. But for my part I am not sure that is what I think, either. I have therefore proceeded in defiance of known explanations, since in choosing to leave the matter open and undefined I have resisted the full implications of the several explanatory possibilities. This defiance is not obscurantism, however, but rather a *resistance to mutually exclusive logical conclusions*. I remain open to possibilities because each of these suggestions, both the normal 'reasonable' conclusion of subliminal amplification and the two paranormal variants (granny-survival and animism), seems to me to have a shade of truth to it, and none of them offends my general orientation. Crucially, therefore, the act of dowsing, and likewise the possibility of moving on any act of a symbolic, ritual or divinatory nature, may occur and be effective without requiring worked out conclusions and without requiring that 'good reasons' are established to justify the act.

This means that in the act of dowsing, to the extent that I am thinking discursively about dowsing, then I am thinking in two or three contradictory ways. This certainly will not do for scientific experiments, but it is surely how human beings decide most things of importance, which, despite our declarations, are only inconsistently worked to their logical conclusions or founded in coherent rational principles. Logical principles are abstractions drawn from consideration of human being, not determinants of human being; where this is not well understood 'good reasons' all too readily become tyrannies of thought.

With the suggestion that one may think in two or three inconsistent ways about a thing, we come to the nub of the idea of knowing that can hold apparently inconsistent possibilities in one and the same act and intention. This is what I mean by 'double-thinking'. I have not come across much satisfactory thinking about double-thinking; we should however avoid the temptation, common in anthropology, of simply equating this phenomenon with Freud's 'primary process'. If we are to follow Freud it might be better described as a quite mindful partial-discursive, a play of secondary cognitive process that evokes affective and imaginative associations but is not bound by them. The discursive threads are lightly held, as in free-ranging conversation, and they are not grasped and rolled up tight towards their conclusions. The effect is to strip the event of any single over-riding explanation. This cedes the authority of the real to the event, the fact of the act.

A comment from Evans-Pritchard is relevant here. The Azande have a termite-oracle where they receive an answer depending on whether termites strip bare one or other (or both or neither) of two branches left overnight. The Azande understand that the termites can hear their question, but they might also address the trees from which the branches are taken. So does the oracle depend on the termites – or on the trees? What is their theory for how the oracle works? From the many conversations Evans-Pritchard records on related matters, it is obvious that the Azande would find it curious and even foolish to push this question very far.[13] Evans-Pritchard says that it must be 'the oracle as a whole' that is taken to provide an answer; this seems true enough, but we need to add that the Azande are very likely adopting the same light-touch double-thinking that has been discussed above, where either *no* explanation is needed or depending on the circumstance several inconsistent explanations could be entertained at the same time, if so desired.

The Chicane and Primitive Mentality

We arrive here at a fruitful comparison with the theories of Lévy-Bruhl. In his terminology, this same phenomenon is characteristic of 'primitive mentality', which likewise eschews what we would term logical consistency when it comes to some of the most significant dealings in life. According to Lévy-Bruhl, this mode is predominant in the realm of the mystical and magical:

> In our thought, the conditions of the possibility of experience are universally valid for every experience, past and to come; what does not satisfy them cannot have been real nor ever become so. In the primitive man's world-view the conditions of the possibility of experience such as we conceive them are valid only for ordinary experience; the mystical experience, the extraordinary experience is not subject to them.[14]

As sometimes occurs, Lévy-Bruhl's use of 'mystical' and 'extraordinary' makes his expression of ideas seem over-dramatic, especially since the Azande generally treat their oracles in a matter-of-fact way. However, his approach brings out a vital distinction, that when it comes to matters of 'medicine', witchcraft and oracles the Azande adopt this open and associative 'non-logical' mode of thinking, a mode

---

13   Evans-Pritchard, *Witchcraft*, p. 353.

14   Lucien Lévy-Bruhl, *The Notebooks on Primitive Mentality*, trans. Peter Rivière (Oxford: Basil Blackwell, 1975), p. 53.

that is neither practical nor necessary for everyday affairs.[15] The background of the modern educated person puts him or her at a disadvantage, because centuries – if not millennia – of abstractive Western philosophy have steeped us in a logic of universal rational categories entirely at variance with such partial and non-concluded double-thinking. As Lévy-Bruhl observes, in contrast to the primitive 'we do not see another sense in which a story may be said to be true or not true; there are not two ways for an event, an act, a thing to be objectively real'.[16] Perhaps the multiple knowing of the primitive real is the message of Granny's Ring.

The Witch-bone Chicane

Evans-Pritchard makes a cardinal observation of the functional relationship of witchcraft, magic and oracles among the Azande: 'the two functions of a witch-doctor are to divine and to extract objects of witchcraft from the bodies of the sick', and sickness is closely bound up with witchcraft, so that any significant illness is held to be a result of its action.[17] This is a common pattern in African culture. The notion of *craft* could mislead us, since its action is an erratic and occasional outcome of ill-intention; in Evans-Pritchard's view, witches are not conscious agents even if their enemies claim they are.[18] Except in very serious instances, the 'witch' is usually forgiven as soon as the error is acknowledged and appropriate ritual and reparation is made. Among the Azande, the power manifesting in the witch is hereditary, and is effective without magical ritual. Where magical ritual is intentionally employed to harm others, this involves bad medicine and is in the distinct category of sorcery; this is a crime that is abhorred. The principal function of witch-doctor divination is to seek out the ill effects of witchcraft and sorcery and to determine the appropriate cure or response.

The witch-doctors come together in an informal but nevertheless tightly knit association in their local area, with a shared understanding and practices known only to them. They have an extensive knowledge of herbs, which includes what the Westerner will term their empirical attributes as well as their magical functions. The witch-doctors' songs and dances are well known and enjoyed in the community, but their most important methods are a closely guarded secret.[19] Leechcraft, the apparent extraction of objects from the bodies of patients, is one of these secrets.

---

[15] Evans-Pritchard, *Witchcraft*, p. 340: 'the main purpose of the oracle and its principal value to the Azande lie in its ability to reveal the play of mystical forces'.

[16] Lévy-Bruhl, *Notebooks*, p. 63.

[17] Evans-Pritchard, *Witchcraft*, pp. 235, 257.

[18] Ibid., part I, ch. VIII, 'Are witches conscious agents?'

[19] Ibid., p. 153: 'In spite of the methods of investigation I employed, my informants did not communicate their entire knowledge to me, even indirectly, and [it] suggests that there were other departments of their knowledge which they did not disclose.'

The practice is common to witch-doctors not just in Africa,[20] but in primitive culture worldwide. As in Azande culture, this practice rests on an understanding that although illnesses are literally embodied, they are nevertheless magical or psychic in origin. In this respect, they are treated in much the same way as other misfortunes befalling a person. The magical interpretation is the cultural norm, the rule rather than the exception, shared by the witch-doctor and the patient.

Before commencing treatment, the Azande witch-doctor privately cuts a small piece of material into a 'witch-bone', or witchcraft object. He hides it between his fingers or under a fingernail. A layman prepares a poultice, and into this the witch-doctor covertly inserts the witchcraft object before placing the poultice on the patient's body. A powerful medicine, *mbiro*, is rubbed across the mouth of the patient, and also into a cut in the affected part of the patient's body. The poultice is removed and examined. When the object is found, the witch-doctor shows it to the onlookers and says 'Heu! Well I never! So that's the thing from which he was dying.'[21] The same act is repeated; according to Evans-Pritchard's informant, Kamanga, 'a man who is good at cheating makes use of the same object about three times'. Some witch-doctors are highly skilled illusionists, comparable to modern stage magicians.[22]

Among a portfolio of other tricks are simulating blood with the juice of red berries, and producing worms.[23] A related procedure is employed where sickness is determined to have occurred because a witch has stolen and hidden the *likikpwo*, a psychic agent belonging to a person. After dancing the dance of divination, its location will be discovered by the witch-doctor, who produces a previously prepared dried rat-gut. This is thumped back into the body of the patient to effect the cure.[24]

Evans-Pritchard gained unique access to these secrets, on account of his immersion in the culture, through the respect in which he appears to have been held and through the fortuitous circumstance of rivalry between two leading practitioners, together with the desire of Kamanga, his servant and informant, to become initiated by them.[25] Evans-Pritchard assisted with the necessary gifts to both Badobo, Kamanga's teacher, and to the formidable Bögwözu, a visiting witch-doctor from the Baka tribe. There seems to be no report of hostility to Kamanga or to Evans-Pritchard as a result of these researches, although it is significant that following the humiliating denouement recounted below, Bögwözu left the district.[26]

---

[20] Ibid., p. 153. In Azande culture leechcraft is also sometimes practised by other healers, both men and women; Evans-Pritchard does not discuss the methods of these healers.

[21] Ibid., p. 235.

[22] See, for instance, ibid., pp. 238–9.

[23] Ibid. p. 236.

[24] Ibid., pp. 237–8.

[25] Ibid., pp. 152–3: 'when informants fall out, anthropologists come into their own'.

[26] Ibid., p. 232.

Given Kamanga's known role as an informant, the witch-doctors held back from his full initiation. The frustrating stalemate lasted until Evans-Pritchard called out 'Badobo's chicanery and Bögwözu's bluff' in an exquisite counter-chicane.[27] One of his houseboys fell mildly ill, and Evans-Pritchard seized the opportunity to suggest that Kamanga should operate immediately, and if this turned out successfully then Bögwözu should receive his full payment for the completion of the training. The procedure necessitated the attendance of Bögwözu. While the trainee was making a cut on the boy's abdomen, Evans-Pritchard saw Bögwözu secrete a small piece of charcoal in the poultice. He intercepted the poultice, and pretending to casually comment on it, he felt for the hidden charcoal and removed it. Bögwözu may not have realized the trick that was being played. The charade continued with Kamanga disagreeably surprised not to find the object that he had from his previous supervised practice come to expect. Evans-Pritchard caught a glimpse of Bögwözu moving his hand over the ground, seeking another piece of charcoal to rescue the situation.[28] At this point he stopped the proceedings and asked teacher and novice to go to a nearby hut where he challenged the deception. The imposture was admitted, Bögwözu was rewarded with part-payment of his fee, and went on his way.

Any concern on Badobo's part about Evans-Pritchard's precipitate intervention appears to have been more than compensated by his relief at seeing the back of a dangerous rival. However, the effect on Kamanga was 'devastating', leaving him in serious doubt about continuing. He soon recovered his poise, and with no further reason for this particular secret to be kept from his European master, Kamanga was granted his initiation. He developed 'a marked degree of self-assurance' so that, like his colleagues, he was well able to rationalize the chicanery of the witch-doctors, and to explain it to Evans-Pritchard.[29] Here is Kamanga's description of what was taught to him about the leech chicane:

> Witch-doctors treat a sick man and deceive him, saying that they have taken an object of witchcraft from his body … but, on the other hand, they have put medicine into the sick man's mouth and cut his skin at the part of the body where he is in pain and have rubbed their medicine across the cut … It is the medicine which really cures people … The people think that healing is brought about by the extraction of objects, and only witch-doctors know that it is the medicine which heals people.[30]

---

[27] Ibid., pp. 230–32.

[28] Ibid., p. 231.

[29] Ibid., pp. 231–2.

[30] Ibid., pp. 235–6. We might speculate on the translation and moral nuance of the word 'deceive' for Kamanga, and we should be alert to the possibility that his response bends to the language and conceptualization of Evans-Pritchard. Such bending to the ethnographer is a problematic issue for participant observation in an alien culture, since it is inherently

Chicane and Embodiment

Why is such a deception necessary? We may speculate that this is because sickness embodies literal truth in a physical dimension that is out in the open, public and undeniable. In an empirical and material sense the witch-doctor must often fail in this embodied half of the work. People will continue to sicken and die, and everyone appreciates this fact of life and death. Despite the qualifiers and caveats that offer leeway, success is measured by health, or at least by amelioration, where failure is suffering. The spectacular ideal is for us to feel with our own bodies and see with our own eyes that we are healed, and for others around us to see this too. Many truths may be symbolized in the body, its woes might be sociopathic, psychic and obscure, but those woes are manifest, so that when the patient says 'I am sick' the literal truth of the matter and the material facts of the case become one.

In this sense, the body does not brook interpretation, but it is exactly at this point that the chicane of the witch-doctor does its work, between seeming and being, matching the material 'given' of the illness with the material given of the witchcraft-object. The patient must perforce attend the material and physical given of the illness, since this is what the pain and discomfort of disease demand of our consciousness. By contrast the witch-doctor works on a double level, carrying over material illness to a material symbol – the witchcraft object – which becomes both the carrier and the representative of the non-material psychic matrix of the illness. There is a dialogical process at work between actor and acted-upon, but different requirements of conscious intention between them, since the witch-doctor knows what the patient thinks, but also knows what the patient *needs*. This presents us with a double mode of interpretation for one and the same act. The patient thinks the illness is *caused by* the object, and its removal removes the illness. The witch-doctor treats the object and its removal as *semblance*, since for him its literal removal does not literally remove the illness, but – crucially – since the removal symbolizes the healing, by the chicane of the whole performance he *effects* the healing. This is a good place to return to the card-playing metaphor with which we started, for witch-doctor and patient are playing this game together. The witch-doctor's trump, his manifest triumph, is the removal of the psycho-spiritual complex, the witchcraft that he and his patient agree is the source of illness. Through chicane the witch-doctor trumps the illness. The trick is played in the sleight-of-hand, and the trick that is taken is at the self-same moment the healing of the patient. This is the instance of empirical healing; honours go to the witch-doctor who performs this feat.

---

unlikely that the European will think like the native. However, this subtle consideration does not seem to me to be of an order that would materially affect the present discussion.

Symbolic Instantiation

In considering how the witch-doctor achieves his healing effect, our ordinary naturalistic and positivist concept of cause and effect may let us down, since there are overlapping and double-thinking senses in which the idea of causality is employed in the compact between witch-doctor and patient. Perhaps we need a more subtle and extended analysis to handle the interpretive moves involved, and Aristotle's approach, foundational for pre-enlightenment philosophy, provides a convincing hermeneutic strategy. For the most literal of possible interpretations by a patient, the witchcraft-object is both the *matter* (the material substance) and the *efficient cause* (the active agent) of the sickness. For the witch-doctor, the same object is not in-and-of-itself either the material or the efficient cause, but is a symbol for both efficient (agent) and *formal* (ideational and intentional) causes. The formal element is the mental reality of the witch's bad motive; this is countered by the intentional mental reality of the healing chicane. That is why the chicane is a symbol, and why healing is a ritual-symbolic act. The *final* cause, to which everything is turned, is the annulling of the malevolent intention of the offending witch, with the consequent well-being of the patient.

The chicane is the symbolic instantiation of the cure in the physical removal of the witchcraft-object. The witch-doctor 'knows' this even if he does not use our words. But what does the patient 'know' about this sleight-of-hand? It is not necessary for patients to be naïve and credulous, even if often they are. Evans-Pritchard is emphatic that many Azande have a healthy scepticism about their witch-doctors,[31] but there is no need to suppose that this hinders engagement in the performance where physical need and emotional affect are invoked. The body and the emotions have their own good reasons to suspend judgement where issues of health, life and death are concerned. Perhaps most witch-doctors cheat and are no use most of the time, but this witch-doctor here-and-now *may* be good, and that is what counts. We infer yet again in the attitude of ordinary Azande the softening of logical generalization and the unbinding of abstraction characteristic of double-thinking and primitive mentality. All that is required is that the patient enters into the one-off performance here-and-now, 'as if' the witch-bone removed from his or her body 'really is' the illness removed.

A sympathetic modern interpretation would allow the witch-doctors an erratic modicum of empirical medicine amplified by suggestion and the placebo effect. This may not be an inaccurate representation within a modern and scientific perspective, yet laying out the case in this way nevertheless falls far short of understanding. This is because the clear distinction we make between pairs such as empirical medicine and placebo, literal and symbolic, is a function of *our* conceptual framework and cultural presuppositions, and therefore of our reality. We face a problem insisted

---

[31] Ibid.; see, for example, pp. 165, 183, 191.

upon by Lévy-Bruhl, and conceded by Evans-Pritchard,[32] that there are elements of the primitive mentality that are opaque to us, and which we are consistently prone to misinterpret. Quite apart from cultural nuances lost in translation into European languages, if we accept the likelihood of double-thinking then even apparently straightforward statements may not grant us a reliable understanding of the mental process at work. We also note that at the time of his acting as an informant to Evans-Pritchard, Kamanga was young in the craft. Given the marked reserve of his teachers, their love of allusion and innuendo and the duplex nature of their thinking, we remain with an uncertain hinterland where the paths, shadowy and mysterious for the witch-doctors themselves, are utterly obscure for us. For us to make any advance into this realm requires the uncommon gift of having at least an inkling of those same paths in our own experience, whether this is attained by symbolic and divinatory practice or whether it springs from inborn *mētis*.

Defining Medicine

Even without treading obscure paths of our own experience, we will recognize with some clarity a fundamental concept that enables us to take the first step into this hinterland. This resides in the understanding of *medicine*, common not just to the Azande but to primitive thought as a whole: 'it is of mystical causes and cures and not physical causes and cures that Azande speak and towards which they chiefly direct their attention'.[33] Evans-Pritchard counters the suggestion that the Azande are 'stating in mystical idiom facts based on observation and experiment'. He allows that some Azande medicines do produce the intended empirical effect, but the Azande do not seek a distinction that we would make between ritual and objective consequences. Medicines that from our pharmacological understanding are wholly ineffective 'are all alike *ngua*, medicine, and all are operated in magical rites and in much the same manner'.[34] This is well brought out in the Azande attitude to the key material agent of the Poison Oracle, *benge*, a red powder prepared from a wild forest creeper; this was used on chickens, and in pre-colonial

---

[32]   Evans-Pritchard's enterprise comes consistently closer to the later Lévy-Bruhlian perspective than he may have recognized, and this proximity of thought emerges in the material on witch-doctor practices discussed here. His position is established in his initial stand against the polarized definition of primitive mentality as 'pre-logical' found in Lévy-Bruhl's early work. There are a number of occasions in *Witchcraft, Oracles and Magic* where he implicitly sets out to counter this earlier definition. There is also a strong possibility that Lévy-Bruhl has himself been influenced by the criticisms of Evans-Pritchard. See Evans-Pritchard, *A History of Anthropological Thought* (London: Faber and Faber, 1981), p. 131.

[33]   Evans-Pritchard, *Witchcraft*, p. 315.

[34]   Ibid., pp. 316, 448. The efficacy of each medicine is self-contained and operative only for the unique situation for which that medicine is intended.

times occasionally on humans.[35] Although from a botanical perspective the creeper of the same name is a poisonous plant, the oracular function of the medicine is not a natural attribute, but depends on it being addressed correctly and employed in the traditional manner, observing appropriate taboos; 'hence Azande say that if it is deprived of its potency for some reason or other it is just an ordinary thing, mere wood'.[36] Evans-Pritchard suggests that the Azande would be 'amazed at the credulity' of the European who might attempt controlled experiments in poisoning chickens in order to determine the natural properties of *benge*.[37] This would show an astonishing ignorance of 'medicine'.

On this basis we may comprehend something of the potent *mbiro* medicine of the witch-doctors, used for both divination and healing.[38] A witch-doctor keeps *mbiro* in a special pot, and mixes it with various herbs and substances; if he falls ill, it is his own *mbiro* that he takes as medicine. There is an intimate relationship between *mbiro* and the witch-bone through *ranga*, which is the name for a plant from which witch-bone is made, and (it seems by extension) for other witchcraft objects manipulated in healing. *Ranga* is eaten to create the *mbiro* in the belly of the witch-doctor. This in turn becomes or produces witchcraft-phlegm; a significant moment in the initiation of the novice involves his swallowing a small amount of this substance retched up by his teacher.[39] It is in this manner that the transmission of *mbiro* magic is effected; and it is a transmission that comes into play in the chicane. Kamanga explained that his teachers had spoken to him 'with hidden meaning in their words' prior to his knowledge of the witch-bone; they said '*mbiro, mbiro*, it is *mbiro* which is the great curer, don't play the fool with *mbiro*'.[40]

The Literal Stop in Interpretation

It is an inescapable element of theory and interpretation that we arrive at a point where we declare what is 'really going on', as opposed to what seems or is commonly thought to be going on. Here is the meeting point of metaphoric and

---

[35] Ibid., pp. 309–12.

[36] Ibid., p. 314, also p. 448: 'it is man who manufactures from it the medicine'.

[37] Ibid., p. 315. From our scientific perspective, the efficacy of *benge* resides in a compound of the strychnine family. Evans-Pritchard established that Azande have no concept of *benge* as 'literally' poisonous in our simple pharmacological sense; when it kills, it kills ritually as an aspect of its function as oracle. This well illustrates the fact that medicines – like illness itself – are all alike taken up by Azande ritually and symbolically, a mode of concern that is not categorially founded in natural properties.

[38] Ibid., p. 227.

[39] Ibid., p. 225: from the account, the term *ranga* may refer also to other objects carrying the same magical potency. There is, perhaps understandably, some ambiguity in Evans-Pritchard's text on the definition of *ranga*.

[40] Ibid., p. 227.

literal knowledge. In talking of the literal, it should be borne in mind that literal expressions may at the same time be entirely abstract, philosophical or theoretical (for example 'kinship structure'); similarly, a symbolic or metaphoric form may be treated literally (for example 'underlying the chicane is the Mercurius archetype').[41] This is a stopping point when we imagine we have to look no further back and behind the phenomena to find another explanation.

This hermeneutic element is itself a device of literal explanation; as such it serves to clarify the several understandings involved in the witch-doctor's chicane. For the most credulous patients, interpretation stops at the surface of events. The chicane has no back-and-behind, and *is not chicane*, since the real happening is the performed event, unseen as chicane. The witchcraft object 'really is' the evil of the illness, its removal literally is the removal of the illness. This is why Kamanga is truly shocked by Evans-Pritchard's exposé of the chicane of Bögwözu; he discovers a hinterland that he never even guessed at, and the veil is torn away without appropriate ritual and without symbolic guards.

The need for a hermeneutic of the chicane becomes pressing as we leave the ordinary villager and seek to penetrate witch-doctor imagination, for we find that the literal stop is moved at least one step back from the surface of things and into the symbolic domain; it is this step above all that distinguishes the initiate. This is readily observed in Kamanga's account, introduced above. As an initiate he now understands that the leechcraft performance is chicane: the 'real' cure is effected by the *mbiro* medicine, rubbed onto the patient's body, 'and only witch-doctors know that it is the medicine which heals people'.[42] But this raises a further puzzling question.

We have well enough established the game of reciprocal intentions in play in witchcraft healing, but the issue becomes more rather than less subtle as we focus our attention on the mode of thought of the witch-doctor. We bump up against the inadequacy of our taken-for-granted distinction between 'literal' and 'symbolic', and likewise between 'objective' and 'mystical' categories.[43] Fluidity across the literal–symbolic bound is part of double-thinking. This is most obvious when we consider the apparent literal stop to interpretation offered by Kamanga, when he

---

[41]   Moving in a complementary direction to the literal, the symbol, recognized as symbol, is equally the stopping point of interpretation. Examples are archetypes *in themselves* and true religious symbols, such as 'Christ'. This interpretive movement is elusive in ordinary parlance, since symbols spontaneously and continuously metamorphose into literals, concrete or abstract, in the process of thinking and talking; and as suggested in this study, the distinction we have learned to make between 'literal' and 'symbolic' may be less secure than we sometimes imagine.

[42]   Evans-Pritchard, *Witchcraft*, p. 236.

[43]   Philip Peek, 'African Divination Systems – Non-Normal Modes of Cognition', in Peek, *African Divination Systems*, p. 8, argues that primitive divination 'makes definite use of both modes of thinking'; there is still a demarcation, but the modes may alternate. This alternation bears comparison with my description of double-thinking.

asserts that *mbiro* medicine is the 'real' agent of healing. But what is *mbiro*? As we have seen, the power of a herb or medicine is essentially psycho-spiritual rather than material, and by psycho-spiritual is meant the efficient agency of knowing and intention, in this case the witch-doctor's healing intent. *Mbiro* 'literally' embodies the transmission of knowledge from initiate to pupil, and it is among the most intimate carriers of the witch-doctor's own power. It is the non-mediated, non-conceptual fabric of ritual and medicine within which he has been initiated. The *ranga* which produces it is at work in the belly of the witch-doctor,[44] but it is also *ranga* that he uses to fashion the witchcraft-object extracted from the patient.

Although Kamanga talks literally as if *mbiro* is the literal stop, we remember the lesson of granny's ring and realize that it is highly unlikely that experienced witch-doctors take all of their devices and rituals 'simply literally' in our positivistic modern sense. I infer – although it seems difficult to imagine a way of proving this – that the movement of thought will be towards non-concluded double-thinking. Perhaps some witch-doctors adopt a simple literalism of *mbiro* much of the time, yet the apparent literalism in Kamanga's statement – or in what Evans-Pritchard has understood from Kamanga – scarcely disguises the fact that in our terms *mbiro* is a participatory complex of psycho-spiritual (symbolic) healing for a psycho-spiritual (symbolic) wound manifesting as a literal bodily ill. The psycho-spiritual (symbolic) wound is the embodied malaise of sociopathic disturbance and ill-intent that Europeans call 'witchcraft'. My parentheses assert that we must take the idea of symbol not simply as a remote signifier but in an immediate and embodied sense; or if we say the medicine is a metaphor, then it is a metaphor that 'carries over' into empirical phenomena – and the ultimate empirical phenomenon of the human body – in the most material of ways. Such embodiment astounds us, it is alien to our ordinary assumptions, making it difficult for us to understand.

It is therefore in the magical thinking of the witch-doctor with his consubstantiality of herbs, medicines, body-fluids and magical objects, and the participation of all of these objects in the field of his conscious intention, that we see the relevance of Lévy-Bruhl's *participation mystique*, for here above all we find the gathering of symbolic and literal, ritual and material metamorphosed in an embodied and empirical worldly goal. Kamanga's self-assured rationalization of the chicane shows that he has imbibed its essential nature, and that is why he has begun to travel the path of the initiate. The witch-doctor's move carries the symbol, known or intuited *as such*, into the body of his patient, where the simple villager – and the simple ethnographer – may cling to more literal interpretations.

---

[44]   Medicine in the belly suggests a mythological motif. Like Mētis, wisdom resides in the belly of Zeus.

The Dance of Divination

I have discussed in some detail the chicane, the symbolic and the literal in the medicine of the Azande witch-doctors in order to suggest that a similar double-thinking is likely to be found in their divination practice. With this suggestion in mind, I focus here on the Azande 'dance of divination'. Evans-Pritchard gives an evocative account and close analysis of the 'séance' and the dance of divination, allowing us to infer something of the cognitive process involved. A group of witch-doctors will perform publicly at the request of a householder who may have suffered misfortune.[45] There is a chorus of boys backing up the songs, but everyone is harangued to take part. Dancing takes place to the beat of drums and gongs. Throughout the whole exuberant performance there is a ceaseless battle against witchcraft; if someone annoys the witch-doctors by a wrong attitude or in their divination they suspect the person of being a witch, they may with a flourish project a witchcraft object into the offender. This is done by the witch-doctor 'raising his leg and sharply kicking out in the direction of his objective'. Following the attack, the witch-doctor 'may walk up to him and theatrically remove his shaft, generally from the forehead when the missile is a black beetle'. There are in addition spectacular mock battles between witch-doctors, with an occasional ill-natured element; in one such incident Kamanga achieved a notable victory, causing the hat and leglets of a jealous rival to fall off by means of his magic ammunition.[46] Projecting witch-bones in a theatrical manner is a feature of the dance and is an explicit and intentional chicane, but it does not directly bear on divination. However, the dance for the *likikpwo* mentioned earlier is an explicit chicane combining both divination and healing. This takes place with a group of unfortunates who have all had this psychic organ stolen and hidden by witches. The witch-doctor has a secret supply of rat-guts on his person while he dances, waiting for his divinations to discover their supposed hiding places,[47] and in this sense the divination itself is a chicane. As with leechcraft, we infer that the embodiment in rat-gut is interpreted in a literal manner by most villagers. For the witch-doctor it exists in ritual-symbolic form, as he metamorphoses the symbol into the patient's body with a thump.

In the usual dance of divination, the witch-doctors dance singly or in twos or threes, taking questions from their audience.[48] The witch-doctor responds by dancing until he is breathless, and stumbling as if drunk. This is the usual moment for him to utter an oracular response, in a strained voice: 'it appears as though the words come to him from without and that he has difficulty in hearing and transmitting them'.[49] As he proceeds, he 'begins to throw off his air of semi-

45 Evans-Pritchard, *Witchcraft*, pp. 163–4.
46 Ibid., pp. 179–80.
47 Ibid., p. 237.
48 Ibid., p. 168.
49 Ibid., pp. 162, 169.

consciousness and to give forth his revelations with assurance, and eventually with truculence'. He may dance again for further revelation, or move to another enquiry. He may run across to gaze into his medicine-pot.[50] Sometimes he halts midstream, and another witch-doctor interjects to assist him with a response.[51] Questions are often gradually answered, bit by bit over many hours, by a drawn-out process of exclusion (it is not this person who is the witch, it is not that person). At the end, it is common for the witch-doctor to whisper the name of the culprit to the enquirer; this is safer for everyone, and the enquirer can then choose to settle the matter by consulting the more authoritative Poison Oracle, apart from the witch-doctor performance.

It is apparent from various accounts that witch-doctor divination commonly involves two principal modes. The core mode is an altered state of consciousness, marked by unusual physiological phenomena. Certain of these gatherings lead to frenzied performances where the witch-doctors enlarge the whites of their eyes, contort and cut themselves, or gash their tongues with knives and foam at the mouth.[52] Cognitive dissociation is induced by drumming, dancing, and exhaustion; this is the *abaissement du niveau mental*, the 'lowering of the mental level' to induce the manifestation of subliminal phenomena.[53]

The witch-doctors, obtaining the names of several potential culprits (that is, witches) by a separate procedure discussed below, enter the core mode of divination by 'dancing to' the name of the individual:

> they keep the names in their memory and repeat them now and again, but otherwise allow their minds to become a complete blank. Suddenly one of the persons to whom he is dancing obtrudes himself upon the witch-doctor's consciousness, sometimes as a visual image, but generally by an association of the idea and the name of the witch with a physiological disturbance, chiefly in a sudden quickening of the heartbeats, which begin to pulsate violently, pit-a-pat, pit-a-pat, pit-a-pat.[54]

This core mode of divination is where participants know the oracle to be active; without this, there may be no oracle. According to the witch-doctors, the dance 'stirs up and makes active the medicines within them, so that when they are asked a question they will always dance it rather than ponder it to find the answer'.[55] The witch-doctor 'goes into the soul of the medicine ... [until it] will stand alert within

---

[50]   Ibid., p. 167.

[51]   Ibid., p. 166.

[52]   Ibid., p. 162. Evans-Pritchard reports Mgr Lagae's observation of witch-doctors walking on burning embers.

[53]   The *abaissement* emerges in psychological theory in the work of Pierre Janet. I suggest this is functionally related to double-thinking.

[54]   Evans-Pritchard, *Witchcraft*, p. 175.

[55]   Ibid., p. 167.

him'.[56] The medicine 'glows in his body and through it he begins to see witchcraft clearly'.[57]

It is difficult to come to a firm view on chicane elements in the core mode in the absence of studies dedicated to this task. Evans-Pritchard provides us with some marvellous descriptions, but he also exemplifies the struggle of classical anthropology to offer an adequate interpretation of divination. He declares that 'a witch-doctor divines successfully because he says what his listener wishes him to say, and because he uses tact'.[58] On the other hand Evans-Pritchard asserts that 'we must allow the Azande witch-doctor a measure of intuition and not attribute his utterances solely to his reason'.[59] The witch-doctors fully believe in their magic,[60] and they will undoubtedly identify with its power at the instant of being seized by a clairvoyant image or a strong mental impression accompanied by physiological sensations. So is this chicane or not-chicane? Evans-Pritchard has to settle for the dance of divination as 'only partly a pose'.[61] This ambiguity perfectly expresses the paradox of double-thinking for the objective observer. In the midst of his ecstasy the witch-doctor keeps his wits about himself sufficiently to avoid causing dangerous offence in what he says, as when he employs innuendo[62] or whispers the name of a witch to the interested party. This shows us that a guiding light of ratiocination passes right through the ecstasy and holds it in an ethical and social compass. It is not an either-or case; both sides of the equation define divination.

Locating the Divinatory Chicane

Beyond the ecstatic state at the core of witch-doctor divination, there is a broader phase or mode involving dialogue, negotiation and interpretation. It is in this broader mode that the divinatory chicane emerges more obviously, and where it has been readily (and negatively) interpreted as chicane by ethnographers. This part of divination is a vehicle or container for the core of divinatory 'realization', establishing the ground and even the possibility of divination and sustaining its meaningfulness for all participants, before and after the event. It is both the precondition for divination and the way in which divinatory meaning is worked out to the satisfaction of everyone involved, including the audience in a public performance. Its first and most important element is that the questioner establishes

---

[56]   Ibid., p. 176.

[57]   Ibid., p. 165, quoting an informant of Mgr Lagae.

[58]   Ibid., p. 170.

[59]   Ibid., pp. 175–6: 'a witch-doctor ... does not simply weigh up the advantages of denouncing this or that man ... there is a measure of free and unconscious association'.

[60]   Ibid., p. 255.

[61]   Ibid., p. 170.

[62]   Ibid., p. 172: Sanza, innuendo, is much appreciated by the Azande, and is a common device in divinatory responses.

a limited field of concern for the diviner, usually by stating his or her misfortune or problem and by negotiating with the witch-doctor several possible witches to be considered.[63] These are the names to whom he will dance.·

The declaring of the problem and a list of suspects is only the most obvious of the preparatory elements for divination; the witch-doctors have other work to do. The following summary of this groundwork is drawn mainly from Evans-Pritchard's deconstructive analysis of the chicane. He observes that the witch-doctors pay considerable attention to moulding the expectations and understandings of client and audience. They build up faith in their powers 'by lavish use of professional dogmatism'.[64] They display great confidence, boast of their prowess and successes, and continually promise that they will discover the secrets that lie behind the various misfortunes in their audience; all this within a dramatic performance of dancing, drumming and singing. Whenever they give answers, these are tailored to provide maximum impact for minimum specificity.[65] Where the diviner is specific, then it is likely to be on a magical or witchcraft topic which of its nature is not open to verification. Here he can speak with the unchallenged authority of the oracle. However, it is in gaining information from his audience and potential enquirers that the diviner is most adept. This is skilfully elicited in exchanges either before the ceremony or during the dance of divination. There is a limited stock of common human concerns to draw on; the witch-doctors know the power and status relationships in their community, and they know most of the local squabbles and scandals in advance. A visiting witch-doctor will get advice from his local colleagues.[66]

In contact with the questioner and an audience, the diviner employs what has come to be known as *cold reading*.[67] This refers to the capacity, which may be subliminal or fully conscious, to pick up clues from the body language of the client and in this case also the audience. In addition clues are garnered from the response to questions. From this information the diviner is able to feed back a plausible interpretation without apparently having been told the relevant details.

---

[63] Ibid., p. 175.

[64] Ibid., p. 171.

[65] This is known as the *Barnum effect*. The diviner offers statements of an almost universal applicability that seem specific yet will be agreed upon by everyone; or, offers a general statement geared to the particular client's situation, yet with no obvious falsifiable detail. The client fills in specific details, crediting the diviner with having a marvellous insight into their situation. See note 67 on 'cold reading' below.

[66] Evans-Pritchard, *Witchcraft*, p. 170·

[67] For cold reading and the Barnum effect, see Geoffrey Dean, Arthur Mather and Ivan Kelly, 'Astrology' in Gordon Stein (ed.), *Encyclopedia of the Paranormal* (New York: Prometheus, 1996), p. 91. These terms come from modern psychology and are common among rationalist sceptics of astrology and divination.

It is worth mentioning here the parallels with Victor Turner's analysis of the Ndembu diviners.[68] His study concerns basket-divination, involving the initiated diviner shaking a basket of symbolic objects (his 'bones'). In terms of the spectrum of divination, 'divination with the bones' does not involve the ecstatic condition of the dance of divination, and falls nearer the objectified end of the continuum. In my view the universal structure of divinatory interpretation is replicated, however, with a negotiating and dialogical element fundamental to the act of divination. Consultants of basket-divination will travel far to ensure that a diviner is not simply relying on local knowledge, but his skill at cold reading will soon overcome their guard: 'he notes the kind and intensity of their reactions, positive and negative, to his questions and statements'; the symbolism of the bones is vague and flexible, allowing him to easily establish a reference to the situation he now infers. When he has fed back a convincing interpretation, he has established a 'certain psychological ascendancy over his audience, "softened them up"'.[69] He even rebukes them when he guesses they are misleading him or withholding vital information. He probes them 'after the manner of the English party game "Twenty Questions"', which allows him to rapidly close on the particulars of a name, such as the undisclosed name of a deceased relative, in a way that appears miraculous. At that point he has increased their credulity to such a pitch that 'the logician is felt to be a magician'.[70] Turner comes to a conclusion that accords closely with the observations of Evans-Pritchard among the Azande, concerning the end point of the divining process. The principal revelation obtained refers to witchcraft, to errors in ritual or to the ancestors: 'the causes of misfortune or death ... are almost invariably mystical or nonempirical in character, although human wishes, desires, and feelings are involved in their operation'.[71] This appears to be a cardinal principle of primitive divination.

Within anthropology there have been two broad directions of interpretation of the divinatory chicane. The rather old-fashioned and simple-minded version is that the phenomena we have discussed show a combination of outright charlatanry (such as the explicit and intentional chicane of witch-doctor healing) and simple ignorance. Simple ignorance is of course shown by the villager, but may be the situation of the diviner who does not understand the power of cold reading and the psychology of dialogue; in this case the chicane is implicit. A more modern version, illuminated by the insight of sociology and structural functionalism, sees in these interactions of diviners and clients the sustainment of social harmony and the social structure: divination is one of several 'institutionalised mechanisms of redress which are ordered towards the maintenance of that social structure'.[72] For sociological interpretations, even the explicit and intentional chicane may

---

[68] Victor Turner, *Revelation and Divination in Ndembu Ritual* (Ithaca: Cornell University Press, 1973)·

[69] Ibid., p. 240.

[70] Ibid., pp. 240–41·

[71] Ibid., p· 209·

[72] Ibid., p. 236·

be explained by this mechanism, while the broader negotiated element of the divinatory process depends on a structural but subliminal and implicit chicane.

In terms of our metaphor of chicane, a feature of the sociological imagination is that the chicane is interpreted more naturalistically, like the function of a baffle-board in a speaker; this tends to downplay the possibility of 'intelligent semblance' by a fully aware diviner, witch-doctor or shaman. Even very subtle and convincing demonstrations of the role of kinship structures in divination, such as that of Devisch,[73] prove beyond doubt that this social structure is foundational, yet tend in my view to underplay the role of the initiate's intelligence. I do not wish to criticize a valid sociological perspective; however, if the approach I have adopted is plausible, then this perspective needs to be augmented by the recognition that these diviners are working at a high level within their culture, moving in the mode of sophisticated double-thinking and negotiating the order that we call 'symbolic'. There is certainly no doubt about the intelligence of the witch-doctors and the diviners, treated as a class. This is a common report from many observers, although depending on the style of interpretation of the chicane, this may also be called 'cunning'.[74] However, Philip Peek speaks for a new generation of anthropologists who completely reject the charlatan tag: 'we have found diviners to be men and women of exceptional wisdom and high personal character'.[75] This new appraisal goes together with the view that diviners and divination embody the epistemology of a culture, in much the same way as a system of law or the interpretations of theology and metaphysics.

The Joker

This brings me to a final remark about current interpretations of the chicane. Apart from scattered heretics,[76] orthodox anthropology has ducked a major epistemological and metaphysical problem. This may be expressed as follows: quite apart from all the rational and functionalist interpretations that might explain the behaviour of witch-doctors, quite apart from the possibility that they have acquired a pharmacological knowledge of some herbs and apart even from psychophysical explanations of placebo – apart from all these, there may be some

---

[73] René Devisch, 'Mediumistic Divination amongst the Northern Yaka of Zaire', in Peek, *African Divination Systems*, pp. 112–32.

[74] Evans-Pritchard, *Witchcraft,* p. 175·

[75] Peek, 'African Divination Systems', p. 3.

[76] A significant heretic in the field of divination studies is Roy Willis; see Willis and Curry, *Astrology,* esp. chs 9 and 10 discussing the breaking of the taboo on the paranormal. There are very few professional anthropologists who will risk their academic careers through a discussion of *their own experience* of divination as valid knowing. We may talk about these things second-hand but not directly, which is perhaps our own weak version of the chicane.

other residuum in their knowledge, for which we can offer no adequate account. With very few exceptions, the explanations that we have adopted fail to give weight to the following possibility: that empirical phenomena of a paranormal (supernatural or preternatural) provenance are at least partial determinants for primitive ritual and divinatory practice.[77] Any such suggestion has been treated as taboo and an absolute non-possibility by most anthropologists; 'witchcraft is imaginary', says Evans-Pritchard, 'and a man cannot possibly be a witch.'[78] To bring in the paranormal is the Joker in the deck, not least because we have almost no way in our present thinking to deal with it. I will, however, appeal to my first mentor in these discussions, Lévy-Bruhl, in his telling observation that primitive mentality is founded in the mythopoeic realm and in what he termed the 'affective category of the supernatural'.[79]

The witch-doctors and their double-thinking chicane may prove to be a significant path for opening the intellectual question of divination and the manner of its revelation. This bears upon the nature of mind itself. Here, I suggest, is a trump card in the apparently empty hand of primitive mentality.

---

[77] We struggle with terms at this point. I use 'paranormal' to encompass two possible classes of occurrence, and to avoid getting stuck in distinctions between them that would take us into a large metaphysical debate. These possible classes are those of the *supernatural*, which is supposed to lie entirely beyond and 'above' our known world and the order of nature, and *preternatural*, which lies beyond the order of nature as known to contemporary science, but which is presumed to fall within the scope of a much-enhanced future science. Telepathy between dogs and their owners may well class as 'preternatural' without us needing to invoke the theological implications that tend to go with the idea of the supernatural. Witchcraft phenomena, if they are considered to be 'real', may arguably be preternatural rather than supernatural, but this question remains wide open.

[78] This *literally stops* any further consideration that there might be a way in which the Azande notion is 'real' (that is, in our terms, has some empirical foundation).

[79] Lévy-Bruhl, *Notebooks*, p. 63: 'It is a reality which is felt at one and the same time as beyond doubt and as having something peculiar to it which characterizes it directly.' In respect of my concluding comments, we may note his dry but revolutionary observation that we need to understand the relations of belief and experience 'in a manner quite different' from the approach adopted in our modern psychology and philosophy (p. 150).

Chapter 9

Darwin's Fortune, Jonah's Shipmates and the Persistence of Chance[1]

Evan Heimlich

When the town of Cave Creek, Arizona faced a tied election for a councilman in 2009, 'a game of chance was called to break the deadlock'. In its article, 'Election at a Draw, Arizona Town Cuts a Deck', the *New York Times* reported that 'Arizona is a modern place. But now and then, the state's Western heritage comes storming through the saloon doors to remind one and all just what this place was like' before it was modern.[2]

Supposedly *Times* readers came to live in modern times when we quit obsolete conventions and banished such chance-channelling to the past. So as it invites its readership to mock Arizona's atavism, the *Times* reports that the town's mayor, officiating at the card-cutting, 'nodded to modern times [by] delaying the proceedings for several seconds so a local television station on commercial break could cover the "historic occasion" live'. Supposedly in places where the doors hang loosely, public divination occasionally resurges into our times. But actually, modern times and places have hardly banished such repertoires.

Like the proverbial elephant that is not supposed to be there, divination's supposed banishment consists of the taboo against recognizing the enormous thing that persists in the room. When people do mention what is undeniably divination, they typically speak as if the wild elephant had suddenly returned: so the *Times'* lead does not report that Arizona's state constitution allows for a town to resolve a tied election by cutting a deck, and the article fails to mention that in almost all

---

[1]   I came to the present chapter's approach through some generous guidance from Jon Barlow, Jonathan Boyarin and Patrick Curry. I thank them as well as Dennis Tedlock, Barbara Tedlock, Michael Davis, Ikeda Riuto, Gina Maduro, Barbara Kimmelman, Ryan Sturgis, Everett Hamner, Bennie H. Reynolds, June O'Connor, Michael Alexander, Jonathan L. Walton, Pawel Jedrzejko, Chico Herbison, Aparecido Donizete Rossi, Tom Ferraro, Tomoko Ashida, Markus Heide, Dick Ellis, Georgia Elliott and the late Emory Elliott. I gratefully acknowledge assistance from the Center for Ideas and Society at the University of California, and leadership by the Center for the Humanities at Wesleyan University. In case of any misrepresentations herein, I take responsibility for failing to follow some of the excellent advice of my teachers.

[2]   Randal C. Archibold, 'Election at a Draw, Arizona Town Cuts a Deck', *New York Times*, 17 June 2009.

US federal court districts, including New York City, officials use a lottery to select a judge for each new case.[3]

When nobody calls attention to them in terms of divination as such, then neither Arizona's constitution nor the federal district-court system merit censure, but when a legal official 'channels' chance openly and unmistakably then authorities crack down. To take a second example, a New York legal commission banished a trial judge who 'in a well-publicized incident in 1982 ... chose between imposing a twenty or a thirty day sentence by publicly flipping a coin while on the bench'. One Yale Law School professor commented that 'the open embrace of chance as determinative was frightening'.[4] Indeed people tend to figure that their social order requires them to shun any such open embrace of unauthorized methods for warranting choices.[5]

Yet the barring of doors begs a few questions. What is at stake in such open embraces of chance, and in their attending taboos? How have taboos influenced how we categorize or characterize the kinds of conventions these acts invoke? In a word, these acts in Arizona and New York invoke certain conventions for cleromancy (also known as sortilege or lottery) and as such they are acts of divination. The censure invokes supersessionism, a rhetoric that seeks to substitute, across the board, a favoured tradition in place of a supposedly obsolete one.

Divination is tricky to define today except in terms of what has supposedly replaced it, because supersessionism works so powerfully in Western scholarship. That is, while monotheists can define divination as a practice used only by unenlightened pagans, similarly scientists can define divination as a superstition (an unscientific, irrational practice) that the dawn of reason made obsolete, worthless or worse.[6] But such definitions reduce divination to terms much narrower than its own. In order to approach it one can hardly proceed as if people perform divination merely as a

---

[3]   Steven Brill, 'When the Government Goes Judge Shopping', *American Law* (November 1988): 3. See particularly also the Southern District of New York law, 'For Division of Business among District Judges 4(b)'.

[4]   E.R. Shipp, 'Friess is Barred From Ever Being New York Judge', *New York Times*, 7 April 1983, p. B3; Judith Resnik, 'Tiers', *Southern California Law Review* 57 (1984): 837–1010, at 841, and notes 18–19, 23. Brill, Shipp and Resnik are all cited by Charles Yablon, 'On the Contribution of Baseball to American Legal Theory', *Yale Law Journal* 104/1 (1994): 227–42, at 231.

[5]   See, for example, Steven Shapin, *The Scientific Revolution* (Chicago: University of Chicago Press, 1996), p. 125.

[6]   See Ethan Allen, *Reason the Only Oracle of Man* (Boston: J.P. Mendum, 1854 [1785]) and conversely, see J.P. Vernant et al. (eds), *Divination et Rationalité* (Paris: Editions du Seuil, 1974). See also Stanley Jeyaraja Tambiah, *Magic, Science, Religion, and the Scope of Rationality* (Cambridge: Cambridge University Press, 1990); Michael Wood, *The Road to Delphi: The Life and Afterlife of Oracles* (New York: Farrar, Straus, and Giroux, 2003); and Shapin, *Scientific Revolution* (p. 94), which notes for example that the physician Sir Thomas Browne in 1646 disparaged divination's appeal to England's masses, unenlightened by reason.

transgression, perversion or ruse against monotheism, rationalism or science. (Nor can one proceed very far after answering that people use divination truly.)

Because we cannot put it behind us, we stand to gain if we can account for how divination can work. Fortunately, approaches that deploy methodological relativism have enabled a few researchers to show how *divination works as an inquiry of the unknown, a tactic for making time cohere, a grammar for turning uncertainty into certainty and a communal procedure for procuring a warrant for a choice.*[7] It tends to require procedural exposure to a ritually pure degree of chance. Divination moreover functions as a kind of *idiom for reading to one's people, aloud*. Paradigmatically it is public fortune-telling.

In order to address a people, an act of divination markedly references itself, as if to say, 'This is how we follow our accepted procedures to make a determination.' It calls for an open embrace because an act of divination must be 'bounded by public, culturally-constituted, clearly-understood rules and procedures'.[8] (This characteristic distinguishes divination from magic.[9]) In this sense divination serves as a vernacular, an idiom common among a people, rather than one characteristic of foreigners' or officials' speech.

Yet, conversely, divination is *not* a vernacular, in the sense that paradigmatically an official divines for the people. Actually such contradiction inheres in the label 'vernacular' itself, and not only because in English if one claims 'I am speaking the vernacular' then one is not speaking it. The term comes from *vernaculus*, Latin for 'native', from *verna*, a slave born in the master's house.[10] Ancient masters used such a label to distinguish the generic slave from one more fully belonging

---

[7]   Barbara Tedlock, 'Divination as a Way of Knowing: Embodiment, Visualisation, Narrative, and Interpretation', *Folklore* 112/2 (2001): 189–97, at 189, describes divination as an inquiry of the unknown. Michael A. Fishbane, *Biblical Interpretation in Ancient Israel* (New York: Oxford University Press, 1985), suggests that typological divination functions to make time cohere. J. Samuel Preus, 'Secularizing Divination: Spiritual Biography and the Invention of the Novel', *Journal of the American Academy of Religion* 59/3 (1991): 441–66, at 444–5, refers to divination as a grammar. Augustine's famous conversion to Christianity is aptly described by Kenneth Burke, *The Rhetoric of Religion: Studies in Logology* (Berkeley: University of California Press, 1961), p. 116, as a movement from uncertainty to certainty; see Aurelius Augustine, *The Confessions of St. Augustine, Bishop of Hippo*, trans. J.G. Pilkington (Edinburgh: T. & T. Clark, 1876 [398]), Book VII. Joel Sweek, reviewing Frederick H. Cryer, *Divination in Ancient Israel and its Near Eastern Environment: A Socio-Historical Investigation* (Sheffield: Journal for the Study of the Old Testament Press, 1994) in the *Journal of Biblical Literature* 116/4 (1997): 725–7, characterizes divination as a procedure for authorizing discourse by procuring a warrant.

[8]   Preus, 'Secularizing Divination', pp. 444–5.

[9]   For an incisive critique of the need to avoid conflating divination with magic, see Sweek, review of Cryer.

[10]   'Vernacular', Merriam-Webster Online Dictionary, http://www.merriam-webster.com/dictionary/VERNACULAR (accessed 24 December 2009).

to a household – in other words, to mark the more familiar version of what is categorically unfamiliar (in German, the *heimlich unheimlich*).

This etymology helps articulate official divination as a paradoxical attempt to co-opt something that by the co-opters' own implicit definition cannot be co-opted. That is, if an idiom were a vernacular, then how could officials reserve it for themselves?

So to approach divination, one might grasp two senses of supersessionism. In the first sense, successive traditions have sought to substitute themselves for divination. More fundamentally, official diviners have always sought to substitute their mastery for a common people's mastery of their own idiom.

The present chapter treats divination as a persistent, common ground. This political tactic counters the propensity of monotheism, or of science, to regard itself as the ground, and divination as an unruly figure – an obsolete subject undeserving much currency. If, instead of supersessionism, we proceed from an axiom of persistence, then each 'moment of supersession' at which some newer tradition supposedly replaced divination becomes legible as an attempt to impose blinders.

Towards accounting for the social role of fortune-telling, broadly construed, the present chapter draws from cultural science, particularly a historical strand of metaphysics, and from discourse analysis, especially speech-act philosophy. It criticizes the critique that finds divination's persistence to profane progress. As one leading cultural theorist observes,

> Profanization – like all idolatry, blasphemy, fetishization, superstition, and kitsch, including the critique that accompanies them – remains irrevocably tied to the very tradition it tends (or intentionally seeks) to subvert or substitute for once and for all, according to a logic and dynamic whose workings and effects we have hardly begun to understand.[11]

Yet it is worthwhile to try to understand this rhetorical regime-making. To bring supersessionism into focus, let us envision an uneven playing field on which universalisms duel over who may tell fortunes.[12]

Across the history of such playing fields, the present chapter takes the form of a peripatetic exploration. It sketches certain moments of supersession often

---

[11]   Hent de Vries, 'On General and Divine Economy: Talal Asad's Genealogy of the Secular and Emmanuel Levinas's Critique of Capitalism, Colonialism, and Money', in David Scott and Charles Hirschkind (eds), *Powers of the Secular Modern: Talal Asad and His Interlocutors* (Stanford: Stanford University Press, 2006), pp. 114–15.

[12]   See Lydia H. Liu, 'Desire and Sovereign Thinking', in Pheng Cheah and Jonathan Culler (eds), *Grounds of Comparison: Around the Work of Benedict Anderson* (New York: Routledge, 2003). Here I am trying to take up Liu's call for a comparative study that does not settle for 'an issue of universalism within the metaphysical tradition of the West', but rather addresses 'the need to account for the scenario of "competing universalisms"' on unequal grounds (p. 213).

claimed in the name of Judaism, Christianity or rationalism after Darwin. The exploration highlights key parries within what I am calling fortune-telling duels, and elucidates paradoxes that attend these duels.

The chapter criticizes discourses of fortune in order to demonstrate how divination has been invalidated, and yet remains valid. So – rather than insist on consistency as a rule – the chapter invites its reader to embrace contradictory positions, unlike Jonah, but like Darwin. That is, the chapter, which particularly examines the function of a metaphysics of randomness often associated with Darwin, further uses the biblical Book of Jonah to illustrate relevant dynamics. Towards its conclusion I will critique some early anthropology of divination for its accounts of chance. But the first task at hand is to sketch the sponsors, contexts and shapes of certain rhetorical duels.

Various historical blocs, vying for hegemony, have duelled at fortune-telling. Early rabbis of ancient Israel and Judea sought to substitute the one God and one scripture, to bind a people, for a heritage of prophecy, lottery and other divinations.[13] In place of the rabbis' orthodoxy, the Church sought to substitute the Good News of the Star of Bethlehem, Jesus' crucifixion, resurrection, the New Testament and the fellowship of the Church. The Reformation later sought to substitute Protestantism for the Church's orthodoxy. But soon enough, Darwin boldly highlighted that neither Judaism nor Christianity had ever fully substituted God for chance – the origin of species was, and is, a matter of chance. Darwin's wake would foster a tradition seeking to substitute itself for all older traditions with, as it were, ultimate, permanent, last finality, by co-opting chance once more and for all time.[14]

---

[13] On scriptural 'divination', see Fishbane, *Biblical Interpretation*, p. 66. On transitional roles of prophecy, see William Schniedewind, *Word of God in Transition: From Prophet to Exegete in the Second Temple Period* (Sheffield: JSOT Press, 1995); see also Alex P. Jassen, *Mediating the Divine: Prophecy and Revelation in the Dead Sea Scrolls and Second Temple Judaism* (Boston: Brill, 2007).

[14] Actually not all, or even most, Christians have read Darwinism as if it threatened to supersede Christianity. According to Gertrude Himmelfarb, *Darwin and the Darwinian Revolution* (London: Chatto & Windus, 1959), pp. 233, 325, relative to Protestants, Catholics were apt to concede science its own sphere in which Darwin's theory was valid; and 'some Calvinists gloried in [an interpretation of Darwinism] because it exalted chance and not design'. Yet in 1862 the French translation of the *Origin* editorially presented Darwinian metaphysics as poised to supersede Christianity. See Charles Darwin, *De l'origine des espèces ou des lois du progrès chez les êtres organisés*, trans. and annot. Clémence-Auguste Royer (Paris: Guillaumin et Cie, 1862). In England meanwhile the chief supersessionist Darwinist was Thomas Huxley; today it is Richard Dawkins. See Dawkins, *The Blind Watchmaker* (New York: W.W. Norton, 1986) and *The God Delusion* (Boston: Houghton Mifflin, 2006). See also the Channel 4 documentaries, *The Enemies of Reason* (2007) and *The Genius of Charles Darwin* (2008), written and presented by Dawkins. But see also Fern Elsdon-Bake, *The Selfish Genius: How Richard Dawkins Rewrote Darwin's Legacy* (London: Icon Books, 2009). In the contemporary United States, see Kenneth R.

Meanwhile a competition had intensified between universalisms when, under a banner of secularism, Europe's civil governments gained control of what had been Church institutions, such as schools, and moreover the new regimes procured their social warrant by means of a narrative of *secularization*. As this narrative divined modern civilization's progress towards its destiny, anything labelled seriously as religion, magic or superstition – that is, anything that could not supposedly be disenchanted – became officially obsolete in the West.[15] In official circles, then, anything still appearing openly as divination became taboo, outside of non-serious entertainments, child's play, 'experimental' arts and certain other specialized repertoires kept more or less under wraps.

In this way the so-called modern West shrugged off any open acknowledgment of its own conventions that procure warrants by channelling chance.[16] Consequently Western research on divination per se has focused almost exclusively on traditions of people framed as incompletely civilized. And even so, Western science has had a very hard time accounting for what diviners do, particularly because science proceeds axiomatically as if no sense of fortune ever were valid. In the nineteenth century, scientific rationalism claimed that thinkers such as Darwin had procured a warrant that invalidated all fortune – so in this sense 'Darwin' became an omen for divining that there is no such thing as an omen.[17]

Where both God and fortune were ruled out, the substitutes were law and arbitrariness. In the twentieth century some anthropologists theorizing divination clearly made such a conceptual substitution (see below). The substitution of arbitrary disorder for fortune – a key parry in a major, historical duel between cosmos-reading regimes – bears closer examination here.

Miller, *Finding Darwin's God: A Scientist's Search for Common Ground Between God and Evolution* (New York: HarperCollins, 1999) and Kenneth R. Miller, *Only a Theory: Evolution and the Battle for America's Soul* (New York: Viking Penguin, 2008), which divines that in the competition over Darwinism, 'America's scientific soul … is truly at risk' (p. x). After Huxley, 'Darwin's Bulldog', Dawkins is nicknamed 'Darwin's Pit Bull' (and Pope Benedict XVI, 'God's Rottweiler').

[15] See John Gray, 'Faith in Reason: Secular Fantasies of a Godless Age', *Harper's* (January 2008): 5; John Gray, *Heresies: Against Progress and Other Illusions* (London: Granta Books, 2004); and Tambiah, *Magic, Science, Religion*. See also Charles Taylor, *A Secular Age* (Cambridge, MA: The Belknap Press of Harvard University Press, 2007).

[16] See J.L. Austin, *How to Do Things with Words* (Cambridge, MA: Harvard University Press, 1963), p. 27, on what it means to 'shrug off' a convention – in his example, the convention of duelling.

[17] See, for example, Ernst Haeckel, *The Riddle of the Universe at the Close of the Nineteenth Century*, trans. Joseph McCabe (London: Harper Brothers, 1900), pp. 273–4. My calling Darwin an omen riffs, so to speak, on Melville's portrayal of abolitionist John Brown as 'the meteor' that portended America's Civil War. See Herman Melville, 'The Portent', in Herman Melville, *Battle-Pieces and Aspects of the War* (New York: Harper & Brothers, 1866).

The Book of Darwin and the Law of Higgledy-Pigglety

Contrary to what one might expect, the 1859 first edition of *The Origin of Species* hardly debunks fortune. It uses the word 'arbitrary' only to criticize other scholars' taxonomies, and never mentions randomness at all. However, it does openly embrace chance and fortune. Consequently the book's reception encountered taboos and confusion. Darwin sent an early copy of the *Origin of Species* to John Herschel, 'his favorite author on the subject of scientific method'.[18] Herschel, who championed the priority of finding nature's laws, tended to valorize law at the expense of any sense of events coming 'at random': indeed he had long associated randomness with the impressions of a newborn infant, which every human immediately outgrew.[19] So facing Darwin's theory that species originated by chance, Herschel derided it as 'the law of higgledy-pigglety'.[20] Darwin felt badly misunderstood,[21] but alas Herschel's misreading became standard.

In order to reduce the *Origin of Species* to a rule of randomness, people needed to misread it unremittingly, so one 1860 reviewer claiming to paraphrase the *Origin* wrote that the transmutations of progeny within a species 'we cannot too often repeat, are first made entirely at random'.[22] In Darwin's theory the prime mover was not mere randomness: such a reductive reading bore repeating if only to confirm a nihilism some people already feared or hoped to see warranted.

To name the cause of transmutations as randomness was a much more extensively debunking claim than Darwin's because unlike 'chance', 'randomness'

---

[18]   Harold Gruber, 'N Notebook Commentary', in Darwin, *Metaphysics, Materialism, and the Evolution of Mind: Early Writings of Charles Darwin* (Chicago: University of Chicago Press, 1974) p. 113.

[19]   John Frederick William Herschel, *A Preliminary Discourse on the Study of Natural Philosophy* (London: Longman, Rees, Orme, Brown & Green, 1840), p. 35, holds that 'The first thing impressed on us from our earliest infancy is, that events do not succeed one another at random.'

[20]   Michael Jonathan Sessions Hodge and Gregory Radick, *The Cambridge Companion to Darwin* (Cambridge: Cambridge University Press, 2003) p. 181.

[21]   After communities of evangelical-rationalists took to championing what Darwin supposedly had said in the *Origin*, Darwin sided with them increasingly, yet without completely abandoning the marks of his own faith. So, though some passages of his autobiography – written in 1871 – eleven years after the first publication of the *Origin* – relate that his machine-like rationalism had replaced any faith, other passages attest that he still occasionally spoke as 'a theist'. See Charles Darwin, *The Autobiography of Charles Darwin 1809–1882*, ed. Nora Barlow (London: Collins, 1958) p. 87, but see also pp. 92–3.

[22]   Francis Bowen, Review of 'On the Origin of Species by Means of Natural Selection', *North American Review* 90 (1860): 474–506, at 498. See also James Mark Baldwin, *Darwin and the Humanities* (Baltimore: Review, 1909). For an overview – itself a misreading Darwin's metaphysics – of Darwin's reception, see Himmelfarb, *Darwin and the Darwinian Revolution*.

could not mean 'fortune'.[23] His argument of course mainly was with a teleology grounded in Genesis, but readers portrayed Darwin as rejecting not only God, but also fortune when they accused Darwin of theorizing a cosmos whose prime moves came merely at random.

Actually, if Darwin had aimed to say that variations came upon species at random, the word was available to him. Indeed his theory of natural selection followed William Paley's 1809 observation that 'Faculties thrown down upon animals *at random*, and without reference to the objects amidst which they are placed, would not produce to them the services and benefits which we see.'[24] Also Darwin himself had used the word 'random' in previous writings.[25]

Yet in the *Origin* he never mentioned randomness at all, or referred to variations as arbitrary or neutral. Instead Darwin asserted that progeny transmute according to a pattern of causes of which 'we are profoundly ignorant. Nevertheless, we can here and there dimly catch a faint ray of light, and we may feel sure that there must be some cause for each deviation of structure.'[26] Rather than assert randomness Darwin held that '*variability is governed by many unknown laws*'.[27] He neither claimed that such governance was absolute, nor that it could become completely legible.

Meanwhile in English, as in French, prior to 1860 'chance' usually meant luck or fortune, and the *Origin* further specified that 'chance' in its usage 'serves to acknowledge plainly our ignorance of the cause of each particular variation'.[28] Darwin did not go so far as to assert that the unknown was disordered, nor that cause might be absent from it.

When Darwin named 'chance' his usage overlapped with Aristotle's ancient gloss, that some people view chance (*tyche*) as a cause 'inscrutable to human intelligence'.[29] Yet, like Aristotle, Darwin did scrutinize certain questions of

---

[23]   'random, *n., adv.,* and *adj.*', *OED Online*, Dec. 2009, http://dictionary.oed.com/cgi/ entry/50197140 (accessed 7 January 2010).

[24]   William Paley, *Natural Theology: or, Evidences of the Existence and Attributes of the Deity* (London: Printed for J. Faulder, 1809), pp. 70–71; emphasis added.

[25]   For example, in his diary aboard the *Beagle*, Darwin wrote of 'houses pitched at random'. Charles Darwin, *Charles Darwin's Beagle Diary*, ed. R.D. Keynes (Cambridge: Cambridge University Press, 2001) p. 146. Although Paley had used 'random' more in the sense of 'purposeless', Darwin used the word more in a sense of 'apparently patternless'. In the *Origin* Darwin often criticizes people's 'arbitrary' classifications (which in a prior publication he called 'random') but never refers to nature itself as random or arbitrary.

[26]   Darwin, *The Origin of Species by Means of Natural Selection: or The Preservation of Favoured Races in the Struggle for Life* (London: John Murray, 1859), p. 132.

[27]   Ibid., p. 43; emphasis added.

[28]   Ibid., p. 131. Genetic mutation was unknown to Darwin, and anyway such explanation still begs the question of what first causes genes to mutate. See also 'chance, *n.* (and *a.*)', *The Oxford English Dictionary*, 2nd edn (1989), http://dictionary.oed.com/cgi/ entry/50197140 (accessed 7 January 2010).

[29]   Aristotle, *Physics*, trans. R.P. Hardie and R.K. Gaye, in William D. Ross (ed.), *The Works of Aristotle Translated into English*, 12 vols (Oxford: Clarendon Press, 1908

chance. Darwin followed Frédéric Cuvier, who in 1828 had written that domestic breeding of livestock depended on 'one of the most general laws of life – the transmission of a *fortuitous* modification into a durable form'.[30] Such theory substituted indeterminism where others had cited determinism. But here the road forked. Paths that approached fortune agnostically were open only to very supple thinkers. In the face of rampant universalisms, others chose to embrace fortune or else reject its reality.

Of course, defenders of Darwin's theory did not openly champion the telling of fortunes, and few were prepared to follow him into accounting for the roles of chance.[31] So the reduction to 'higgledy-piggledy' effectively cornered Darwin's defenders. Could they reject fortune? Although substituting law for God may be conceptually simple for some, it is far harder for people to disclaim the reading of any signs of cosmic favour or disfavour, particularly because both monotheists and evangelical-rationalists tend to be blinkered to the ways that they themselves tell fortunes.[32]

Of course, the ascendant evangelical-rationalist consensus declined to embrace fortune. (If more rationalists had done so in Darwin's wake, then 'Darwinism' could have come to label the embrace of a hermeneutic of chance, decoupled from monotheistic orthodoxy. Indeed, more expressly to align science with divination would have been a reunion, because the fathers of early-modern science were astrologers.[33])

Meanwhile Darwin used the term 'chance' with some slippage. According to his theory, evolution proceeds mainly according to two steps: first some progeny happen to vary while certain deadly conditions happen to bear on a given population, and then over time, the conditions' deadly pressures tend to select for advantageous variants. As if to unify his explanation, Darwin characterized both steps in terms of chance. That is, typically he wrote that facing various contingencies, 'individuals having any advantage, however slight, over others, would have the best chance of surviving and of procreating',[34] and in most of his usages, 'chance' similarly refers to contingency or probability of survival: but elsewhere in the *Origin* Darwin used

---

[350 BCE]), vol. 2 (1930), Book 4.

[30]   Frédéric Cuvier, quoted by Sir Gavin de Beer, 'Introduction', in Charles Darwin, *Darwin's Notebooks on Transmutation of Species*, Part I, First Notebook (July 1837–February 1838), ed. Gavin de Beer (Cambridge: Cambridge University Press, 1960); my emphasis.

[31]   Among the few were nineteenth-century America's two greatest philosophers, William James and Charles Pierce.

[32]   The term 'evangelical-rational consensus' comes from T.J. Jackson Lears, *Something for Nothing: Luck in America* (New York: Viking, 2003). See his discussion particularly on pp. 62 and 168–9.

[33]   See Shapin, *Scientific Revolution*.

[34]   Darwin, *Origin*, p. 81. Darwin also uses 'chance' in a sense of contingency or probability on pp. 41, 82, 105 and 125, and elsewhere uses 'chance' as a verb, for example referring to 'when a slightly better variety has chanced to appear' (p. 37; see also pp. 82, 177).

'chance' differently, to characterize progeny's variations themselves or to name the variations' cause.

This slippage matters because it has helped people to misread Darwin as if he made claims about patternless chance (or randomness). Actually he was very careful to avoid making any such claims in the 1859 *Origin*, and wrote instead of 'fortunate chance'. Darwin told fortunes, but readers have tended to turn a deaf ear, not only by ignoring his references to fortune, but also by misstating his theory's role for 'chance'. In this way Darwin became the whipping boy of Creationists and the patron saint of more than a few materialists who would characterize all serious talk of fortune as nonsense.

Reading Darwin's 'Fortune'

In only one instance does the *Origin* debunk a propensity to read fortune: 'I have seen it gravely remarked', Darwin chides in 1859, 'that it was most fortunate that the strawberry began to vary just when gardeners began to attend closely to this plant' circa 1825. Darwin argues that the commencement of 'those many admirable varieties' of domestic strawberry actually resulted from the increased selection effected by the gardeners themselves, and not from any fortunate change in the propensity of the strawberry to transmute.[35] Still, Darwin's strawberry lesson hardly asserts that variation always stands apart from fortune.

Far more confounding is that although Darwin characterizes speciation as amoral, he still tries to reconcile his theory within a cosmic sense of moral order. Indeed an Aristotelian might say that Darwin's manifold use of the term 'chance' itself evinces Darwin's concern for moral significance of the cosmos. That is, according to Aristotle, 'chance [*tyche*] and what results from chance are appropriate [only] to agents that are capable of good fortune and of moral action generally', because 'what is not capable of moral action cannot do anything by chance'.[36] Such concern by Darwin shows most pointedly in the *Origin*'s account of queen bees who instinctively eat their daughters, a propensity he calls 'maternal hatred'.

Just as Darwin claims that maternal love or maternal hatred is 'all the same to the inexorable principle of natural selection', with the same breath he allows that maternal hatred *'fortunately is most rare'* among species.[37] Darwin's use of 'fortunately' here invites readers to appreciate that the natural world, some of which violates our moral sense, would violate our present moral sense more unfavourably in a possible counter-reality. Though natural selection does not care about anything, still when this relatively lovely cosmos became actuated, fortune smiled.

---

[35]   Darwin, *Origin*, pp. 41–2.

[36]   Aristotle, *Physics*, trans. R.P. Hardie and R.K. Gaye, in Ross (ed.) *Works of Aristotle*, vol. 2 (1930), Book 6.

[37]   Darwin, *Origin*, p. 203; my emphasis.

Now if one applies here Darwin's own fortune-debunking lesson on strawberry cultivation, one can conclude that – properly speaking – only Darwin's new *attention* to the maternal love/hate ratio – and his ongoing *cultivation* of a strain of morality – led him to attribute the present cosmic case mistakenly to fortune. Moreover one could resolve any contradictions between the various positions Darwin embraces simply by disqualifying any senses of Darwin's writings that seem inconsistent with a canonical sense of his theory – for example as if science obviated any inscrutable, cosmic pattern, therefore Darwin surely did not mean all he said, and we can safely ignore those of his statements that are unsuited to reigning notions of what he might have said.[38]

Yet Darwin openly embraced metaphysical positions unsuited to a univocal, universal, disenchanted metaphysics. On the whole he demonstrated that it was extremely useful to speak as if laws and probabilities were self-sufficient without invoking an inscrutable, cosmic pattern of conscious design; and then he also invoked an inscrutable, cosmic pattern. When he read the traces of the unseen, he invoked fortune in order to invite readers to share a sense of privilege and wonder that we live in this cosmos rather than one less favourable to us and our ideas. Although Darwin spoke from outside the community of strawberry cultivators, ultimately he read the cosmos from within a human community, an 'us'. The *Origin*'s Conclusion proclaimed it is a wonder that people have not observed more of creatures' adaptations that are morally 'abhorrent to *our* ideas of fitness'.[39]

He knew that his theory stood to revolutionize metaphysics,[40] and felt fortunate that he had learned to become the leading reader of traces of nature's scheme – traces that 'nature may be said to have taken pains to reveal'.[41] To wit, in Darwin's narrative of his own research, it advanced particularly when he was in the right place at the right time, as if the cosmos had aligned faint rays of light for him to catch what they indicated. He writes, 'One day I *fortunately chanced* to witness a migration from one nest to another', and again, 'I have been enabled, *by a fortunate chance*, elsewhere to prove that two individuals, though both are self-fertilising hermaphrodites, do sometimes cross.'[42] In the *Origin* Darwin presented himself not only as an evangelical-rationalist, but also as a reader of the signs of life, in flashed traces of 'hidden' patterns of our cosmos.[43]

---

[38]   According to Himmelfarb, *Darwin and the Darwinian Revolution* (p. 332), his contemporaries generally thought Darwin had proved cruelty 'the governing force of nature'.

[39]   Darwin, *Origin*, p. 472; my emphasis.

[40]   See Charles Darwin, 'N Notebook', in *Metaphysics, Materialism, and the Evolution of Mind*, p. 5.

[41]   Darwin, *Origin*, p. 480.

[42]   Ibid., pp. 221, 101. My emphasis.

[43]   For example, 'I believe that something more is included; and that propinquity of descent, – the only known cause of the similarity of organic beings, – is the bond, hidden as it is by various degrees of modification, which is partially revealed to us by our classifications' (Darwin, *Origin*, pp. 413–14).

Darwin was able to embrace both law and fortune because he was a supple thinker, not bound by an all-or-nothing duel of religion versus irreligion. For his investigation he found it useful to read unknown, favourable causes as fortune. But out of the uncanny triangles of mischaracterizations between the metaphysics of Darwin's *Origin*, the metaphysics of its critics and the metaphysics of its champions, for many this book warranted the ruling out of both God and fortune.[44] Supposedly it marked a moment of supersession.

An Ancient Chain of Would-Be Substitutes

Even if Darwin had aimed to speak of a charmless cosmos, such rhetoric was hardly available before a post-*Origin* consensus substituted, for the *Origin*'s metaphysics, a less supple metaphysics of higgledy-pigglety.[45] This misreading of Darwin has been pointedly political – a supersessionist move with grand historical scale.[46]

That is, attempts to substitute randomness for a tradition of fortune joined a very long chain of such substitutions. Ancient monotheism had substituted 'God' for chance when the Hebrew Bible (Proverbs 16:33) insisted that lotteries channel, not chance, but actually God. Then, after Darwin bracketed the doctrine that God determined speciation, his theory reverted to chance and re-substituted it in place of God as the origin of species.

For many modern people, the unknown could neither be left bracketed nor be marked as 'chance' or 'God' so, in place of God or the charmed uncertainty of fortune, some substituted the certainty of cosmic, intrinsic, absolute randomness. That is, some insisted on substituting, for the significance of the inscrutable unknown, a 'known unknown' of patternlessness. (In contrast to randomness merely as an observer's perspective on the indeterminacy of, say, a shuffled deck of cards, what I am calling 'cosmic, intrinsic, absolute randomness' overlaps with what some mathematicians and quantum physicists call 'ontic, irreducible randomness', and here refers to an attribute ascribed to the universe itself.[47]) However the concept of absolute randomness may be paradoxical, because if a thing is in the universe then it must connect to the universe's fundamental order if there is one; and if there is no such order, 'random' then would name the absence of something that never existed.

---

[44]   See Himmelfarb, *Darwin and the Darwinian Revolution*, p. 373.

[45]   On the history of 'randomness', see O.B. Sheynin, 'The Notion of Randomness from Aristotle to Poincaré', *Mathématiques et Sciences Humaines* 114 (1991): 41–55, at 47.

[46]   I suggest Creationism has often helped tie its own rope by exaggerating Darwin's supersessionism.

[47]   For a basic gloss of ontic, irreducible randomness, see 'vanesch', blogged 20 July 2006, 03:44 p.m., under 'Looking for Explanation of Randomness', Physics Forums, © 2000–2009, Jelsoft Enterprises Ltd, http://www.physicsforums.com/showthread.php?t=126272&page=4 (accessed 19 December 2009).

Although randomness is crucial to useful models of mathematics and science, and indeed can often validly substitute for 'fortune', ultimately one cannot construct a logically consistent system by substituting 'randomness' for 'fortune' across the board – any more than one can avoid contradiction when substituting 'God' for 'fortune'.[48] In sum, a metaphysics of 'randomness' makes sense in the context of an agnostic approach to the question of fortune, but if one uses 'randomness' as a banner under which to shrug off any talk of an inscrutable pattern, the term hardly refers to much beyond such a shrug.

In the duel pitting monotheists against evangelical-rationalists, Darwin realized his framing of cosmic 'chance' and 'fortune' blasphemed against sacred tenets not only of partisans of monotheism, but also of some partisans of science. So he apologized for characterizing transmutation with 'a wholly incorrect expression':[49] chance. Elsewhere in the *Origin* when he calls transmutation 'accidental', in each and every instance Darwin disclaims his own usages as if 'accidental' were an even more wholly incorrect expression.[50] Of course he did not foresee that people would manage to denature the term 'chance' in the wake of his usage of the term, in order to resolve metaphysical contradictions.

People who described transmutation in terms of randomness shrugged off the older meanings of 'chance' as 'fortune'. They could do so because the supersessionisms duelling for hegemony were rather less mutable than the meaning of any one word. Soon it made sense to say that the obverse of fortune was 'random chance'.

Monotheists at first hardly panicked over Darwin's open embrace of chance, because they purported to have won their duel against fortune decisively, long ago.

---

[48]   On various ways modern people tend to make sense of randomness, see R. Falk and C. Konold, 'Making Sense of Randomness: Implicit Encoding as a Basis for Judgment', *Psychological Review* 104 (1997): 301–18 and Carmen Batanero, Juan D. Godino and Rafael Roa, 'Training Teachers to Teach Probability', *Journal of Statistics Education* 12/1 (2004).

[49]   Darwin, *Origin*, p. 131.

[50]   Darwin labels an 'imaginary case' as 'accidental', before he uses the term in a conditional clause; then moreover he refers to '*what would commonly be called an accident*' and '*what may be called accidental variations ... produced by .... unknown causes*', and then '*so-called accidental variations*' (pp. 94, 188–9; 165, 209, 213; my emphasis here and below). Next he mentions variations that 'first appeared from *what we must in our ignorance call an accident*', yet finally terms them '*as we must call them accidental, variations*' (pp. 216, 242). See also Aristotle's *Metaphysics*, trans. William David Ross, in Ross (ed.), *Works of Aristotle*, Book V. When the *Origin* says a breeder takes 'care to prevent accidental crosses' of strains (p. 142; see also p. 93), Darwin's usage overlaps with Aristotle's definition of accident (*maten*) as an act, in the sphere of purposeful actions, whose effect differs from its aim. Lest anyone still suppose Darwin meant simply 'patternless', he notes, when he characterizes the contingencies that occasionally distribute seeds, that 'These means of transport are sometimes called accidental, but this is not strictly correct: the currents of the sea are not accidental, nor is the direction of prevalent gales of wind' (p. 364), because they are patterned.

For them, Darwin's metaphysics 'must mean one of two things', with 'no third alternative': either 'a fortuitous Cosmos [or] a designed Cosmos', and officially a fortuitous cosmos was 'simply inconceivable'.[51] The third alternative was all but unspeakable, not least because nobody before 1860 had said much about a cosmos lacking purpose or fortune.

Meanwhile monotheisms had made accommodations for telling fortunes even after officially invalidating such practices. The *Atlantic Monthly* neatly embodied such contrivance when it pronounced Darwin's fortuitous-cosmos terminology 'unfortunate'.[52] As thinkers after 1860 have continued to struggle to come to terms with the metaphysics of chance, these contrivances – ascribing randomness or unfortunateness – have hardly lost their currency. As Stephen Jay Gould wrote in 1980, 'Darwinians speak of genetic variation, the first step, as "random." This is an unfortunate term.'[53] Such Darwinian usage is not, of course, accidental: it is *anti-'fortunate'* in the sense that it seeks to invalidate fortune by substituting 'randomness'.

Darwin vs. Jonah

As one consequence of all this supersessionism, science has particular difficulty accounting for the kinds of inquiry it has supposedly replaced. So some anthropologists have struggled to contain the open embrace of chance as determinative. They could hardly explain the work by which diviners channel fortune, however, because professional imperatives bound the anthropologists instead to explaining the function of randomness.

---

[51]   Asa Gray, 'Darwin and his Reviewers', *Atlantic Monthly* 6 (October 1860): 406–25, at 413, 415–16.

[52]   Ibid., p. 416.

[53]   Stephen Jay Gould, *The Panda's Thumb* (New York: Norton, 1980), p. 79. For latter-day, interminably botched conversations on the role of 'randomness' in evolution, see 'Why Natural Selection is not Random', blogged at 'For the Sake of Science', starting 25 October 2008, at http://forthesakeofscience.wordpress.com/2008/10/25/why-natural-selection-is-not-random/ (accessed 1 December 2009). See also the following, all blogged at RichardDawkins.net: 'Random Mutations are a Big Joke', starting 27 October 2006, at http://forum.richarddawkins.net/viewtopic.php?f=46&t=923&start=75 (accessed 18 November 2009); 'How Evolution is not Pure Random Chance', starting 27 January 2007, at http://forum.richarddawkins.net/viewtopic.php?f=4&t=7428 (accessed 18 November 2009); 'Richard Dawkins' Views on Non-random Natural Selection', beginning 20 November 2009, at http://forum.richarddawkins.net/viewtopic.php?p=2473287 (accessed 10 January 2010); 'Is Natural Selection Random?', starting 10 January 2010, at http://forum.richarddawkins.net/viewtopic.php?f=4&t=105953 (accessed 14 January 2010); and 'The Infamous "Chance" and "Random" Canards', starting 27 December 2009, at http://forum.richarddawkins.net/viewtopic.php?f=46&t=104525&start=50 (accessed 14 January 2009).

Generally, the paradoxes that have long attended encounters between divination systems and universalisms cannot be understood on any single, consistent set of terms, so before addressing anthropology from a perspective of divination, or vice versa, I offer a relevant exercise in methodological relativism. My retelling below of the biblical Book of Jonah highlights the conflicting rationales of the tale's characters, mainly Jonah and his God (Yhwh-Elohim, also referred to here as Yhwh, the Lord, or God) in their conversations about reading omens and chances.

Darwin's approach was, in some key ways, congruent with the biblical Jonah's, in that each tried and failed to rationalize the Lord's role in the world. They each became aggrieved by the moral paradoxes that attended their attempts – in a letter about his perplexity Darwin confessed, 'the more I think the more bewildered I become'.[54] So each became dissatisfied with the received word of the Lord, and went in a different direction than it indicated.

As their reasoning at first ran parallel, from the same rule that God's actions are always consistently benign, Jonah and Darwin each proceeded into paradox. Jonah faced God's potential as a destructive punisher, and then God sent a malignant worm to consume Jonah's benevolent vine; Darwin faced the malignant queen bee who instinctively consumes her own daughters, and the malignant, parasitical wasp that paralyses a caterpillar then slowly consumes it.[55] Further, not unlike Jonah, who in his book read the growth of a vine as an omen, Darwin read the growth of 'the great Tree of Life', on which 'we here and there see a … branch … [that] by some chance has been favoured', a branch 'which has apparently been saved from fatal competition by having inhabited a protected station'.[56]

But unlike Jonah, whose conundrums drove him to flee and go mad, Darwin instead resolved that he could proceed rationally if instead of naming God as the creator of prototypes for each new species, he substituted something amoral, namely chance.

Perhaps all heirs of evangelical-rationalism should wrestle with the contradictory senses of the *Origin*, because these sorts of paradoxes attend the struggles not only of Darwin, but of any thinker concerned with universal consistency who ever reads signs sent by Providence or chance.[57] A reading of the Book of Jonah can illustrate, and perhaps sketch some background here.

---

[54] Darwin, Letter to Asa Gray, 22 May 1860, archived by the Darwin Correspondence Project, Cambridge University, at http://www.darwinproject.ac.uk/entry-2814 (accessed 2 December 2009).

[55] On the ichneumon wasp as Darwin's conundrum, see ibid. See also Darwin, *Origin*, pp. 199–206.

[56] Darwin, *Origin* p. 130.

[57] In the wake of the first edition of the *Origin*, Darwin's friend and American champion Asa Gray ('Darwin and his Reviewers', p. 425) articulated such inevitability of paradox for a Providentialist theist: 'Whoever would be a consistent theist should believe that Design in the natural world is coextensive with Providence, and hold fully to the one as he does to the other, in spite of the wholly similar and apparently insuperable difficulties

The Book of Jonah[58]

Now the word of Yhwh came to Jonah. Jonah divined it directed him east to Nineveh to declare doom upon that city, because Yhwh saw the Ninevites' wickedness. Instead Jonah fled. He sailed west towards Tarshish. During the voyage Yhwh sent a violent storm. Jonah's shipmates heard the ship crack and understood it would break.

Each prayed to his own gods for rescue, and the sailors also jettisoned the ship's cargo to make the ship lighter, but the ship continued to founder. Meanwhile Jonah slept. The helmsman awoke Jonah and commanded him to pray to his gods to intercede, in order that they might have a chance to survive.

Then the shipmates said to each other, let us have a lottery to determine on whose account this calamity approaches. This inquiry, they could not pose to a mere human being.[59] They all understood the procedure and that hitting this lottery would mark the misfortunate shipmate.

When the lottery fell to Jonah, his shipmates interviewed him and learned he was a Hebrew worshipper of Yhwh, God of the heavens, Creator of sea and land. Jonah said he had fled Yhwh. Now that their lottery had diagnosed the cause, they asked Jonah to divine how to treat the problem. *They asked him, 'What must we do to you to make the sea calm around us?'* Jonah too declared the storm portended their collective misfortune. *He prescribed that the sailors throw him in the sea. But instead the sailors attempted fruitlessly to row him to shore while the sea got wild against them.*

Finally his shipmates did jettison Jonah, and the sea immediately calmed. Then the sailors, fearful of Yhwh's power, made sacrifices and vows to Yhwh. Meanwhile Yhwh sent a large fish that swallowed Jonah. In his poetic prayer (omitted here), Jonah thanks Yhwh for rescuing him. He promises to offer Yhwh a sacrifice, to

---

which the mind encounters whenever it endeavors to develop the idea into a complete system, either in the material and organic, or in the moral world.'

[58]   My account here draws from John R. Kohlenberger III, *Interlinear NIV Hebrew-English Old Testament* (Grand Rapids, MI: Zondervan, 1979); Jack M. Sasson, *Jonah: A New Translation with Introduction, Commentary, and Interpretation* (New York: Doubleday, 1990); and from *The Jewish Study Bible: Jewish Publication Society Tanakh Translation*, trans. Adele Berlin, Marc Zvi Brettler and Michael A. Fishbane (London: Jewish Publication Society, 2004 [1985]), pp. 1200–1204. The quotations within my account are from the latter source.

[59]   According to Barbara Tedlock, 'Divination as a Way of Knowing', p. 189, divination's use aims to elicit an answer to a given question that seems, to the askers, not amenable to their other forms of inquiry. Tedlock, listing the typical kinds of inquiries divination poses, concludes with 'making choices of persons for particular tasks'. Preus, 'Secularizing Divination', pp. 444–5, notes that people tend to use it particularly when they 'find themselves … in "dicey" situations of uncertainty in which usual forms of inquiry do not apply'. Roy G. Willis and Patrick Curry, *Astrology, Science and Culture: Pulling Down the Moon* (New York: Berg, 2004), p. 12, define divination as a dialogue with the unknown.

make vows and to keep them. His prayer concludes that rescue must always be divined as Yhwh's.

At Yhwh's command, the fish vomited Jonah onto dry land. Again Yhwh commanded Jonah to declare Yhwh's message to Nineveh. So Jonah entered the giant city and prophesied: 'Forty days more, and Nineveh overturns!'

Then the Ninevites believed in God. They all fasted and wore sackcloth to repent for their wickedness. Their king immediately sat in ashes, and ordered all Nineveh's inhabitants – including herds and flocks – to fast, wear sackcloth, and pray urgently. He commanded them to forsake evil and violence. The king finally declared that Nineveh might have a chance to survive.

Indeed God relented. Then Jonah, upset, begged Yhwh to kill him. Now Jonah recounted for God a flashback to when Jonah, in his homeland, first received Yhwh's judgment on Nineveh. Jonah said he had fled because he realized Yhwh would eventually relent from his wrathful pronouncement, which Yhwh's benevolent heart did not match.

That is, from Jonah's claimed perspective, Yhwh's decree of Nineveh's fate did not correspond to any inner act of dooming.[60] In response, omniscient Yhwh rhetorically asked Jonah whether Jonah's own aggrieved words matched Jonah's inner act: *'Are you that deeply grieved?'*

Outside Nineveh, Jonah sat to see what would happen. There a vine grew to shade his head. Jonah became overjoyed when he correctly read the vine's growth as having been sent by Yhwh.[61] But the next morning a worm attacked the vine so that it withered, and in the sun Jonah swooned.

Jonah became aggrieved about this omen of Yhwh's disfavor. Again he begged Yhwh to kill him.

Yhwh responded with an analogy, in a question as a moral lesson: just as Jonah is sorry to lose the ephemeral vine, so would Yhwh not be sorry to lose Nineveh,[62] which Yhwh has cultivated, and which contains not only myriads of people who do not know their right hand from their left but 'many beasts as well'?

---

[60]   See Austin, *How to Do Things with Words*, pp. 5–10. Axiomatically '*our word is our bond*', because any claim to the contrary puts the claimant in league with a 'welsher' who disclaims a bet he has made by citing his 'fictitious inner act', that is, that, despite his words, in his heart he did something other than wager.

[61]   See Sasson, *Jonah*, p. 317.

[62]   See G.M. Butterworth, 'You Pity the Plant: A Misunderstanding', *Indian Journal of Theology* 27 (1978): 32–4. See also Hans Walker Wolff, *Obadiah and Jonah: A Commentary*, trans. Margaret Kohl (Minneapolis: Augsburg, 1986 [1977]), pp. 83–8. Wolff categorizes the comic lesson of the Book of Jonah as 'wisdom didactic'. On the translation 'sorry to lose', see Butterworth as well as Thomas N. Bolin, *Freedom Beyond Forgiveness: The Book of Jonah Re-Examined* (Sheffield: Sheffield Academic Press, 1997), p. 162.

Reason the Only Oracle of Jonah?

At the start of his tale, Jonah (he later claims) foresaw no chance that Yhwh would overthrow Nineveh. So Jonah denied Yhwh the chance to punish, and denied Nineveh the chance to change its fate. But in order to give the Ninevites their chance, Yhwh gave Jonah no chance to flee from paradox.[63]

In the basic paradox – Yhwh doomed Nineveh yet will not overthrow it[64] – the sense of doom is classically divinatory. An inscrutable power, personified as a god, decrees what will happen. In such reading of fate – from 'fatum', Latin for 'it has been spoken' – a diviner's public task is to proclaim the decree outright or interpret it by its traces.

However, Jonah's reading of non-doom shrugs off ancient conventions by which fate is always whatever the gods decree, and in their place Jonah substitutes the axiom that God must always act benevolently.[65] Furthermore Jonah imposes a hindsighted logic of consistency, according to which what eventually has transpired (forty-plus days after Jonah's proclamation, Nineveh still stands) must have been fated, regardless of Yhwh's decree.

Jonah's logic here first mistakes prophecy as if an incorrect prediction would mark it as false and worthless.[66] Yet the value of a prophecy, like any warrant (or answer, oracle or verdict) from divination, does not come from its eventually

---

[63]   On Jonah's flight from the paradoxes of his role as what I am calling a prophetic diviner, see Uriel Simon, *The JPS Bible Commentary: Jonah* (Philadelphia: Jewish Publication Society, 2003). 'The Book of Jonah seeks to teach us about the educational purpose of prophecies of doom (see Ezekiel 3:16–21 and 33:1–9) through the medium of a story that criticizes a prophet who viewed announcing future events as his role and full realization of the prophecy as his only test', according to Simon, who notes that this view was adopted by Saadiah Gaon in the ninth century, Rashi in the eleventh century and many others, including many modern scholars.

[64]   Many modern scholars of the Hebrew Bible claim that the Book of Jonah primarily targeted Hebrew audiences who knew that Nineveh eventually was indeed overthrown, so such knowledge determines the meaning of the narrative. However, nobody has determined when the story was crafted: this might have been before the fall of Nineveh. Moreover, perhaps Hebrew audiences took the Book of Jonah not as history, but as something closer to what modern academics call 'a national literature'. Relevantly, see H.M. Orlinsky, 'Nationalism-Universalism and Internationalism in Ancient Israel', in *Essays in Biblical Culture and Bible Translation* (New York: Ktav, 1974), pp. 78–116, at p. 113. Anyway, even if 'original' audiences understood that Nineveh eventually did meet its doom, other biblical precedents help establish that Yhwh overthrows cities, such as Sodom, because of the wickedness of their present inhabitants rather than the wickedness of their distant forebears, so in this sense Yhwh's initial verdict against Nineveh was not necessarily open-ended. Moreover still, no audience requires historical knowledge of Nineveh's fall in order to make ironic sense of Jonah.

[65]   See J. Mather, 'The Comic Art of the Book of Jonah', *Soundings* 65 (1982): 280–91. See also Sasson, *Jonah*, pp. 334–5.

[66]   Deuteronomy 18:21–2 also expresses this viewpoint of Jonah's.

proving correct: rather, it comes when a community, according to its conventions, honours it.[67] For instance, because the conventions of Jonah and his shipmates overlap concerning lottery, they can agree to accept their lottery's verdict. Someone fully party to such conventions does not insist that a warrant, to be valid, must eventually match what transpires. Rather, the convention works when one joins the communal enactment that makes such determinations count. So Jonah's shipmates, and later the Ninevites, collectively seize their chance to avert misfortune: but Jonah instead tries to stand on his perceptiveness, foresight and reason, as if these things were universal and prime, apart from any community.

Jonah's worst mistake is that, even while rejecting the social responsibility that divination entails, he insists on trying to indulge in solo omen-reading. Of course one might try to distinguish divination from prophecy by claiming that true prophecy is merely direct service as God's mouthpiece, but anyway Jonah, who is not averse to joining a lottery, is loathe to serve as a mere mouthpiece. Instead he tries to flee, then at the end of the tale he reads the signs from Yhwh without telling his fortunes to anyone else.[68]

Jonah's rationale is based on some accurate findings, and is consistent enough as far as it goes, yet his basic approach is wrong because it denies chance. The Book of Jonah indicates that Yhwh averts his wrath not, as Jonah claims, because His benevolence allows no other choice, but rather because He cultivates Nineveh's

---

[67]   In divination 'incorrect prognosis is not regarded as a challenge to the system' (Preus, 'Secularizing Divination', pp. 444–50). See also Martin Holbraad, 'Gauging Necessity: Ifá Oracles and Truth in Havana', *Mana* 9/2 (2003): 39–77. (According to typical Cuban users of an Ifá divination system, 'in Ifá there are no lies' (*en Ifá no hay mentiras*). See also the vernacular wisdom of players of sports with penalty shots, such as basketball, in which 'Ball don't lie!' (that is, the ball never lies) means that a given shot has channelled chance properly to yield the verdict of a penalty point, or none.) So, in order to use a divination system properly, one must join a community that honours its verdicts. My general understanding of the function of a reading community is indebted to Nicholas Howe, 'The Cultural Construction of Reading in Anglo-Saxon England', in Jonathan Boyarin (ed.), *The Ethnography of Reading* (Berkeley: University of California Press, 1993), pp. 58–79, at p. 67; to Brian Stock's argument that Christianity itself 'emerges as a textual community built around shared principles of interpretation', in *Augustine the Reader: Meditation, Self-Knowledge, and the Ethics of Interpretation* (Cambridge, MA: Harvard University Press, 1996), p. 196; and to Geoffrey Cornelius's findings, in *The Moment of Astrology: Origins in Divination* (New York: Arkana, 1994), p. 20, that because 'an omen is only an omen if it is recognized as such', and 'an omen's significance is dependent on the participation of those for whom it is present', there can be no such thing as an intrinsically universal omen.

[68]   Scholars of divination after Bottéro will map 'a mere mouthpiece' onto the category of 'inspired divination', which purports to tap revelation directly, and is supposedly distinct from deductive divination, which requires interpretation. See the gloss but see also the critique cited in Maria Michela Sassi, *The Science of Man in Ancient Greece* (Chicago: University of Chicago Press, 2001) p. 140.

chances to survive. Ultimately Jonah rejects his own life and ends alone with Yhwh's disfavour: because he denies chance, Jonah lacks hope.

Finally, in the very act of supposedly enlightening Jonah, Yhwh actually persists in torturing him with a botched conversation about divination.[69] That is, in response to Jonah's insistence on a consistent rationale, Yhwh does deign to explain His own actions, but His punch line, about Nineveh's repentant beasts, parodies reason with a farcically pat moral.[70] As the punch line burlesques the expectations of Jonah and of his co-religionists reading the tale, Yhwh's priorities extend finally to the beasts that the Ninevite king commanded to repent.

If the Lord plays farceur and makes his own prophet a comic dupe, where is the common sense?[71] Not only does Yhwh here favour the outlandish conventions of this chance-seizing king who, after one warning from a foreign prophet, leapt from his throne into ashes and commanded repentance even of beasts. Moreover, as Yhwh easily shrugs off both the paradox Jonah faces and the rationale Jonah tries to impose, Yhwh's analogy – 'I read Nineveh like a cultivator reads the vine, Jonah' – is tricky. Yhwh presents himself here as subject to losses of crops, by chance: that is, in order for Yhwh's analogy to make sense, Yhwh must have not known the outcome for Nineveh in advance. Does Yhwh accept the outcome – Nineveh successfully atoned – as a sign of favour from His cosmos? One lesson here is that instead of applying a universalist rationale, one should apply empathy in order to make sense of what happens where divination meets the one, omniscient-yet-anthropomorphic Lord.

---

[69]   See D.F. Rauber, 'Jonah – the Prophet as Schlemiel', *Bible Today* 49 (1970): 29–38 and G.M. Butterworth, 'You Pity the Plant'. The phrase 'botched conversation' concerning divination comes from Martin Holbraad, 'Definitive Evidence, from Cuban Gods', *Journal of the Royal Anthropological Institute* 14/s1, *Special Issue on 'The Objects of Evidence'*, ed. M. Engelke, published online 18 March 2008, S93–S109.

[70]   See N. Habel, *The Book of Job: A Commentary* (Philadelphia: The Westminster Press, 1985), and the critique of Habel in Bruce Zucherman, *Job the Silent: A Study in Historical Counterpoint* (Oxford: Oxford University Press, 1991), pp. 146, 166, 265, which says the Book of Job frames Job's task as a fool's errand. Zucherman, who reads Elihu as taunting Job, frames the conclusion of Elihu's section of the Book of Job as 'a sham conclusion' that sets up a meta-lesson about inscrutability. On parodic aspects of the Book of Jonah, see Gildas Hamel, 'Taking the Argo to Nineveh: Jonah and Jason in a Mediterranean Context', *Judaism* (Summer 1995); and see E.M. Good, *Irony in the Old Testament* (Sheffield: Almond Press, 1981 [1965]). Good (p. 55) finds 'The alternative to Jonah's absurdity is the absurdity of God.' See also Wolff, *Obadiah and Jonah*. Wolff, who suggests that the figure of Jonah may caricature a typical Jewish figure of the early Hellenistic period, moreover finds that the lesson of the Book of Jonah concerns the history of monotheism, facing paradox of prophecy (pp. 85–6). And see Sasson, *Jonah* (p. 331), who notes that Jonah's name 'has entered our dictionaries to describe a personality with farcical potential'; as well as Herman Melville, *Moby Dick* (New York: Harper & Brothers, 1851), ch. 84, which concludes that Jonah's lesson relates to a sceptic's 'foolish pride of reason'.

[71]   See J. Mather, 'Comic Art of the Book of Jonah'; and Sasson, *Jonah*, p. 347.

Yhwh's punch line ironically shows a lack of empathy between Jonah and Yhwh. On his part, Jonah first fails to divine that Yhwh's actions transcend human reason, or that His prophecies, omens and stories function to deliver moral lessons. Meanwhile if anyone should understand why Jonah was glad to see the vine appear and sorry to see it go, it is Yhwh, who indeed sent it and then the worm that ate it, yet Yhwh shrugs off any convention by which Jonah reads these omens of divine favour or disfavour. So when Yhwh declines to recognize Jonah as a reader of omens, he ultimately botches the conversation, in order to deliver a reading lesson.[72]

Ultimately the Book of Jonah teaches that the significance of a sign must come from dialogue between a diviner and his human community. Otherwise one's conversation with one's God gets botched and one lands beyond the perimeter of a foreign city, like mad Jonah all alone raving wrongly over a vine.

Overall then, the Book of Jonah champions itself as the Hebrews' communal story of the demise of a Hebrew who tried to flee his God and follow his own conventions of reason. The narrative, which progresses from lottery to prophecy, neither castigates Jonah for joining his shipmates' lottery nor casts divination as merely an obsolete version of monotheism, but it shows that a prophet's verdict is more extensive than the lottery's. Finally, however, trumping lottery and prophecy, foresight and reason, comes the biblical story itself.

The Book of Jonah pointedly omits Jonah's co-religionists from the narrative, in order to emphasize its implied audience – the tale was crafted for Jewish audiences – who must provide Jonah's Jewish context. The tale prompts its readers to subordinate lottery, prophecy, foresight and even reason, all to Judaism's lessons. Unlike Jonah's shipmates, readers should not serve God only as an empirically justified response to fair weather. Ultimately success or failure at their own cosmic ordeal, including struggle with paradoxes such as those the tale itself embodies, will reveal whether or not the Hebrew people deserve Yhwh's favour. And meanwhile the process helps constitute their peoplehood.[73] The Book of Jonah invites its readers to divine peoplehood from this biblical tale about honouring conventions, and to accept the absurdity that comes with trying to rationalize inscrutable conundrums.

From Lottery to Oral Prophecy to Divination by Biblical Interpretation

Like Darwin's fortune-telling, the Book of Jonah illustrates legacies of divination. Indeed by portraying a movement from lottery to oral prophecy to divination by scriptural interpretation, the Book of Jonah allegorizes the historical development of the ancient Israelites' characteristic, priestly practices. That is, 'for inquiry of

---

[72] My interpretation opposes the contention of Sasson, in *Jonah* (particularly on p. 298), that the Book of Jonah resolves itself neatly with 'pedagogic instruments that are too obvious to be misunderstood by Jonah'.

[73] See Orlinsky, 'Nationalism-Universalism', p. 113.

Torah, and on to Midrash',[74] they developed newer conventions of reading that 'functionally co-opted older divinatory techniques of divine inquiry',[75] particularly lottery.[76]

Some books of the Hebrew Bible speak as if some of the very early Israelites had prohibited, then abandoned, divination. But such prohibitions came much later than might appear: they were projected anachronistically to portray a moment in the distant past when the newer tradition supposedly had substituted for the ancient, cultic role divination had played.[77] This supersessionism aimed to help foster a monotheistic, tribalized identity amid polytheistic competition, so it downplayed the very old conventions shared by polytheists – conventions that had persisted through the adoption of monotheism by the people of Israel and Judea. That is, the more ancient, cultic rites of Israelites featured priestly divination by the Urim and Tummim (objects that may have been stones), a convention the Torah does not differentiate terminologically from that of 'a Babylonian king consulting omens (Ezek 21:26) or the like (Hos 4:12)'.[78]

The revisionism on one hand succeeded in bringing the Hebrew Bible, in some passages, to firewall its people's practices from what they should count as divination, but in other passages conversely the Hebrew Bible endorses divination, notably when Yhwh commands the High Priest to cast lots (Lev. 16:8). Relevantly the patriarch Joseph was a professional oneiromancer (a diviner by dreams) who, when he confronts his brothers with their conspiracy against him, asks rhetorically whether they do not know that a man like him can learn secrets through divination. So, when Yhwh prohibits divination (Lev. 19:26) and specifies that He will cut off from His people anyone who consults a medium (Lev. 20:27; see also Deut. 18:14, Isa. 2:6, and 2 Kgs. 21:6), such prohibitions conflicted with older endorsements.

In another tactic, Proverbs 16:33 declares that lotteries happen, but their every decision comes from Yhwh. This declaration, while acknowledging that indeed anyone is party to conventions of using lotteries, moreover co-opts these conventions as monotheistic. So Proverbs 16:33 can frame the biblical Hebrews' use of lotteries to divine guilt (for example 1 Sam. 14:40–43) or settle disputes (Prov. 18:8); or mainly, to warrant the selection of persons for a special role, for example, as Israel's first king (1 Sam. 10:19).[79]

---

[74]   Preus, 'Secularizing Divination', p. 441.

[75]   Fishbane, *Biblical Interpretation in Ancient Israel*, p. 66, referring to 1 Kg. 22:8 and Ezra 7:10. Preus, 'Secularizing Divination', p. 442, further notes that 'the very idiom used to describe Ezra's activity … is a precise reworking of an ancient formula used to indicate oracular activity … Since Ezra's textual task is to seek from the Torah new divine teachings (or explanations of older ones) for the present', this is an exegetical divination.

[76]   Burke O. Long, 'The Effect of Divination upon Israelite Literature', *Journal of Biblical Literature* 92/4 (1973): 489–97, at 496.

[77]   For this point concerning revisionism I am indebted to Bennie Reynolds.

[78]   Long, 'Effect of Divination', p. 490.

[79]   For a full list, see J. Lindblom, 'Lot Casting in the Old Testament', *Vetus Testamentum* 12 (1962): 164–78.

Yet the tensions regarding lottery have yielded within Judaism a lastingly marked ambivalence towards it – an ambivalence that shows in *Purim*, the carnival-like festival centred on a scriptural story featuring a lottery. According to the Book of Esther, the Jewish people's ancient arch-enemy Haman used a lottery to select a day to wage genocide against the Jews of his kingdom, but Haman's attack backfired, unfortunately for him but fortunately for the Jews. Today each Spring many congregations celebrate the festival of *Purim* in part with a raffle (that is, a lottery), as if to highlight the hope of chance.[80]

Such channelling of chance might mitigate oppression, and likewise so could oral prophecy, which divined by a voice that spoke 'in ways that are entirely unpredictable and which no one can control'.[81] The oral prophets historically did not even preach from scripture, nor use scripture to authorize their divinations.[82]

However, from the first centuries of the Common Era, 'rabbinic Judaism donned the mantle of prophecy and instructed a new generation'[83] when in place of oral prophecy it sought to substitute divination-by-scriptural-interpretation.[84] The latter featured elaborate uses of typology, 'the hermeneutical aspect … which sees in persons, events, or places the prototype, pattern, or figure of historical persons, events, or places that follow it in time'.[85]

That is, typology can trace the links between three things: a figure in the present age; its prefigurement in a long-gone age; and its fulfilment in an age that will replace the present age. Thus it can serve 'as the means whereby the deeper dimensions perceived to be latent in historical events are rendered manifest and explicit'.[86] The scriptures of the Hebrew Bible, as Michael Fishbane highlights, were ready-made for such divining because they featured 'inner-Biblical typology'. This internal cross-referencing made a *traditum* (content of tradition) into 'the screen upon which national hope and renewal is contextualized, even imagined', and moreover – through exposure to the chance that hope embodies – divinatorily 'warranted'.[87]

Even more deeply, by tracing correspondences of identities across ages, typology sutures the past to the present and future. To put it another way, typology works because 'what is ultimately put at stake is the very rational order which gives cognitive coherence to time and its terrors'.[88] It is a social process of making

---

[80]   Sasson, *Jonah*, pp. 108–9. Sasson further notes that Purim taught Judaism 'the Babylonian word for "lot" (*pur*)'. See also Theodor Herzl Gaster, *Purim and Hanukkah in Custom and Tradition: Feast of Lots – Feast of Lights* (London: Sutton Press, 2007).

[81]   Gerald L. Bruns, *Hermeneutics Ancient and Modern* (New Haven: Yale University Press, 1992), p. 72.

[82]   Julius Wellhausen, *Prolegomena to the History of Israel*, trans. J. Sutherland Black and Allan Menzies (Edinburgh: Adam & Charles Black, 1875).

[83]   Fishbane, *Biblical Interpretation in Ancient Israel*, p. 439.

[84]   See Bruns, *Hermeneutics Ancient and Modern*, p. 69.

[85]   Fishbane, *Biblical Interpretation in Ancient Israel*, p. 350.

[86]   Ibid., p. 360.

[87]   Ibid., pp. 459, 413, 362 and 375. Fishbane here mentions hope, not chance.

[88]   Ibid., p. 511.

sense via paradox, whenever users of typology divine 'a counter-reality of promise or anticipation that is already lived proleptically in the present'.[89]

This logic is as old as divination, and moreover older than what counts as reason today: so rather than supposing that 'counter-reality' violates the value of consistent reason, it is perhaps less anachronistic to say that the value of consistent reason itself fits poorly with the divination of a counter-reality. On one hand, if one is bound to proceed by applying universalistic reason then one must – like Jonah and like many scientists after Darwin – shrug off any talk of counter-reality. But on the other hand if one's oracle indicates a counter-reality, then one needs to approach it agilely.

Overall the conflicting voices within the Hebrew Bible need not resolve into any single message, nor crumble in contradiction. Instead their inverse distinctions and historical syncopations can be heard as musical counterpoint.[90]

In the Hebrew Bible's treatment of divination, at odds with itself, layers of traditions have arrayed a deeply textured, contrapuntal dialogue. The Book of Jonah's reading lessons, then, can help one towards hearing its music. Such reading lessons also have served here to approach *The Origin of Species*.

Conventions for Reading Signs of the Times

The Classical oracles legendarily fell silent the moment Jesus was born,[91] yet Christianity followed Judaism in co-opting divination. According to Matthew, who himself was chosen as the twelfth apostle by lottery (Acts 1:23–6), at first only a few astrologers from the East divined the significance of the Star of Bethlehem (Matt. 2:1), but moreover, like Paul, Matthew constituted a community of socially universal potential for reading the portents that he (in Matt. 16:4) called the 'signs of the times'.

While Rabbinical Judaism continued to champion divination-by-interpretation-of-Hebrew scripture, early Church authorities framed Christianity as the *ultimate* form of reading, the end of the line. These authorities insisted that the New Testament was the last, non-allegorical word, largely in order to parry a competing cult, Gnosticism, which was reading the New Testament itself as an allegory.[92] In other words, when the Church divined that its truth was the endpoint of all reading, it prohibited anyone from reading the Christian Bible the way the Church was reading the Hebrew Bible. (The term 'supersessionism', which this chapter uses broadly, comes specifically from a critique of Christianity's framing of the Hebrew Bible as 'The Old Testament'.) Christian authorities read the Hebrew Bible, and all

---

[89]   ibid., p. 518.

[90]   Zucherman, *Job the Silent*, pp. 22–4.

[91]   See Wood, *The Road to Delphi*, pp. 136–51.

[92]   See Wilhelm Dilthey, 'The Rise of Hermeneutics', trans. Frederic Jameson, *New Literary History* 3/2 (1972): 229–44, at 236.

portents anywhere since the dawn of time, as portending King Jesus.[93] All competing forms of divination meanwhile were actually not competing at all, insofar as they were obsolete and Christian divination did not count as divination.

If one can consider fortune-telling as omen mongering, then in this sense the early Church tended towards monopolizing truth by monopolizing divination. As Michael Wood suggests impiously in *The Road to Delphi: The Life and Afterlife of Oracles*, Christianity's universalism effectively claims 'Anything that looks like another religion is really just the bad side of our religion.'[94]

Moreover Christianity made divination a less public kind of act. By the fourth century CE most soothsaying had been banned in the Roman Empire: 'public divination was forbidden … Therefore, one had to interpret one's own dreams; one had to be a self-interpreter.'[95] The Church spurred each person to focus on inner acts, 'to try to know what is happening inside him … to recognize temptations, to locate desires', and 'to decipher himself in regard to what was forbidden'.[96] Still, as a category of human action, procedures markedly exposed to ritually pure chance persisted. So instead of a lottery, some – like Augustine – used other aleatory procedures, in semi-privacy, to classify themselves.

According to Augustine's *Confessions*, his conversion (and Alypius' conversion) to Christianity came when he was 'torn asunder with grievous perplexities',[97] and via divination his 'very uncertainties suddenly were made the basis of his new certainty'.[98] In his moment of dire uncertainty about his worth, Augustine addressed an inquiry to the unknown: 'Why not now? Why is there not this hour an end to my uncleanness?'[99] When he overheard a child's voice chanting repeatedly, 'Take up and read', he took these words as an omen – according to a convention of

---

[93]   I apologize for here caricaturing traditions strictly in terms of their supersessionisms and their co-options of divination. Some disclaimers are in order. Though providing an overall assessment of these traditions would exceed this chapter's scope, actually I find Judaism, Christianity, evangelical-rationalism and science irreducible to such repertoires. I do not champion the use of divination over anything else. I hasten to add further that I criticize here the polarities and taxonomies of rhetorics of purity and universalism: so, rather than dismiss any traditions as too impure or parochial, my critique aims to vex such judgements. Neither do I fault these traditions for having sought to replace anything, nor for having failed. I find that supersessionism – like divination itself – can do good, and sometimes may even be necessary. I do not promote 'persistence-ism' as if it might supersede supersessionism.

[94]   Wood, *The Road to Delphi*, p. 144.

[95]   Michel Foucault, 'Technologies of the Self', in Michel Foucault, Luther H. Martin, Huck Gutman and Patrick H. Hutton (eds), *Technologies of the Self: A Seminar with Michel Foucault* (Amherst: University of Massachusetts Press, 1988); reprinted unpaginated at http://www.thefoucauldian.co.uk/tself.htm (accessed 1 February 2007).

[96]   Ibid.

[97]   Augustine, *Confessions*, Book VIII, ch. 10.

[98]   Kenneth Burke, *Rhetoric of Religion*, p. 116.

[99]   Augustine, *Confessions,* Book VIII, ch. 12.

cledonomancy, or divination by overheard words. Although Augustine elsewhere scoffs at bibliomancers,[100] at this moment he took up his Bible to perform *Sortes Biblicae*. He opened his Bible at an indeterminate page, where a verse struck him deeply enough for him to place himself as a Christian; and Alypius, Augustine's student, followed suit. This indeed is how divination works: it enacts the fortunate conversion of uncertainty to certainty.

Heritage Comes Storming Through?

Like the early rabbinate's bid to substitute divination by scriptural interpretation for oral prophecy and lottery, subsequently each supposed substitute for divination actually was itself a convention of divination. So although Rome forbade 'public divination', by the Middle Ages repertoires of divination structured European societies with ordeals, duels, trials, inquisitions and medical diagnoses. These repertoires all channelled chance in 'an entire network of functions' for testing and sorting the social body.[101] Their conventions deployed 'rules for producing an unequivocal outcome' to warrant 'a clear decision about social relations'.[102]

Later, much as early Christianity supposedly had superseded Judaism and divination, Protestantism followed suit. In the wake of Renaissance humanism's divinatory conventions for textual purification,[103] Protestantism divined the unadulterated core of Christianity itself. Moreover, according to J. Samuel Preus, 'Divination in the broad sense of obtaining the divine knowledge necessary for salvation became *the* quintessential religious act of Protestant Christianity.'[104]

Next, when early-modern science emerged, it largely joined Protestantism's battle against obsolete conspirators.[105] The joint, 'severe inquisition of truth'[106] fiercely hunted and judged improperly warranted truths. But eventually much of

---

[100]   Augustine, *Confessions*, Book IV, ch. 3.

[101]   Talal Asad, *Genealogies of Religion: Discipline and Reasons of Power in Christianity and Islam* (Baltimore: Johns Hopkins University Press, 1993), pp. 122, 113. Though Asad refers here only to the 'monastic body', he argues for its relevance to the encompassing, social body.

[102]   Ibid., p. 90. Unlike Foucault, Asad does not name divination as such.

[103]   See Dilthey, 'Rise of Hermeneutics'.

[104]   Preus, 'Secularizing Divination', p. 442; emphasis in original. On typology as a 'dodge' by which Protestantism continued the work of allegory even while prohibiting it, see David Dawson, *Allegorical Readers and Cultural Revision in Ancient Alexandria* (Berkeley: University of California Press, 1992), p. 15 and Thomas H. Luxon, *Literal Figures: Puritan Allegory and the Reformation Crisis in Representation* (Chicago: University of Chicago Press, 1995), pp. ix, 40.

[105]   See Shapin, *Scientific Revolution*.

[106]   Francis Bacon, *The Advancement of Learning*, ed. Joseph Devey (New York: P.F. Collier and Son, 1901 [1605]), ch. IV, sec. 4.

science claimed reason for itself, as if reason were a disenchanted replacement for all superstition and religion including even Protestantism.

Among Protestants, meanwhile, the British and American Puritans were notable diviners. They practised divination by earthquake, *Sortes Biblicae* and oneiromancy (dream interpretation).[107] They found 'the hand of God could be discerned not only in major historical events (the discovery of America, the Reformation)', but also 'in the most apparently trivial happenstance'.[108]

Particularly they tended to divine by their own life narratives,[109] so the Puritans adapted typology in order for individuals to divine whether they were headed for heaven or hell. Already, Jewish typology interpreted biblical characters as the prefigurements of subsequent historical persons:[110] now as Puritans read their own life stories typologically, biblical characters came each to function as a potential exemplar of the elect or reprobate individual.[111] A Puritan divined 'which of those Biblical characters *applies to me* here and now?'[112]

More broadly, American jeremiads, a rhetorical form first mastered by Puritans, reached determinations via exposure to individualism and the degree of chance it entails.[113] These jeremiads followed the Puritans' basic, divinatory practice of interpreting current events, which had jelled by 1679 when a synod of leading clerics, in 'something of a ritual incantation', would 'set up the doctrine that God avenges the iniquities of a chosen people ... bringing the list up to date by inserting the new and still more depraved practices an ingenious people kept devising'.[114] By the 1730s, Jonathan Edwards used 'obsessive speculation about current events'[115] to read America as opening 'the way for the future, glorious times'.[116]

Such conventions persisted for sorting social relations. Regarding the War for Independence, American conventions of reading found 'every fact that touched upon the war was pregnant' with portents.[117] By the end of the 1770s, in Massachusetts, Maine, South Carolina and Virginia, July Fourth orators motivated their countrymen by systematically divining 'the correspondence between local

---

[107]   See Lears, *Something for Nothing*, p. 42.

[108]   Ibid.

[109]   Sacvan Bercovitch, *The American Jeremiad* (Madison: University of Wisconsin Press, 1978), p. 101, n.

[110]   Fishbane, *Biblical Interpretation in Ancient Israel*, p. 350.

[111]   Preus, 'Secularizing Divination', pp. 447, 449.

[112]   Ibid., p. 449. Hollywood's star system, designed for users to constellate identities in relation to certain stars, works similarly today. See Evan Heimlich, *Divination by The Ten Commandments: Its Rhetorics and Their Genealogies*, doctoral dissertation (University of Kansas, 2007).

[113]   See Bercovitch, *American Jeremiad*, pp. 24–5.

[114]   Perry Miller and Thomas Herbert Johnson, *The Puritans* (New York: American Book Co., 1938), pp. 8, 15.

[115]   Bercovitch, *American Jeremiad*, p. 99; see also pp. 115, 117.

[116]   Ibid., p. 99.

[117]   Ibid., p. 116.

progress and "the vast designs of providence"'.[118] They could read such traces
because Americans are 'persons endowed with the ... gift of detecting ... the most
appalling portents'[119] – diviners. In the nineteenth century 'as evangelical rationality
spread', idioms divining destiny and fortune in America increasingly 'became a
means of legitimating worldly developments: the emergence of a new nation, the
westward course of empire, the steady ascent of a successful entrepreneur' and
basically progress, of an individual or a civilization.[120]

Users of these conventions dare not admit their continuity with pre-modern
or non-Western conventions of divination, because each supersessionist tradition
had joined an age-old cycle when it abominated the tradition for which it sought
to substitute itself. Judaism, early Christianity and Protestantism each co-opted
what it could not replace, and in their turn, the regimes championing Reason
were no exception. The Enlightenment was hardly less divinatory than Europe's
supposedly Dark Ages, because efforts to replace practices of divination were
themselves divinatory. Notably, a 'witchcraft craze that raged for two centuries' of
inquisitions accompanied the era 'many scholars have regarded as ushering in the
dawn of modern rationality and civilization'.[121]

Europe and America have engendered cultural hegemony through idioms
that tell fortunes even while censuring any open embrace of fortune-telling.[122] So
thinkers in the wake of Thomas Jefferson have hailed 'the standard of reason at
length erected, after so many ages, during which the human mind has been held
in vassalage'.[123] Under this standard, to deny the role of fortune is supposedly to
guard mental freedom.

Putatively, a firewall separates the authentic-but-invalid old diviners from
modernity's users of denatured figures of speech. Supposedly modern people no
longer believe in fortune, hence no longer really mean what our words say. That is,
supposedly 'the outward utterance is a description, *true or false*, of the occurrence
of the inward performance',[124] yet somehow our disclaimers of certain kinds of
inward performance can invalidate our utterances' function of reading 'fortune'
or channelling chance. But we never denatured fortune-telling: indeed we cannot

---

[118]   Ibid., p. 141.

[119]   William Evans Arthur, on July Fourth, 1850, in Covington, Kentucky, quoted by
Bercovitch, *American Jeremiad*, p. 146. Among other appalling portents, Americans have
read traces of conspiracy. See Bercovitch, *The American Jeremiad*, p. 125 and note; and see
Barack Obama, *The Audacity of Hope: Thoughts on Reclaiming the American Dream* (New
York: Random House, 2006), p. 24.

[120]   Lears, *Something for Nothing*, p. 62.

[121]   Tambiah, *Magic, Science, Religion*, p. 47.

[122]   See Bercovitch, *American Jeremiad*, p. 28.

[123]   Thomas Jefferson, letter to James Madison, 1786, quoted in Adrienne Koch and
William Peden (eds), *The Life and Selected Writings of Thomas Jefferson* (New York: The
Modern Library, 1944), p. 371.

[124]   Austin, *How to Do Things with Words*, p. 9. Emphasis in original.

substitute mere idioms for divination, because divination has always been an idiom for a performative speech act.

Anthropologists of Fortune

Vassalage supposedly still held the minds of those people who lived outside the civilization that upheld the modern standard of reason, and held the minds of those who, even within modern civilization, persisted in openly embracing obsolete ways. Accordingly, in the Social Darwinism of anthropologist Edward Burnett Tylor's *Primitive Culture* (1871) the primitives retained cultural 'survivals', vestiges of no further use to humanity.[125] These vestiges' perverse survival was supposedly interfering with modern progress, so people should eliminate them. Tylor was here referring expressly to the persistence of divination.

Nevertheless divination's logic remained worth studying, for a few bold researchers including Omar Kayham Moore, an anthropologist who in 1957 authored a pioneering argument on chance. In his article, 'Divination – A New Perspective', his paradigmatic diviners were neither tennis players in London nor circuit-court justices in New York. Instead they were hunters among the Naskapi tribe of Labrador who, in preparation for a caribou-hunting expedition, conventionally burn a caribou's bone in order to make legible some traces of the unknown.[126] They interpret the burned bone's emergent pattern of spots and cracks systematically as their map. (Such conventions, common to many hunting tribes around the world, anthropologists call osteomancy; and when diviners like the Naskapi use a shoulder bone it is scapulimancy.)

Moore tried to take divination seriously on its own terms of chance. First he held that the Naskapi rely on divination for effective guidance when they are uncertain.[127] Finally he suggested that the key to its method was its randomness. Overall Moore bravely helped establish that chance matters but, as a so-called Darwinist, in place of fortune Moore substituted randomness. Although the hunters' scapulimancy surely enacted the tracing of patterns of their world, Moore argued that it deployed patternlessness. That is, according to Moore's evolutionary hypothesis, divination functions to randomize human behaviour, which helps hunters by preventing their overhunting any one area; plus it prevents the caribou from predicting and thereby avoiding the hunt.

---

[125] Edward Burnett Tylor, *Primitive Culture; Researches into the Development of Mythology, Philosophy, Religion, Language, Art, and Custom* (New York: Brentano's, 1924 [1871]).

[126] Omar Khayyam Moore, 'Divination – a New Perspective', *American Anthropologist* 59/1 (1957): 69–74; reprinted in William Armand Lessa and Evon Zartman Vogt (eds), *Reader in Comparative Religion: An Anthropological Approach* (New York: Harper & Row, 1979), pp. 376–9.

[127] Moore, 'Divination – a New Perspective', in *Reader*, p. 377.

A century after Darwinists first denatured Darwin's 'chance', Moore here denatured scapulimancy congruently: if the diviners were using what looked like chance, this must mean they were actually using randomness. If they were using randomness, there must be some good reason, so then the question for Moore became, *What evolutionary advantage could their deployment of randomness be giving these hunters?* His creative hypothesis responded reasonably to the question he had posed. His answer drew on randomization – a methodology familiar to his fellow scientists – as well as ecology and economics, to rationalize a tactic in a struggle for food.

But Moore's model of the hunter unfortunately was far more like a machine than a member of a human community. Moore's question had ignored the procedure by which the Naskapi bands used conventions to warrant determinations of where to hunt. Actually Moore's '"probability theory" of divination' was rather boneheaded, suggested George Park in his 1963 article 'Divination and Its Social Contexts': the Naskapi hunters would not use osteomancy to hunt in random directions.[128]

Park, who analysed divination, especially in various parts of Africa, influentially described how 'the employment of chance or chance-like mechanisms in the rendering of decisions' insulates an act of divination from merely expressing a user's own wish.[129] Although there indeed might be tactical advantages to random hunting, Park pointed out that there is perhaps no parallel advantage to randomization in other categories of aleatory divination, for example in the determination of guilt.

By naming 'chance-like mechanisms' Park sidestepped struggles over the meaning of 'chance'. Anyone could accept that aleatory mechanisms such as lotteries are *like* determinants of fortune (if fortune really existed), or that these mechanisms are akin to those of randomization. Moreover, when Park tried to describe indeterminacy from a diviner's own perspective, he cogently found that diviners used chance not to produce control so much as to transcend any one human person's control.

Yet not even Park was able to bracket the law of higgledy-pigglety, so instead of dismissing it, he stood Moore's randomization hypothesis on its head. Park reasoned that diviners use chance mechanisms not to produce unpredictability, but instead hegemonically, to foster a more predictable social order. In Park's words, 'Paradoxically, divination appears to have a derandomizing function; establishing consensus, it renders action more predictable and regular.'[130] Actually, though Park's fellow anthropologists could allow that diviners imposed order on disorder, osteomancers hardly 'derandomized' things if they did not face social disorder as a first principle.

---

[128] George K. Park, 'Divination and Its Social Contexts', *Journal of the Royal Anthropological Institute of Great Britain and Ireland* 93/2 (1963): 195–209, at 198, 201.

[129] Ibid., p. 198.

[130] Ibid., p. 200.

The law of higgledy-pigglety unfortunately continues to appeal to anthropologists and other thinkers. Some even fixate on Moore's account of divination as randomization – framing a tactic of competition between hunter and hunted, rather than a communal act of reading aloud.[131] Relevantly, classics scholar Sara Iles Johnston, in her important essay 'Divining Divination', walks the high wire at first by holding that 'in one way or another, all forms of divination partake of randomization';[132] however to her credit she then pirouettes to clarify that 'what scholars of divination call "randomization" actually is *not* randomization, but instead is the establishment of conditions beyond human control', or indeterminacy.[133] Finally she jumps off the high wire and into the safety net, though, by claiming that clients of Apollo's dice oracles 'were trying to domesticate the unpredictable (we would say "random") forces that drove both their dice throws and their lives'.[134] Yet the ancient patrons of dice oracles did not try to tame chance.

Rather, if they were attempting to domesticate anything it was themselves, in the sense of becoming at home in the cosmos by orienting themselves in relation to chance. Diviners and their clients always aim to trace an inscrutable pattern, never cosmic patternlessness. Historically, rhetorics for reading cosmic randomness gained currency not in ancient Greece, but only after Darwin's *Origin*, as if insistence on randomness could substitute for a pesky propensity to speak of fortune.

Denatured Fortune?

When one has spun or tossed an object to make a decision, or honoured the results of someone else's toss – for example by allowing that the player who won the toss deserves to decide who plays first – then one has divined. When one has used a procedure such as 'Eenie Meenie Minie Moe' or when one reads the signs of the times, when one mentions the fate or destiny of anything, or when one honours the privilege that one's society accords its winners, then one is party to divination.[135] When one calls someone fortunate, then one is telling a fortune.

---

[131] See John Geirland, 'Complicate Yourself' [interview with Karl Weick], *Wired* (April 1996). See also John Geirland, 'Moving Forward When There is No Visibility', *M World: The Journal of the American Management Association*, Spring 2002 Inaugural Issue.

[132] Sara Iles Johnston, 'Introduction: Divining Divination', in Sarah Iles Johnston and Peter T. Struck (eds), *Mantikê: Studies in Ancient Divination* (Boston: Brill, 2005), pp. 1–28, at p. 15.

[133] Ibid.

[134] Ibid., p. 16.

[135] On the sorting of winners and losers in America, see Scott A. Sandage, *Born Losers: A History of Failure in America* (Cambridge, MA: Harvard University Press, 2005) and Lears, *Something for Nothing*. See also Barrett Wendell, *Stelligeri, and Other Essays Concerning America* (New York: C. Scribner's Sons, 1893), p. 119. Wendell found, 'What

Perhaps one still reasons that one cannot really be a diviner because one simply does not believe in divination, so let us turn to an example from the world of sports, where players use a conventional procedure to enable a match to begin. If I have challenged someone to a tennis match, to start it I customarily spin my racket on the ground, and the other player calls it 'up' or 'down', like a tossed coin's 'heads' or 'tails'. According to this procedure, if the other player calls correctly then they will choose who serves first, and if not, I will choose. When tennis players the world over honour the determinations this procedure yields, they are using an ancient form of divination to select someone for a role. One might cry that tennis players embrace a mere superstition as if a supernatural power guides the racket, yet regardless of what else anyone may believe about divination, players spin a racket mainly because it works as a convention more or less required of players.

Even so, perhaps people today retain only the old forms from an unenlightened age, which at some point have become denatured? Modern people have substituted new beliefs in place of what our predecessors used to believe, no? So when we say something happened 'fortunately' or when we channel chance to make a choice, such acts no longer mean what they used to mean, do they?

The first problem with such questions is that they tend to posit an unlocatable historical moment when, across the board, a new meaning was substituted for an older meaning of chance-channelling. Moreover, regardless of users' beliefs, communities do honour the warrants people procure via conventions of divination. And even when communities actively dishonour given conventions, verdicts or warrants, their dishonour does not cancel out what communities signify when they honour divined warrants.

Today, debunkers of fortune often try to explain coin tossing procedures simply as an expedient to fairness – if someone tosses a coin and I call it, the probability of my success is 50 per cent, which is evenly fair – but this rationale of a fair selection system cannot disenchant the toss of the coin. In seeking to denature it, debunkers in vernacular English will insist that readings of any chance are valid only in terms of probability and randomness, therefore technically there is no such thing as a fortunate or unfortunate chance. So even if everyone can agree unofficially that the winner of a certain coin toss is fortunate, still some will claim that when they say 'fortunate' they merely mean privileged, without alluding to anything inscrutable about social privilege. If one guards what counts as reason, one may well insist that at some point our civilization denatured the divinatory conventions we inherited, simply by virtue of the new understanding that in an absolute sense the universe really does not favour anyone.

Yet perhaps anyone might occasionally call out something like, 'May the best man win', calling for a competition to reveal no mere accident, but instead the competitors' relative standing in the cosmic rankings. Moreover in a society that tends to honour its winners as the best, if one actively dishonours all such

---

[Calvinism] regarded as evidence for the doctrine of election is very like what people have in mind nowadays when they talk about the survival of the fittest.'

conventions of a cosmic order, one's own community brands one as a bad sport, and one can hardly get through social life.

Historically, when our 'pre-modern' predecessors used a coin toss to make a determination, they honoured a way of reading cosmic favour and hardly shared our agenda for positing randomness, so to cite random fairness as the whole function of divination is to put the cart before the horse. Despite active disbelief in superstition, today people still honour divinations of cosmic favour much like the ancients did. How does it make sense, then, to claim that because we know better than our predecessors, we use their same old procedures and terms now to invoke the absence of any pattern of cosmic favour?

It makes sense because a supersessionist tradition must continually insist on the obsolescence of the tradition it seeks to replace. In other words, one marks the absence of inscrutable cosmic pattern only *because human beings 'always already' have honoured cosmic pattern, but one officially can no longer honour such blasphemy.*

Overall, mantology, 'the study of material which is ominous or oracular in scope and content',[136] is a special kind of semiotics: it serves to foreground metaphysical issues of community, performance and authority. Its pursuit calls for a critical history of cosmologies. Mantology particularly helps show that no moat insulates monotheism from other conventions if divination is actually a common ground. Particularly, no firewall separates evangelical-rational science from monotheism, because historically these universalisms – which seek to substitute themselves for all older claimants of belief and claimants of the mantle of human inquiry itself – continue their intercourse.

The Grace of Fortune-Telling

One who reasons as if standing apart from the enchantment of the social is hardly well-positioned to address what people do socially.[137] Because the human cosmos is social, our terms of privilege, and of encounter, resonate cosmically, like it or not. For example, even if one insists that the cosmos is intrinsically random and that privilege lacks any cosmic dimension, still one may count oneself fortunate that one does not believe in luck.

Meanwhile, though the evangelical-rational consensus largely has reversed the meaning of 'chance' now as 'random', a parry by the English vernacular next is reversing the meaning of the word 'random'. For example, suppose on an airplane abroad you encounter your former roommate, who happens to be holding a copy

---

[136] Fishbane, *Biblical Interpretation in Ancient Israel*, p. 443.

[137] See Giambattista Vico, *The New Science: Principles of the New Science Concerning the Common Nature of Nations* (New York: Penguin, 1999 [1725]). See also W.H. Auden, 'Under Which Lyre', in *W.H. Auden: Selected Poems*, ed. Edward Mendelson (New York: Vintage Books, 2007 [1946]): 'Thou shalt not commit a social science, nor sit with statisticians.'

of the book *The Lost Domain*, just like you are; and you have encountered each other under exactly the same circumstances a few years prior, each carrying a copy of *The Scientific Revolution*. He exclaims, 'Hey, what the heck? Good to see you again … out of the blue! But, how random is this?!' In reply it would hardly be humane to shrug and say flatly that there is nothing baffling or marvellous about a merely random encounter. Rather, a fitting response would be to chuckle and agree that the encounter is 'pretty random!' – as if it were disconnected from any apparent pattern but connected to an inscrutable pattern.

For mantology the suitable way forward is to account for social processes of truth-making on their own terms, using methodological relativism. Although the evangelical-rational consensus, in its universalism, may tend to reject methodological relativism in cultural science and at large, still, other than poetics or musicology there is no other proper methodology to make sense of fortune-telling in an officially fortuneless cosmos.[138]

Without methodological relativism one can hardly see past 'mistaken beliefs' – an all-too-common pitfall that obscures divination's actuality. 'The assumption that the only way of having oracles is by "believing in them"', writes anthropologist Martin Holbraad, is 'a baseless projection, due to a lack of ethnographic imagination combined with a remarkable self-confidence that our own conceptual framework is rich enough to describe that of all others.' He finds 'it is remarkable how prevalent this muddle is in anthropological thinking'.[139]

Moreover, let us ask how our own authorized discourses might lack the richness to describe *our own* honouring of oracles. The present chapter's genealogy of divination's co-optation, most recently by claimants to reason-as-progress, perhaps has helped contextualize this muddle, elucidate its prevalence in and beyond anthropology, and relate its rhetoric to a long history of supersessionisms.

For mantology, belief or disbelief is hardly at issue for approaching how people use divination to authorize a discourse, so an investigator need not proceed by classifying oneself apart from believers (nor, for that matter, need one conclude as a true believer). Inasmuch as belief may be relevant, one need not model it as an all-or-nothing affair of conversion,[140] or as determinative, nor need one locate belief upstream from discourses.

---

[138] On the methodological necessity of relational thought experimentation, or meta-theorizing, see Martin Holbraad, 'Ontology, Ethnography, Archaeology: An Afterword on the Ontography of Things,' *Cambridge Archaeological Journal* 19 (2009): 431–41, at 434.

[139] Martin Holbraad, 'Defining Anthropological Truth', paper presented at Truth Conference, Cambridge, 24 September 2004; available at http://sites.google.com/a/abaetenet.net/nansi/abaetextos/defining-anthropological-truth. See also Martin Holbraad, 'Ontography and Alterity: Defining Anthropological Truth', *Social Analysis* 53/2 (2009): 80–93.

[140] See James Davidson, 'I Told You So!' [review of Wood, *The Road to Delphi*], *London Review of Books* (2 December 2004): 12–18, at 18, col. 4. On the inconstancies of belief, see also William James, *The Varieties of Religious Experience* (New York: Penguin, 1985 [1902]), p. 65.

The challenge here is not to promote or resist the lottery of Jonah's shipmates or the fortune-telling of Darwin: rather it is to acknowledge, situate and explore such conventions and their legacies. No people has substituted another convention for divination, across the board, so as a category of human action it has never been a throwback, and perhaps will always persist.

Human beings cannot dispense with divination if, as poet Wallace Stevens suggests, 'we live in a constellation/Of patches and pitches,/Not in a single world.'[141] In any case, societies maintain and honour various conventions for reading different kinds of hidden patterns, in order for their members to locate themselves socially.

Such pattern-reading is 'crucial to understanding what it feels like to be human', according to leading neurologists who increasingly focus on a prune-sized lobe of the cerebral cortex near each ear – the insula, 'a crossroads of time and desire'.[142] The human insula, larger and more complex than those of other mammals, is 'a sort of receiving zone' where 'simple body states or sensations are recast as social emotions', warranting decisions. It is the seat of empathy, as well as the seat for processing events that have yet to happen.[143] It primes human beings to divine.

Finally divination matters because each human being must navigate a sea of social play. According to a medieval Sanskrit text, 'It is a marvel! In me the eternal ocean, the person-waves rise, strike one another, play together, and finally die, each according to its destiny.'[144] Such marvelling is not an epiphenomena of outlandish beliefs, but a crucial, ordinary affect for navigating social life.[145]

When one insists that nobody can really channel chance to tell a fortune, one dismisses the possibility of grace, in a sense of grace as 'what happens when openness to chance yields a deeper awareness of the cosmos or one's place in it'.[146] Yet such dismissal can hardly override the marvel-reading by which we act recognizably human. Moment to moment one can hardly stop acting as if fortune matters, because when locating oneself socially each human being attunes to an ocean of possibilities.

---

[141] Wallace Stevens, 'July Mountain', in *Opus Posthumous: Poems, Plays, Prose* (New York: Knopf, 1989). Quoted by Kathleen Stewart, *Ordinary Affects* (London: Duke University Press, 2007).

[142] Sandra Blakeslee, 'A Small Part of the Brain, and Its Profound Effects', *New York Times*, 6 February 2007.

[143] Ibid.

[144] Jeffrey Moussaieff Masson, *The Oceanic Feeling: The Origins of Religious Sentiment in Ancient India* (Dordrecht: D. Reidel, 1980), translates the medieval Sanskrit text, the *Astavakra Samhita*, also known as the *Astavakra Gita*. Masson argues that the Freudian term 'oceanic feeling' derives from this text.

[145] See Stewart, *Ordinary Affects*.

[146] Lears, *Something for Nothing*, p. 7.

Chapter 10

Arrows, Aiming and Divination: Astrology as a Stochastic Art

Dorian Gieseler Greenbaum

'The right art', cried the Master, 'is purposeless, aimless!
The more obstinately you try to learn how to shoot the arrow for the sake of hitting
the goal, the less you will succeed in the one and the further the other will recede.
What stands in your way is that you have a much too wilful will.
You think that what you do not do yourself does not happen.'

(Eugen Herrigel)[1]

Unlike the modern connotation of stochastic processes, which deal with randomness and probability in many different fields, my focus in this chapter concerns the ancient definition of stochastic and its use in ancient science and divination. The word 'stochastic' comes from a Greek word (στοχάζομαι) meaning to 'aim at', 'conjecture' or 'guess'. It was used both for aiming at a target and, by extension of this primary meaning, for guessing or conjecturing. The image of aiming at a target is also used metaphorically in antiquity to describe certain ancient practices, and to highlight the use of conjecture and interpretation in those practices.

The ancient concept of *stochasmos* moves down two different paths: one that leads to 'science' (that is, 'stochastic' arts which aim towards and eventually approach our modern concept of science) and the other that leads to divination (described as an art of conjecture in antiquity).

The art of aiming can also be connected to the concept of metaphor and its role in divination. Since my main interest is in divination and, particularly, the intersection of astrology with divination, this chapter will also explore how metaphor might be used to explain what diviners, and astrologers as diviners, do.

Thus the aim of this chapter is to see, first, whether we can call astrology a stochastic art and, second, whether it is in a 'scientific' or in a 'divinatory' way that we should view this 'stochasticism'. Lastly, we shall think about the connection of the stochastic concept with metaphors, poetry and divination, and how this may be relevant to astrological practice. My target audience for this chapter is not primarily astrologers (though they may be interested in my thoughts on how

---

[1]   Eugen Herrigel, *Zen in the Art of Archery*, trans. R.F.C. Hull (New York: Random House, 1953, repr. 1999), p. 31. I am indebted to Garry Phillipson for alerting me to this most apt quotation.

astrologers do what they do), but rather those readers who have not considered that astrological perspectives and methods of interpretation have any value. I am offering an approach to astrology that takes it out of the realm of the literal and into a different, but no less present, reality: a reality that includes the metaphorical as a valid way of looking at the world.

Precise Prediction and Astrology

How is it possible to make astrological prediction precise and consistent? The ability to forecast correctly is a concern of both astrologers and their critics. Astrologers desire ways to make their art more accurate, while critics use its inconsistency in an attempt to invalidate it. For millennia, astrologers used the following or similar justifications for failure in astrological prediction:

- The technique used by the astrologer did not properly reflect a physical mechanism.
- The doctrine or technique was applied incorrectly.
- The practitioner's knowledge and skill were inferior.

In touting their own, superior systems, astrologers frequently resorted to denigrating their colleagues and blaming their inaccurate forecasts on the reasons outlined above, especially the last.[2] Those faulty skills, and not the art itself, are to blame if the predicted outcome does not occur.[3] Such a justification is demonstrated in the description Cicero's brother, Quintus, gives in *De divinatione* about the efficacy of divination by signs: 'ea quibus bene percepta sunt, ii non saepe falluntur; male coniecta maleque interpretata falsa sunt non rerum vitio, sed interpretum inscientia' ['Those who properly perceive are rarely deceived. The falsehood of bad conjectures and bad interpretations is due, not to any fault in the world, but to the scientific ignorance of the interpreters'].[4]

---

[2]   Among other examples, see Vettius Valens, *Anthologiarum libri novem*, ed. David Pingree (Leipzig: B.G. Teubner, 1986) [hereafter *Anthology*], III, 9.1–6; IV, 11.1–5; V, 8.113–117; Julius Firmicus Maternus, *Matheseos libri VIII*, ed. Wilhelm Kroll, Franz Skutsch and Konrat Ziegler, 2 vols (Leipzig: B.G. Teubner, 1897–1913) [hereafter *Mathesis*], I, 3.6.

[3]   Claudius Ptolemy, Ἀποτελεσματικά, ed. Wolfgang Hübner, *Opera quae exstant omnia*, vol. III 1 (Stuttgart and Leipzig: B.G. Teubner, 1998) [hereafter *Tetrabiblos*], I.2, 12–13 (as cited in Joanna Komorowska, 'Astrology, Ptolemy and technai stochastikai', *MHNH* 9 (2009): 129–40). I am grateful to Komorowska for her previous research on this topic, though my approach is different from hers.

[4]   Cicero, *De divinatione*, I, lii.118 = SVF 2.1210; trans. A.A. Long and David Sedley, *The Hellenistic Philosophers*, 2 vols (Cambridge and New York: Cambridge University Press, 1987), vol. 1, 42E, p. 261; vol. 2, 42E, p. 261.

In antiquity, scientific ignorance, especially of the workings of the physical world, was a particular concern for Ptolemy, who supposed that if he could find rational, physical explanations for astrological doctrines and their effects, he would be contributing to an increase in accurate prediction. Ptolemy, who considered astrology to be stochastic, saw similarities between the art of astrology and the art of medicine: he may have been the first to compare astrology to the practice of medicine in which, like the physician, the astrologer applies his skill and proper technique to predict an outcome. The physician's goal is also to use her skill to provide the proper remedy to heal the patient, while the astrologer's equivalent goal is to provide astrological remedies, for instance in the form of katarchic charts.[5] Like the art of medicine, Ptolemy says, astrology cannot predict successfully every time, because of factors beyond the control of the astrologer and astrology. These include things like (the ancient equivalents of) genetics and environmental factors.[6]

However, in contrast to Ptolemy's attempt to find natural rules governing astrological practice, astrological techniques were more often purported to be revealed wisdom (for example in the writings of Vettius Valens).[7] The divinatory origins of astrology are corroborated by such perceptions of its ancient doctrines.

A general set of rules for interpretation arises from this acquisition of revealed wisdom. Divination's rules are based on the medium through which the divination is made (whether flights of birds, the fissures in livers, the casting of lots or the patterns in the heavens). The Stoics too describe divination as rule-based (theoretical as opposed to practical), as Arius Didymus relates: 'Εἶναι δὲ τὴν μαντικήν φασιν ἐπιστήμην θεωρητικὴν σημείων τῶν ἀπὸ θεῶν ἢ δαιμόνων πρὸς ἀνθρώπινον βίον συντεινόντων. Ὁμοίως δὲ καὶ τὰ εἴδη τῆς μαντικῆς' ['They say that the prophetic art is a rule–based knowledge of signs from the gods or *daimones* which apply to human life. They say the same about the forms of the prophetic art'].[8] These rules become a jumping-off point, not necessarily consistently applied in all cases, from which the diviner uses his interpretive skill to predict an outcome. Thus the astrologer may interpret the symbolism differently in each *particular* case, even though following a general set of rules. Different rules can be applied in different

---

[5]   One use of 'katarchic' astrology is to find the best possible moment astrologically for beginning a ritual or other event, in order to secure the best outcome for that event.

[6]   Ptolemy, *Tetrabiblos* I, 2.17–19; Valens, Anthology, IV, 16 talks about the Sun and Moon causing different changes under similar astrological conditions but different natural ones.

[7]   For example, *Anthology* IV, 11.7; V, 6.16; VI, 1.7.

[8]   Arius Didymus, *Epitome of Stoic Ethics*, ed. and trans. Arthur J. Pomeroy, *Texts and Translations* 44, *Graeco–Roman Series* 14 (Atlanta: Society of Biblical Literature, 1999), 5b12, pp. 24–7. Pomeroy translation slightly modified.

cases; for example, Saturn might be used to represent the father in the interpretation of one chart, but the Lot of the Father may signify the father in another.[9]

Ancient astrologers were aware of the distinction between the general and the particular. Vettius Valens, for example, describes the Ascendant and angles from it as 'universal' and 'cosmic centrepins', while the Lot of Fortune and angles from it are 'genethlialogical' (that is, natal, unique to that person).[10] Ancient astrology offers several ways of dealing with the two categories:

1. It explains mass disasters both naturally and astrologically (both Ptolemy and Valens do this).[11]
2. It uses different techniques to take both the general and the particular into account (as in the Valens example above, where lots become a way to account for particular outcomes).
3. It approaches each chart as a unique portrait/prophecy, tailored by time, space and interpretation as a particular 'take' matching (changing) symbol to circumstances (see the use of aphorisms as guides, not axioms, below).

Astrology differs in some respects from other forms of divination, in that its medium is the planets and stars in the sky, whose movements can be measured and consistently predicted (unlike, for instance, the casting of lots, which change each time they are thrown). Also, once a chart is written down, it becomes a stable and enduring record of a fleeting moment, whereas once the flock of birds has passed, or the liver cools, the divination ends. Because it is based on the physical representation of the universe, people like Ptolemy theorized a mechanism of physical causation; if such is the case, then astrology becomes a proto-science. As a science, it should be susceptible to predictable results. However, like medicine, its results are not consistently correct, so it therefore has a commonality with that and other disciplines, like rhetoric, which depend on the practitioner's experience, skill and creative interpretation in a unique situation.

---

[9]   Astrological lots are considered to be sensitive predictive points in a chart. They are usually calculated by taking the arc between two planetary positions in a chart and projecting that arc from a third point (often the Ascendant, the zodiacal degree where the ecliptic and eastern horizon intersect).

[10]   Valens, *Anthology* II, 18.6 (p. 76.18–20 Pingree): 'ὑφίστανται γὰρ τινες μυστικῶς τὸν μὲν καθολικὸν ὡροσκόπον καὶ τὰ τούτου τετράγωνα κοσμικὰ κέντρα, τὸν δὲ κλῆρον καὶ τὰ τούτου τετράγωνα γενεθλιαλογικὰ κέντρα' ['Some have mysteriously laid down the universal Hour–marker [i.e. Ascendant] and its squares [points directly opposite and perpendicular] as the cosmic centrepins [*kentra*, modern 'angles'], but the Lot and its squares as the genethlialogical centrepins']. All astrological translations are my own unless otherwise specified.

[11]   See, for example, Ptolemy, *Tetrabiblos* I, 1–3; Valens, *Anthology* VII, 6.127ff. Furthermore, one could say that the two categories of mundane astrology (called universal or general by the ancients) and natal astrology are an attempt to deal with this issue on a broad scale.

In *De divinatione* (I, xiv.24), Cicero's brother Quintus tells us that divination is allied with other arts which depend on 'conjecture and deduction' (*quae coniectura continentur et sunt opinabiles*) such as medicine, navigation, military strategy and statecraft. It grows into an art capable of a certain level of prediction through experience 'derived from everlasting eternity' (*ab omni aeternitate repetita*) (I, xiv. 25).[12] The same signs over time are shown to have consistent results (though this does not necessarily prove physical causation).

The words 'conjecture' and 'consistency' bring us to the first aim of this chapter, which is to look at what a 'stochastic' (or 'conjectural') art is, and to see whether we can apply it to astrology, as Ptolemy suggested.[13] We shall examine this word (with its variations), and what it represents in Greek culture, in relation to astrology and its practices. In doing so, we shall take up ideas about aiming (including the target, the goal and the ability of the aimer) and conjecture. These will be applied to astrology in particular, and compared with other disciplines usually described in antiquity as 'stochastic', such as medicine and rhetoric. We shall also look at the philosophical interpretations of this word, especially those of the Stoics (for whom it was an important concept). In the Greek of the late Hellenistic period, a word for a diviner was not only *mantis*, but also *stochastēs*.[14]

Targets and Goals

The first definition of the verb στοχάζομαι (*stochazomai*) in the Greek lexicon is 'aim' or 'shoot at'.[15] These primary meanings pertain to the literal shooting of arrows at a target, but the term was adopted and applied in both Aristotelian and Stoic philosophy.

In particular, both of these philosophic strands widely use the metaphor of an archer aiming at a target. Aristotle, in the *Nicomachean Ethics*, states that 'every art' aims at some good, and aiming at that objective helps us, like the archer, to

---

[12] Both quotations from Marcus Tullius Cicero, in *De senectute. De amicitia. De divinatione*, trans. W.A. Falconer (Cambridge, MA: Harvard University Press, 1923, repr. 2001), pp. 250–53. The last cited quotation is my translation.

[13] The relevant Ptolemaic text is his Ἀποτελεσματικά, commonly known as the *Tetrabiblos*, especially Book I.

[14] The earliest usage of *stochastēs* appears to be in the Greek translation of *Isaiah*, with a date probably in the 2nd century BCE. It is then mostly used in commentaries on this passage by theological writers. In *Isaiah* it is paired with the word *prophetēs*. (For the dating of the Septuagint translation of *Isaiah*, see I.L. Seeligmann, *The Septuagint Version of Isaiah: A Discussion of its Problems* (Leiden: E.J. Brill, 1948), p. 91: 'the middle of the second century *ante* would be the most likely date to assign also to this chapter (ch. 23) of the translation'.)

[15] Henry George Liddell, Robert Scott and Henry Stuart Jones, *A Greek–English Lexicon*, 9th edn (Oxford: Clarendon Press, 1996), s.v.

hit the target (1094a). In the *Rhetoric* (1360b 4–7), he uses the same metaphor: 'Σχεδὸν δὲ καὶ ἰδίᾳ ἑκάστῳ καὶ κοινῇ πᾶσι σκοπός τις ἔστιν οὗ στοχαζόμενοι καὶ αἱροῦνται καὶ φεύγουσιν· καὶ τοῦτ' ἐστὶν ἐν κεφαλαίῳ εἰπεῖν ἥ τ' εὐδαιμονία καὶ τὰ μόρια αὐτῆς' ['Nearly everyone has a kind of target, both privately for each person and in common, in aiming at which they make their choices and avoidances, and this is, in brief, happiness and its parts'].[16] Later, 'conjecture' (*stochasmos*) was described as the first task a rhetorician undertakes, determining facts from signs and suspicions: 'Ὧν στοχασμὸς τὸ πρότερον· ὑπάρχει δ' οὗτος, ἄναξ,/ἔλεγχος οὐσιοποιὸς ἐκ φανεροῦ σημείου/ἢ τῆς περὶ τὸ πρόσωπον ἀκριβοῦς ὑποψίας' ['The first of these is conjecture: this is, master, an examination that establishes what is the case from a clear sign, or from particular suspicions about a person'].[17]

Other philosophers use the archer metaphor to explain the attainment of virtue. Thus, in Cicero's *De finibus*, 3.22:

> ... primum error tollendus est ne quis sequi existimet, ut duo sint ultima bonorum. Etenim, si cui propositum sit conliniare hastam aliquo aut sagittam, sicut nos ultimum in bonis dicimus, sic illi facere omnia quae possit ut conliniet. Huic in eius modi similitudine omnia sint facienda, ut conliniet. Et tamen, ut omnia faciat quo propositum adsequatur, sit hoc quasi ultimum quale nos summum in vita bonum dicimus, illud autem, ut feriat, quasi seligendum, not expetendum.

> ... [one must at the outset remove the mistake of supposing that there are two final goods. For if a man's object were to aim a spear or an arrow straight at something, his doing everything in his power to aim it straight would correspond to our doctrine of the final good. On that kind of analogy, this man must do everything to aim straight. And yet his doing everything to attain his object would be his end, so to speak, analogous to what we are calling the final good in life, whereas his striking the target would be something 'to-be-selected', as it were, not 'to-be-desired'.][18]

Antipater, a Stoic commentator, also used the example of an archer shooting at a target to articulate the difference between Stoic targets and goals about obtaining happiness. It is generally interpreted to mean that an archer can still succeed by

---

[16] Trans. Julia Annas, *The Morality of Happiness* (New York and Oxford: Oxford University Press, 1993), p. 364.

[17] Michael Psellos, *Synopsis of Rhetoric (Poem 7)*, trans. Jeffrey Walker (2006), at https://webspace.utexas.edu/jw2893/www/PsellosSynopsisRhetoricWebtext.pdf (accessed 13 January 2010), Poem 7.32–4.

[18] Trans. Long and Sedley, *Hellenistic Philosophers*, vol. 1, p. 403; Latin, vol. 2, pp. 397–8.

shooting skilfully, even if he does not hit the target.[19] Julia Annas points out that this depiction of archery is just a metaphor, and that archery in itself is not a stochastic art[20] (which claims that target and goal are different). Be that as it may, the archery metaphor is widely used to illustrate the difference for the Stoics between target and goal, and thus becomes almost a commonplace for the definition of a stochastic art.

The Stoics are looking for the attainment of happiness (*eudaimonia*). They make a distinction between *aiming* for happiness and *being* happy, and this is the distinction between a *skopos* and a *telos*; as Annas indicates, the *telos* involves *doing* or *obtaining* something (actions expressed by verbs); the *skopos* the thing *done* or *obtained*, expressed as a noun.[21]

The Greek words for target and goal also illustrate their differences. The word often translated as 'target' is *skopos*, literally the mark, or the thing aimed at; the goal (*telos*) (famous as Aristotle's 'final' cause, for which something is done), is literally the end, the completion. As Arius Didymus says about the relationship between *skopos* and *telos*, 'Καὶ ἔστι σκοπὸς μέν, τὸ προκείμενον εἰς τὸ τυχεῖν, οἷον ἀσπὶς τοξόταις· τέλος δέ, τοῦ προκειμένου τεῦξις' ['A *skopos* is a target to be hit, like a shield for archers; a *telos* is the hitting of the target'].[22] Applied to medicine, Galen says that the stochastic nature of the art is such that the target is doing what is humanly possible to cure the patient, but the goal is the actual cure.[23] Since the art is stochastic, there is no shame and no failure in failing to achieve the goal.

Can we apply these conceptions to astrology? On a literal level, *skopos* and *telos* (and related forms) are common in the ancient astrological vocabulary. The astrologer is often advised to 'mark' a particular point or position of a planet (from which an interpretation will be made); the moment of birth, translated into a corresponding position in the sky, is even called the *Hōroskopos*, the 'Hour-marker'; and the outcomes forecast by the interpreting astrologer are called '*apotelesmatika*', derived from the root '*telos*'. From this perspective the goal is

---

[19]   F.H. Sandbach, *The Stoics*, 2nd edn (London: Hackett, 1975, repr. Indianapolis, IN, 1994), p. 57. Gisela Striker, 'Antipater, or the Art of Living', in Malcolm Schofield and Gisela Striker (eds), *The Norms of Nature: Studies in Hellenistic Ethics* (Cambridge: Cambridge University Press, 1986), p. 192, interprets thus: 'it is simply meant to say that the archer is not concerned with hitting the mark, but only with shooting skilfully'. Brad Inwood, citing Roswitha Alpers-Gölz, points out that Antipater reshaped the difference between *skopos* and *telos*, which previously distinguished between 'the happy life ... as a physical object ... and the attainment and living of that life' (see Brad Inwood, 'Goal and Target in Stoicism', *Journal of Philosophy* 83/10 (1986): 547–56, at 551, n. 9).

[20]   Annas, *Morality of Happiness*, p. 402.

[21]   Ibid., p. 34.

[22]   Arius Didymus 47.8–10, quoted in Annas, *Morality of Happiness*, p. 34.

[23]   Paraphrased from M. Frede, in discussion following the paper of Véronique Boudon, 'Art, science et conjecture chez Galien', in Jonathan Barnes and Jacques Jouanna (eds), *Galien et la philosophie, Entretiens sur l'antiquité classique*, Tome XLIX (Geneva: Hardt, 2003), p. 300.

the outcome, which one aims at by 'marking' the positions of the stars and then interpreting them in line with the goal.

On a broader, philosophical level, we can look at the *skopos* and *telos* of astrology in two ways. The ancient position, I think, would be analogous to that of the target and goal in medicine: the goal (*telos*) is the correct prediction and the target (*skopos*) is doing whatever humanly possible to aid the client by achieving the correct prediction. If astrology is a stochastic art like medicine, then as long as the astrologer does everything in his power to achieve a correct prediction, it is no failure not to achieve it.

The other way of looking at this issue is by inverting the ancient position on what the target and goal is.[24] The *target* is the correct prediction, and the *goal* is aiding the client in life decisions to the best of the astrologer's ability, taking into account the conjectural nature of the art. This position could be described as pragmatic, and an ontological change from the ancient view.[25] In adopting this view, we can examine it in the light of Aristotle's four causes. Astrologically:

- the material cause is the stars, planets and celestial phenomena
- the formal cause is the patterns formed by the above
- the efficient cause is the correct prediction
- the final cause is the aiding of the client.

Let us think about the target in archery. Materially, it is the cloth, the stuffing and the paint used to make the target (astrologically the stars, planets and celestial phenomena). Formally, it is the actual object of the stuffed, cloth-wrapped circle with lines and a bull's eye drawn on it (astrologically the astrological patterns). But the target is also the means by which the goal is achieved, and so we could also call it the efficient cause. Therefore, if the target is the efficient cause, and correct prediction in astrology is the target, then prediction is the efficient cause. It is just something to be hit until one invests it with meaning (the final cause). Helping the client with life decisions is the goal, the final cause. Even if the target, the correct prediction, is not achieved, the goal, helping the client, can still be achieved.

Accepting this other approach does not mean that astrology, with its goal and target reversed from medicine's, should no longer be considered a stochastic art, because it still depends on informed conjecture and the judgement and skill of the practitioner, and it can still be practised successfully even if the goal is not achieved.

In medicine, a cure is not always achieved, but improvement is aimed at. Because medicine is widely acknowledged and accepted as a stochastic art, it is not required that 'perfection' be achieved for the art or the practitioner to be successful. The practice is 'perfect' (that is, complete), even if the cure does

---

[24]   I am grateful for the insights and feedback of Marcia Butchart in this section.

[25]   My thanks to Guido Giglioni for discussing these points with me, and helping me to clarify my positions.

not occur. In another archery analogy, the Stoic Panaetius discusses aiming at different virtues and describes the target as possessing rings of different colours – different shooters, with different goals, may aim at different rings – but all hit the target.[26] We could think of astrologers as being like the different shooters who aim at the target, but achieve, with their astrology, different ends based on which of the (metaphorical) colours they hit.

However, some paradoxes involved in marksmanship must be considered and applied to astrological practice. First, the shooter does not aim precisely at the middle of the target in order to hit the bull's eye, but must take into account the trajectory of the arrow and the speed of its flight, the distance from the target, the flatness of the terrain one is shooting on and so on. So we could say the aim is true when the aim is not true. In astrology, it is the apparent, not the 'real', on which the interpretation is based. Astrological rules are based on our human perceptions of a geocentric universe, which of course is not scientifically true. For example, in both astronomy and astrology, the 'conjunction' of a planet with the sun does not actually occur in the heavens, as the two bodies, in reality, are millions of miles from each other. From our earth-bound perspective, we only see what 'appears' to be a conjunction, and even that is not visible to us at the exact moment when sun and planet join, because the brightness of the sun swallows up our sight of it. We can only know that the conjunction has happened after the planet has moved far enough away from the sun to be visible (this is true *phasis* versus visible or apparent *phasis*). (This very example may show that astrology is founded on, and moves in, a figurative (metaphorical), not literal, space.)

Second, there is a psychological component to consider, involving a mental stance which must be taken in shooting for a bull's eye. This involves skill and desire in proper proportions. Here I shall use an example from the sport of baseball: when trying to get a home run in baseball, there is a certain detachment, or *not* trying to get a home run, that is necessary to hit a home run. We saw this in the USA during the summer of 2007, when the baseball player Alex Rodriguez, famous for his prowess in hitting home runs, went ten days between his 499th home run and his 500th.[27] During that period, the press kept the pressure on by reporting each

---

[26] Panaetius, fr. 109 (part) in Stobaeus, 2.63, 25–64, 12; quoted in Long and Sedley, *Hellenistic Philosophers*, 63G, vol. 1 (trans.), p. 396; vol. 2 (original), p. 392. 'ὅμοιον γὰρ ἔλεγεν εἶναι ὁ Παναίτιος τὸ συμβαῖνον ἐπὶ τῶν ἀρετῶν, ὡς εἰ πολλοῖς διαφόρους τοῖς χρώμασιν· εἶθ' ἕκαστος μὲν στοχάζοιτο τοῦ τυχεῖν τοῦ σκοποῦ, ἤδη δ' ὁ μὲν διὰ τοῦ πατάξαι εἰς τὴν λευκὴν εἰ τύχοι γραμμήν, ὁ δὲ διὰ τοῦ εἰς τὴν μέλαιναν, ἄλλος <δὲ> διὰ τοῦ εἰς ἄλλο τι χρῶμα γραμμῆς' ['Panaetius said what happens in respect of the virtues is similar to a single target set up for many archers, which contains within itself lines of different colours. In that case each archer would aim to hit the target, but one would do so, if he were successful, through striking into the white line, and another through striking into the black line, and another through doing so into a line of different colour'].

[27] Though Rodriguez had similar stretches of time between hitting home runs when the record was not an issue, in 2007 he usually hit a home run an average of every four or

failed attempt at breaking the record.[28] Thus, in addition to hitting home runs in general, Rodriguez also had to think about specifically hitting *the 500th home run*. Perhaps the more he thought about 'hitting the 500th home run' the less he was able to do it; only by letting 'hitting the home run' go could he hit the home run. He acknowledged as much when he said on 28 July 2007 (three days after hitting his 499th home run), 'They're [the pitchers] being extra careful, and I'm kind of playing into their hands a little bit. There's not much I can do with the pitches I'm swinging at. Basically, I've just got to get a good pitch to hit and *try not to do too much*.'[29] This is an example of what Herrigel meant in the quotation beginning this chapter, also expressed poetically by the Daoist Chuang Tzu:

When an archer is shooting for nothing
He has all his skill.

If he shoots for a brass buckle
He is already nervous.

If he shoots for a prize of gold
He goes blind
Or sees two targets –
He is out of his mind!

His skill has not changed. But the prize
Divides him. He cares.
He thinks more of winning
Than of shooting –
And the need to win
Drains him of power[30]

---

five days (one home run per 10.8 at bats). See the Major League Baseball website statistics on Alex Rodriguez at http://newyork.yankees.mlb.com/team/player_career.jsp?player_id=121347&y=2007 (accessed 3 January 2010).

[28] See the game summaries for this period at http://mlb.mlb.com/news/wrap.jsp?ymd=20070726&content_id=2112071&vkey=wrapup2005&fext=.jsp&team=away (insert the relevant date in the url to see subsequent days until 4 August 2007, when Rodriguez hit the 500th home run). See also http://bats.blogs.nytimes.com/2007/07/31/alex-rodriguez-0-for-1/ (both sites accessed 13 January 2010).

[29] Quoted by Tyler Kepner, 'Stuck on 499, It's Just Like Old Times for A-Rod', 'Bats' blog, *New York Times*, 29 July 2007, online at http://bats.blogs.nytimes.com/2007/07/29/stuck-on-499-its-just-like-old-times-for-a-rod/ (accessed 13 January 2010); my emphasis.

[30] Chuang Tzu, *The Way of Chuang Tzu*, compiled by Thomas Merton (New York: New Directions, 1969), p. 107. Again I am grateful to Garry Phillipson for giving me this quotation. For more astrological discussion on this topic, see Garry Phillipson, *Astrology in the Year Zero* (London; Flare, 2000), pp. 191–2. See also Garry Phillipson, *Tales from*

If an astrologer goes into a consultation aiming (metaphorically) to 'hit a home run', in almost all cases what occurs is a mediocre reading; he fails to hit the target. This is true not only of astrology but of any art involving skill and desire. We shall return to these ideas at the end of this chapter, when we talk about metaphor, aiming and divination.

Stochastic Arts vs. Productive Arts

The stochastic arts involve learning technique (or 'rules'), being able to apply those rules based on an intuition guided by experience and taking into account that particular situations will require a particular, not general, application of technique. As James Allen puts it,

> Thus, if they were to succeed at their art, stochastic artists needed to do more than acquire a mastery of the formal precepts of their art; they also needed to develop a sensitivity to the peculiar features of particular situations, a sense of the opportune moment (ὁ καιρός) which enabled them to undertake the right procedures, at the right time, in the right way (cf. *Phaedr.* 272a). Since this ability cannot be incorporated into the formal precepts of an art, it has to be built up by practice and hands-on experience (Isoc. *Antid.* 15, 184; cf. Aristotle, *EN* 1104a 3–10).[31]

Alexander of Aphrodisias, in his commentary on Aristotle's *Topics*, distinguishes stochastic arts from 'productive' arts like building, weaving or any of the technical crafts. Katerina Ierodiakonou has nicely demonstrated these distinctions.[32] In examining Ptolemy's assertion that astrology is a stochastic art, I shall apply the distinctions between stochastic and productive arts to astrology. We shall see that astrology has more in common with stochastic arts, but historically (other than by Ptolemy) often appears to be judged as a productive art. In Table 1 I duplicate Ierodiakonou's definitions (taken from Alexander). Let us look at these more closely.

Babel, especially the section entitled 'A Quest for Quality #3: Self-Concern', online at http://www.astrozero.co.uk/articles/tales_from_babel.htm (accessed 13 January 2010).

[31] James Allen, 'Failure and Expertise in the Ancient Conception of an Art', in Tamara Horowitz and Allen I. Janis (eds), *Scientific Failure* (Lanham, MD: Rowman and Littlefield, 1994), pp. 81–108, at p. 88.

[32] Katerina Ierodiakonou, 'Alexander of Aphrodisias on Medicine as a Stochastic Art', in Philip J. van der Eijk, H.F.J. Horstmanshoff and P.H. Schrijvers (eds), *Ancient Medicine in Its Socio-cultural Context* (Amsterdam: Rodopi, 1995), pp. 473–85, at p. 474.

Table 1   Astrology as a Stochastic or Productive Art[33]

Stochastic art	Astrology		Productive art
1 Proceeds in a systematic, but not fully determined manner	Yes		1 Proceeds in a fixed manner
2 Its function is to aim at doing everything possible to achieve its end	Yes		2 Its function is to aim at reaching its end
3 Its success is not to be judged by the final outcome		Yes	3 Its success is evaluated by the end product
4 Its failure is due to the nature of the art itself, which is such that its objects are also influenced by external factors	Yes	Yes	4 Its failure is due solely to the practitioner's faulty performance

•   Number 1: A stochastic art proceeds in a systematic, but not fully determined manner.

Astrology creates a set of rules that are followed in general, but not uniformly applied in every case. So we cannot say that astrology, or good astrology, proceeds in a fixed manner, like productive arts where a sequence of steps is precisely followed in order to achieve a successful outcome. Ierodiakonou reminds us that Alexander calls medicine a stochastic art in that the rules for a cure apply 'for the most part' and follow syllogistic reasoning.[34] Astrology's rules, as well, bring success 'only for the most part'[35] and in this way may be said to be contingent:

---

[33]   Definitions taken from ibid.

[34]   Ibid., p. 480. Astrology's rules are also logical and rational within their symbolism, whatever one might want to say about their causal properties. The rationality of divination (especially including astrology) is discussed in R.J. Hankinson, 'Stoicism, Science and Divination', *Apeiron* 21/2 (1998): 123–60. See also Daryn Lehoux, 'Tomorrow's News Today: Astrology, Fate and the Way Out', *Representations* 95 (2006): 105–22.

[35]   Alexander of Aphrodisias, *On Aristotle's Prior Analytics 1.1–7*, trans. Jonathan Barnes, Susanne Bobzien, Kevin Flannery, S.J. and Katerina Ierodiakonou (Ithaca: Cornell University Press, 1991), 39.17–40.5; see especially p. 98, n. 61: 'The rules or general principles of an art guarantee success in the sense that if you apply them correctly you will

they can be modified according to the particular situation and the judgement of the astrologer. Thus in this definition astrology follows the stochastic, not the productive, model. In supporting Ptolemy's argument that astrology is stochastic, Joanna Komorowska interprets this statement from the Ptolemaic viewpoint, that the rules do not always bring success because a complete and certain system for the successful practice of astrology had not yet been attained, and therefore that system is not completely defined.[36] But, as Allen points out,[37] success must also depend on what amounts to proper interpretation of a particular situation based on experience and judgement.

- Numbers 2 and 3: A stochastic art's function is to aim at doing everything possible to achieve its end –AND– a stochastic art's success is not to be judged by the final outcome.

It could be said that astrology's end must be a successful prediction (or character delineation), and often even its practitioners act as if this is the case. If the prediction does not come true, then astrology fails. But this treats astrology solely as a productive art. The building of a house is judged to be successful if the house is well constructed, all the steps necessary in the building of the house have been followed and the house meets standards of habitability; if these criteria are not present, the house is not considered to have been successfully finished. By contrast, in medicine, healing is not always possible, but generally medicine is not blamed when the patient is not cured: the disease may be beyond present methods of healing, circumstances beyond medicine's control may be contributing factors and so on. This aligns with the stochastic principle of 'doing everything possible to achieve its end'.

When astrology is treated like a productive art, it is judged by the success of what is assumed to be the end product: the correct prediction. As a productive art, success would be consistently achievable by following the right procedure (Number 1, 'proceeding in a fixed manner'), and its results could be judged by those standards. Because of astrology's symbiotic relationship with astronomy, both ancients and moderns may fall into the trap of considering astrology as an exact science.[38] However, a competent astrologer may do everything 'right'

---

achieve your end. An art is conjectural if it can only guarantee success *for the most part*'; emphasis in original.

[36] Komorowska, 'Astrology'.

[37] See note 31.

[38] For example, astrology and its relationship with astronomy is included in O. Neugebauer, *The Exact Sciences in Antiquity*, 2nd edn (New York: Dover, 1957, repr. 1969). If astrology fails to be 'exact', it becomes labelled a 'pseudo-science', with all the pejorative connotation that word can muster. For discussions of the history of astrology as pseudo-science, with more sympathetic approaches, see Hankinson, 'Stoicism, Science and Divination', pp. 123–4; Tamsyn S. Barton, *Power and Knowledge: Astrology, Physiognomics,*

in judging the chart, but not make a correct prediction. Or, the astrologer may satisfactorily answer the questions of the client, but not predict something else about which the client did not ask.[39] If we think of astrology as a productive art, then we may fault the astrologer for not predicting something as obvious as a pregnancy. Failure is not an option in a productive art.

However, if astrology is stochastic, then the failure to predict correctly does not mean *ipso facto* that the practitioner is incompetent. Uncertainty within the art itself brings interpretation into play; in astrological interpretation, there is a unique interplay between astrologer and client which involves a dance between the needs of the client and the intuition and skill of the astrologer. If the client asks for a tango, it is not the astrologer's job to provide a waltz. Furthermore, as we have discussed above, is the goal really just that of correct prediction? We have compared the ancient goal and target in astrology to that of medicine: goal as cure (prediction) and target as help. But the inversion of these as outlined above (in my discussion of targets and goals) may be more fruitful philosophically for understanding the underpinnings of astrological theory and practice. It may even be that the adherence to the former position through the ages by both sceptics and practitioners has led in part to the consideration of astrology purely as a 'science' (and eventually as 'pseudo–science') which must ultimately be more like a productive art than a stochastic one.[40] It is a misinterpretation, I suggest, of what astrology is.

If astrology is inherently stochastic – if the astrologer is not just 'following directions' – then failure to hit the target is not failure of the art itself. (And every practising astrologer has experienced the mystery of having greatly aided a client, while a prediction went wide of the mark.) Uncertainty is built in (the conjecture), and the aim is, though risking failure, to use that uncertainty to create a freedom to act outside the boundaries of the rules. The stochastic art practitioner, by her interpretation, creates a solution that takes into account both the unique circumstances of the situation and the creative application of the 'rules'.

---

and Medicine under the Roman Empire (Ann Arbor: University of Michigan Press, 1994, repr. 2002), pp. 15–17, 175; also Liba Taub's discussion of Barton, in her review of Power and Knowledge: 'Review: The Rehabilitation of Wretched Subjects', *Early Science and Medicine* 2/1 (1997): 74–87, at 82–3, 86–7.

[39] An astrologer remarked to me recently that a client, giving feedback about her consultation, had reported her satisfaction about astrological advice on her business prospects (which she had asked for); but she wondered why the astrologer had failed to predict her pregnancy!

[40] The view of astrology as a science carried into the Arabic era: for example, see Charles Burnett, 'The Certitude of Astrology: The Scientific Methodology of al–Qabīsī and abū Ma'shar', *Early Science and Medicine* 7/3 (2002): 198–213. The importance of the Arabic viewpoint on the later development of medieval and Renaissance astrology was such that the paradigm of astrology as a science has been maintained even into the modern era.

- Number 4: The failure of a stochastic art is due to the nature of the art itself, which is such that its objects are also influenced by external factors.

Ptolemy specifically claims that outcomes are influenced by more than astrological factors. This follows the stochastic art model. But often the blame for an incorrect prediction is laid not on factors outside of astrology's purview, but on the astrologer/practitioner (and especially by other astrologers). This follows the productive art model, which blames failure on the practitioner's faulty performance. While few would take issue with suing an incompetent carpenter for a failed building, in a stochastic art the lines are less clearly drawn (witness the high incidence of medical malpractice suits whose outcomes favour the medical defendants). If rhetoric fails to persuade, one does not sue the speechwriter.

The problem is that astrology seems to have more in common with the accepted precepts of a stochastic art, but is often judged as a productive art. This instantly damages its credibility, because it is expected to live up to standards impossible to achieve by its own natural limitations. When astrologers blame the practitioner's competence they reinforce this position.[41] Valens hurts the cause of astrologers when he claims that faulty predictions are to be blamed on the incompetence of other astrologers, and not on ascribing to astrology a function of which it is not capable. Ptolemy here is correct when he says that outcomes cannot be predicted by astrological methods alone, because some things are beyond the influence of the stars. Yet he does not consider (or ignores) the divinatory aspects of astrology; he has concentrated on the 'productive' and physically causal side (for example the planet Mars 'makes' soldiers) and relinquished the 'semantic' and 'symbolic' side (the seventh house 'signifies' marriage).[42] The 'physically' caused trumps

---

[41] This is not to say that it does not matter whether the astrologer is competent. But solely using the competence of the astrologer to judge the success of the art does not take into account other reasons for its failure, or the stochastic nature of astrology. Furthermore, the competence of the astrologer depends on more than merely following the rules without exercising her own judgement.

[42] I do not mean to imply that Ptolemy is the only one to use words of physical causation about astrological technique. All the Hellenistic astrological writing uses words like 'make' or 'produce' to describe astrological configurations which 'bring about' certain effects. In fact, the verbs *semainō* and *poieō* seem often to be used interchangeably in astrological texts. Without doing an intensive study on the frequency and context of these verbs, I can only suggest that, in the manuals designed to teach astrology, the writers were not necessarily paying attention to the way in which they were using the verbs that conveyed the outcomes of various astrological figures; they were simply correlating those heavenly figures with their possible counterparts on earth. It remained for philosophical writers like Plotinus to take up the questions of 'making' versus 'signifying', and to nudge astrology back to its religious and divinatory roots. (For a discussion of these issues in Plotinus, see Marilynn Lawrence, 'Who Thought the Stars are Causes? The Astrological Doctrine Criticized by Plotinus', in John F. Finamore and Robert M. Berchman (eds), *Metaphysical Patterns in Platonism* (New Orleans: University Press of the South, 2007), pp. 17–33.)

'significance'. Ptolemy has also sacrificed the final cause (the *telos*) for the efficient cause (the *skopos*).[43]

We must also consider the fact that the interpretation itself can be aligned, ambidextrously, with both external and internal factors. External, because the astrologer – who brings her own judgement to the astrological configuration – is herself the outside variable in the astrological interpretation. Internal, because the interpretation is intrinsic to the practice of astrology. Interpretation is the crucial factor in a stochastic art. A productive art may be successfully practised by strictly following the rules without the necessity of personal interpretation.[44] But a stochastic art cannot be practised without interpretation of the undetermined and external factors involved, and the consideration of the unique (particular) case. Thus, even though astrology has some features of a productive art it cannot, in the end, be practised without the freedom allowed by a stochastic art.

These theories on the nature of astrology as stochastic or productive can be substantiated in the works of ancient astrologers themselves. How did ancient astrologers consider the exercise of their art? Can we discover evidence of 'productive' or, especially for our purposes, 'stochastic' practices among them? Surviving astrological manuals, aside from Ptolemy's, contain few attempts by astrologers to categorize their art, but examining the way they describe what they do and how they do it yields a surprising amount of evidence.

Astrology, Aiming and Conjecture

Most surviving astrological texts are concerned with practical techniques, not philosophical reflections. Nevertheless, these technical manuals can provide some illumination on whether, philosophically, Hellenistic astrologers viewed their art as stochastic or productive (even if they do not use those particular words). Since one of the purposes of a technical manual is to present techniques that give consistently correct results, one might expect that hard and fast rules, without any chance for deviation, would be the order of the day. There is, however, due emphasis on the importance of judgement, as well as other kinds of 'stochastic' practices. I shall give examples from four astrologers (Valens, Hephaestio, Ptolemy and Manilius) which demonstrate the subtlety of their thought about what astrology is and how it should be practised.

Vettius Valens and his Target

Valens, as a practising astrologer, is generally more concerned with passing along technique to his readers than with addressing the philosophical foundations of

---

[43] Thanks to Geoffrey Cornelius (private communication) for suggesting this.

[44] I do not mean to imply that interpretation can never be used in a productive art.

astrology. He uses 'stochastic' words only once in the *Anthology* proper,[45] and once in an appendix to the *Anthology*,[46] without any philosophical sense. However, on a number of occasions he gives glimpses of his philosophical positions. I want to examine a particular passage in Book IV, Chapter 11, whose ostensible topic is the technique of profections (a predictive technique). Within this chapter, however, Valens shares how he came to find astrology and how he employs it in his personal life. He also uses the target and goal analogy. Here is the passage, separated into three sections for ease of commentary.

Valens tells us he was searching for correct guidance in astrology (IV, 11.7):

καὶ δὴ πολὺν μὲν χρόνον ἀνιαρῶς διήγομεν, καὶ ἐπιλύπως τὰς μεταβολὰς τῶν τόπων ποιούμενοι, τοῖς περὶ τὰ τοιαῦτα ἐσπουδακόσι συμμίσγοντες, διάπειραν ἐλαμβάνομεν, μέχρις οὗ τὸ δαιμόνιον βουληθὲν διά τινος προνοίας τὴν παράδοσιν ἔν τινι τόπῳ πεποίηται διά τινος φιλομαθοῦς ἀνδρός.

[And at that point, we spent much time wretchedly, and while we were sadly moving from place to place, associating with those who have seriously studied such things, we kept on experimenting, until the wished-for *daimonion*, through a certain providence (*pronoia*), made the transmission in a certain place through a certain man who loved learning.][47]

Because of his *daimōn* and Providence, Valens was able to find the right astrology teacher for himself. Here the acquisition of the knowledge came about because of a divine intervention. As in prophecy,[48] the signs from the *daimones* point Valens to the human teacher of wisdom. He continues, using the target and goal analogy (IV, 11.8):

ἀρχὴν οὖν λαβόμενοι καὶ πολὺν πόνον εἰσενεγκάμενοι κατελαβόμεθα τοῦ σκοποῦ ὃν καὶ ἐκτησάμεθα ἐπεισενεγκάμενοι καὶ αὐτοὶ πολλὰς δυνάμεων εὐχρηστίας.

[And so making a start and applying much effort, we *seized on a target which we got for ourselves* when we brought to bear many advantages rendered from these productive agencies.][49]

---

45   VIII, 3.2, p. 284.11 Pingree.
46   Appendix 16, p. 426.7 Pingree.
47   Valens, *Anthology*, p. 163.13–17 Pingree.
48   See the quotation from Arius Didymus, 5b12 above.
49   Valens, *Anthology*, p. 163.17–19 Pingree; my emphasis.

Here Valens says that he was able to realize his goal, that is, hit the target (*skopos*) of being a good astrologer, and a good teacher of astrology, by using the very astrology (the 'productive agencies') that he has so arduously learned. Valens goes on, after articulating his goal, to say that by practice and experience he was able to 'discern a holy and immortal theory' in astrology, using the verb *krinein*[50] (IV, 11.9–10):

ἐκ γὰρ τῆς καθημερινῆς τριβῆς καὶ πολυάνδρου συμβολῆς καὶ τῆς τῶν παθῶν αὐτοψίας ἱερὰν μὲν καὶ ἀθάνατον τὴν θεωρίαν ἐκρίναμεν, ἄφθονον δὲ τὴν μετάδοσιν ποιησόμεθα .. γὰρ ἄνευθεν οὐδὲν οὔτε ἐστὶν οὔτε ἔσται· ἀρχὴν γὰρ καὶ τέλος ἔχει προγινωσκόμενον.

[For from daily practice, meeting with many people and seeing what happens with our own eyes, we discerned (*krinō*) a holy and immortal theory, and we will share it unbegrudgingly ... For without this nothing either is or will be; for what is foreknown has a beginning and an end.][51]

Here is astrology, the stochastic art, invoked as a goal (a stochastic word) and wrapped up in the cloak of divination and daimonic visitation, leading to the articulation of a technique of the art as a 'holy and immortal theory'. The craft shows its divinatory links, the technique melded with dependence on the will of the gods, via the aid of the *daimōn*, to share their knowledge. The goal is realized through personal practice, through hands-on application that leads to the theory – not the other way around, with theory informing practice. With the last sentence in this section, we have the sense that Valens is no longer talking just about a particular astrological technique,[52] but about the art of astrology itself.

Hephaestio and Conjecture

Certain passages in Hephaestio suggest that he may have taken for granted the status of astrology as a stochastic art. This position makes sense because Hephaestio frequently quotes Ptolemy, the purveyor of astrology as stochastic; also, Hephaestio was writing in the early fifth century, subsequent to any discussions on productive versus stochastic arts that may have occurred concerning astrology in the second century. In almost the first sentence of his work, Hephaestio brings up the distinction of whether astrology works through signs or causes 'or something

---

[50] Manilius (see below) uses the same verb (in its Latin form, *cernere*) in his poem *Astronomica* (5.293–94). It is clear that the astrologer's judgement is crucial to astrological practice.

[51] Valens, p. 163.19–22, 23–4 Pingree.

[52] The topic of discussion was ostensibly profections (a predictive technique).

else'.[53] (It appears that for the most part he bears the same opinion as Ptolemy about its causality.) We have seen in rhetoric a correlation of *stochasmos* with being able to establish situations by interpreting signs.[54]

Further on in the preface, he makes a distinct bid for considering astrology as a stochastic art, and also clearly correlates it to medicine:

ὥσπερ δὲ οἶμαι καὶ ἐπ' αὐτοῦ τοῦ προγνωστικοῦ, καὶ εἰ μὴ διὰ παντὸς γοῦν ἄπταιστον ἦν, τὸ γοῦν δυνατὸν αὐτοῦ μεγίστης σπουδῆς ἄξιον κατεφαίνετο, τὸν αὐτὸν οἶμαι τρόπον καὶ ἐπὶ τοῦ φυλακτικοῦ, καὶ εἰ μὴ πάντων ἐστὶ θεραπευτικόν, ἀλλὰ τό γε ἐπ' ἐνίων, κἂν ὀλιγάκις μικρὰ ᾖ, ἀγαπᾶν καὶ ἀσπάζεσθαι χρή. τούτοις δὲ ὡς ἔοικε συνεγνωκότες οἱ παλαιοὶ Αἰγύπτιοι οὕτως ἔχουσι συνῆψαν πανταχῇ τῷ δι' ἀστρονομίας προγνωστικῷ τὴν ἰατρικὴν διὰ τῶν καλουμένων παρ' αὐτοῖς ἰατρομαθηματικῶν συντάξεων ἐξ ὧν προσφόρως ἑκάστῳ τὰ βοηθήματα προσφέρουσιν.

[But just as I think about prognostication itself, that even if it is not in all circumstances infallible the possibility of it at least is plainly worthy of the greatest attention, in the same way I think of it also as protective; and if it is not therapeutic for all things, but at least for some, even if it may be seldom and in a small way, it is [still] necessary to regard and greet it with affection. The ancient Egyptians, so it seems, agreeing with these things, have thus wholly joined medicine to prognostication by astronomy through their so-called iatromathematical systems, from which they convey remedies in a way suitable to each person.][55]

This is akin to Ptolemy's position (as we shall soon see). Even though he does not use the stochastic buzz words here, earlier in the preface Hephaestio has called astrology an 'inquiry and knowledge based on contingency'.[56] It is plain that he

---

[53]   Hephaestio, *Apotelesmaticorum libri tres*, ed. David Pingree, 2 vols (Leipzig: B.G. Teubner, 1973), I, Preface.1, p. 1.7–8 Pingree, 'περὶ τῶν ἄστρων ἤτοι σημαινόντων ἢ ποιούντων ἢ καὶ ἑτέρῳ τρόπῳ'.

[54]   See above, note 17, the quotation from Michael Psellos about conjecture being the ability to determine a case from a 'clear sign'.

[55]   Hephaestio, *Apotelesmaticorum libri tres*, I, Preface.7–8, vol. 1, pp. 2.28–3.10 Pingree.

[56]   Hephaestio, *Apotelesmaticorum libri tres*, I, Preface.2, vol. 1, p. 1.12–13 Pingree, 'τὴν κατὰ τὸ ἐνδεχόμενον ἐπίσκεψίν τε καὶ γνῶσιν'. This is similar, but slightly altered, from Ptolemy's statement in *Tetrabiblos* I, 1.2. The statement echoes remarks made by Alexander of Aphrodisias, *Analyticorum priorum librum I commentarium*, ed. Maximilian Wallies (Berlin: Georg Reimer, 1883), p. 39.27–40.5: 'περὶ δὴ μόνου ποιεῖται τὸν λόγον τοῦ ἐνδεχομένου καὶ δυνατοῦ τοῦ ὡς ἐπὶ τὸ πλεῖστον καὶ τοῦ πεφυκότος τε καὶ κατὰ φύσιν, ὃ καὶ αὐτὸ ὡς ἐπὶ τὸ πλεῖστόν ἐστιν, ἐπειδὴ ἐκ τῶν τοιούτων καὶ δείκνυταί τινα τῶν κατὰ

thinks of it in the same way as medicine, an art of possibilities that is worthy of practice even though it is not consistent. Notice here that he also makes a distinction between general rules and particular therapies even, perhaps, putting the emphasis on astrology (rather than medicine) for a remedy uniquely suited to a patient.

When Hephaestio moves on to astrological technique, we see occasional use of *stochazomai* merely meaning 'to conjecture' without any special overt philosophical meaning. But one particular passage sheds additional light on the way he views astrology as stochastic. It appears in his third book, on katarchic astrology, which might be significant in itself, as that branch of astrology is arguably the most divinatory in nature. The passage comes in the middle of interpretations of various astrological configurations for katarchic charts, and is followed immediately by more interpretations. Between the two, however, there is an astonishing statement on the nature of astrology, and about the role of the astrologer as interpreter:

Καὶ οὗτοι μὲν οἱ στοχασμοὶ ἔκ τε τῶν ἀστέρων καὶ ἐκ τῶν ζῳδίων ἔστωσαν εὑρίσκεσθαι, ἀλλ' οὐ δεῖ πάντα τὰ σημεῖα ἀνελλιπῶς ἐφ' ἑκάστου εὑρίσκεσθαι νομίζειν ἀλλ' ὅσα ἐνδέχεται ἐντέχνως ἐπεξιέναι ἔκ τε τῶν συσχηματιζομένων ἀστέρων συνεπικρίνειν τὸν στοχασμόν. ἐὰν δὲ τῷ σημαίνοντι τὸν κλέπτην ἀστέρι ἀγαθοποιὸς μαρτυρῇ ἐλεύθερος ἔσται ὁ κλέπτης, ἐὰν δὲ κακοποιὸς δοῦλος ἢ πένης ἢ μισθωτός. ἐὰν δὲ Ἀφροδίτη σημαίνῃ τὸν κλέπτην αἰτία τῆς κλοπῆς ἔσται γυνή, ἐὰν δὲ Ἑρμῆς παῖς, ἐὰν δὲ Ἄρης ἀκμαῖος, ἐὰν δὲ Ζεὺς μεσῆλιξ, ἐὰν δὲ Κρόνος γέρων.

[And let these conjectures from the stars and from the zodiac signs be found, but one must not believe that all the meanings for each have been found without fail; but one may also proceed in such matters by skilfully using the art to help judge the conjecture from the configurations of the stars. [*The aphorisms continue*] If a benefic witnesses the star which signifies the thief, the thief will be a free man; but if a malefic, a slave, a

---

φύσιν γινομένων, καὶ εἰσί τινες τέχναι περὶ τὸ οὕτως ἐνδεχόμενον, ὡς αἱ στοχαστικαί· λαβὼν γὰρ ὁ ἰατρὸς τὸ τὸν οὕτως νοσοῦντα ὡς ἐπὶ τὸ πλεῖστον ὑπὸ πλήθους ἐνοχλεῖσθαι καὶ τὸ τὸν ὑπὸ τοῦ πλήθους ἐνοχλούμενον ὡς ἐπὶ τὸ πλεῖστον διὰ φλεβοτομίας θεραπεύεσθαι συνάγει τὸ τὸν οὕτως νοσοῦντα ἐνδέχεσθαι ὑπὸ φλεβοτομίας θεραπευθῆναι, ὃ λαβὼν χρῆται τῇ φλεβοτομίᾳ. διὸ καὶ ἔστιν ἐν συλλογιστικῇ χρείᾳ' ['Thus he deals only with the kind of contingency and possibility which holds for the most part and which is by nature or according to nature (which itself holds for the most part). For some natural events are indeed proved on such a basis, and there are some arts concerned with what is in this way contingent – for instance, the conjectural arts [*stochastikai*]. A doctor assumes that someone who is ill in such-and-such a way is for the most part unwell from surfeit, and that someone who is unwell from surfeit is for the most part cured by venesection; and he deduces that it is contingent that someone who is ill in this way will be cured by venesection. Taking this to be so, he performs a venesection. For this reason, there is syllogistic utility in these things']. Trans. Barnes, Bobzien, Flannery and Ierodiakonou in *Alexander of Aphrodisias, On Aristotle's Prior Analytics 1.1–7*, p. 98.

poor man or hired servant. If Aphrodite signifies the thief, a woman will be responsible for the theft, but if Hermes a child, if Ares a person in the prime of life, if Zeus middle-aged, if Kronos old.][57]

We see here the highest use of stochastic technique to arrive at a correct outcome. Like the physician, the astrologer uses his *personal judgement* and *experience* to make the prediction. Like Valens and Manilius (see below), the Theban astrologer uses a form of the verb *krinein* (here *sunepikrinein*, 'help judge'). Hephaestio is telling us that aphorisms are not definitive. He is telling us that we must use our own skill and judgement to create an interpretation suited to the symbolism of the astrological factors, but to make it particular to the situation. He is countering one of the most common objections to astrology by both modern and ancient critics, that aphorisms seemingly *are* definitive. Here is evidence that ancient astrologers did not think of aphorisms in that way at all. Aphorisms were merely examples of the symbolism, not hard and fast descriptions of astrological outcomes. The astrologer hits the target by using his *own* skill at interpretation to discern the answer suited to the unique situation, at the right and opportune (kairotic) moment.

Ptolemy and Astrology as a Stochastic Art

Of all the Hellenistic astrologers, Ptolemy is certainly the most interested in deriving a philosophical foundation for astrology, in addition to understanding why it works. It is clear that he likes the medical model as an analogy for astrology and that, by his lights, astrology generally aligns well with the stochastic model.

First, Ptolemy points out the natural influences of the Sun, Moon and stars on the earth (I, 2.1–6). These clear physical connections lead him to the second part of his argument (I, 2.7), that farmers and herders observe natural conditions, and from these make conjectures *(stochazontai)* about the fertility of their crops and herds; and that obvious configurations of the Sun, Moon and stars signify general events on earth. From this, Ptolemy says, comprehensive study of the heavens can lead, in many cases, to successful conjectures – aiming well *(eustochōs)*, based on physical data and educated guesses (I, 2.10): 'ἱκανὸν δὲ πρὸς τοιαῦτα ὄντα φυσικῶς ἅμα καὶ εὐστόχως ἐκ τῆς συγκρίσεως πάντων τὸ ἴδιον τῆς ποιότητος διαλαβεῖν' ['competent, in regard to all such things, to grasp, both from natural [indications] and by aiming well, the specific characteristic quality from the commixture of them all'].[58] This fits the definition of a stochastic art, especially in Stoic terms.

---

[57] Hephaestio, *Apotelesmaticorum libri tres*, III, 45.10–15, vol. 1, p. 315.10–19 Pingree. Regarding the aphorisms, here and in general: they show the *de facto* metaphorical status of planets in astrological interpretation. The attributes of the planet translate into an earthly equivalent (here Aphrodite = woman, Hermes = child and so on). Such passages are ubiquitous in astrological writing.

[58] Ptolemy, *Tetrabiblos* I, 2.10, pp. 8.133–9.135 Hübner.

And Ptolemy seems to acknowledge the importance of the unique situation ('the specific characteristic quality') and an accordingly unique interpretation.

Ptolemy goes on to give the arguments that we have seen laid out by Alexander of Aphrodisias in his differentiation between stochastic and productive arts:

- that the art itself is difficult to pin down precisely (astrology is many-sided and only able to be estimated: *polumerēs* [I, 2.12] and *eikastikos* [I, 2.15])
- that its practitioners are not skilled enough (I, 2.12–13)
- that heavenly configurations are scarcely repeated in exactly the same way, and so cannot lead to exact prediction (I, 2.15–16)
- that environmental factors are also causes (I, 2.17–19).

It is for these reasons, he says, that astrology should be considered in the same way that we consider navigation and medicine. And in this concluding paragraph of the chapter (I, 2.20), he says that these systems, which cannot be fully comprehended, still must be embraced as one embraces what can be understood of divine things; in addition, he uses words that recall archery: *diamartanomai*, entirely miss the mark (the word is used of spears missing their target) and *estochasmenōs*, hitting the mark: 'προσῆκον ἂν εἴη μήτε, ἐπειδὴ διαμαρτάνεσθαί ποτε τὴν τοιαύτην πρόγνωσιν ἐνδέχεται, καὶ τὸ πᾶν αὐτῆς ἀναιρεῖν ... μήτ' αὖ πάλιν πάντα ἡμῖν ἀνθρωπίνως καὶ ἐστοχασμένως αἰτεῖν παρ' αὐτῆς' ['it would not be fitting, although it is possible for such foreknowledge to miss the mark entirely, to do away with all of it ... nor, in turn, would it be fitting for us, as humans who aim but do not always hit the mark, to demand all things from it'].[59]

In a remarkable passage in Book III, 2, in the middle of a chapter on conception and birth, Ptolemy again uses strikingly Stoic terminology and applies the archery metaphor to the way astrology should be apprehended:

τὰς δὲ πραγματείας αὐτάς, δι' ὧν ἕκαστα τῶν εἰδῶν κατὰ τὸν ἐπιβλητικὸν τρόπον συνορᾶται, καὶ τὰς κατὰ τὸ ἰδιότροπον καὶ ὁλοσχερὲς τῶν ἀστέρων πρὸς ἕκαστα ποιητικὰς δυνάμεις, ὡς ἔνι μάλιστα, παρακολουθητικῶς τε ἅμα καὶ ἐπιτετμημένως κατὰ τὸν φυσικὸν στοχασμὸν ἐκθησόμεθα, τοὺς μὲν τοῦ περιέχοντος τόπους, πρὸς οὓς ἕκαστα θεωρεῖται τῶν ἀνθρωπίνων συμπτωμάτων (καθάπερ σκοπὸν οὗ δεῖ καταστοχάζεσθαι) προυποτιθέμενοι, τὰς δὲ τῶν τοῖς τόποις κατ' ἐπικράτησιν συνοικειουμένων σωμάτων ποιητικὰς δυνάμεις (ὥσπερ ἀφέσεις βελῶν) κατὰ τὸ ὁλοσχερέστερον ἐφαρμόζοντες, τὸ δὲ ἐκ τῆς συγκράσεως τῆς ἐκ πλειόνων φύσεων περὶ τὸ ὑποκείμενον εἶδος συναγόμενον ἀποτέλεσμα καταλιπόντες, (ὥσπερ εὐστόχῳ τοξότῃ) τῷ τοῦ διασκεπτομένου λογισμῷ·...

---

[59]   Ibid., p. 13.208–10, 213–14 Hübner. This is similar to Hephaestio's remarks at *Apotelesmaticorum libri tres*, I, Preface.7–8.

[We shall lay out the systematic treatments themselves, as much as possible, and at the same time both consciously and succinctly in accordance with natural conjecture, through which each of the forms is seen together in direct apprehension [i.e. intuition], and the productive powers according to the unique and general characteristics of the stars in relation to each. Preliminary to this we shall lay out the places of the surrounding [heavenly] atmosphere, in relation to which each of the human events is beheld (*just as if it were a target at which one must aim*), and adapting in a general way the productive powers for the places according to their predomination over bodies affiliated to them (just like *the releasing of arrows* [in a general direction]). But we shall leave the outcome reconciled from the commixture of many natures to the underlying form – just as to a *well–aiming archer* – to the calculation of the one who has thoroughly examined the situation.][60]

Here, using the archery metaphor, Ptolemy stresses the stochastic method, taking what can be apprehended in a general way from the physical world, and applying it with the intuition of the stochastic practitioner, who relies on skill and experience to make a correct judgement. The physical configurations of the stars are aligned to human events – the events are the target aimed at by the arrows of astrological technique – and the astrologer, the 'well-aiming archer', provides the skill to hit the target. It is worth remarking that the astrological 'arrows' that are 'released' – have a counterpart in an actual astrological technique called 'releasing', described by Ptolemy later in Book III. This may not be a coincidence.

By treating astrology as a stochastic art, Ptolemy aligns it with medicine and paradoxically helps to cement its trajectory as a proto-science.[61] Some 'stochastic' arts, like medicine and navigation, can become, through refinement of theory and innovation in technique, more like 'productive' arts such as carpentry, as their results become more consistent and replicable.[62] The productive arts, though,

---

[60] Ptolemy, *Tetrabiblos* III, 2.6, pp. 171.99–172.112 Hübner; my emphasis.

[61] I say paradoxically because there is a stochastic component in divination as well (as we saw in the quotation of Quintus Cicero above), but identifying a practice as stochastic historically appears to lead it in the opposite direction from divination, towards science.

[62] It seems that modern scholarship has, for the most part, been ready to follow in the footsteps of Ptolemy by forging a strong bond between the 'productive' function of astronomy and the 'stochastic' function of astrology. By focusing on the treatment of ancient astronomy and astrology as one discipline, modern scholars therefore emphasize it as an 'exact science' (see note 38 on exact science). This has been helpful in creating a respectable milieu for the study of ancient astrology, but along with that advantage, it has done a disservice to astrology in terms of what astrology actually is and what it can do.

are more like modern crafts, while it is the stochastic arts that contribute to the establishment of the modern sciences.[63]

But something stochastic, by its very nature, must involve a certain amount of conjecture, of aiming for but not always hitting, the target; must contain a bent towards metaphor that allows, even requires, spontaneous creativity. The interpretive component, and therefore the interpreter, is also essential. But there are two spurs towards the use of interpretation in stochastic arts, only one of which we have discussed so far. In the next part of this chapter, we turn from interpretation as a product of experience and judgement to another kind of creative interpretation using intuition, symbol and metaphor. This kind of interpretation arises from the association of the stochastic with the divinatory model: (divine) signs interpreted. It is an especially useful way to look at astrological practice. Our last example of stochastic components in astrological writings, Manilius' *Astronomica*, demonstrates this use of metaphor in astrological practice.

Stochastic Arts and Divination

Φέρε δὴ οὖν ἐπὶ τὸν διὰ τέχνης ἀνθρωπίνης ἐπιτελούμενον τρόπον μετέλθωμεν, ὅστις στοχασμοῦ καὶ οἰήσεως πλείονος εἴληχε. λέγεις δὲ καὶ περὶ τούτου τοιαῦτα· οἱ δὲ ἤδη καὶ διὰ σπλάγχνων καὶ δι' ὀρνίθων καὶ δι' ἀστέρων τέχνην συνεστήσαντο τῆς θήρας τοῦ μέλλοντος.

[Come then, let us turn to the mode of divination accomplished by human skill, which partakes largely of guessing and supposition. About this you say the following: 'some have already established a technique for pursuing the future by means of entrails, birds and stars.'][64]

Manilius, Archery and Metaphor

As a poet, Manilius makes metaphorical allusions for astrological interpretation. Wolfgang Hübner has pointed out, in his interesting article on tropical points of the

---

[63]   In antiquity, stochastic *technai* like medicine, navigation and agriculture are also considered to be *epistēmai*, 'kinds of knowledge' or 'sciences'; subsequently, in modern iterations these ancient practices have become sciences (in the way we understand science today). By contrast, shoemaking and weaving did not evolve into modern sciences. Even productive arts like sculpture or carpentry, while they can be clearly artistic, are not sciences.

[64]   Porphyry, *Lettera ad Anebo*, ed. A.R. Sodano (Naples: L'arte tipografica, 1958), II, 2g (= Iamblichus, *De mysteriis* III.15 [135]). Translation in Iamblichus, *On The Mysteries*, trans. and comm. Emma C. Clarke, John M. Dillon and Jackson P. Hershbell, *Writings from the Greco-Roman World* 4 (Atlanta: Society of Biblical Literature, 2003), p. 157.

zodiac and *paranatellonta* in Manilius,[65] that there is ample imagery and metaphor concerning the shooting of arrows, judgement, aiming and the practice of astrology in the Roman author's astrological poem. In Hübner's examples of correlations between the cardinal points and stars co–rising with them, we see that co-rising with the cardinal points (important points in astrological technique) are a number of stars and constellations that have to do with arrows and shooting. Moreover, Hübner suggests a connection between the 'stochastic' nature of archery and that of both medicine and astrology.[66]

The archery metaphor is thus as usefully applied to the practice of astrology as to the practice of Stoic ethics. I shall point out some of the intersections here between the 'stochastic' words used by Manilius and the references he makes to archery, archers and hunters, following Hübner's exegesis.

Archery and hunting images are particularly strong with the equinoctial signs, Aries and Libra. Julius Firmicus Maternus tells us (*Mathesis*, II, 10.3) that the very word 'Κριός' (Aries in Greek) is derived from κρίνειν, the Greek word which means 'judge' or 'discern', from which the Latin *cernere* is also derived. It also has a medical meaning, 'to come to a point of crisis' (from which the word 'crisis' itself comes; the medical *krisis* is the moment of judging the course of the disease).[67] Right away the first sign of the zodiac is associated with judging and discernment, exactly what an archer must do as she prepares to shoot; and what an astrologer must do as well. At about 10 degrees of Aries (roughly the sidereal vernal point when Manilius wrote), according to the poet, Orion the hunter co-rises, the first association with hunting to the tropical points.

Turning now to the sign opposite to Aries, Libra, Hübner reminds us[68] that its name arises from the verb 'librare', which means 'to balance'. It is used to describe the balancing of a missile like a spear or a javelin. Sagitta, the arrow, co-rises with the 8th degree of Libra[69] (again, close to the sidereal autumnal equinox), and Manilius recalls Aries by introducing it to us with the verb *cernere*: 'sed parte octava surgentem cerne Sagittam/Chelarum' (5.293–4). He goes on to mention hurling javelins and shooting arrows and missiles (5.294–7). As well as literally producing archers, Manilius adduces metaphorical associations for those born under these conditions with the triumph of Greece over Troy, as well as the parent who saves his child from harm by shooting an attacking serpent.

---

[65]   Wolfgang Hübner, 'The Tropical Points of the Zodiacal Year and the *Paranatellonta* in Manilius' *Astronomica', Culture and Cosmos* 11/1 and 2 (2007): 87–110. This paper was originally given at a workshop on ancient astrology held at the Warburg Institute, London in February 2007.

[66]   Ibid., p. 90: 'Archers used a "stochastic" art … this was applied – in a figurative sense – to the art of doctors and astrologers as well.'

[67]   Hübner (ibid.) also speaks of these associations.

[68]   Ibid., p. 89.

[69]   As Hübner notes (ibid.), according to Hipparchus the arrow actually rises with Sagittarius, but we shall continue with Manilius' metaphorical system here.

Here the Roman poet also mentions Teucer, the renowned archer from Homer, but in this astrological context one cannot help thinking also of Teucer of Babylon, the astrologer who, Hübner states, is a source for both Manilius and Firmicus.[70] Teucer the astrologer was known, among other things, for his writings on the co-risings of the fixed stars.[71] Teucer himself tells us that a constellation called the 'Three Shooting Heroes' (οἱ Τρεῖς Ἥρωες οἱ καὶ Βαλλισταί, *Tres Heroes qui vocantur Ballistae*) co-rises with 16–18 degrees of Libra.[72] Teucer explains that those born when the 16th degree is rising will be, among other things, physicians and astrologers![73] Thus the sign of the autumnal equinox contains more associations with arrows and shooting, including Manilius' metaphorical connection between the archer Teucer and the astrologer Teucer.

Note that when these hunting and arrow constellations co-rise with the equinoctial points, they are also approximately culminating and anti-culminating with respect to the solsticial points, and thus remain connected to all four cardinal signs. For instance, when Libra rises and Cancer culminates, we see the arrow, and then the three heroes, rising while Orion, the hunter, culminates.

Even these few examples demonstrate the direct application of metaphorical technique to the interpretation of astrological patterns, even including the particular metaphor of the arrow aiming at the target as a metaphor for astrology itself. With his use of the archery metaphor, Manilius thus emphasizes the stochastic nature of astrology as an art of aiming. Let us now turn to the idea of metaphor itself as a component of interpretation, for divination in general and astrology in particular.

Metaphor, Aiming and Divination

The way Manilius uses metaphor leads us to ask: Is metaphor a medium through which astrology can – even must – work? We normally associate metaphor with poetry and creative prose, but the way in which metaphor is created may say

---

[70]   Ibid., p. 91.

[71]   These can be found, excerpted by Rhetorius, in *Catalogus Codicum Astrologorum Graecorum* [hereafter *CCAG*], vol. VII, ed. Franz Boll (Brussels: Henri Lamertin, 1908), pp. 192–213; see also the *Liber Hermetis*, ch. 25, in Simonetta Feraboli (ed.), *Hermetis Trismegisti: De triginta sex decanis*, Hermes Latinus IV/1 (Corpus Christianorum) (Turnhout, Belgium: Brepols, 1994).

[72]   As cited in Hübner, 'Tropical Points', p. 92 and n. 21; see also *CCAG* VII, p. 204.14, 'οἱ λεγόμενοι Βαλλισταί' 'the so-called shooters'. The Latin version is in Feraboli, *Hermetis Trismegisti*, ch. 25.17, p. 111.40–42. An English translation can be found in *Liber Hermetis*, trans. Robert Zoller (Salisbury, Queensland: Spica, 1998), ch. 25, 'On the Fixed Stars and Degrees of Libra', p. 37.

[73]   Feraboli, *Hermetis Trismegisti*, ch. 25.18, p. 111.44–45; *Liber Hermetis* (Zoller), ch. 25, p. 37. Has Teucer thus made an oblique connection between medicine and astrology as stochastic arts?

something about the way we practise astrology. Interpreters of divinatory signs and and interpreters of poetry were functionally linked by Cicero in *De divinatione* I, xviii.34 (end): 'Quorum omnium interpretes, ut grammatici poetarum, proxime ad eorum quos interpretantur divinationem videntur accedere' ['The interpreters of all these signs, like the commentators who are interpreters of the poets, seem to come very near to the divine foresight of the gods whose wills they interpret'].[74]

Metaphor is already at work in the way that omens are interpreted, using physical-world events (such as the burning of a temple) or actions in dreams (a statue running blood) to predict events in the future (in these cases, the conquest of Asia by Alexander and the cruelty of Phalaris).[75] In astrology, the interpretation of celestial appearances shows evidence of a metaphorical outlook as well.[76] Though Aristotle does not endorse the use of metaphor or metaphorical expressions in all cases,[77] he does find it useful in philosophy, where someone who hits the mark (εὔστοχυς) can realize the similarity between things that are apart.[78] It is equally valid in poetry, he says, where the poet's skill can be measured by his use of metaphor and his ability to find resemblances between things dissimilar on their face.[79]

Through metaphor in poetry, the artist strives to make the topic of her poem more meaningful by a specific form of analogy that melds two things. The image is carried from one thing to another; the literal meaning of metaphor is to carry across, transfer or translate. Metaphor does not use the comparison of simile (something is *like* something else); it makes a transference which brings two things together into one thing (Aristotle defines the difference between simile and metaphor in *Rhetoric* III, 1406b20, using the Homeric simile 'Achilles springs like a lion' and making the metaphor of Achilles called 'the lion [who] springs').[80]

---

[74] Trans. (slightly modified) Peter Struck, The Birth of the Symbol: Ancient Readers at the Limits of Their Texts (Princeton and Oxford: Princeton University Press, 2004), p. 169.

[75] These descriptions appear in *De divinatione* I. xxiii.

[76] As with other kinds of omens, the correlation between astrological and terrestrial circumstances can be almost literal in nature, and can also be coupled with mythological symbolism. The way in which astrological components are aligned symbolically with terrestrial concerns (for example Sun = king, Saturn = old man, Mercury = child or thief) encourages this metaphorical approach. (For the *de facto* metaphor in astrology, see the section above on Hephaistio and n. 57.)

[77] For instance, he says 'one should not use metaphors or metaphorical expressions in definitions' in *Posterior Analytics* 97b37–8, quoted in G.E.R. Lloyd, *The Revolutions of Wisdom: Studies in the Claims and Practice of Ancient Greek Science* (Berkeley: University of California Press, 1987), p. 185.

[78] *Rhet.* III, 1412a11 ff., quoted in Lloyd, *Revolutions of Wisdom*, p. 185, n. 47.

[79] See Aristotle, *Poetics* 1459a5 ff. as cited in Lloyd, *Revolutions of Wisdom*, p. 185 and n. 47.

[80] See the discussion of metaphor and simile in Aristotle in Paul Ricoeur, *The Rule of Metaphor*, trans. Robert Czerny, with Kathleen McLaughlin and John Costello, S.J. (Toronto, Buffalo and London: University of Toronto Press, 1977, repr. 2008), pp. 24–7; see also Patrick Curry's discussion of Ricoeur and metaphor in Chapter 7 of this volume.

The French scholar Jackie Pigeaud has examined this concept of metaphor,[81] and here I shall explore some of his arguments in relation to what they can tell us about astrology. First, he makes some intriguing connections between metaphor and familiarity (*oikeiōsis*): whether a sign of a good metaphor is that it shows a real familiar likeness between the objects linked by it:

> Metaphor therefore actualises a landscape with two objects, and a spectator who observes, judges, appreciates whether the similar is really similar; who acknowledges whether, finally, there is a real family likeness (Greek: *oikeiôsis*), between the objects that metaphor links together. The spectator may be the author of the metaphor himself, or the reader. We may even think that there are, so to speak, quiet metaphors, waiting eternally for somebody to wake them up, for his own pleasure.[82]

For 'author and reader' we substitute, in our iteration, 'astrologer and client'. The 'quiet metaphor' of the last sentence evokes the idea of the symbolism lying quiescent in the chart until the questions posed by the client or astrologer bring its metaphorical power into consciousness.[83] It takes both the astrologer, working with astrological symbolism, and the client, whose life it is, to see the appropriateness of the metaphor. The concept of *oikeiōsis* Pigeaud mentions can correlate to the way astrology generally works by finding familiarity between a terrestrial event and a heavenly pattern. More specifically, the concept of familiarity extends to astrological technique: the coordinated system of relationships between planets and zodiac signs is even called *oikeiōsis* by Ptolemy.[84]

Familiarity is an important component of metaphor, but so is the idea of conveying together two things that may be literally or figuratively distant from one another (Ricoeur reminds us that 'to transfer is to ap-proximate, to suppress distance').[85] Pigeaud also brings up the power of a good metaphor to connect two things that one might normally see as remote from each other.[86] In doing so, he

---

[81]   Using Aristotle's *Poetics* and *On Divination through Dreams*; see Jackie Pigeaud, '"To Shape into One": Aristotle's Poetics and the Poet as Melancholic' (Public Lecture, Warburg Institute, London, 10 May 2006). I am using a transcript of this lecture. I thank Professor Pigeaud for permission to quote his work.

[82]   Ibid., pp. 9–10.

[83]   See Dorian Gieseler Greenbaum, 'Rising to the Occasion: Appearance, Emergence, Light and Divination in Hellenistic Astrology', in Angela Voss and Jean Hinson Lall (eds), *The Imaginal Cosmos: Astrology, Divination and the Sacred* (Canterbury: University of Kent, 2007), pp. 9–24, esp. p. 20.

[84]   See *Tetrabiblos* I, 12–23.

[85]   Ricoeur, *Rule of Metaphor*, p. 194.

[86]   Pigeaud, '"To Shape into One"', p. 11. See also the discussion in Ricoeur, *Rule of Metaphor*, pp. 194–5.

analyses a passage from Aristotle's *On Divination through Dreams* (464a–b), which again utilizes the archer analogy:

οἱ δὲ μελαγχολικοὶ διὰ τὸ σφοδρόν, ὥσπερ βάλλοντες πόρρωθεν, εὔστοχοί εἰσιν, καὶ διὰ τὸ μετα- (464b) βλητικὸν ταχὺ τὸ ἐχόμενον φαντάζεται αὐτοῖς· ὥσπερ γὰρ τὰ Φιλαινίδος ποιήματα καὶ οἱ ἐμμανεῖς ἐχόμενα τοῦ ὁμοίου λέγουσι καὶ διανοοῦνται, οἷον Ἀφροδίτην φροδίτην, καὶ οὕτω συνείρουσιν εἰς τὸ πρόσω. ἔτι δὲ διὰ τὴν σφοδρότητα οὐκ ἐκκρούεται αὐτῶν ἡ κίνησις ὑφ' ἑτέρας κινήσεως.

[Melancholics, because of their intensity, as those who shoot from afar, are those who make good shots. And because of their ability to change quickly, the contiguous appears to them; for just as the poems of Philaigides and the insane say and have the contiguous of the similar in mind, such as Aphrodite (phrodite), so they go on stringing things together. And moreover, because of their intensity, their movement is not distracted by another movement.][87]

Pigeaud points out the ability of the good metaphorist to be unaffected by distance, or even by aiming[88] (is aiming, in fact, a distraction?). He particularly notices that the mark itself is not even mentioned in this passage, from which he makes this brilliant observation: 'It is necessary to think that this mark exists; but it is only revealed as soon as the arrow hits it, and, hitting it, reveals it as a mark, as *the* mark. We must even say: *as the good mark.*'[89]

There are two important points here: the immateriality of distance to accurate shooting, and the revelation of a mark only when it is hit. The poet, like the melancholic, has the ability to change so quickly, and to move without being distracted, that she can make metaphorical connections without regard to space or time. The metaphor revealing a mark that wasn't even seen shows the poetic genius.[90] We can apply these concepts to divination in general and astrology in

---

[87] Aristotle, On Divination through Dreams, 464a–b. My translation partially following Pigeaud, '"To Shape into One"', p. 12. My main difference with Pigeaud here is that he translates the Greek *sphodros* as 'strength', whereas I follow Philip van der Eijk's translation of *sphodrotēs* as 'intensity' (see Philip van der Eijk, 'Aristotle on Melancholy', *Medicine and Philosophy in Classical Antiquity: Doctors and Philosophers on Nature, Soul, Health and Disease* (Cambridge: Cambridge University Press, 2005), pp. 139–68, at p. 144). We should remember that (the Aristotelian, but probably not by Aristotle) *Problems XXX, 1* says that poets are melancholic (van der Eijk discusses this treatise, including its authorship, in the article just cited). I thank Peter Pormann for alerting me to van der Eijk's work.

[88] Pigeaud, '"To Shape into One"', p. 13.

[89] Ibid., p. 12; emphasis in original. See also his analysis on p. 14.

[90] Pigeaud (ibid., p. 17) reminds us of Schopenhauer's remark, 'Talent is the shooter who hits a mark that other people cannot hit; genius is the shooter who hits a mark that other

particular, and to the ability of the astrologer to make 'hits' even when she does not know that this will happen. We are drawn back to the idea of aiming without aiming which we discussed earlier in this chapter, to the ability to make the hit only when we are not focused on making the hit.

Pigeaud sees this as bound up with the ability to move quickly and, with that ability, to see an image that makes contiguous two things that may not be, two things that are sequent but not consequent.[91] The poet and the diviner/astrologer are themselves the change that creates the metaphor. Put another way, the poet is the link between the two things that create the metaphor. Because of her ability to move quickly, to be 'metabletic', able to be transported,[92] she is able to transport (*metaphorein*). In this, time and space are both immaterial; the poet (and diviner/astrologer) is able to put contiguous and similar instantly together, no matter what their actual (chronological or spatial) distance. They grasp the future in an image linked with the present. Pigeaud quotes the modern poet Torquato Tasso, who comments on this Aristotelian passage: ' I have grasped the quarry before I have got the beast in my hands; and it seems to me that I anticipate, from a long distance, the similar and the consequent; and by dint of making images and dreams ... in the way of an archer who shoots all day long, perhaps I shall hit the mark of my thoughts.'[93]

Conclusions

We have covered a lot of ground in this chapter. We have introduced the idea of astrology as a stochastic art, and given some of the history of the concept of stochastic arts in antiquity. We have defined the word 'stochastic' and the connection of stochastic arts with targets and goals. We have talked about stochastic arts versus productive arts, and outlined some of the arts most commonly referred to as stochastic, namely medicine, navigation and rhetoric. We have speculated on what astrological targets and goals might be. We have looked at astrology in relation to the aims of productive and stochastic arts to see where it falls along that continuum. We have looked at the writings of the Hellenistic astrologers for evidence of stochastic methods. Finally, we have examined metaphor and its connection with aiming and divination, particularly in regard to astrology. Throughout, our connecting thread has been the metaphor of the archer, which has kept appearing in each of the areas we have explored.

The stochastic concept, the art of conjecturing through signs, has its first associations with divination, as Quintus Cicero tells us. But with Ptolemy and those who follow him, the stochastic seems to lead to science, and it is that association which becomes firmly cemented in the scientific model. It has been

---

people cannot even see.'
   [91]   Ibid., p. 14.
   [92]   I am following Pigeaud's argument here, ibid., pp. 14–17.
   [93]   Ibid., pp. 16–17.

the aim of this chapter, however, to show that it is useful, even necessary, to think of the stochastic in astrology as harking back not only to ancient science (and leading to modern science), but also to its association with divination and the aleatory function. From this association with the symbolic and metaphorical in divination, we find new ways of looking at astrology as an art that uses metaphor and symbolism in its own interpretations.

Euripides said that 'the best diviner is the one who guesses well' ('μάντις δ᾽ ἄριστος ὅστις εἰκάζει καλῶς').[94] Here, the word 'guess' is *eikazō*: approximate, estimate, literally 'make like'; this is the word Ptolemy uses to describe astrology, and which fits the definition of a stochastic art. Our examination of metaphor shows the importance of likeness and similarity; in astrology we find the concept of *oikeiōsis* linking astrological components. All of these aid in our 'guessing'.

Yet there are additional qualifications that improve the 'guessing'. As Plutarch tells us in *De defectu oraculorum* (432c–d), the best of seers is the one who guesses well because he is intelligent, and also able to receive 'impressions and presentiments' ('φαντασιῶν ... καὶ προαισθήσεων'), and 'inconsequently grasps at the future when it is farthest withdrawn from the present' ('ἀσυλλογίστως ἅπτεται τοῦ μέλλοντος, ὅταν ἐκστῇ μάλιστα τοῦ παρόντος') – able to do this, Plutarch says, by having an ability 'by temperament and disposition' to 'change (*metabolē*), which we call inspiration' (*enthousiasmos*) ('ἐξίσταται δὲ κράσει καὶ διαθέσει τοῦ σώματος ἐν μεταβολῇ γιγνομένου, ἣν ἐνθουσιασμὸν καλοῦμεν').[95] This is akin to the ability of the creator of metaphor, who herself, as 'metabletic', becomes the link between two things. This is the astrologer as well who, as the prophet-interpreter of the heavenly pattern, links heaven and earth and brings them into contact by his own 'move' of interpretation.

---

[94] Euripides, fr. 973 Nauck, quoted in Plutarch, *De defectu oraculorum*, trans. Frank Cole Babbitt, in *Moralia*, vol. V (Cambridge, MA: Harvard University Press, 1936, repr. 2003), 432c; also quoted and discussed in Plutarch, *De Pythiae oraculis*, trans. Frank Cole Babbitt, in *Moralia*, vol. V (Cambridge, MA: Cambridge University Press, 1936, repr. 2003), 399a; see also Cicero, *De divinatione* II, 4.12.

[95] *De def.* 432d, trans. Frank Cole Babbitt, in Plutarch, *Moralia* V, p. 469. 'φαντασιῶν ... καὶ προαισθήσεων, ἀσυλλογίστως ἅπτεται τοῦ μέλλοντος, ὅταν ἐκστῇ μάλιστα τοῦ παρόντος. ἐξίσταται δὲ κράσει καὶ διαθέσει τοῦ σώματος ἐν μεταβολῇ γιγνομένου, ἣν ἐνθουσιασμὸν καλοῦμεν.' Note that *metabolē* is a variation on the same word (*metablētikos*) that Pigeaud considered important for the poet.

Chapter 11
Life between Lives Therapy:
A Mystery Ritual for Modern Times?

Angela Voss

When you are about to die ... [The guardians of Hades] will surely ask you ... for what reason you seek out the darkness of dank Hades. Say 'I am the child of Earth and of starry Sky, and I am parched with thirst and I am perishing. But give me quickly cold water to drink from the lake of Memory'. And above all, they will announce you to the king under the earth. And above all, they will give you to drink from the lake of Memory. And what is more, when you have drunk, you will travel a road, a sacred road, which other famous *mystai* and *bakchoi* also tread.[1]

Prelude

The theme of this chapter arose through a strange coincidence and a dream, which I shall briefly relate. Some time ago a friend introduced me to the work of Michael Newton, and I spent a session with my MA students[2] discussing the question of regression therapy and spiritual encounter in relation to Hermetic texts and the *mundus imaginalis* of Henry Corbin. Shortly after this, I received an email, quite out of the blue, from Michael Newton himself. He was looking for a university department where he could develop his client work into a doctoral thesis, and this initiated a flow of personal communication on the subject of life between lives (LBL) therapy. It was also during this time that I had a dream of particular relevance: I was walking through the medieval streets of Canterbury, which metamorphosed into the skyscrapers of New York. I saw the twin towers of the World Trade Center on fire and, as I watched, people were jumping from the towers. I focused in on one young woman who was falling, and noticed with surprise that she was very happy; indeed, when she hit the ground, she did not die, but simply got up, dusted

---

[1]   Orphic Gold tablet from Hipponion, fifth–fourth century BCE, quoted in Susan G. Cole, 'Landscapes of Dionysos and Elysian Fields', in Michael Cosmopoulos (ed.), *Greek Mysteries: The Archaeology and Ritual of Ancient Greek Secret Cults* (London: Routledge, 2003), pp. 193–217, at p. 200. *Mystai* and *bakchoi* were initiates into the mysteries of Eleusis and Dionysus respectively (see Cole, 'Landscapes of Dionysos', p. 201).

[2]   MA in the Cultural Study of Cosmology and Divination, University of Kent, Canterbury.

herself down and went on her way with a smile. I walked back into Canterbury, carrying a precious bundle which was at first a cat, then turned into my son as a young baby. I knew I must not put it down, for it couldn't yet walk, but that I must carry it safely back to the university.

I am not going to interpret this dream, but simply let it serve as an introduction, for in relation to the encounter with Michael Newton it indicated to me that it was time to venture into a new area of research – one that would require careful handling, for the territory it maps poses many challenges to both conventional academic methodology and our prevalent materialist view of reality.

Life between Lives Therapy

Michael Newton uses the term 'spiritual regressionist' to describe his vocation.[3] A doctor of psychology, he has worked in counselling and hypnotherapy for over forty years, during which time he has developed a technique of leading clients to remember not only their previous lives, but an existence purportedly in between lives, where they learn about the mistakes and achievements of their former incarnations and prepare for their next journey to the earth plane. Through assimilating information from thousands of case studies, Newton has compiled a detailed picture (which is remarkably consistent) of the interaction between souls that have left their bodies and the spiritual beings they meet, who guide and advise them and above all reveal to them the nature of the spiritual world.[4] The unanimous realization of his clients is that this place is their true home, and that their earthly lives are training periods during which they work towards eventual release from the cycle of birth and death. Most importantly, they gain a sense of their soul's immortality and appear to undergo a healing or resolution of karmic issues when they return to 'normal' life.[5]

---

[3]   Michael Newton, *Journey of Souls: Case Studies of Life between Lives* (St Paul, MN: Llewellyn, 1994), p. 256.

[4]   In Newton, *Journey*, and *Destiny of Souls: New Case Studies of Life between Lives* (St Paul, MN: Llewellyn, 2006).

[5]   Of course this is not the only contemporary source of such accounts. There is a vast amount of literature on otherworld or shamanic journeys, near-death experiences (NDEs) and out-of-body experiences (OBEs) in the fields of psychical research, parapsychology, history and anthropology which provides a broadly consistent picture (however it may be interpreted) of individuals' revelations in what they understand to be the afterlife, and their sense of well-being on return to normality. A selection of such texts includes Theodore Flournoy, *Spiritism and Psychology*, trans. Hereward Carrington (New York: Harper & Bros, 1911); G. Murphy and R. Ballou (eds), *William James on Psychical Research* (New York: Viking, 1960); Frederic Myers, *Human Personality and Its Survival of Bodily Death* (London: Longmans, Green, 1920). More recent enquiries into afterlife experiences include David Fontana, *Is There an Afterlife? A Comprehensive Overview of the Evidence* (Ropley, Hampshire: O-Books, 2005); *Life beyond Death: What Should We Expect?* (London: Watkins,

When I first encountered this work, I was immediately struck by two things: firstly, the thoroughness and detail of Michael Newton's analysis of these 'divinatory dialogues' and secondly, the significant parallels between the experiences of his clients and those of the participants in mystery rituals in the ancient world, who were led over the threshold of death while fully alive, returning with a knowledge that set them apart from the uninitiated. In this chapter I am not setting out to 'prove' an infallible, objective and universal 'truth' regarding the afterlife and the destiny of souls, but I do want to look closely at the phenomenon of spiritual revelation – and the question of initiation – in relation to the 'verity' of the experience for the individuals involved. Can we indeed view Michael Newton's work as a contemporary means of initiation, giving access to the hidden realms of being formerly identified as Hades or Paradise, in the guise of new-age therapy?[6]

In our secular age, LBL presents an anomaly. It appears to be a psychological technique, yet induces profoundly religious experiences. It requires no particular

---

2009); Raymond Moody, *Life after Life: The Investigation of a Phenomenon – Survival of Bodily Death* (San Francisco: Rider, 2001); Carol Zaleski, *Otherworld Journeys: Accounts of Near-Death Experience in Medieval and Modern Times* (Oxford: Oxford University Press, 1987). From a phenomenological perspective, many elements of these accounts are also corroborated by 'channelled' communicators in their descriptions of the topographies of the spiritual world and the nature of the intelligences that inhabit it. Of these, the most striking must be the 'Seth' communications to Jane Roberts in the 1960s and 1970s (eg. Jane Roberts, *The Nature of the Psyche* (New York: Prentice Hall, 1979); see also http://www.sethcenter.com/pages/bookstore.htm), the *Awakening Letters* of Cynthia Sandys and Rosamond Lehmann (vol. 1, Jersey: Neville Spearman, 1978; vol. 2, Saffron Walden: C.W. Daniel, 1986) and Grant and Jane Soloman, *The Scole Experiment: Scientific Evidence for Life after Death* (London: Piatkus, 1999). It is not the purpose of this chapter to critique the 'mechanics' of these experiences, as I believe this would detract from the question of their 'truth' for the participant. I agree with Carole Zaleski, who states that 'there is no sensory, imaginative, or intellectual form capable of fully expressing the transcendent ... such understanding as we do receive of the transcendent comes to us through symbols, and it is through symbols that we communicate this understanding to one another' (*Otherworld Journeys*, p. 191).

[6] The association of the terms 'subconscious' and 'superconscious' with the 'underworld' and 'upperworld' realms of Hades and Paradise is easy to make, as is the association of the umbrella term 'unconscious', in the Jungian sense, with the entire visionary realm. I will, however, avoid a definition of these terms in relation to visionary experience, preferring to regard both Hades and Paradise as expressions of different stages of the soul's development after death (see Fontana, *Is There an Afterlife?*, chs 6 and 7, on the seven planes of after death existence in the Western esoteric tradition). We could suggest that 'Hades' in ancient literature tends to be echoed in what contemporary researchers call the 'etheric' realm, while 'Paradise' corresponds more fully with the less material plane of the 'astral' body and beyond (these terms being founded in the Western esoteric tradition and taken up by the theosophical and anthroposophical schools at the beginning of the last century). But perhaps they could both be more accurately described as 'through-worlds' which lie beyond yet simultaneously within this one.

belief or ritual practice, yet leads individuals to understand the meaning of immortality – while sitting calmly in the therapist's office. It is available to all who are prepared to pay for it, with little or no preparation, and it undoubtedly changes people's lives profoundly. As one client reports:

> I have gained an indescribable sense of joy and freedom from learning my true identity. The amazing thing is that this knowledge was in my mind all the time. I now have a knowing rather than a feeling about why I am here and where I am going after death.[7]

These words could easily have been uttered by a new initiate at Eleusis.

Let us now look in some detail at the LBL therapist's techniques and the visionary experiences described by his or her clients, before we draw comparisons to ancient practices and address the question of initiation. Michael Newton sees his role as Hermetic, with the task of leading souls to another world, although he insists that he is not 'a religious person'.[8] He says 'I feel truly blessed to be chosen as one of the messengers for this significant work.'[9] It should be noted that the training for LBL practitioners is extensive – hypnotherapy and counselling training followed by several years of past-life regression experience before they are considered skilled enough to undertake this specialized vocation. Furthermore, 'the hypnosis facilitator should be well versed in the field of metaphysics in order to be able to analyze the karmic influences in the client's existence from both a psychological and historical perspective'.[10]

Such a skill would require a spiritual maturity surely beyond the remit of most training programmes in therapeutic techniques, and would seem more akin to that of a spiritual director. Under hypnosis, the client is engaged in a dialogue designed to lead them back through their memories in the manner of visualizations, while their conscious mind is still alert. Dr Newton describes the process thus:

> I use a systematic approach to reach the soul by employing a series of exercises for people in the early stages of hypnotic regression. This procedure is designed to gradually sharpen my subject's memories of their past and prepare them to analyze critically the things they will see in the spirit world.[11]

(Note the phrase 'analyze critically' – to which we will return later.)

---

[7]   Newton, *Destiny*, p. 10.

[8]   Ibid., p. 5.

[9]   Ibid., p. xiv.

[10]   Newton, *Life Between Lives: Hypnotherapy for Spiritual Regression* (St Paul, MN: Llewellyn, 2004), p. xiii.

[11]   Newton, *Destiny*, p. 3.

The secret to taking them so far is, he stresses, 'the deepening' of the hypnotic trance from alpha to theta stages.[12] From there, clients report what they see as 'literal observations'.[13] They often undergo a death-experience, which can be disturbing or even traumatic, and then find themselves liberated as disembodied souls, able to see clearly into both the earthly realm they have just left and the spiritual one they are about to enter.

Central to both the mystery rites and the LBL experience is the vision of and/or communication with spiritual beings, in a place that is beyond the earth yet shares some of its characteristics. In both cases it is described in terms of an enhanced reality, full of light, beauty and tranquillity. Topographically, clients describe the spirit world as a huge tier of shaded sections or layers, 'they curve away from me as I float through them' says one.[14] Some see light and dark coloured sections, some hear sounds akin to wind chimes, vibrations, bells or strings, or humming or buzzing sounds.[15] They may use the imagery of radio frequencies or vibrations, but common to all is the sense that successions of astral planes are experienced as diminishing in density the further the soul moves away from the earth, until they merge with the immateriality of spiritual planes. Subjects describe travelling through the arms of a 'galactic cloud' to a place of pure thought, carried along as if on a current, to the place where they belong, and where they meet their group of kindred souls. One describes being inside a 'giant bowl' or upside down sphere. There is never any suggestion that this is a place of punishment or even

---

[12]   See ibid. and Newton, *Life Between Lives*, part 3, 'Beginning the LBL Hypnosis Session'. The alpha state is the state of light trance induced by total physical and mental relaxation. The theta state is recognized as one of deeper tranquillity where images such as daydreams are consciously experienced (normal waking consciousness is the 'beta' state, whereas 'delta' designates deeply unconscious states).

[13]   Newton, *Destiny*, p. 4. One should be suspicious of the term 'literal' here. The client is reporting an 'inner' visionary journey that is taking place in a reality removed from ordinary sense-perception. It is perhaps akin to the *mundus imaginalis* described by Henry Corbin, a place of revelatory vision and theophany, perceived through the active imagination (see Corbin, *Mundus Imaginalis or the Imaginal and the Imaginary* (Ipswich: Golgonooza Press, 1976)). To be communicable, in LBL such experiences are expressed through a common language and familiar conceptual framework which appear to have a literal or 'objective' dimension. However, although such discourse informs the reader, it is of a different order from the symbolic power of music, poetry or art to directly evoke a realm beyond rational apprehension. Carole Zaleski suggests that the desire to establish objective accuracy in terms of afterlife experiences is misplaced, and that 'it might ... be more fruitful for theologians to consider near-death visions as works of religious imagination, whose function is to communicate meaning through symbolic forms rather than to copy external facts' (*Otherworld Journeys*, p. 187).

[14]   Newton, *Journey*, pp. 20–22. Cf., for example, Plato, *Republic*, 616d.

[15]   On the sounds heard by initiates in ancient rituals, see Peter Kingsley, *In the Dark Places of Wisdom* (Inverness, CA: Golden Sufi Center, 1999), pp. 129–33, referring to references in Plutarch, *Moralia*, 590-b-d and Iamblichus, *De mysteriis* 3.2.

purgatory; rather it is a place of healing and reunion – although there are places of solitary contemplation for those who have seriously erred.[16] The descriptions certainly recall the common motifs in ancient literature of post-mortem journeys up through the planetary spheres to the stars,[17] and of hearing planetary harmonies or whistling sounds.[18] One of the most interesting aspects of the LBL clients' accounts is their common understanding that the spiritual world is strictly hierarchical in the developmental sense, in a similar way to the hypostases of Neoplatonic and Gnostic cosmology. The metaphor is given of souls being like threads woven into a fabric, or as passengers on a train, some nearer the front than others, meaning that some are nearer the point of freedom from the wheel of rebirth than others.[19] Spirit guides are differentiated through their levels of experience and expertise, exhibiting differently coloured auras according to their rank and tasks. Michael Newton concludes that 'the entire ladder serves as one unbroken conduit to the source of all intelligent energy'.[20] What this 'source' might be I will consider below. It would also appear that 'the awareness level of the soul determines to some extent the degree of advancement of the guide assigned to them',[21] which evokes the Platonic notion of *sympatheia* between human and divine worlds, and reminds us of Plotinus' seance at the Iseum, where his individual 'genius' was revealed to be a god, and not a common or garden *daimon*.[22]

Despite the 'secular' context, the clients use common religious terminology. They speak of souls, guardian angels and heaven, and use various terms to denote a further source of power which they sense to be the generator of the whole process, such as the Source, the Over-Soul or the Presence. This unknowable essence is

---

[16] Newton, *Journey,* p. 58. Unlike ancient and medieval after-death accounts, contemporary accounts generally do not refer to hell or severe punishments. No doubt, to a certain extent, individual experiences are coloured by the collective expectations and convictions of the age as well as the context of the vision (see Fontana, *Is There an Afterlife?*, pp. 97–102). On medieval return-from-death stories, see Zaleski, *Otherworld Journeys*, chs 3–5.

[17] For example, *Corpus Hermeticum*, Book 1; 'The Myth of Er' in Plato, *Republic*, Book X; Cicero, 'The Dream of Scipio', *De re publica*, Book 6. See also Macrobius, *Commentary on the Dream of Scipio*, trans. William Harris Stahl (New York; Columbia University Press, 1952).

[18] As in Plato, 'Myth of Er', *Republic* 617b. One should also note various accounts by 'communicators' who describe travelling through the etheric solar system and recognizing different planets as power-points of cosmic energy, all of which sustain different forms of spiritual life. See for example *Corpus Hermeticum*, I; trans. Brian Copenhaver, *Hermetica* (Cambridge: Cambridge University Press, 1992), pp. 1–7; Sandys and Lehmann, *Awakening Letters*, vol. 2, pp. 5–8, 45.

[19] Newton, *Journey*, p. 167.

[20] Ibid., p. 120.

[21] Ibid., p. 107.

[22] Recounted in Porphyry, *Life of Plotinus*, 10; trans. A.H. Armstrong, *Plotinus*, I (Cambridge, MA: Loeb Classical Library, 1989), pp. 33–5.

beyond direct perception, yet it is glimpsed in what is the most important episode of most clients' sessions, the meeting with the Council of Elders.[23] Elders are understood to be higher spiritual beings before whom individual souls appear after incarnation and before rebirth – Michael Newton describes them as 'mythological figures who have cosmological functions as mediators'.[24] These functions include assessment and review rather than judgement. Before the Elders, souls relive the life just left and are pointed towards their faults and wrong choices, as well as praised for their good deeds and the choices that furthered the working out of karmic issues. At this divinatory encounter, the soul is questioned and in turn may question the Elders on matters such as intractable issues in this present lifetime, in order to gain advice and encouragement – there seems to be a sense in which the Elders want to ensure that souls understand the consequences of their actions and will not repeat the same mistakes. They are visualized by clients as elderly men (although occasionally there is a woman), bald, white-haired, bearded, in hoods and robes, although more advanced souls may experience them as androgynous, or as bodies of light energy in human shape. Michael Newton points out that in the interpretation of these inner visions, clients can only feedback information through their inbuilt cultural ideas and stereotypes, so here we find the *senex* or Saturnine archetype of the wise old man, revered and venerated, compassionate and wise.

One characteristic of these advanced spirits is that they wear medallions with emblems or signs on them which have particular relevance for the soul they are questioning, usually to instil in them a specific quality such as valour or independence. The showing of this symbol is often the key to the soul's healing process, and the clients usually want to create a similar medallion to remind them of this in everyday life. It is also at this meeting that souls choose their own next incarnation in order to work on unresolved karmic issues, and it has a profound and lasting effect. 'When I leave them, I feel they have absorbed all my self doubt and cleansed me' says one, and another came away with a sense of 'awe, penitence and the need for atonement'.[25] It is also at this point that there is awareness of a higher Source that exists to help the work of the Council, together with a sense (in more advanced subjects) that the purpose of all incarnations is to eventually merge back with it.[26] One client calls it a 'Oneness', composed of 'many who are one'; another, when asked who created her, replied 'the One'.[27] It should be stressed again that these observations remain consistent, without the clients having any former knowledge of or interest in philosophical traditions Platonic or otherwise, or any particular religious affiliation. Interestingly, they never report meeting religious figures such as Jesus or Buddha, unlike ancient mystery visions which

---

[23]   See Newton, *Destiny,* ch. 6.
[24]   Ibid., p. 250.
[25]   Ibid., pp. 239 and 253.
[26]   Ibid., p. 243.
[27]   Ibid., p. 126.

depended on specific mythologies for their context and drama, in which the spirit apparitions might be identified as Demeter, Persephone or Dionysus.[28]

What about the souls themselves? They are variously described as 'blobs of energy',[29] 'half-formed human shapes', 'transparent', 'myriads of sharp star lights',[30] 'patches of light bobbing around'[31] or 'bunches of moving lights'.[32] They 'buzz around as fireflies',[33] radiating different colours ranging from bright yellow to dark purple. Souls are allocated to specific groups based on 'levels of understanding'.[34] It appears that 'as souls, the density, colour and form of light we radiate is proportional to the power of our knowledge and perception as represented by increasing concentration of light matter as we develop'.[35] It is also stressed by the observers that when a soul incarnates, part of its spiritual essence remains in the spirit world, so that under hypnosis an individual may meet the soul of a friend or relative, even though that person is still alive. It also means that after death they unite with their own 'higher self' and become whole, reconnecting with their essence and spiritual source, although this may take a considerable amount of further work 'on the other side'.[36] They also meet and merge with loved ones who are true 'soul mates'; souls with whom they work in various ways over many lifetimes. The fact that souls may be in two places at once, dividing and leaving

---

[28]   The question of auto-suggestion on the part of Michael Newton cannot be avoided here. There is no evidence from other channelled accounts of after-death experience that all disembodied souls meet a Council of Elders shortly after death. It would seem that such common factors as life-review, soul-mate encounters and telepathic communication are expressed through a variety of images which may derive in part from the individual's cultural expectations and in part from the common language established by the particular therapist or guide. Fontana writes 'we must suppose that there is an objective coherent potential "out there" which is the same for all, but which is in some ways sensitive to the wishes and expectations of the individual who can – within certain limits – create a personal illusory reality within it which others can see and share' (*Life beyond Death*, p. 107).

[29]   Newton, *Journey*, p. 31.

[30]   Ibid., p. 72.

[31]   Ibid., p. 75.

[32]   Ibid., p.79. On spiritual beings perceived as light entities, see, for example, Plutarch 'The Myth of Timarchus', in *De genio Socratis* 501d, where the *daimones* are likened to darting stars; Michael J.B. Allen, 'Summoning Plotinus: Ficino, Smoke and the Strangled Chickens', in *Plato's Third Eye* (Aldershot: Variorum, 1995), XIV, p. 68, on Marsilio Ficino's description of *daimones* as spherical lights, like 'stars of the sphere of air'; and most famously *Paradiso* from Dante's *Divina Commedia*, trans. Mark Musa (Harmondsworth: Penguin Classics, 1986), where angelic spirits are described as 'shooting sparks' (VII, line 8), 'revolving lights', 'sparks in a fire' (VIII, lines 16, 19) and 'flashes of living light' (X, line 64).

[33]   Newton, *Journey*, p. 98.

[34]   Ibid., p. 105.

[35]   Ibid., p. 102.

[36]   Ibid., p. 212.

part of their energy behind in the spirit world as an exact duplicate, has interesting resonances with Neoplatonic theories of the undescended soul.[37] Some souls have memories of being elements of nature or mythical beasts, or of visiting other worlds as alien life forms. Earth is certainly not experienced as the only planet – there are myriads of worlds, each with their own lessons for the ongoing development of the soul throughout thousands of incarnations.

When the time comes for reincarnation, souls agree with their spirit advisors not to remember their other lives, in order to start with a clean slate and not inhibit self-discovery. They choose their next one, in consultation with the Elders, and are allowed to watch their future lives unfold as on a movie screen. It is given to understand that each life has an overall plan or blueprint, but that individuals are continually required to take risks and make choices. As one client says, 'Oh there is destiny all right. The life cycles are in place. It's just that there are so many alternatives which are unclear.'[38]

I cannot possibly do justice here to the wealth of details presented in Michael Newton's many case studies, but I hope to have highlighted the most important themes. One can of course find resonances and correlations with aspects of these accounts in the afterlife traditions of mainstream religions, in Platonic and Pythagorean mythology, theosophy and other esoteric movements, or in shamanic journeying. They emerge from what seems to be a collective consensus of metaphysical or imaginal reality, glimpses of which are facilitated through many consciousness-expanding practices such as ritual, visionary experience, dreaming, NDEs and OBEs, absorption of entheogens, hypnosis or active imagination techniques.

But any comparative analysis will not touch the quick of the significance of the encounters to those who participate in them – a mystery of which ancient initiates were forbidden to tell. I am more interested in pursuing the implications of the moment of realization, the meeting of two worlds, in a way that involves travelling on a vertical axis of connection, if you like, between the phenomenon and the human response to it. It seems to me that one should not extricate oneself from the deeply personal implications of these otherworld journeys, for to do so would obscure the possibility of truly understanding their impact on the lives of ordinary people past and present. We will all – even academics – arrive at the point of no return, we all have a vested interest in what might be in store. As Linda Fierz-David has suggested, death itself is the supreme unknowable symbol, 'forever on the other side of the boundary which is set for consciousness: it is an eternally

---

[37] See Plotinus, *Ennead* IV.8.8: ' even our soul does not altogether come down, but there is always something of it in the intelligible; but if the part which is in the world of sense-perception gets control, or rather if it is itself brought under control, and thrown into confusion, it prevents us from perceiving the things which the upper part of the soul contemplates'; trans. A.H. Armstrong, *Plotinus* IV (Cambridge, MA: Loeb Classical Library, 1984), p. 421.

[38] Newton, *Journey*, p. 212.

impenetrable mystery'.[39] In approaching this mystery through the mythologies and metaphors of those who have encountered it, one avoids the danger of reducing it to the explanations of a material science that attributes spiritual revelation to brain function as its 'ultimate truth'. The *mystai* of the ancient world – and their modern counterparts – stand by the conviction that they are being shown a reality of a totally different order, one more suggestive of the narratives of science fiction than conforming to the physical laws of conventional science.[40]

Altered States of Consciousness

All initiatory rituals in the ancient world were designed to induce an altered state of awareness. In the early (that is, pre-Platonic) incubation rituals of the Orphics and Pythagoreans, sick people, guided by priests, lay down in underground caves and had dreams of the spirit world which healed them. Peter Kingsley describes this state as 'like sleep but not sleep, not waking, not ordinary dream'; it was beyond time and space, and was often induced through the hypnotic power of incantations and music.[41] Indeed cultivation of a music which imitated the perfect harmonies of the spiritual world came to be regarded as a powerful means of ascent (or descent) in itself.[42] The shamanic poet/musician Orpheus became a cult figure because he

---

[39] Linda Fierz-David and Nor Hall, *Dreaming in Red: The Women's Dionysian Initiation Chamber in Pompeii* (Putnam, CT: Spring, 2005), p. 133.

[40] I cannot explore here the implications of the new physics for the mind/matter debate, which is indeed pushing back the boundaries between mysticism and science; see, for example, Amit Goswami, *The Self-Aware Universe: How Consciousness Creates the Material World* (New York: Tarcher, 1993); Trish Pfeiffer, John E. Mack and Paul Devereux (eds), *Mind before Matter: Visions of a New Science of Consciousness* (Ropley, Hampshire, O Books, 2007). However, the crucial point is that of the appropriate *mode of enquiry* for transpersonal experience: rational/empirical or symbolic//imaginal. Regarding science fiction, our space-exploration narratives could be seen as a way of giving a concrete image to psychic reality for the modern age, a fact that may contribute to their enduring fascination. On this topic, and the prevalence of UFO sightings as a contemporary manifestation of archetypal images, see Patrick Harpur, *Daimonic Reality* (London: Penguin, 1994, repr. Ravensdale, WA: Pine Winds Press, 2003), ch. 2.

[41] Kingsley, *Dark Places*, p. 82 and *Reality* (Inverness, CA: Golden Sufi Center, 2004), pp. 41–3.

[42] See Cicero, *Somnium Scipionis* (*De re publica*, 6.18): 'By imitating [the music of the spheres] on their strings and in song, learned men have opened the way for themselves to return to this place (heaven), like others of outstanding gifts who have devoted earthly life to studying the divine.' A theurgic technique originally attributed to Pythagoras, developed by the later Pythagorean Neoplatonists and revived in the fifteenth century by Marsilio Ficino in Florence. See Angela Voss, 'Orpheus Redivivus: The Musical Magic of Marsilio Ficino', in Michael J.B. Allen and Valery Rees (eds), *Marsilio Ficino: His Theology, His Philosophy, His Legacy* (Leiden: Brill, 2002), pp. 227–41; 'Father Time and Orpheus', in Angela Voss

journeyed to the underworld, where, in the words of Kingsley, 'he saw the things to be seen there just as they are'.[43] He knew how to use music and song to invoke a vision of Persephone and to understand the divine nature of the Sun as Apollo,[44] and in one Orphic poem he makes this journey at the site of a dream oracle next to a volcanic crater.[45] The symbolic significance of Orpheus' attempt to rescue Euridice – who can be seen as the personification of the feminine psyche – from the depths of Hades is a profound one which I cannot develop here,[46] except to point out that the purpose of all mystery rituals was the realization – or bringing to light – of the divinity hidden within nature. Kingsley has also demonstrated that both Empedocles and Parmenides were shamanic figures whose poetry reveals first-hand knowledge of the underworld; indeed he suggests that Parmenides' poem *The Mares* was designed to shift the parameters of the reader's normal consciousness in the manner of an incantation and lead them 'into another world' as an initiation into spiritual knowledge.[47] 'To go down to the underworld when you're dead is one thing', says Kingsley; 'To go there while you're alive, prepared and knowingly, and then learn from the experience – that's another thing entirely.'[48]

Mystery rituals did not necessarily involve incubation, but at their heart was a direct encounter with spiritual reality. Jeremy Naydler has shown how the origins of such 'death in life' experiences lies in ancient Egypt, where ritual practices facilitated 'a crossing of the threshold of death while still alive in order to stand

---

and Jean Hinson Lall (eds), *The Imaginal Cosmos: Astrology, Divination and the Sacred* (Canterbury: University of Kent, 2007), pp. 139–56; Martin L. West, *The Orphic Poems* (Oxford; Clarendon Press, 1983), pp. 30–32.

[43] Kingsley, *Dark Places*, p. 89. On Orpheus and the Orphic mysteries, see W.K.C. Guthrie, *Orpheus and Greek Religion* (London: Methuen, 1952; repr. Princeton: Princeton University Press, 1993); Jane Ellen Harrison, *Prologomena to Greek Religion* (Cambridge: Cambridge University Press, 1903; repr. Princeton: Princeton University Press, 1991), ch. IX; John Warden (ed.), *Orpheus: The Metamorphosis of a Myth* (Toronto: University of Toronto Press, 1982); West, *Orphic Poems*.

[44] West, *Orphic Poems*, pp. 12–13, Kingsley, *Dark Places*; Harrison, *Prologomena to Greek Religion*, pp. 455–60.

[45] West, *Orphic Poems*, p. 90; this is recalled in Virgil, *Aeneid*, Book VI, where Aeneas' journey to the Underworld takes place near the Oracle of Cumae, in the volcanic region near Naples.

[46] See Fierz-David and Hall, *Dreaming in Red*, p. 94.

[47] Kingsley, *Dark Places*, p. 118, *Reality*, p. 63. Kingsley's *Reality* presents Parmenides' text as an initiatory journey to the Underworld. He argues that the Western philosophical tradition has misinterpreted (or ignored) its true roots in the visionary and incubatory experiences of the ancient *magi*, and he seeks to re-instate the spiritual significance of these roots for the modern reader. On Empedocles, see Kingsley, *Ancient Philosophy, Mystery and Magic* (Oxford: Oxford University Press, 1995).

[48] Kingsley, *Dark Places*, p. 101.

within the spirit world and to know oneself as a spirit'.[49] He adds, 'The experience of spiritual rebirth required that one consciously undergo the experience of dying.'[50] For the Egyptians, death was a hidden realm – the *Dwat* – which interpenetrated the world of the living, containing active spiritual powers and energies in the form of gods and daemons as well as the spiritual life energy of the living. 'In the Dwat … the essential forms of things exist inwardly in a more interior space – a space that is prior to the external space into which they will unfold when they enter the world of physical manifestation.'[51]

It is this interior space that is accessed via the trance state, induced in the Egyptian tradition of temple incubation via rituals of burial and proto-death. This technique is preserved in the texts of the Hermetic corpus, in which the initiate undergoes a transmission or revelation from a teacher while in a dream or trance, during which he or she attains a knowledge of immortality and eventual *gnosis* or union with the divine source of being itself.[52] This 'hidden' reality is described as an intermediate realm between temporality and complete transcendence. Greek traditions refer to it as Elysium or the Islands of the Blest,[53] and it is interesting to note that LBL clients see the place they go to immediately after physical death manifesting as a 'heightened reality' version of earthly buildings or landscapes with which they are familiar, peopled by souls of loved ones and by beings they recognize to be spiritual guardians. They have a sense that there is somewhere 'beyond' all this, but it is not accessible at the initial stage of transition between worlds.[54]

At Eleusis, candidates for initiation underwent a nine-day fast and drank a powerful (and alcoholic) brew of barley groats, water and fresh herbs called

---

[49]   Jeremy Naydler, *Shamanic Wisdom in the Pyramid Texts: The Mystical Tradition of Ancient Egypt* (Rochester, VT: Inner Traditions, 2005), p. 48. Herodotus says the doctrine of reincarnation was borrowed by the Greeks from Egypt (*Histories*, 2.123): 'The Egyptians were the first to introduce the doctrine that the soul of man is immortal, but that at the death of the body it enters into one animal after another, as they are born. Then when it has gone the round of all creatures of land or sea or air it enters again into the body of a new-born man. This cycle is accomplished in three thousand years' (Guthrie, *Orpheus and Greek Religion*, p. 170). See also Arthur Versluis, *The Egyptian Mysteries* (London: Penguin Arkana, 1988), ch. 1.

[50]   Naydler, *Shamanic Wisdom*, p. 48.

[51]   Ibid., pp. 83–5; see also Versluis, *Egyptian Mysteries*, pp. 105–7.

[52]   On the Egyptian tradition of temple incubation and consultation of dream oracles informing the *Corpus Hermeticum*, see Peter Kingsley, 'Poimandres: The Etymology of the Name and the Origins of the *Hermetica*', *Journal of the Warburg and Courtauld Institutes* '56 (1993), pp. 1–24.

[53]   See Homer, *Odyssey* 4.561ff.; Plato, *Georgias*, 523b, 526c; *Menexenus*, 235c; *Republic*, 7.519c, 540b; *Symposium*, 179e, a180b; Cole, 'Landscapes of Dionysos', p. 196, on Hesiod's and Pindar's references to the Islands of the Blest, which are described in terms of a perfected natural world.

[54]   David Fontana characterizes these 'places beyond' as the 'formless planes' or places of pure consciousness, beyond all image (*Life beyond Death*, ch. 10).

the *Kykeon*, which is likely to also have had hallucinogenic properties.[55] At the sacramental heart of the ceremony, when symbolic objects were shown to the initiates, the *Eumolpidae* or hierophants sang or recited 'in solemn and melodious tones'.[56] The *mystai* then received a vision of the goddess Persephone in the sacred fire, and underwent a profound realization, the nature of which I will consider later. In some Dionysian or Bacchic ceremonies, divine vision was achieved through ecstatic dancing. In both cults, the initiates re-enacted a journey through darkness and fear before they could emerge into the light and 'see' – the altered state of awareness had to be carefully prepared through ritual means. Hypnosis has its own ritual – Michael Newton uses candles, music and a carefully modulated tone of voice to unlock clients' memories – but there is no sense in which the visions depend on any artificial stimulant, or on the cultivation of intense emotional states. There is no required lifestyle, such as the Pythagorean or Orphic regulations for diet and abstinence, and hence no suggestion that the LBL vision will confer freedom from the wheel of rebirth if the client lives a life of purity.[57] But we can certainly say that, just as at Eleusis, the experience heals the fear of death, and clients return to their lives safe in the knowledge that it is simply a transition to another mode of being.

---

[55]   See Karl Kerenyi, *Eleusis: Archetypal Image of Mother and Daughter* (Princeton: Princeton University Press, 1967), pp. 177–80, 'The Preparation and Effect of the *Kykeon*'. He suggests the herb used may have been a variety of pennyroyal, which is related to the hallucinogenic Mexican plant commonly known as *salvia divinorum,* used by diviners. Walter Burkert in *Ancient Mystery Cults* (Cambridge, MA: Harvard University Press, 1987), pp. 108–9, disagrees that drugs were used, suggesting that it would have been impossible to organize this for thousands of people, and would require individual supervision under a master. He thinks it more likely that the sense of bliss was produced by communal festivity. Kerenyi also suggests that only a few chosen initiates were given the potion, but this is contradicted by Shawn Eyer, 'Psychedelic Effects and the Eleusinian Mysteries' in *Alexandria,* vol. 2 (Grand Rapids, MI: Phanes Press, 1993), pp. 64–93, who makes a plausible case for the collective use of hallucinogens. He points out that barley may attract the fungus ergot, which in turn contains the psychoactive alkaloid ergine, the source of LSD (pp. 74–5), and argues that all the textual evidence regarding the state of mind of the initiates – and the reliability of the mass vision – points to an altered state of consciousness such as that resulting from lysergic acid-based drugs (p. 79). He concludes: 'It is, then, by no means a sacrilege to think that the mysteries of Demeter and Kore might have utilised the naturally-occurring compounds which sporadically appeared on the heads of grain which were sacred to the goddesses' (p. 86). See also R. Gordon Wasson, Albert Hofmann and Carl A.P. Ruck, *The Road to Eleusis: Unveiling the Secret of the Mysteries* (New York: Harcourt Brace Jovanovich, 1978; repr. Berkeley: North Atlantic Books, 2008).

[56]   West, *Orphic Poems*, p. 23.

[57]   On Orphic beliefs about living in their final incarnation, see Guthrie, *Orpheus and Greek Religion*, p. 175.

Eleusis

> For among the many excellent and indeed divine institutions which your
> Athens has brought forth and contributed to human life, none, in my opinion,
> is better than those mysteries. For by their means we have been brought out of
> our barbarous and savage mode of life and educated and refined to a state of
> civilization; and as the rites are called 'initiations', so in very truth we have
> learned from them the beginnings of life, and have gained the power not only to
> live happily, but also to die with a better hope.

Thus wrote Cicero on the Eleusinian mysteries.[58] Celebrated since around
1500 BCE, these mysteries attracted thousands of individuals, of any profession
or religious persuasion. So what happened there? Eleusis means 'the place of
happy arrival',[59] and the rituals centred on the myth of the rape of Persephone,
the grief of her mother Demeter and her eventual rescue from the underworld and
restoration to her mother. In the Homeric Hymn to Demeter, the Mother Goddess
is the inaugurator of the mysteries, which may not be recounted or altered by
human beings. Demeter's own initiation was the finding of her daughter, and this
event became the ineffable, unspeakable secret, the *arrheton*, at the heart of the
ceremony – so secret, in fact, that Persephone's name was considered too dreadful
to pronounce and she was generally referred to simply as 'the goddess'.[60] All other
surrounding rituals were *aporrheton*, or subject to the strictest law of silence. We
could suggest an analogy here with the stages of hypnosis described earlier: the
initial public sacrifices in the temples could be seen to correspond to the *beta* stage
of 'ordinary' consciousness, the *apporheton* (lesser mysteries) to the *alpha* stage
and the *arrheton* (greater mysteries) to the *theta* stage.[61]

Karl Kerenyi emphasizes the impossibility – for the historian – of penetrating
to the inner experience which 'moves beyond word and image or mythological
representation'.[62] All we know is that at a small shrine, the *Anaktoron*, in the central
sanctuary or *Telesterion*, the hierophant 'made things appear' to a small number
of initiates.[63] After undergoing night-time wanderings in imitation of Demeter's
search for her daughter, the initiates gathered around a central fire where they

---

[58]   Cicero, *Laws,* II, xiv, 36.

[59]   Kerenyi, *Eleusis*, p. 23. It was at Eleusis that Demeter finally ended her wanderings
in search of her daughter, and where a temple was built in her honour. See Homeric *Hymn
to Demeter* (sixth–seventh century BCE), lines 295ff.; trans. in Helene P. Foley, *The Homeric
Hymn to Demeter: Translation, Commentary and Interpretative Essays* (Princeton:
Princeton University Press, 1994).

[60]   See Cole, 'Landscapes of Dionysos', p. 196, Kingsley, *Poimandres*.

[61]   See n. 12 above.

[62]   Kerenyi, *Eleusis*, p. 38.

[63]   'Hierophant' means 'he who makes the holy things appear' (Kerenyi, *Eleusis*, p. 90.
See pp. 88–94 on the proceedings in the Telesterion).

were taken through a threefold process of initiation.[64] At the climax, the high priest called for Persephone – and she was seen to rise up out of the fire to the terrifying sound of a huge gong.[65] Now there is no doubt from the accounts that the initiates saw the goddess in a shared experience, taking place in 'external' reality, and we should resist rational attempts to explain how this could be. As Otto remarks, 'the scholar must learn to see that it is absurd to suppose we can understand anything so great by the mere application of a philological method and a little modern psychology'.[66] Later the hierophant showed an ear of grain, and

> all who had seen turned, at the sight of this concrete thing, as though turning back from the hereafter into this world ... to those that had seen Kore at Eleusis, this was no mere metaphor proving nothing, but the memento of an encounter in which the goddess of the underworld showed herself in a beatific vision.[67]

I shall consider the significance of the 'turning' via the symbolic showing later in this chapter. Evidently it had the effect of breaking the hypnotic trance and restoring the initiate to 'normal' vision. The word 'mystery' derives from *myesis* denoting the closing of the lips or eyes, and this word was used for the first stage of the ritual, or the 'lesser mysteries'. The *mystes* would then return for the rituals of the 'greater mysteries', the *teletai* (literally, 'rites of fulfilment') after which they would attain to *epopteia*, or 'having seen', the highest level of vision, implying that their eyes had been opened to a new kind of sight.[68] Kerenyi states that 'there is undeniable evidence' that the *epopteia* conveyed happiness, hope and anticipation, suggesting that the vision was not an objective 'outer' event such as a theatrical performance or displaying of a statue, but arose through the kindled imaginations of the participants, whose minds had been made empty and receptive. Otto remarks that the overwhelming effects of the vision could not have been achieved if it were merely a dramatic re-enactment: 'the truth', he says, 'must have been something absolutely new, astonishing, inaccessible to rational cognition'.[69] Indeed we learn from Aristotle that the initiate was put into a passive condition in which he or she

---

[64] The *Dromena* (drama), *Legomena* (sayings) and *Deiknymena* (displaying). See Eyer, 'Psychedelic Effects', p. 68.

[65] Kerenyi, *Eleusis*, p. 84.

[66] Walter F. Otto, 'The Meaning of the Eleusinian Mysteries', in Joseph Campbell (ed.), *The Mysteries: Papers from the Eranos Yearbooks*, Bollingen series XXX/2 (London: Routledge & Kegan Paul, 1955; repr. Princeton: Princeton University Press, 1990), pp. 14–31.

[67] Kerenyi, *Eleusis*, p. 94.

[68] On the stages of initiation, see Kevin Clinton, 'Stages of Initiation in the Eleusian and Samothracian Mysteries', in Cosmopoulos, *Greek Mysteries*, pp. 50–78; Cole, 'Landscapes of Dionysos', p. 193.

[69] Otto, 'Meaning of the Eleusinian Mysteries', p. 24.

did not 'learn' but 'experienced' and underwent a 'change of mind'.[70] Kerenyi suggests that 'in psychological terms, there must have been an experience of the "other" in a change of consciousness, moving far beyond what could be found in everyday life',[71] adding 'who can tell what the experience is like without having undergone days and days of fasting, purifications, exhaustion, apprehension and excitement?'[72]

According to Plutarch, the acting out of the initiatory rituals was a direct imitation of the moment of death, when

> the soul suffers an experience similar to those who celebrate the great initiations ... Wanderings astray in the beginning, tiresome walkings in circles, some frightening paths in darkness that lead nowhere, then immediately before the end all the terrible things, panic and shivering and sweat, and amazement. And then some wonderful light comes to meet you, pure regions and meadows are there to greet you, with sounds and dances and solemn, sacred words and holy views, and there the initiate, perfect by now, set free and loose from all bondage, walks about, crowned with a wreath.[73]

A description not dissimilar to those of LBL clients reliving a death-experience from a past life, who describe the terror of dying followed by release from the body and a sensation of travelling through a tunnel to a place of light, where they feel surrounded by benevolence.[74] Similar, too, is the impact of the vision. To quote a few ancient authorities: Aristotle, 'all who use these rites experience relief mixed with joy';[75] Cicero, at Eleusis it is shown 'how to live in joy, and how to die with better hopes';[76] and on the epitaph of a Hierophant, that he has shown in the mysteries 'that death is not only not an evil, but good'.[77] One of the very few accounts of the event itself comes from Apuleius, who describes his initiation in the mysteries of Isis:

> Then the High Priest ordered all uninitiated persons to depart, invested me in a new linen garment and led me by the hand into the inner recesses of the sanctuary itself ... I approached the very gates of death and set one foot on Persephone's threshold, yet was permitted to return, rapt through all the elements. At midnight

---

[70] Aristotle, fragment 15; Burkert, *Ancient Mystery Cults*, p. 89; also see Kerenyi, *Eleusis*, p. 90.

[71] Kerenyi, *Eleusis*, p. 90.

[72] Ibid., p. 91.

[73] Plutarch, fragment 168, quoted in Kerenyi, *Eleusis*, pp. 91–2; see Burkert, *Ancient Mystery Cults*, p. 162.

[74] For example, Newton, *Journey*, pp. 10, 17–19.

[75] Aristotle, *Politics,* 1242a.

[76] Cicero, *De legibus*, 2.36.

[77] From 200 CE, quoted in Burkert, *Ancient Mystery Cults*, p. 21.

I saw the sun shining as if it were noon, I entered the presence of the gods of the Underworld and of the Upperworld, stood near and worshipped them.[78]

Those who underwent initiation were blessed, and could expect a better lot in the afterlife than those who did not. They certainly no longer feared death, but looked forward to it as the beginning of a new life[79] – they also seemed to gain a sense of the purposeful unfolding of many lives, judging from a remark by Isokrates: 'Those who take part in [the Eleusinian rites] possess better hopes in regard to the end of life and in regard to the whole *aion*.'[80]

Orphism

We find the same sentiments in texts associated with the Dionysian mystery rituals celebrated by Orphic cults in Italy from the fifth century BCE onwards. The role of Orpheus as initiator of the Dionysian rites has been thoroughly explored by Jane Harrison,[81] so suffice it to say here that they are rites of redemption, of entering the underworld to reclaim the divinity of the soul through encounter with the god. The myth of the dismembering of Dionysus in Greek tradition provided an explanation for the conflict human beings experience between their Titanic human nature and the divine part of their soul.[82] As Linda Fierz-David puts it, 'The Orphic mystery cult seeks to atone for the Titan guilt and to free humans from their conflict, as they ceremonially relive the fate of the god. If the humans die in the mystery ceremonial, as the god did, their divine spark is freed and unites itself with the god.'[83]

Small gold tablets have been found in graves, with engraved texts, evidently designed to protect the soul after death. The texts on the tablets give specific instructions for souls to identify themselves to the gods or beings they meet in

---

[78]   Apuleius, *The Golden Ass*, trans. Robert Graves (Harmondsworth: Penguin Classics, 1990), pp. 285–6.

[79]   See Burkert, *Ancient Mystery Cults*, p. 289; Cole, 'Landscapes of Dionysos', p. 197; Kerenyi, *Eleusis*, pp. 13–16.

[80]   Isokrates, *Panegyric on Athens*, IV 28, quoted in Kerenyi, *Eleusis*, p. 15.

[81]   Harrison, *Prologomena to the Study of Greek Religion*, ch. X.

[82]   'According to Orphic tradition, [Dionysus] is the son of the chthonic Zeus in the form of a snake and of Persephone, and as such is called Dionysus-Zagreus. Jealous Hera incites the Titans against the young huntsman, and it is said that during the flight from them he takes on the forms of animals: he becomes a kid, a deer, and a bull. The Titans nevertheless overtake him, tear him apart, and eat the pieces. Only his heart is saved by Pallas Athene, she brings it to Father Zeus. Zeus shatters the guilty Titans with his lightning-bolt, and they burn to ashes. From these ashes, however … human beings originate; and this is the Orphic teaching – that human beings have thereby inherited the nature of the Titans and their guilt' (Fierz-David and Hall, *Dreaming in Red*, p. 28).

[83]   Fierz-David and Hall, *Dreaming in Red*, p. 28.

the underworld (as, for example, the epigraph to this chapter).[84] Some imply that rebirth will follow, others give passwords and ritual responses for the soul as it reaches the gates of Hades.[85] Some report dialogues between the soul and the gods, others give pronouncements such as 'blessed and most happy you will be god instead of mortal', or a common metaphor for the finding of spiritual nourishment, 'A kid, you fell into the milk'.[86] Several of the texts describe the newly arrived soul as thirsty, needing to drink from the cool springs of the 'waters of memory' in order to become fully conscious of its divinity.[87] Susan Cole, in her analysis of these tablets, suggests that they were generated by ceremonies which were 'privately organized, performed in obscurity, and under no official control'.[88] An example of such a ceremony may be found in the frescoes of the Initiation Chamber of the Villa of the Mysteries in Pompeii, which reveals the stages of a Roman woman's initiation into the mysteries of Dionysus. Fierz-David has interpreted the images through the metaphor of the Jungian journey towards individuation, concluding that the value of the transformatory and painful awakening to one's inner divinity offered by these rituals lies in the memory one takes back to everyday life:

> In the dramatic course of the initiation, [the woman] has come to know how human life passes to death and over beyond death as a way between height and depth, danger and help – a way which can be trodden according to a divine pattern toward a divine goal. The human being who can remember is no longer given over to blind fate. She has, indeed, seen the eternal symbols which in all conditions of life mediate the right demeanor and lend meaning to all events.[89]

Fierz-David implies here that the soul's memory of the deeper spiritual patterns governing its earthly existence opened up an awareness for individuals of an underlying responsibility for their own life-events, and concludes that that same is true for modern people, for 'in the course of inner development, once the world

---

[84]   See Guthrie, *Orpheus and Greek Religion*, pp. 171–82; Cole, 'Landscapes of Dionysos', pp. 200–213; Harrison, *Prologomena to the Study of Greek Religion*, pp. 572–4; Radcliffe G. Edmonds III, *Myths of the Underworld Journey: Plato, Aristophanes and the Orphic Gold Tables* (Cambridge: Cambridge University Press, 2004), ch. 2; Fritz Graf and Sarah Iles Johnston, *Ritual Texts for the Afterlife: Orpheus and the Bacchic Gold Tablets* (London: Routledge, 2007), for detailed discussions of the texts on the gold plates.

[85]   See Cole, 'Landscapes of Dionysos', pp. 201–9.

[86]   Ibid., p. 207; see Guthrie, *Orpheus and Greek Religion*, pp. 178–89, for a further analysis of this metaphor, and also Fierz-David and Hall, *Dreaming in Red*, pp. 63–5, on the symbolism of the kid as representative of the initiate's animal nature which must be fully experienced before redemption.

[87]   Guthrie, *Orpheus and Greek Religion*, p. 177; Harrison, *Prologomena to the Study of Greek Religion*, pp. 575–82.

[88]   Cole, 'Landscapes of Dionysos', p. 206.

[89]   Fierz-David and Hall, *Dreaming in Red*, p. 146.

of archetypal images has arisen in a dramatic, moving inner drama, individuals need never again lose connection with it if they do not forget their most valuable experiences and, with that, themselves'.[90] There is no doubt that LBL invokes such a world, but unlike the *Dionysia*, it does not require the suffering of the *katabasis*, the wandering 'through a darkness full of terror' before it can be glimpsed.[91] Such psychological torment can be likened to the alchemical *nigredo*,[92] and involved facing the peril of annihilation before the divine spark could be freed from its material imprisonment and union with the god achieved. Fierz-David suggests that the drama of the *katabasis* can now be contained within the 'private, methodical activity' of inner dialogue with a guide-image in the Jungian practice of active imagination – a means of confronting the shadow aspects of the personality without literally acting them out.[93] Certainly LBL clients are presented with difficult and challenging insights into their own patterns of behaviour by the Elders, but there is no sense of terror, fear or torture – only compassion.[94]

Plato

There were many variations in cult expressions of Dionysian mythology, but the gold tablets certainly confirm the fundamental convictions of the Orphics that the soul is immortal, that life on earth is a punishment and trial from which it is eventually purified, and that it undergoes reincarnation with the possibility of ultimate escape from the cycle of births:

> They (i.e. Orphics) say that the soul of man is immortal, and that at one time it comes to its end (which they like the rest of men call dying), and at another it is reborn, but is never finally exterminated. For these reasons it is necessary to live a life as sinless as possible ... The soul then, being immortal and often reborn, and having seen all things, both things here and in Hades, has learned everything that there is.[95]

---

[90]   Ibid., p. 147.

[91]   Ibid., p. 93.

[92]   The first stage of the alchemical process, the blackening, before the separation of the elements and their purification has taken place. For an overview of alchemical procedure and a selection of texts, see Stanton J. Linden, *The Alchemy Reader, from Hermes Trismegistus to Isaac Newton* (Cambridge and New York: Cambridge University Press, 1993).

[93]   Fierz-David and Hall, *Dreaming in Red*, p.115. See also C.G. Jung, *Jung on Active Imagination*, ed. Joan Chodorow (London: Routledge, 1997), which contains key readings from Jung on the purpose and techniques of active imagination.

[94]   The Pompeii fresco depicts the distraught initiate being whipped by the 'angel of darkness' before her final revelation.

[95]   Plato, *Meno,* 80e.

We find all these ideas recounted fully by Plato, who presents us with Socrates as hierophant of the mysteries of philosophy.[96] For Socrates, it is through the contemplation of Beauty that the inner realization of the soul's immortality may be achieved, and the path of love becomes the soul's *katabasis,* another way of entering the underworld of the trapped soul and learning how to free it. The states of mystery initiation become a metaphor, in the *Phaedrus,* for the purification of the soul through the yearnings of erotic love and its final realization of divinity.[97] The pain and difficulty of the immortal soul trapped in a mortal body and forced to shed its wings is one of Plato's most graphic and enduring images, and he describes the initiation process as the regrowth of the wings which enables the soul to fly back to its true home 'beyond the heavens' where true being dwells.[98] This higher sphere is the abode of the stars and, in the *Timaeus,* Plato speaks of each soul being assigned to a star, furthermore 'the one who lived his appointed time well would travel again to dwell in his proper star, and live a blessed life according to his true nature'.[99] We may recall that the etymology of the word 'desire' (*desidere*) is 'from the star', and desire for union with Beauty is the underlying force propelling Plato's philosophical lover towards the Good.

In the *Phaedrus* also we find a detailed explanation of reincarnation and the laws of karma, for souls will, according to Plato, reincarnate into different kinds of lives depending on how righteously they have lived, and how much they have remembered spiritual truth through 'following in the train of a god'.[100] He specifies that souls must spend ten thousand years between incarnations, unless they are philosophers in which case the whole process becomes speeded up, for the philosopher alone is able to recover his wings and 'approach the full vision of the perfect mysteries':[101]

> Beauty it was ours to see in all its brightness in those days when, amidst that happy company, we beheld with our eyes that blessed vision ... then were we all initiated into that mystery which is rightly accounted blessed beyond all others; whole and unblemished were we that did celebrate it, untouched by the evils that awaited us in days to come; whole and unblemished likewise, free from all alloy, steadfast and blissful were the spectacles on which we gazed in the moment of final revelation.[102]

---

[96]   On Socrates as hierophant of the philosophic mysteries, see Gregory Shaw, 'Living Light: An Exploration of Divine Embodiment', in Patrick Curry and Angela Voss (eds), *Seeing with Different Eyes: Essays in Astrology and Divination* (Newcastle: Cambridge Scholars Press, 2007), pp. 59–87.

[97]   Plato, 'Myth of the Charioteer', in *Phaedrus,* 250d–256e.

[98]   *Phaedrus,* 247c–d.

[99]   Plato, *Timaeus,* 31d, see Guthrie, *Orpheus and Greek Religion,* pp. 180–81.

[100]   *Phaedrus,* 248c–e.

[101]   *Phaedrus,* 249c–d.

[102]   *Phaedrus,* 250b.

Souls take full responsibility for choosing their next life, which may well be that of a beast if they have not 'beheld truth' through the pursuit of philosophy, which Plato defines as 'passing from a plurality of perceptions to a unity gathered together by reasoning', a 'recollection of those things which our souls beheld aforetime as they journeyed with their god'.[103]

It is, I hope, very obvious that these ideas have sprung, fully formed, into the twenty-first-century LBL consulting room. Even more startling are the correlations between the after-death journey of Er in the *Republic* and his modern counterpart.[104] Er was a warrior who was slain in battle, but he was evidently not clinically dead for his body did not decay, and on his funeral pyre he revived and told of his vision of the afterlife. He speaks of spiritual beings or judges who tell him to be a messenger to mankind, and to recount truths of the other world; he observes a dialogue between newly arrived souls and souls already there, greeting each other as old acquaintances; he learns the laws of karma, and he is taken to a place called the 'meadow' where he sees a beam of light like a pillar extending from heaven to earth 'most nearly resembling a rainbow, but brighter and purer'.[105] From the extremities of the light stretched the spindle of Necessity, through which all the orbits of the planets turned. The whorl of the spindle, as a metaphor for the topography of the 'intermediate' spirit world, is remarkably similar to the curved layers described by several LBL clients:

> Its shape was that of those in our world ... but we must conceive it to be as if in one great whorl, hollow and scooped out, there lay enclosed, right through, another like it but smaller, fitting into it as boxes that fit into one another, and in like manner another, a third, and a fourth, and four others, for there were eight of the whorls in all, lying within one another, showing their rims as circles from above and forming the continuous back of a single whorl about the shaft.[106]

On the rims of the whorls stand the Sirens, singing notes that combine into a perfect harmony. Er speaks of choosing lots for his next incarnation, again stressing the responsibility of humans to choose wisely in accordance with the deeds of their previous life. Socrates comments here that this choice should be 'our main concern' in this lifetime, and that humans should study everything that enables them to 'distinguish the life that is good from that which is bad' to prepare for this crucial moment in which their next life is determined. Er tells of souls being sent their individual genius or guardian spirit, and of being allotted their destiny for their next life, which is made irreversible.[107] They are then required to drink of the River of Forgetfulness and they waft their way towards their birth 'like shooting

---

[103] *Phaedrus*, 249b–c.
[104] *Republic*, 614b-621d.
[105] *Republic*, 616b.
[106] *Republic*, 616c–e.
[107] *Republic*, 621a.

stars'.[108] Er, however, is not allowed to drink the water, and he wakes up on the funeral pyre. This tale, says Socrates, 'will save us if we believe it'.[109]

Here we find the notion that the salvation of the soul lies in its power of memory and imagination, and crucially, that *faith* in the 'truth' offered by such revelations (rather than their provability) is the key to fully realizing them oneself in the afterlife. That there may be a soteriological dimension to LBL work is not considered by Michael Newton who is more concerned with its healing effects in this life, but Socrates' comment deserves our attention. It implies that the power of symbolic narrative, if entered into on its own terms, has far-reaching implications for the karmic journey of each individual.

Initiation

Let us now look more closely at the meaning of the term 'initiation'. We have seen that it involves a death-experience, and how at the apex of the mystery vision an immediate knowledge of immortality was conferred upon the initiate through the visible presence of the deities. Fierz-David calls it 'a call to awakening',[110]and Mircea Eliade gives one characteristic of such initiation as a transcendence of the human condition, the attaining of a super-human or divine state.[111] But how can this come about through a vision, or even through a divinatory encounter? One key may be that the 'seeing' is, simultaneously, a knowing, achieved through the power of the symbolic representation to bring together in a flash of insight material form and its immaterial significance. Through visual image, what Jung would term unconscious contents and Plato the lost memories of the soul are revived and re-membered as the soul is infused with a knowledge of its own hidden potential to transcend its embodied condition. Fierz-David describes this as consciousness 'accepting' the unconscious, just as Apollo as lord of the Delphic oracle acknowledges the opposing power of Dionysus.[112] The coming together of the conscious and unconscious, light and dark, waking and dream life, male and female, soul and body constitutes the work of integration symbolized by the dramatic narratives underlying all ancient initiations.

Eliade argues that this is a perennial and universal experience, the mysteries being capable of being 'indefinitely re-animated and enriched with new values' according to the context and society in which they are enacted.[113] He describes

---

[108] *Republic,* 621b.

[109] *Republic,* 621c.

[110] Fierz-David and Hall, *Dreaming in Red,* p. 85.

[111] Mircea Eliade, *Rites and Symbols of Initiation* (New York: Harper & Row, 1958), p. 112.

[112] See Fierz-David and Hall, *Dreaming in Red,* pp. 74–7; at Delphi Dionysus was revered as the 'winter sun' and Apollo as the 'summer sun'.

[113] Eliade, *Rites and Symbols,* pp. 113–14.

the Hellenistic mysteries as 'a ritually guided experience of the regeneration of the soul'[114] suggesting that in modern man 'the unconscious is religious', and that our present-day initiations are undergone in psychological contexts. Fierz-David sees the ancient way of initiation as 'a close parallel to the way of individuation for modern people, who through it are also always presented with fundamental moral problems'.[115] These problems are existential ones, springing from 'the original ground of the soul itself', and in that sense, I would suggest, can only be addressed through freeing the understanding from its normal limited parameters of judgement and leading it to a place where a greater, deeper and more universal perspective may be attained.

As I have pointed out, the goal of all ancient mystery cults was union of human and divinity through the *realization* of that unity within the individual, while fully embodied. This would also appear to be the key to LBL's aim to heal psychic wounds through bringing a spiritual perspective to bear on human problems. But we certainly do not find the same emphasis on the secrets of sexuality at the heart of the revelation. The significance of the erect phallus for the Dionysian initiate *was* part of the 'ineffable secret', the secret that in the sexual act matter and spirit are united.[116] In the Pompeii fresco, suggests Fierz-David, the initiate is warned of the dangers of becoming pure soul and forgetting to return to the body – an inevitable temptation, when in the cold light of day the 'mystery' is no longer accessible or comprehensible. It was kept secret precisely because it could not be translated into worldly terms without gross misrepresentation or even ridicule. In LBL, one of the most powerful and ecstatic experiences related by clients is that of merging with a loved one's soul without the encumbrance of the body, or of all the emotional 'baggage' of an earthly relationship. It is then very difficult for the individual to return to their life where the loved one may well be inaccessible or estranged. It is as if they must taste unity and then allow this knowledge to inform the hard and slow everyday work of 'divinizing' the mundane. There is no 'divine madness' of being taken by a god, or instantaneous granting of freedom from the wheel of rebirth. But there is something very important that both ancient and modern practices have in common, and that is the *mode of revelation* that effects such a dramatic and shattering change in consciousness.

This depends, I suggest, on the turning point between allegorical representation and symbolic perception. Something happened in the mysteries, and something happens in the LBL consulting room, when individuals grasp a 'truth' through visionary experience which involves seeing through the veil that separates conscious awareness from unconscious memory. In differing ways, this involves both manifestation of spiritual life-forces and the showing of objects and, in the case of LBL, it is revealed through a two-way dialogue between client and spirit, and client and therapist. In both cases, the 'truth' would seem to derive from the

---

[114] Ibid., p. 114.
[115] Fierz-David and Hall, *Dreaming in Red*, p. 120.
[116] Ibid., p. 105.

convergence of literal and spiritual realities, and in both cases, initiates have been led deep into a state of altered awareness, through ritual incantation or hypnosis. At Eleusis they have been led to the central fire by the hierophant who invokes Persephone and Demeter (and many other deities along the way),[117] in Orphic rituals they have been taken into the underworld to awake their Dionysian spark of divinity, and in LBL they have been led by the therapist into the spirit world, and by spiritual guides to the Council of Elders – in all cases, they come to know with unshaking conviction that they are immortal.

Symbols

Particularly intriguing is the function of the symbolic objects in both processes, for it would seem that they perform a central role in the 'seeing'. To ponder this role leads us to Neoplatonic theurgy and the symbol or *synthema* as a 'bait' for focusing the attention of the celebrant and leading them to apprehend the sacred dimension to which the symbol points (and indeed in which it participates).[118] This involves making the transition, as I remarked earlier, from an *allegorical* understanding of significance to an inner grasp of *symbolic* meaning, the distinction being eloquently expressed by the Romantic poet Samuel Taylor Coleridge:

> Now an allegory is but a translation of abstract notions into a picture-language which is itself nothing but an abstraction from objects of the senses ... On the other hand a Symbol ... is characterised by a translucence of the Special in the Individual or of the General in the Especial or of the Eternal through and in the Temporal. It always partakes of the Reality which it renders intelligible; and while it enunciates the whole, abides itself as a living part in that Unity, of which it is the representative.[119]

---

[117] Kerenyi, *Eleusis*, p. 28, mentions that in the *aporrheta* they encountered 'even more deities', whereas in the *arrheton* only 'the two deities' of Demeter and her daughter were revealed.

[118] On the Neoplatonic symbol, see Peter T. Struck, *Birth of the Symbol: Ancient Writers at the Limits of their Texts* (Princeton: Princeton University Press, 2004), chs 6 and 7; on theurgic ritual, see Gregory Shaw, *Theurgy and the Soul: The Neoplatonism of Iamblichus* (University Park: Pennsylvania State University Press, 1995).

[119] In Coleridge, 'The Statesman's Manual' in *Lay Sermons,* ed. R.J. White, vol. 6 of *The Collected Works of Samuel Taylor Coleridge,* ed. Kathleen Coburn (Princeton: Princeton University Press, 1972), p. 30. On symbol and the numinous, see also J. Robert Barth, 'Symbol as Sacrament', in *The Symbolic Imagination: Coleridge and the Romantic Tradition* (Princeton; Princeton University Press, 1977), pp. 3–21; Paul Tillich, 'Religious Symbols and Knowledge of God', *Christian Scholar* 38/3 (1955): 189–97; and Stephen Wasserstrom, 'On Symbols and Symbolising', in *Religion after Religion: Gershom Sholem, Mircea Eliade and Henry Corbin at Eranos* (Princeton: Princeton University Press, 1999), pp. 85–99. On the etymology of 'symbol', see Pietro Negri, 'Knowledge of the Symbol'

At Eleusis, certain objects were contained within a large basket and were ceremoniously revealed at the height of the ritual. These apparently included a womb, a phallus, a snake and a pomegranate, although their identity was never revealed to the non-initiated.[120] In some ceremonies, the initiates themselves handled the objects and transferred them from one basket to another. Of more public knowledge was the displaying of the ear of grain (*epoptikon*), which from an outsider's perspective might seem to be of minor importance, or even 'crude and meaningless'.[121] But Kerenyi points out that 'nothing about the Eleusinian mysteries was so striking as the initiates' awe of Demeter's gift, the grain, and their hope of life after death'.[122] To the celebrants, having just beheld the secret of secrets, the grain symbolized the knowledge they had just gained, knowledge that for life to flourish anew there must be death.[123] The humble ear of grain, the 'concrete thing', enabled the initiates to connect material and immaterial reality in one stroke, to come back into their bodies and their awareness of the natural processes of Demeter, while also understanding the transcendent aspect of the feminine in the resurrection of Persephone. In the same way as the initiates experienced the finding of Persephone, so they understood that eternal life is never extinguished and is fully present as a secret within the world of generation. A similar message may have presented itself in the revealing of the phallus in the Dionysian mysteries.[124]

In the case of LBL, the most conspicuous objects observed by subjects are the medallions worn by the Council of Elders.[125] These mysterious pendants are described in great detail.[126] They consist of gold discs inscribed with images or emblems, with mysterious indecipherable writing around the rim. The images and emblems are understood as 'messages of inspiration' to the soul which are far more powerful than verbal communication, and enable them to feel they are an 'active participant' in the questioning of the Council. For example, one young woman is shown an image of a fleeing gazelle with a human carrying a torch on its back, which she interprets as a reminder 'to have the courage and strength to continue on with my life with a greater sense of purpose. The gazelle also represents freedom

---

in Julius Evola (ed.), *Introduction to Magic* (Rochester, VT: Inner Traditions, 2001), pp. 83–96.

[120] Kerenyi, *Eleusis*, pp. 75, 106 and n. 6; Eyer, 'Psychedelic Effects', p. 69.

[121] Eduard Meyer, *Geschichte des Altertums*, 4th edn, IV, p. 215, quoted in Kerenyi, *Eleusis*, p. 205.

[122] Kerenyi, *Eleusis*, p. 106.

[123] See ibid., pp. 106–7, for relevant parables from Christian and Jewish traditions.

[124] See Fierz-David and Hall, *Dreaming in Red*, p. 76; a winnowing basket was filled with fruits, under which Dionysus was believed to be hidden in the form of a phallus: 'it is a symbol that, if it does *not* remain hidden, has a grotesque and obscene character' (p. 104).

[125] See Newton, *Destiny*, pp. 224–43.

[126] Ibid., pp. 230–31.

to conquer fear and have faith in myself.'[127] Or, an Elder may use an image to correct an unhelpful pattern of behaviour: 'like the oracles of old, the Elders may show a sign as a warning of impending trouble if what we strive for in life is set aside'. This is undoubtedly the divinatory heart of the encounter, giving the client a specific task to bring back to their life: 'The impact of viewing these signs and symbols under hypnosis is so compelling with some clients that after their sessions they have ordered duplicates on personal jewelry to remind them of their karmic path.'[128] Again we have the notion of a physical object, the item of jewellery, containing a talismanic function of bearing a message from another dimension that is relevant to material existence. Like the concrete realization of a dream, such objects facilitate a journey between worlds, being simultaneously here and there.

J. Robert Barth has pointed towards the sacramental nature of the symbol, suggesting that an act of faith is required to perceive the unity of outer image and inner meaning. This act he describes as a 'commitment of self' to the revelation. As in traditional religious sacraments, symbols can be seen as ways in which divine power is shared with human beings, a 'making present' of that which they represent.[129] Barth also stresses the notion of 'encounter', that sacraments are the mode in which humans encounter God, or divinities, in the same way that symbols convey a dynamic, timeless and *active* property that demands constant relationship in order to stay alive and 'work' on the consciousness of the perceiver. Indeed the quality of revelation will be inextricably related to the commitment and belief of the individual.

Can we call the spirit world itself a 'symbolic' reality, then? It is certainly not literal (in the sense of material) or allegorical, or purely mystical (in the sense of being without image), but it does use familiar forms to convey the presence of a dimension of experience normally inaccessible. The Council of Elders, the meetings with ancient deities, could be described as all taking place in what Henry Corbin termed the *mundus imaginalis*, the imaginal space where divine essence takes on form in order to be present to human vision.[130] Paradoxically this place is experienced as more 'real' than the ordinary world; it is, in the words of Tom Cheetham, like a 'world turned inside out'.[131] This is the place where the soul encounters its angel or spiritual counterpart, or a mode of vision in which the human and divine eyes are drawn into single focus. The Islamic sages who inspired Corbin were able to live fully in both worlds, 'dreaming with open eyes'. I think we could suggest that what LBL clients 'see' exists in this imaginal place, and

---

[127] Ibid., p. 236.

[128] Ibid., p. 243.

[129] Barth, 'Symbol as Sacrament', pp. 13–14.

[130] See Corbin, *Mundus imaginalis*.

[131] Tom Cheetham, *The World Turned Inside Out: Henry Corbin and Islamic Mysticism* (Woodstock, CT: Spring, 2003). The experience of the ontological 'super-reality' of the spiritual world is confirmed by many communicators. See Fontana, 'Life beyond Death', ch. 9.

they certainly encounter their angel there; but where are the fastings or fires, drugs or gongs, frenzied dancing or sacrifices, burial rites or philosophical training? Michael Newton asks why this easy method of visionary travel should be available now to anyone without any ritual or religious context, and concludes 'I believe the spiritual door has been opened to our immortality because to deny us this knowledge has proven to be counterproductive ... The benefits of amnesia may no longer outweigh the drawbacks of lives existing within a vacuum of chemically-induced apathy.'[132] Unlike the *mystes* of old, these modern day travellers to the other world may speak freely of their experiences – and this very communicability has led Michael Newton for one to believe that he is tapping into the 'objective', universal reality that will await us all.

Postscript: Rudolf Steiner

One cannot address the question of initiation in the modern age without acknowledging the spiritual science of Rudolf Steiner, in which he advocates a method for human beings to develop and extend their powers of perception to the higher realms of spirit.[133] Following Plato, initiation for Steiner is a path of knowledge that will enable people to bring an Apollonian clarity of thought to bear on worlds normally inaccessible to the consciousness. In this he is an heir of Swedenborg[134] and embodies the enlightenment ideal of the attainment of truth through objective observation – indeed he insists that this is the most appropriate mode of knowledge for our time.[135] In his lecture 'Knowledge and Initiation' of 1922,[136] he points out that all initiatory sciences are peculiar to their age, and their purpose is 'to investigate and understand what is eternal in the human being and the universe'. The aim is to develop a process of 'imaginative', 'inspirational' and finally 'intuitive' thinking through intensive meditative exercises which empty

---

[132] Newton, *Destiny*, p. 397.

[133] Rudolf Steiner, 1861–1925, esoteric teacher, founder of the anthroposophical movement. Of his many writings *Occult Science: An Outline* (1925, repr. London: Rudolf Steiner Press, 1963) gives a comprehensive exposition of the aims of spiritual science and the path of 'thinking' as a spiritual discipline.

[134] Emanuel Swedenborg, 1688–1772, protestant visionary whose angelic communications gave rise to a detailed taxonomy of the spiritual realm and the condition of the human soul after death. For an introduction to his works, see Michael Stanley (ed.), *Emanuel Swedenborg*, Western Esoteric Masters Series (Berkeley: North Atlantic Books, 2003).

[135] 'Anthroposophy ... seeks to develop a knowledge and perception of the spiritual worlds which is no less exact, no less conscientious in the sense of exact science, than is the best tendency and striving of our natural scientific age.' R. Steiner, *'Knowledge and Initiation'* Lecture, 14 April 1922, at Rudolf Steiner Archive: http://wn.rsarchive.org/Lectures/GA/GA0211/19220414p01.html (p. 1).

[136] As above. All following quotations are from this lecture.

the consciousness of all interfering thoughts, so that an awareness of what he calls 'super-sensible reality' can emerge. This is not like ordinary memory, reflection or conception, but requires a shift in consciousness, a 're-visiting' the realm of spirit through cultivating 'the forces of the soul'. In this way, 'we are led to what is essentially the soul and spiritual being of man that lived in the spiritual worlds before it united with the physical substance of heredity ... We come to know our own eternal being, our life of soul and spirit in the spiritual worlds before birth.'

These are exactly the claims of LBL, with remarkably similar techniques of consciously 'going backwards' in memory until one passes through birth, and through the moment of death 'in full consciousness'. Steiner stresses that this vision is not a hallucination, and that the subject retains full presence of mind, full control and 'firm and sound judgement'. He claims that ancient mystery forms of initiation such as those at Eleusis had 'vision without knowledge', and that participants in this kind of ritual were completely identified with their 'visions and hallucinations' and thus unable to maintain full independence of mind. It is the task, he believes, of modern man to gain a higher knowledge of spiritual soul-being in the universe while holding together the opposites of critical thinking (and I refer back here to Michael Newton's comment that clients should be able to 'analyze critically' the things they see) and observation of spiritual phenomena. Through developing faculties of imagination and inspiration, one may arrive finally at the intuitive knowledge where 'we pass in conscious experience out through the gate of death and experience our immortality'.[137] Steiner makes a clear distinction between 'faith or belief' and 'clear knowledge', and is distrustful of 'vague kinds of mysticism' which cannot give rise to 'exact knowledge'. In fact he states that 'imagination, inspiration and intuition' are 'the very opposite' of 'visionary, hallucinatory, or mystical experiences' and he would therefore no doubt be distrustful of 'knowledge' obtained under hypnosis, if the individual did not maintain a fully conscious awareness at all times.

It is difficult to judge whether the visions obtained through LBL would be regarded as hallucinations by Steiner, and indeed the very question of how authentically imaginal vision can be relayed as 'objective knowledge' in this world gives rise to a post-Cartesian epistemological dilemma.[138] However, I would suggest that Steiner's model has deep resonances with LBL therapy, indeed it is the model that informs most psychical research today. It would seem that the spiritual world is

---

[137] Michael Newton also mentions that his method involves a consideration of 'the I signs of the soul: insight, imagination and intuition' (*Life between Lives*, p. 9), but he makes no acknowledgement of Steiner's similar threefold scheme.

[138] It would be absurd to any ancient initiate to differentiate between 'objective' and 'subjective' truth. See Gerhard Wehr, *Jung and Steiner* (Great Barrington, MA: Anthroposophic Press, 2002), particularly Appendix 3, 'Depth Psychology and Anthroposophy'. Wehr suggests that Jungian 'active imagination' would be akin to the first stage of anthroposophical knowledge, the 'imaginative', and would be preparatory to the higher levels of inspiration and intuition (p 305).

making itself known to Western men and women through models of consciousness-expansion, psychological therapy and technology.[139] Yet the archetypal roles of the players in the game remain the same: hierophant or therapist, client or *mystes*, spirit guide or *daimon*, Source or God. At the heart of the LBL experience lies the divinatory encounter, as the messages of the gods are revealed and communicated in a ritual of dialogue. Ancient mystery rituals may not involve interaction and encounter in the same way, but whether formally asked or not, the implicit question 'am I immortal?' is answered in no uncertain terms in both cases. There may no longer be a secret that cannot be told on pain of death (although the question of *how* to speak of it still remains), but the knowledge that is given to the modern *mystes* who parts with a large sum of money to spend several hours under hypnosis would appear to be every bit as life-changing as the *visio beatifica* in the *Telesterion* at Eleusis.[140]

My conclusion in this brief overview is that we cannot dismiss the possibility that life between lives therapy is of comparable significance, in terms of extending the capacities of human perception to the dimension we call 'spiritual', to the rituals of antiquity. But is it truly initiatory? Are techniques such as LBL merely comforting illusions, 'quick fixes' that may remove certain existential anxieties, but will never lead the individual to a true *catharsis* in this life? What is the 'real' message of the dialogue with the 'other' that is opened up here, for contemporary men and women? And perhaps most importantly of all, how can *any* transcendent experience be adequately articulated through forms which are necessarily limited by the constraints of sense-perception on the one hand, or the conceptual mind on the other? We can only glimpse the place 'beyond' in the terms of this one, and since we live in an age of literalization, of academic, scientific and religious fundamentalism which has no room for imaginal modes of knowledge, spiritual entities are now required to present themselves 'literally' to be believed, to be photographed, videoed and recorded to 'prove' their existence.[141] They are even speaking through computers and radios.[142] Psychic consumerism abounds; guardian angels can be conversed with under the guise of therapy or neo-shamanic workshops, mediums are two a penny. Access to the spiritual realm has been removed from the domain of sacred ritual and made available on internet sites and phone lines, and as a result the gulf grows ever wider between 'new age' and orthodox religious mentalities. Finally, I remain in agreement with Carol Zaleski,

---

[139] See n. 142 below.

[140] Kerenyi uses this term to denote the supreme vision of the deity, as in Christian mysticism (*Eleusis*, p. 95).

[141] See, for example, Solomon and Solomon, *Scole Experiment*.

[142] This phenomenon is called 'instrumental transcommunication'. See D. Gullà, 'Computer-based Analyses of Supposed Paranormal Voices', in A. Cardoso and D. Fontana (eds), *Proceedings of the First International Conference of Current Research into Survival of Physical Death, with Special Reference to Instrumental Transcommunication* (Vigo, Spain: ITC Journal Publications, 2004).

who pleads for an approach to contemporary otherworld vision that is based on a
pragmatic attention to individuals' experience and a re-location of such experience
within an imaginal framework, so that, like the ancient mysteries, its healing and
transformatory potential rather than the mechanics of its operation (the 'why'
rather than the 'how') becomes the primary focus of research:

> If we fully recognized the symbolic nature of near-death testimony (and accept
> the limits that imposes on us), then in the end we will be able to accord it a value
> and a validity that would not otherwise be possible; this in turn will yield further
> insight into the visionary, imaginative, and therapeutic aspects of religious
> thought in general.[143]

Primary Sources

Cicero, *Laws,* trans. Niall Rudd, *Republic and Laws* (Oxford: Oxford University
  Press, 1998).
Cicero, 'The Dream of Scipio', *De re publica,* Book 6, trans. Niall Rudd, *Republic
  and Laws* (Oxford: Oxford University Press, 1998).
Homer, *Odyssey,* ed. D.C.H. Rieu and Peter Jones (Harmondsworth: Penguin
  Classics, 2002).
Iamblichus, *On the Mysteries,* trans. E. Clarke, J. Herschbell and J. Dillon (Atlanta:
  Society for Biblical Literature, 2003).
Plato, *Collected Dialogues,* ed. E. Hamilton and H. Cairns (Princeton: Princeton
  University Press, 1961).
Plutarch, *On the E at Delphi (Moralia,* vol. V*), On the Daimon of Socrates, The
  Myth of Timarchus (Moralia,* vol. VII*) (*Cambridge, MA: Loeb Classical
  Library, 1936 [vol. V], 1959 [vol. VII]).
Virgil, *Aeneid,* trans. W.F. Jackson Knight (Harmondsworth, Penguin Classics,
  1956).

Further Reading

Collins, John J. and Fishbane, Michael (eds), *Death, Ecstasy and Other Worldly
  Journeys* (Albany: State University of New York Press, 1995).
Fontana, David, 'Why the Opposition to Evidence for Survival?', *Scientific and
  Medical Network Review* (Spring 2007), pp. 3–6.
Godwin, Joscelyn, *Mystery Religions of the Ancient World* (London: Thames and
  Hudson, 1981).
Kerenyi, Karl, *Dionysos: Archetypal Image of Indestructible Life* (Princeton:
  Princeton University Press, 1976).

---

[143] Zaleski, *Otherworld Journeys,* p. 192.

Meyer, Marvin W. (ed.), *The Ancient Mysteries: A Sourcebook of Sacred Texts (1987, repr.* Philadelphia: University of Pennsylvania Press, 1999).

Sandys, Cynthia and Lehmann, Rosamund, *Letters from our Daughters, Part 1, Sally* (London: College of Psychic Science, 1957).

Shaw, Gregory, 'Containing Ecstasy: The Strategies of Iamblichean Theurgy', *Dionysius*, vol. XXI (Dec. 2003), pp. 53-88.

Steiner, Rudolf, *Life Beyond Death* (Forest Row: Rudolf Steiner Press, 2003).

Ulansey, David, *The Origin of the Mithraic Mysteries* (Oxford: Oxford University Press, 1991).

Chapter 12

Talking and Walking with Spirits: Fresh Perspectives on a Medieval Necromantic System

Paul Devereux

We know of various forms of medieval necromancy. One was *utiseta*, the Norse practice of 'sitting out' on prehistoric burial mounds or in cemeteries for divinatory purposes. Variations on this practice occurred all over Europe. Another Norse tradition was crossroads divination, particularly well recorded in Iceland, though it happened throughout northern Europe if not further afield. In Iceland, the seer would resort to a lonely crossroads from which a church was visible, or where one of the roads ran *straight* to a church, put on an animal skin and go into a trance by staring at a polished axe blade while lying perfectly still. When, in a trance state, he perceived that spirits had glided up to the crossroads he would interrogate them for divinatory purposes. In Britain, there was the church-porch watch tradition, in which the local 'ghost seer' would hold a vigil between 11 p.m. and 1 a.m. at certain times of the year at the church door or in the graveyard, at the lych-gate (where the funeral party entered the churchyard) or in a nearby lane. The seer would look for the wraiths of those who would die in the following twelve-month period entering the church. A yet further variant was stile divination, in which passing spirits could be interrogated at certain stiles on particular nights of the year.

Resulting from research over the last few years, this chapter will suggest that these necromantic practices were all aspects of a *single system* of medieval necromancy related to the nearly forgotten landscape features known as 'corpse roads' or 'church-way paths' (terms used interchangeably in this chapter), the features that tied together the divinatory use of crossroads, stiles, burial places and churches, and were themselves sites of seership.

Corpse Roads and Church-way Paths

The basic, material facts concerning corpse roads are straightforward enough: they provided a functional means of allowing walking funerals to transport corpses to cemeteries that had burial rights. In England in the tenth century, for instance, burial rights became an issue with the beginning of a great expansion of church building which inevitably encroached on the territories of existing mother churches or minsters. There was a demand for autonomy from outlying settlements, which minster officials felt could erode their authority, not to mention their revenue, so they decided to institute corpse ways that led from outlying locations to the mother church at the heart of the parish, the one that alone held the burial rights. For some parishioners this meant corpses had to be transported quite long distances, sometimes over difficult terrain. 'Corpse roads' developed as a special class of footpath because of this. They were also known by other names such as bier roads, burial roads, coffin lines, funeral roads or lychways. Reference to such paths is also found as far back as Saxon times as *deada waeg*, presumably the etymological roots of the Dutch term for corpse roads, *Doodwegen* ('deathroads'). A corpse road was usually synonymous with a church-way path or church-way – that is, a road specifically for going to and from a church ('mass roads' in Ireland) – but that was not necessarily always the case. (It was popularly believed that if a walking funeral crossed someone's land then it would thereafter become a public right of way, and though this never seems to have been the case in law many landowners were not keen on allowing such funeral processions passage across their property. Consequently, corpse ways tended to follow established routes to the church, and these were typically the church-way paths used by worshippers from outlying farms and communities to attend church on Sundays and holy days.)

Corpse roads are therefore primarily medieval features – though some are later, dating to the early modern period. Many have disappeared while the original purpose of those that survive as footpaths has been largely forgotten. Survivors still possessing overt reference to their original purpose include the Lych Way on Dartmoor, Devon, which runs from roughly the centre of the moor to Lydford Church on the perimeter, crossing the Rive Tavy by means of the Cataloo Steps near Coffin Wood; the Old Corpse Road that once linked Mardale Green (now submerged beneath Haweswater) to Shap in Cumbria; the Old Hell Way on the North York moors, linking the valley of Fryup to St Hilda's churchyard in Danby Dale; and Burial Lane which links a now defunct chapel at Cruise Hill, Worcestershire, with the village of Feckenham.

Some corpse roads now exist as recreational routes but their former purpose can sometimes be noted by certain features along them. For instance, a path that connects Rydal (of Wordsworth fame) with Grasmere in the Lake District is used by tourists who are oblivious as to its original purpose, but halfway along it is a massive rock with a seat around it – the place where the cortege would stop, allowing the bearers to rest while singing hymns and saying prayers. Again, church-way paths in Penwith, the Land's End district of Cornwall, are typically marked with low, round-headed wayside Celtic crosses. As W. Haslam remarked in 1847, the function of many of the crosses was to 'guard and guide the way to the church'. He went on: 'In several parishes there are "church paths", still kept up by the parish, along which crosses, or bases of crosses, yet remain, and generally it will be found that they point toward the church.'[1] Fields crossed by church-way paths often had names like 'Churchway Field' to identify the special routes passing through them, and it is sometimes possible to plot the course of a church-way by old field names even after the path itself has disappeared.

A Deeper History

In simple terms, then, church-way paths or corpse roads were simply the routes used to take the dead to cemeteries that had burial rights. But our research indicates that there is a deeper and more complex association with them. This is hinted at by Shakespeare, in fact, in *A Midsummer Night's Dream*, where he has that mischievous nature spirit Puck say:

> Now it is the time of night,
> That the graves all gaping wide,
> Every one lets forth his sprite,
> In the church-way paths to glide. (V. i. 375–8)

The Bard was referring to the remnants of a very ancient spirit lore tradition in Europe, which still survived in England in Shakespeare's time. This spirit lore had attached itself to the corpse roads, because they ran not only through the physical landscape but also through the mental geography of the folk mind. This lore stated that spirits, whether ghosts of the dead or nature spirits like fairies (or like Puck!), travelled through the land along special routes. It was thought that *straightness* facilitated the passage of spirits and that convoluted pathways, such as stone or turf labyrinths, crossroads or even tangles of threads, hindered their progress.

Vestigial evidence of this archaic spirit lore is revealed by a variety of physical and 'virtual' features across Europe. The virtual features were invisible paths that existed only in the folk mind but were accorded a geographical reality. An example existed in Nemen, Russia, where there was the belief in a *Leichenflugbahn*, literally 'corpse flight path'. There were two cemeteries in the town and spirits were believed to be able to travel between the two places. These ghosts were said to fly along on a direct course close to the ground, so a straight line connecting the two places was kept clear of fences, walls and buildings in order that they would not be obstructed. The Germans had similar virtual paths they called *Geisterwege* that linked actual, physically real cemeteries. Although conceptual, these spirit paths likewise had a definite geography in local folklore, and people would be sure to avoid them at night. They were also straight. The *Handwortbuch des deutschen Aberglaubens* describes them thus:

---

[1]   W. Haslam, cited in Arthur Langdon, *Old Cornish Crosses* (Truro: Joseph Pollard, 1896), p. 7.

The paths, with no exception, always run in a straight line over mountains and valleys and through marshes ... In towns they pass the houses closely or go right through them. The paths end or originate at a cemetery. This idea may stem from the ancient custom of driving a corpse along a special dead man's road, therefore this way or road was believed to have the same characteristics as a cemetery; it is a place where spirits of the deceased thrive.[2]

In Ireland and other Celtic lands there were 'fairy paths' that were considered as being straight even though invisible – they had such perceived geographical reality in the minds of the country people that building practices were adopted to ensure they would not be obstructed.

Fairies and the spirits of the dead held a curiously ambiguous relationship in the peasant mind: for instance, American folklorist W.Y. Evans-Wentz was told about paths of the dead in Brittany that he could not distinguish from the beliefs about fairy paths elsewhere. The specific Breton tradition related to the *Ankou*, the last man to die in a parish during the year. For the next twelve months he was King of the Dead, and he and his subjects 'like a fairy king and fairies, have their own particular paths or roads over which they travel in great sacred processions'.[3]

The actual, physical corpse roads of Britain and Continental Europe vary between being dead straight and not particularly straight. Notably straight ones include the Medieval Dutch *Doodwegen* (death roads), which were officially checked on an annual basis to ensure their straightness and regular width.

There are fragments of evidence and lore that indicate the actuality of an association between corpse roads and spirits. A documented contemporary tradition relating to a corpse road at Aalst, Belgium, informs that mourners had to intone: 'Spirit, proceed ahead, I'll follow you'. This suggests that the spirit connection was alive and well when the roads were being used, and is not some falsified folk memory added later. This is further indicated by the fact that another Dutch term for a corpse road was *Spokenweg*, spook or ghost road. Furthermore, ghostly happenings were thought to occur on death roads in the Netherlands, and that they should be avoided at night because of this. German lore similarly maintained that corpse roads took on the 'magical characteristics of the dead' and should not be obstructed.

There is also an abundance of generalized lore about how the dead had to be conveyed along corpse roads to avoid their spirits returning along them to haunt the living. It was a widespread custom, for example, that the feet of the corpse be kept pointing away from the family home on its journey to the cemetery. Other minor ritualistic means of preventing the return of the dead person's shade included ensuring that the route the corpse took to burial would take it over bridges or stepping stones across streams (for spirits could not cross open, running water),

[2]   *Handwörterbuch des deutschen Aberglaubens* (Berlin: de Gruyters, 1933), trans. Ulrich Magin.

[3]   Y.W. Evans Wentz, *The Fairy-Faith in Celtic Countries* (Gerrard's Cross: Colin Smythe, 1977), p. 218.

stiles and various other liminal locations, all of which had reputations for hindering the free passage of spirits. In old Europe, crossroads were included as another such place (the corpses of suicides were buried at crossroads, for example, so that their spirits would be 'bound' there, and for similar reasons gallows were often erected at them). It was generally considered 'unlucky' to take a corpse to burial by a route other than the customary corpse way, and what this meant was that if the body was not taken by this route the ghost of the departed might return to haunt its neighbours and relatives, or would wander the land as a lost soul – or even as an animated corpse, for the belief in revenants was widespread in medieval Europe. It was further believed that church paths leading to and from cemeteries needed to be swept at certain times of year so as to dislodge spirits haunting them. Occasionally, 'spirit traps' (webs of thread – typically red thread – on a framework) were placed on them to snare flitting phantoms.

Divination

There was a Dutch tradition concerning a class of diviners called *voorlopers* or *veurkieken*, 'precursors', who were specifically associated with the Dutch death roads. They were seers able to tell who was going to die soon in the community because they had the ability to see spectral funeral processions pass along the death road they visited or lived alongside. Evans-Wentz recorded a similar tradition near Carnac in Brittany. There is fragmentary evidence that there was a similar church-way seer tradition in Britain too. In his book *Forty Years in a Moorland Parish*, the eighteenth-century vicar of Danby Dale, John Atkinson, told of 'Old Margaret', at Fryup, Yorkshire, who was well-known locally for keeping the 'Mark's e'en watch' (church seership) and who lived directly alongside the corpse way known as the Old Hell Road mentioned above. Eventually she saw her own wraith and warned her neighbours that she would die shortly, and that her body was to be taken to burial in the church cemetery in Danby Dale along the 'old road', the corpse way, or else she would return to haunt them.[4] As the church-seers observed spectral funeral processions coming into the church, it is reasonable to assume they too were observing the corpse roads with their 'second sight'.

There are other hints of a link between corpse roads and divination. Crossroads divination, for instance, was also conducted in former times in Britain and other parts of Europe, and as already noted crossroads were one of the types of location favoured as stopping points on funeral processions. Also conducted was stile divination. An old Cornish folk tale (documented from oral sources in the seventeenth century) tells that the ghost of a widow's husband carried her over the tree-tops and deposited her on Ludgvan church stile where she was able to interrogate passing ghosts about a domestic matter. The stile referred to in the folk tale still exists (it is a granite stile), and is close to Ludgvan church near Penzance.

---

[4]   J.C. Atkinson, *Forty Years in a Moorland Parish* (London: Macmillan, 1891).

That this is a folk-gloss of necromantic tradition associated with a corpse road is indicated by the fact that Ludgvan church stile is positioned on a church-way path.

Concluding Remarks

Behind all these fragments the outlines of a coherent body of spirit lore can be discerned, a corpus of spirit beliefs that persisted in the 'virtual' spirit paths traversing the folk mindscapes of old Europe and which also became attached to the actual, physical corpse roads, even if in a disjointed manner. Though corpse roads are in themselves medieval or early modern features, the spirit lore that became attached to them probably had its roots in ancient shamanic traditions, for contact with the ancestral spirits and spirit flight are quintessential shamanic themes. Throughout medieval and early modern Europe, from Hungary and Italy in the south-east to Ireland and Scandinavia in the north-west, and almost everywhere in between, there was for untold generations various traditions concerning trance practitioners in the form of village specialists who could enter an ecstatic mode of consciousness – the hallmark of shamanism – in order to conduct divination, or to protect the fertility of the fields, livestock and vineyards by means of 'night battles' against hostile sorcerers, or to obtain magical power. These specialists from different countries and periods of history often shared similar characteristics, and some scholars, such as Carlo Ginzburg and Eva Pocs, claim that they belonged to a common origin of great antiquity: an agrarian shamanism that stretched from Asia to Western Europe.[5]

This chapter suggests that the full context of crossroads, cemetery, stile and church divination has been overlooked and that they were in fact aspects of a single system of necromancy that was unified by corpse roads or church-way paths, which themselves were also used for divination by specialist seers.

Further Reading

Caciola, Nancy, 'Wraiths, Revenants and Ritual in Medieval Culture', *Past and Present* 152 (1996): 3–45.
— 'Spirits Seeking Bodies: Death, Possession and Communal Memory in the Middle Ages', in Bruce Gordon and Peter Marshall (eds), *The Place of the Dead* (Cambridge: Cambridge University Press, 2000), pp. 66–86.
Davies, Jonathan Caredig, *Folk-Lore of West and Mid-Wales* (Lampeter: Llanerch, 1992).

---

    [5]   Carlo Ginzburg, *Ecstasies: Deciphering the Witches' Sabbath* (London: Penguin, 1992); Eva Pocs, *Between the Living and the Dead* (Budapest: Central European University Press, 1999).

Devereux, Paul, *Spirit Roads* (London: Collins & Brown, 2007).

Evans, E. Estyn, *Irish Folk Ways* (London: Routledge & Kegan Paul, 1957).

Gordon, Bruce, 'Malevolent Ghosts and Ministering Angels: Apparitions and Pastoral Care in the Swiss Reformation', in Bruce Gordon and Peter Marshall (eds), *The Place of the Dead* (Cambridge: Cambridge University Press, 2000), pp. 87–109.

Harte, Jeremy, 'Show me the Way to Go Home', *3rd Stone* (April–June 1998).

Hinze, C. and Diederichs, U., *Sagen aus Ostpreussen* (Reinbek: Rohwohlt Taschenbuich Verlag, 1994).

Menefee, Samuel Pyeatt, 'Dead Reckoning: The Church Porch Watch in British Society', in Hilda Ellis Davidson (ed.), *The Seer* (Edinburgh: John Donald, 1989), pp. 80–99.

Palmer, John, 'Notes on Church and Corpse Roads in Holland', *The Ley Hunter* 127 (1997).

— 'The Folklore of Death: The Precursors', *The Ley Hunter* 129 (1998).

Puhvel, Martin, *The Crossroads in Folklore and Myth*, American University Studies (New York: Peter Lang, 1989).

Rees, Alwyn and Brinley, *Celtic Heritage* (London: Thames and Hudson, 1961).

Saward, Jeff, 'The Labyrinth as Spirit Trap', *The Ley Hunter* 133 (1998).

Simpson, Jacqueline, *Icelandic Folktales and Legends* (Berkeley: University of California Press, 1972).

Thomas, W. Jenkyn, *The Welsh Fairy Book* (Cardiff: University of Wales Press, 1995).

Chapter 13

Clarifying Divinatory Dialogue: A Proposal for a Distinction between Practitioner Divination and Essential Divination[1]

Anthony Thorley, Chantal Allison, Petra Stapp and John Wadsworth[2]

It seems to us that contemporary academic presentations of divinatory practice tend to fall into three broad categories or basic positions. These are (1) academics who are not practitioners of divination; (2) academics who are practitioners but who present their material as if genuinely separate and detached from their practice; and (3) academics who are practitioners and who acknowledge a more personal divinatory involvement in the material they present.

By personal divinatory involvement we mean that the academic material, while viewed externally, dispassionately and objectively, has in addition been acknowledged and admitted as being intruded upon and influenced by powerful and significant divinatory processes experienced by the individual, such as pertinent dreams and marked synchronicities, so that the boundary between the academic material and personal experience has become blurred. A clear example of this sharing of personal divinatory experience is to be found at the beginning of the chapter in this volume by Angela Voss on 'The Descent of Orpheus'.[3] This raises the question as to how much divinatory experience, or experience that we might best come to consider or categorize as divinatory, might be acknowledged as incidental to all normal personal and social functioning.[4] Indeed, we might speculate that such experiences as a divinatory phenomenon can be viewed as a rich but relatively unacknowledged feature of normal Western life.

---

[1]   Attending the 'Divination and Dialogue' conference at the University of Kent in October 2007 provided the stimulus for the ideas and subsequent discussion among the authors which has led to the construction of this chapter.

[2]   The authors are the founder members of *The Imaginals*, an independent academic study group established in 2005 to develop a philosophical framework that can accommodate the imaginal experience. Study areas include astrology, divination, phenomenology, animism and shamanism. See http://www.theimaginals.com

[3]   See Angela Voss, Chapter 11 in this volume, 'The Descent of Orpheus and Life between Lives Dialogue: Divination, Initiation or Therapy?'

[4]   See, for example, Roy Willis and Patrick Curry, *Astrology, Science and Culture: Pulling Down the Moon* (Oxford: Berg, 2004), p.148.

Before pursuing this idea of 'normal' or 'natural' divination further, it is perhaps necessary to examine a number of cogent definitions of divination which are reflected in the academic debate.

Some Definitions of Divination

We might start with that of Michael Loewe and Carmen Blacker in their valuable survey of divination and oracles:

> By divination we mean the attempt to elicit from some higher power or supernatural being the answers to questions beyond the range of ordinary human understanding.[5]

Blacker refines this in her own contribution on Japanese divination.

> By the terms divination and oracles I refer to the methods of communication between two worlds or dimensions which are usually divided from each other. We are trying to put questions which we are unable to answer for ourselves to another order of beings whose knowledge transcends the limitations of our own.[6]

Loewe in his chapter on Chinese divination also provides his own refinement:

> Divination ... may be regarded as an attempt to ascertain truth on a level other than that of verifiable analysis or quantifiable proof, and by means other than those which depend on reason. The process is possible thanks to the personal powers of an initiate to form or contact with external verities, by means, and towards ends, which he may or may not be able to control. Such is divination in its true form.[7]

In each of these definitions the enquirer is seeking truth (1) not usually accessible through normal rational thinking and (2) from a source that is variously considered as 'supernatural', a 'higher being', 'another order of being whose knowledge transcends the limitations of our own', 'external verities' or in another 'world' or 'dimension'.

Patrick Curry, who has carried out a carefully considered exploration of astrology as a divinatory process in *Astrology, Science and Culture*,[8] never actually presents a precise definition of divination in that account, but in Chapter 7 in this volume, on 'Embodiment, Alterity and Agency', he advances a more certain and

---

[5]   Michael Loewe and Carmen Blacker (eds), *Divination and Oracles* (London: George Allen and Unwin, 1981), p. 1.

[6]   Blacker, 'Japan', in Loewe and Blacker, *Divination*, pp. 63–86, at p. 63.

[7]   Loewe, 'China', in Loewe and Blacker, *Divination*, pp. 38–62, at p. 39.

[8]   Willis and Curry, *Astrology, Science and Culture*; see esp. ch. 5.

clarified statement of the nature of divination.[9] This is almost a formal operational definition, telling us precisely which practical and operational components must be present in order to satisfy the concept. Hence without any or all of them being satisfied, divination, by inference, is possibly not present or actually impossible to find. He writes:

> Divination is a ritual (synchronically) and a tradition (diachronically) constituted by, and constituting, an ongoing dialogue with more-than-human agents. It is enacted in order to ask them for guidance and/or discern their will in the matter at hand, to enable them to respond, and to permit intelligible interpretation of the response. An indefeasible part of the ritual, following from those requirements, is an act of aleatory randomization.[10]

Elsewhere, Curry has explored the basic tenets of astrology as divination and in particular how it relates to a 'more-than-human agency', and suggested that a natural dialogue utilizing the symbolic, and usually with nature in some form or with natural events (which may become signs), is a fundamental process lying behind divination. He draws attention to Lama Chime Radha's essay on Tibetan divination to emphasize this relationship of divination with natural events:

> As one works with the symbolism and penetrates more deeply into its meaning, one learns to arrive at an integral view of the world ... In doing so one develops an intuitive insight into the workings of the world of nature, which reflect universal principles, and that insight is the basis of the art of divination.[11]

Practitioner Divination

All these surveys of basic principles and definitions have been constructed and written in the main with a view to clarifying divination as an art or a specific practice, or as Curry has noted, a ritual event in a longstanding tradition.[12] This sort of divination can be clearly identified with a specific divinatory technique or practice, for example astrology, oracular consultation, the Tarot, Ifá, the *I Ching* or chieromancy, an identifiable mantic art, indeed possibly named as one of the innumerable 'mancies'. For simple reference, we might term these mantic techniques of divination, which require a specialist interlocutor or practitioner coordinating the ritual and interpreting the response between the querent, enquirer or client and the 'more-than-human agency', as *practitioner divination*.

---

[9] See Patrick Curry, Chapter 7, this volume, 'Embodiment, Alterity and Agency: Negotiating Antinomies in Divination'.

[10] Ibid., pp. 85–117.

[11] Lama Chime Radha, 'Tibet', in Loewe and Blacker, *Divination*, pp. 3–37, at p. 25.

[12] See Curry's definition above.

We are aware, however, that in characterizing practitioner divination we may be perceived as investing in such experts, as a kind of elite group, a special power or skill to make predictions of a fixed and immutable fate. However, we do not consider divination to carry such a fixed and non-negotiable quality and judge that it is important to de-mystify any concept of absolutism attached to such an elite group. For us, divination is more about the surrendering of individual will and opening to the experience of guidance from more-than-human agency, with or without the intercession of practitioner divination.[13]

Encultured Divination

Therefore we consider that there are settings where divination and a divinatory framework of explanation (and possibly cosmology) do not seem only to apply to or require practitioner divination but to extend to a whole culture and society and encompass everyone. We refer of course to those many indigenous and traditional cultures, worldwide, in which survives, to use Curry's words, the 'mode of a divinatory relationship with the natural world'.[14] Here, there may be specialist practitioner diviners, shamans and medicine men, but outside of their specialist role ordinary people in those cultures exercise their own divinatory enquiry by being acutely sensitive to the natural world, its events and the symbolic signs that can (and do) ensue in the context of a natural (and continuous) dialogue.[15]

In these cultures, asking for a sign to illuminate a query or specifically assist in finding an answer to a dilemma (or, for example, merely enquiring where animal game may be successfully hunted) is part of the natural process of life. And the signs are acknowledged, whether literally or symbolically, as carrying some form of information from the world, dimension or more-than-human agency that is beyond rational enquiry, and are acted upon accordingly. In these societies, ordinary people are using their own divinatory insights totally naturally as part of their psychology and culture. Such cultures are often seen as animistic, where natural dialogues between all forms of persons-other-than human are acknowledged as a given, and underpin the structure, organization and governance of the individual and the social group.[16] In such cultures, the divinatory relationship with nature is

---

[13]   See in addition, Curry's useful discussion of the 'essential condition' of divinatory processes in Willis and Curry, *Astrology, Science and Culture*, pp. 57–8.

[14]   See Curry, Chapter 7, this volume, pp. 85–117.

[15]   For example, see Willis and Curry, *Astrology, Science and Culture*, chs 10 and 11; Gerado Reichel-Dolmatoff, *The Forest Within: The World-View of the Tukano Amazonian Indians* (Dartington: Themis Books, 1996); Gerado Reichel-Dolmatoff, *Rainforest Shamans: Essays on the Tukano Indians of the Northwest Amazon* (Dartington: Themis Books, 1997).

[16]   See David Abram, *The Spell of the Sensuous: Perception and Language in a More-Than-Human World* (New York: Vintage, 1997), esp. ch. 1; Reichel-Dolmatoff, *Rainforest,*

for everyone, but more complex questions or culturally and ritually established petitioning (when will the rains come?) may require specialized practitioner diviners in the form of shamans or specially identified individuals.

As Alan Campbell has pointed out of even shamanism seen as a divinatory process, if it is viewed as 'a quality rather than an office, then it admits of degrees. You can have a lot of it, or a little of it ... You are either a chief or are not – that's an office – but you can be more or less shamanistic.'[17] Campbell states that 'the point is to loosen up the distinctions in our thought between the role (shaman), the attribute (shamanistic), and the act (shamanising), and allow an easy passage between them'.[18] It might be that in our Western culture, rather forgetful of our own indigenous roots, we deny the truth of this 'easy passage' and too easily attribute and split off and even invest in the power of divinatory 'office' (the astrologer, the Tarot reader and so on) and in doing so neglect (or avoid) our own 'divinatory responsibility' and the ability to 'tune in' and make coherent choices for ourselves.

Such divinatory responsibility, experienced and expressed by everyone in a society, also tends to be omitted from academic discussions of divination in Western cultures, and yet, as Curry has pointed out in his story of Karen Blixen 'reflecting on a spontaneous (and desperate) act of divination',[19] it is not extraordinary (at all) for intelligent rational persons in our own secular and materialist culture to ask (perhaps particularly when in crisis) for a sign. However, Blixen's act of divination is not practitioner divination, but something more everyday and personal, carrying an almost Gnostic quality in that there is no human intermediary but a direct experience of a more-than-human presence.

In 2004, when recounting Blixen's experience and the related experience of Val Plumwood as examples of bidden and unbidden contemporary divinatory dialogue, Curry tentatively ventured 'that divination is a *natural human faculty*, however unevenly distributed, which will appear spontaneously in the right circumstances', but commenting that 'the ideal conditions ... surely remain an indigenous/aboriginal animistic society'.[20] Curry did not develop the idea of a 'natural human faculty' of divination any further but speculated that 'if the wellspring of divination is a fundamentally human and ultimately animal faculty, however, it might well find and/or create new forms which allow it to happen'.[21]

---

esp. chs 1 and 2.

[17] Alan T. Campbell, *To Square with Genesis: Causal Statements and Shamanic Ideas in Wayapi* (Edinburgh: Edinburgh University Press, 1989), p. 110.

[18] Ibid.

[19] Curry, Chapter 7, this volume, pp. 85–117.

[20] Paper presented at the international conference on 'The Imaginal Cosmos', University of Kent, Canterbury, October 2004, published as Patrick Curry, 'Divination, Enchantment and Platonism', in Angela Voss and Jean Hinson Lall (eds), *The Imaginal Cosmos: Astrology, Divination and the Sacred* (Canterbury: University of Kent, 2007), pp. 35–46, at pp. 42–3; emphasis in original.

[21] Ibid., p. 42.

Curry's remarks were part of a broader paper contrasting, as he saw it, conceptual difficulties for Platonic-based Western monism to provide a fertile medium for divinatory enrichment as compared with more pluralistic traditions. This distinction drew a critical riposte from Maggie Hyde who was concerned to defend the richness, as she perceived it, of a Platonic perspective in divination studies.[22] It is not our purpose here to enter into this monist/pluralist argument, which will probably run for some time until it is suitably clarified, but to draw attention to Hyde's concern about how she perceived Curry apparently locating the basis of divination in aboriginal society (which he may not have actually said). She writes:

> This approach to divination roots it in the aboriginal and does not address its manifestation in contemporary western culture … The Londoner who uses the Tarot … or the west coast New Ager who throws I Ching coins … are worlds apart from the indigenous aboriginal shaman. For modern man, divination does not appear to be animistic or local.[23]

She further comments:

> Not *all* authentic divination either originates in, or comes to fruition through indigenous aboriginal practices. This is especially so with astrology, the Tarot and above all, the sophisticated metaphysics of the I Ching.[24]

Discounting at this point the tantalizing opportunity of further debate about the probable authenticity of the indigenous and animistic roots of practices like astrology and the *I Ching*, we note that in this statement Hyde seems to be perceiving the natural human faculty of divination in Western culture as *only* manifesting in complex divinatory practice such as astrology and the *I Ching*; in other words, as practitioner divination rather than the everyday *non*-practitioner divination exemplified by the Blixen and Plumwood examples used by Curry. Surely, if we are to pursue the possibility of a natural human faculty of divination evenly distributed in Western culture, we have to be open to it manifesting on a wider basis than only what can be identified in specialist practitioners?

If in 2004 Curry does not take his observation of a *natural human faculty* of divination any further, in his chapter in this volume he has suggested that 'it is possible to maintain a practice of divination which is integral to developing what Jung called "a symbolic attitude": an ongoing dialogic way of life in which the more-than-human world and/or its parts can symbolically answer enquiries

---

[22]   Maggie Hyde, 'The Cock and the Chameleon: Divination, Platonism and Postmodernism', in Voss and Lall, *Imaginal Cosmos*, pp. 47–54.

[23]   Ibid., p. 48.

[24]   Ibid.; emphasis in original.

which arise (consciously or unconsciously) in the course of living'.[25] Curry is not questioning whether such an ongoing divinatory dialogue is possible as a matter of basic principle, for it is clearly evidenced in indigenous and traditional cultures, but whether such a form of dialogue is possible in our own everyday Western culture. We address this question more specifically below, but first it is useful to deal with the issue raised by Lama Chime Radha that divination is closely related to the workings of the natural world.

Divination and Nature

There is a problem when seeking evidence of natural faculty of divinatory dialogue in our Western urban culture simply because such dialogue, as stated above by Lama Radha, does tend to get associated with nature, as if it can only happen in the natural circumstances of being outdoors in the countryside or in a rural setting, where, for example, a flock of birds or a deer running across one's path is considered to be more likely and somehow (falsely, we consider) more inherently *natural*. We note that even David Abram, in his enthusiastic celebration of the natural sentient world, has written of the difficulty of locating that world and experience of the more-than-human agency in a Western urban setting.[26]

Thus as we walk the busy path of urban freeways, packed pavements and crowded bus-stops, bathed in artificial light and within a web of electrical gadgets and technology, in what Abram calls 'the very structure of our civilised existence',[27] there seems little place for the flocks of birds or the random cry of a noted animal to guide us in our divinatory quest. And yet this tendency to exclude the *natural*, the sentient world and random event from our urban culture is inconsistent (and bordering perhaps on a sentimental view of the very idea of nature). We have plenty, indeed untold richness of opportunity in our urban culture to access more-than-human agency and natural randomness. For example, the number of red cars that pass before our bus arrives; the number of times the traffic lights will change before five o'clock. Will I drive safely through these green traffic lights before they change to red, to answer my question: yes or no? Will my mobile phone ring in the next five minutes: yes or no for my decision? The next song from the shuffle function on my iPod will be the sign. And even raw 'nature' can intervene: the pigeon that explodes into flight at our feet on the pavement, the rat that we see slipping between the sleepers on the underground rail-track on our evening journey home, the money spider[28] that runs across our hand in the business meeting, the splashed puddle from a passing car that drenches our clothes and ruins our élan.

---

[25]   Curry, Chapter 7, this volume, pp. 85–117.

[26]   Abram, *Spell of the Sensuous*, pp. 26–8.

[27]   Ibid., p. 28.

[28]   A money spider is a common form of very small spider found in Europe and worldwide associated with financial good fortune when it runs across one's skin.

These are all examples in the urban setting of significant natural events carrying as signs potential symbolic information worthy of our interpretation.

Essential Divination

We would suggest that such so-called 'magical thinking', seen as the linking of a question and the request for a sign which will be used for guidance, is not rare and unusual, but commonplace (if sometimes rather private) in our own culture and that it reflects a natural tendency to utilize a simple divinatory process on an everyday basis.

There are also other features of everyday divination in ordinary people's lives which need to be explored further. For example, as noted, Curry has proposed that it is very possible to live in a Jungian-flavoured 'symbolic attitude' utilizing conscious or unconscious requests in the course of everyday living. We consider that this is not a question of possibility but a fact of real ordinary universal experience. Just as Karen Blixen asked for a sign, so do many of us do exactly the same if we are honest about it. And more importantly, if we acknowledge unconscious processes of enquiry (as Jung most certainly would) we are unwittingly engaged in a natural dialogue with the more-than-human world as commonplace. Our unconscious enquiries and requests, needs, wishes and desires may certainly satisfy (1) the request, of Curry's definition and (2) the response, but whether (3), an interpretation or even an awareness of the response is transacted in the normal everyday experience (an exception would be something equivalent to active dream analysis in psychotherapy) is of course deeply questionable, particularly if the unconscious is literally of its essence un-cognized. There are important moments of course where our hidden thought processes do become externalized and we recognize the process (sometimes in a state of shock or wonder), and with some further thought and contemplation we can perceive the whole unconscious divinatory process successfully at work.

If we can consider or accept the tenet that our most natural thinking processes are richly gifted with potential for the symbolic, there may be other important ways in which everyday divinatory experience and dialogue can be recognized in Western culture. For example, there are those who set considerable store on life's strange coincidences, seeing them as meaningful, replete with symbolism and externalized information, indeed, essentially synchronistic. Such synchronicities and serendipity (not always advantageous) can be seen as the formal responses to conscious and unconscious requests arising from what appears to be randomized events or even chaos. Maggie Hyde, in her admirable account of Jung and astrology, has valuably explored the complexities of synchronicity between the querent, the astrological chart and the astrologer, showing how the external separation and 'objectivity' of the astrologer is virtually illogical as unconscious divinatory processes and dialogue ensue in what Jung aptly terms 'secret mutual connivance'.[29]

The tendency, strongly supported by anecdote and evidenced by best-selling books such as the recent *The Secret*,[30] of ritually prepared requests or desires to be responded to in relevant and powerfully significant ways, the so-called 'Law of Attraction',[31] may produce derisory comments from philosophers deeply uncomfortable with processes that deny logical causality,[32] but they are nonetheless part of the real and vital psychology of ordinary Western lifestyle and culture. No one who follows the preparations (certainly a ritual element) for asking a question or making a request as they leaf through their copy of *The Secret* is asked to be a practitioner-diviner, but simply an ordinary person.

There are of course many strange psychological experiences and unusual perceptions well outside rational thinking occurring in ordinary normal Western life that defy easy classification and may find themselves subsumed under terms like psychism, the paranormal, mysticism or even at a stretch, the psychopathology of delusional illness.

These classificatory havens and especially the infinite purview of psychology will always provide refuge and reassurance for the more sceptical enquirer who must necessarily reject any claim for the reality of widespread divinatory dialogue in Western society. However, many of these personal experiences could be considered, particularly after careful phenomenological analysis, as some kind of dialogue with a more-than-human world and in essence divinatory, but in this chapter we are not making that extreme claim. We are simply drawing attention to the reality in Western culture of ordinary people who are not adept at some divinatory skill such as astrology or the use of the *I Ching* utilizing natural divinatory dialogue in the course of effective decision-making in normal personal and social functioning.

The acknowledged psychological function that comes closest to irrational thought and always carries some degree of mystery and often profound creative novelty is, of course, intuition. This is not the place to enter into a detailed examination of the status and form of that function; suffice to say that although Jung paid great attention to the idea and saw it as one of the four primary psychological functions, it has received little academic attention since, possibly because such a

---

[29]   Maggie Hyde, *Jung and Astrology* (London: Aquarian Press, 1992), pp. 132, 163–7; C.G. Jung, *Synchronicity: An Acausal Connecting Principle* (London: Routledge & Kegan Paul, 1972), p. 85.

[30]   Rhonda Byrne, *The Secret* (New York: Atria Books, 2006).

[31]   Esther Hicks and Jerry Hicks, *The Law of Attraction: How to Make It Work For You* (London: Hay House, 2006); see also Dawne Kovan, 'Astrology and the Law of Attraction', *Astrological Journal* 50/1 (2008): 13–20.

[32]   See for example Julian Baggini, 'No Success Please, We're British', *Courvoisier: The Future 500* supplement of *The Observer*, 22 November 2007, p. 13; available at http://observer.guardian.co.uk/cvtf500/story/0,,2215135,00.html (accessed 18 March 2008).

capricious and unbiddable process does not easily lend itself to the experimental situation and the test of science.[33] When it is considered, intuition tends also to get rather idealized as a process that, when it can be evinced (by active question or unconscious process), is actually going to produce 'the truth', when in reality it commonly proves to be most unreliable and often plain unhelpful and disastrous.[34] This may, however, be no different from any other divinatory process, equally as unbiddable and capricious in response and content. Indeed Michael Loewe's definition of divination as 'an attempt to ascertain truth ... by means other than those which depend on reason' could easily be construed as intuition. It may be therefore that intuition, hunch and issues around heady creativity and powerful enthusiasm (from the Greek *en theos*, 'in the divine') are all features of a divinatory language that is absolutely normal and part of successful navigation through life's challenges. These are, however, wider questions that can only be clarified by further consideration and enquiry.

We are proposing therefore that in our own Western culture, as in any culture, we have the capacity to think symbolically and to have a symbolic attitude. This is the process that fires so much of the richness of our language, poetry, humour and creativity. Utilizing that symbolic attitude, we suggest that everyone to some degree or other engages in a divinatory dialogue with a more-than-human world, often consciously and certainly unconsciously, and makes requests and receives responses, whether they are recognized or not. When there is conscious recognition, there is subsequently the opportunity for interpretation and considered action. We see this process as inherent to the human psyche, and indeed of its essence. Not only is it essential in this regard, but it is also essential in the sense of being an irreducible component of normal effective functioning and everyday survival.[35] Without this essential divinatory function we would barely manage to chart a course through life. For this reason we would suggest that such normal inherent divination should be termed *essential divination* to distinguish it from *practitioner divination*. It goes without saying that all those astrologers, Tarot readers and other professionals who practise or research practitioner divination also experience essential divination in their everyday lives.

---

[33] C.G. Jung, *Psychological Types*, vol. 6, *Collected Works of C.G. Jung* (London: Routledge & Kegan Paul, 1971), pp. 366, 369; D. Myers, *Intuition: Its Powers and Perils* (New Haven: Yale University Press, 2004).

[34] Myers, *Intuition*, pp. 76–85.

[35] Essential as informed by the philosophical term *essentialism*: '(in logic and metaphysics) the view that some properties inhere necessarily in the individuals to which they belong'. See Thomas Mautner (ed.), *Dictionary of Philosophy* (London: Penguin, 2005), p. 199.

Essential and Practitioner Divination: A Relationship for Discussion

'Essential divination' is therefore the term we are proposing to encompass Curry's 'natural human faculty' of divination and, as he observed in 2004, '*A fortiori,* it can potentially be encouraged and developed.'[36] If everyone carries essential divination to some degree or another, operating recognized and unrecognized, conscious and unconscious, it follows that this natural faculty when recognized can be refined and developed by study and training in specific techniques and practices which would eventually lead to the status of practitioner divination, for example the astrologer, the Tarot reader or a recognized shaman. One is an inherent capacity, the other a developed and structured technique, each for divinatory dialogue, the latter possibly even carrying qualities of Hyde's 'sophisticated metaphysics'. However, we would suggest that neither facet of divination, the *essential* or the *practitioner*, has any certain claim to superiority in accessing the wise knowledge that divination is able to deliver. Both are equally rich in their capacity to present us with confounding and profound insight: the private dream or the well-interpreted astrological chart carries the same potential.

We are aware that the distinction we are making between essential and practitioner divination is a matter of degree, perhaps even a spectrum of potential complexity, and that it carries all the conceptual and technical problems of artificial separation. However, we see value in making this distinction (remembering that all forms of divination inevitably grow out of essential divination) as a way of advancing and clarifying academic dialogue and discussion about divination as a subtle and complex phenomenon.

In addition, we are emphasizing this distinction between essential and practitioner divination in order to draw attention to appreciating the fact that discussion and exploration of concepts of divination in the academy requires acknowledgement and admission of the importance of personal experience of essential divination by the academic researcher. Essential divination may have been a key component in the creation of the hypothesis or hunch that is being academically followed up; synchronicities and other unconsciously (or consciously) requested signs may have had great significance in the formation and crafting of the academic contribution or paper.[37] Because it is evident that such essential divination commonly contributes to the academic consideration and expressed study of practitioner divination, so that in reality the two processes are not entirely or always separate but actually merge or overlap, it is perhaps important for academics to say a little about their experience of natural divinatory dialogue as a prelude to or as an integrated part of their contribution.

---

[36] Curry, 'Divination', p. 42.

[37] For example, those of Voss (Chapter 11) and Grillo (Chapter 4) in this volume.

Academic Exploration of the Verity of Divination

There are clearly echoes here of the classic etic/emic distinction in the conduct of research into experiential belief systems.[38] Do emic practitioner-diviners such as astrologers make better researchers into astrology than etic non-astrologers? There are clearly valuable (and possibly differing) contributions from both sides and as Curry cautions us 'while an experience of astrology from the "inside" is invaluable to its analysis from the "outside", the former is no guarantee of the excellence of the latter'.[39] However, Curry has more recently offered a methodological prescription that the academic historian or researcher ideally 'should have experienced, for him- or herself, the truth of astrology in action, in practice, and without any *post hoc* "reaching after fact or reason" to disqualify such an experience as metaphysically, ideologically or personally unacceptable', as a valuable adjunct to asking academic questions about astrology.[40] Geoffrey Cornelius, in his important paper on 'Verity and the Question of Primary and Secondary Scholarship in Astrology', makes a strong case that primary scholarship into the verity – the essential and unique truth of the experience and effect – of astrology can only be carried out in the academy by practising astrologers and that the etic perspective can only provide a level of secondary scholarship which will inevitably fall short of authentic illumination of the verity.[41] What we are suggesting in this chapter is that although the verity (using Cornelius's meaning) of divination may also be elusive to those academics of divination who are not practitioner-diviners, it will probably be more securely examined and revealed if all academics, whether practitioner-diviners or not, freely acknowledge their experience of essential divination in their academic journey. In that sense, essential divination makes us all, to some degree, naturally emic.

We wish to make it clear at this point that we are not drawing attention here to the need for qualitative research into divination, when appropriate, to make use of autoethnography, personal narrative and reflexivity techniques so that the researcher can be seen as the subject.[42] This is a separate issue (which may indeed have its own relevance) which already enjoys a full academic literature and its own

---

[38]   K.L. Pike, 'Etic and Emic Standpoints for the Description of Behaviour', in R. McCutcheon (ed.), *The Insider-Outsider Problem in the Study of Religion* (London: Cassell, 1999), pp. 28–36.

[39]   Willis and Curry, *Astrology, Science and Culture*, p. 91.

[40]   Patrick Curry, 'The Historiography of Astrology: A Diagnosis and a Prescription', in K. von Stuckrad, G. Oestmann and D. Rutkin (eds), *Horoscopes and History* (Berlin and New York: Walter de Guyter, 2005), pp. 261–74, at p. 267.

[41]   Geoffrey Cornelius, 'Verity and the Question of Primary and Secondary Scholarship in Astrology', in Nicholas Campion, Patrick Curry and Michael York (eds), *Astrology and the Academy* (Bristol: Cinnabar Books, 2004), pp. 103–13.

[42]   C. Ellis and A. Bochner, 'Autoethnography, Personal Narrative, Reflexivity: Researcher as Subject', in N.K. Denzin and Y.S. Lincoln (eds), *Handbook of Qualitative Research* (London: Sage, 2005), pp. 733–68.

advocates. Our appeal is for academics studying divination, whenever possible, to acknowledge their experience of essential divination as an integral part of the presentation of research findings. How they actually do this may of course utilize techniques of narrative, reflexivity and autoethnography. Similarly, our appeal for divination researchers to acknowledge personal divinatory experience relevant to their work is to be clearly distinguished from any suggestion that every type of researcher, for example a psychologist writing about depression, should necessarily declare their personal experience (or not) of that illness, or whatever part of their personal life is reflected in their academic research material. Such non-divination subject matter may or may not benefit from personal declarations.

What we are saying is that to enquire academically into the specific matter of divination, that is to create hypotheses, follow up hunches, be gifted with intuitive breakthroughs and so forth, is to actively acknowledge that the creative process in the research endeavour can be credibly perceived as a contributing divinatory dialogue and therefore is inseparable from the specific aspect of divination that is being hypothesized, studied or written about. We are suggesting that divination (unlike depressive illness or aircraft design) is therefore a special case for research because the personal process of creative inspiration with all the myriad phenomena that inform and drive it is posited as divinatory in itself.

We appreciate that this is a challenging idea which many academics researching divination instinctively may wish to avoid in order to protect or conserve their sense of 'objectivity', or escape personal revelation, but we suggest that carefully integrated material about personal divinatory experience pertinent to the academic question being pursued may be of great value in helping to open up clearer and more honest thinking in the field of divination studies. At least we might suggest that if academics do not wish to integrate or reflect on such material they should state so at the beginning of their paper or contribution.

A Preliminary Conclusion

It is important to appreciate that this is a preliminary account born out of some general observations of academic presentations of studies on divination. We are not attempting to present an exhaustive and critical analysis of these two facets of divination but are simply laying before the reader a broad and provisional proposal which we believe may have merit in the field and about which we invite comment and discussion.

In summary, we are proposing that divination, as commonly defined as a form of request or dialogue with a more-than-human agency, intelligence or power and when practised in some form of recognized mantic process, for example astrology, *I Ching* and so on, can be usefully designated as *practitioner divination*; but more fundamentally, that divination can also be found universally present in all individuals in all cultures as a natural inherent and everyday process of divinatory dialogue (conscious and unconscious) which we have tentatively termed *essential divination*. We have briefly discussed the relationship and connections between these two aspects of divination and urged that academic discussion and the development of academic study of divination in general would benefit from acknowledgement and thoughtful integration and expression of both forms by those working in the field.

Personal Statement

Finally, while developing these ideas, we are unable to report with certainty any spectacular divinatory events, secret mutual connivance or marked illumination of the verity of divination. There was, however, one remarkable moment of synchronicity. While Thorley was intensely working mid-morning on his computer on a particular issue in this chapter (without any contact with the editor or other authors for over a week), Patrick Curry unexpectedly phoned specifically about a query over its publication, and as the handset was put down the phone immediately rang again. It was Wadsworth, again unexpected, able to answer another query about the chapter. The intensity of the *moment* of textual construction seemed to elicit a web of support and interconnection with key involved figures – which didn't *feel* like 'sheer coincidence'! Only two of us are practitioner-diviners (Allison and Wadsworth) but we all freely acknowledge and indeed welcome the part our own essential divination has played and is playing in our creative lives and in the constructive dialogue we have had in preparing and writing this chapter.

Afterword
Of Ises and Oughts:
An Endnote on Divinatory Obligation

Martin Holbraad

Truth, body and spirit. In his introductory overview, Curry singles out these as the three most promising paths for thinking opened up by this remarkable collection of studies in divination. More as an endnote than an afterword, I would like to add ethics as a fourth one. The theme, which is latent in a number of the volume's chapters, falls squarely within the analytical frame in which Curry places divination in the Introduction (and in greater and more wide-ranging philosophical detail in his own substantive chapter). What brings the chapters of the volume together, he notes, is a common urge against the temptation to 'accommodate divination … in what "we" already "know"'. A temptation that, as he explains, inevitably issues in attempts to account for what 'they' (that is, the practitioners of divination) cannot possibly know, because it is blatantly false, and can therefore only be said to 'believe'. This, in Curry's great phrase, is the analytical activity of 'describing and adjusting conditions of native error'. To the contrary, Curry argues, to the extent that the practice of divination does indeed contradict what we may, as analysts, consider to be properly knowable, taking divination seriously as an object of study must involve 'the hard work of revising our inappropriate starting concepts accordingly'. I want to suggest, then, that one of the things that we know in just this way, which is indeed contradicted by the practice of divination and therefore invites the hard work of analytical self-revision, is the putatively axiomatic distinction between fact and value – Hume's fabled contrast of 'is' versus 'ought'.

The omission of this line of inquiry from Curry's list of 'promising paths' may well be connected to the tenor of the book's critical agenda. As Curry notes, the concern with ethics – or at least with normativity – has featured prominently in the scholarly literature against which the book's argument is pitched. Indeed, its role in this literature exemplifies exactly the kind of analytical tack the book seeks to avoid, and this in the guise of 'social functionalism'. Importing into the analysis of divination Durkheim's Judeo-Christian (not to say peculiarly French) onto-theology of society as a moral force, authors who have found the 'belief' in divination sufficiently scandalous to warrant explanation have often resorted to finding value in its social effects. So: divinatory beliefs may be epistemically flawed, but they nevertheless make sense insofar as they can be shown to be socially useful. For example, as Mary Douglas remarked, while E.E. Evans-Pritchard's book on Zande divination became a landmark in broader epistemically minded debates about the 'rationality' of primitive 'modes of thought', within social anthropology it also provoked a whole series of arguments regarding the social and political efficacies of divination in varied ethnographic contexts.[1] From the point of view of this book's concern with taking divinatory practices seriously on their own terms, this strategy for 'explaining them away' ranks as a form of analytical displacement: since divination *cannot* be taken seriously by the analyst in this way, it had better be understood on terms that the analyst can take seriously on its behalf (in this case, questions of social order and organization, political power and legitimacy, and so forth).

So, contributors to this book may be said to resist this kind of displacement by seeking to tackle head on the notion that divination cannot be taken seriously on its own terms. The epistemic assumptions that have made divination appear so unreasonable (and not least the idea that divination is to be understood as an epistemic exercise in the first place) are put up for revision, and more appropriate ideas about what such things as truth, body and spirit might amount to in divination are proposed. Certainly, from a moral and political point of view, this spirit of engagement is more laudable than the smarter-than-thou conceptual imperialism (*sensu* Viveiros de Castro)[2] of much scholarship on divination, not to mention infinitely more imaginative intellectually.

A possible shortcoming of this approach, however, is that in seeking so positively to avoid sociological 'reductions' of divination, it effectively buys into the distinction that makes such reductions possible in the first place, namely the distinction between normative 'oughts' and factual 'ises'. If the reductionist strategy boils down to the idea that epistemically deficient practices can nevertheless have normatively useful effects, then the counter-strategy of refuting the premise that divination is epistemically deficient can easily end up affirming, if only by implication, the underlying assumption, namely that epistemic and normative aspects of divination can be treated separately. Arbitrating on the matter of how 'is' and 'ought' are best demarcated may best be left to philosophers. But it is

---

[1]   Mary Douglas (ed.), *Witchcraft Confessions and Accusations* (London, Tavistock, 1970), p. xvi; cf. E.E. Evans-Pritchard, *Witchcraft, Oracles and Magic among the Azande* (Oxford: Clarendon Press, 1937). Examples include J.C. Mitchell, *The Yao Village* (Manchester: Manchester University Press, 1956); J. Middleton and E.H. Winter (eds), *Witchcraft and Sorcery in East Africa* (London: Routledge & Kegan Paul, 1963); George K. Park, 'Divination and Its Social Contexts', *Journal of the Royal Anthropological Institute* 93 (1963): 195–209; Jack Goody (ed.), *Succession to High Office* (Cambridge: Cambridge University Press, 1966); and, more recently, Stephan Feuchtwang, *Popular Religion in China: The Imperial Metaphor*, rev. edn (London: Routledge, 2001).

[2]   Eduardo Viveiros de Castro, *(anthropology) AND (science)*, Manchester Papers in Social Anthropology 7 (Department of Social Anthropology, University of Manchester, 2003).

worth noting that the injunction to move on from the epistemological policing of divination towards a more serious inquiry into its ontological foundations (truth, body and spirit) would seem to keep things mainly in the court of the 'is'. What *is* truth, what *is* body and what *is* spirit in divination, go the ontological questions. And one might add that, as the tenor of many of the chapters of this book would suggest, answers to these questions tend to turn primarily on cosmological considerations (of planets, twins, gods, dreams and so on, fascinatingly), and cosmology too seems to belong most comfortably to the realm of fact rather than that of value. Unless, that is, one sets out to show that it need not.

My suggestion, then, is that part of what makes divination peculiar enough to warrant analytical exercises in ontological revision is that it transgresses habitual distinctions between the sociological (the normative ought) and the cosmological (the factual, or even the ontological, is). Indeed, I suspect that the ease with which scholars have been able to reduce the truth-claims of divination to their sociological effects is owed partly to the peculiar way in which divinatory phenomena so often seem to fuse these levels. In other words, it is arguably because divinatory phenomena *themselves* incorporate features that the analyst would recognize as normative that they so easily lend themselves to sociological reduction. However one might feel about its theoretical agenda, after all, the literature on the social roles of divination shows amply that a concern with what looks like normativity is hardly exclusive to the analyst. Most typically, it extends to the practitioners of divination themselves. From matters of royal succession, public dispute settlement and secret strategy in warfare, to questions of curing, comportment in love and the harmings of sorcery, divination seems to be an eminently moral act, if by that we understand – loosely for now – that in some sense it pertains to what ought to be done even as it pertains to what is the case. Diviners' pronouncements, one might say, are as much edicts as they are verdicts.

While the preceding chapters do not problematize the question of what may count as normativity in this context, they give plenty of clues as to its presence in sundry divinatory practices. Even on their own, Peek's and Tedlock's erudite cross-cultural surveys of the role of twin symbolism and dreaming, respectively, are replete with such references, particularly to the curative injunctions of divination. As for diviners' and their sponsors' explicitly political purposes, the most poignant example is Heimlich's report of the State of Arizona's constitutional provisions for settling tied election results by cutting a deck – not least for the issues it raises for the role of divinatory impulses in the contemporary world.

Following Cornelius's lead back to Evans-Pritchard's masterpiece on Zande oracles, the point can also be made with reference to a recent paper by James Laidlaw, which shows convincingly that Evans-Pritchard's book can be read as much as a study of the Azande's conception of ethics as a study of their epistemology.[3] Laidlaw writes:

---

[3]   James Laidlaw, 'Agency and Responsibility: Perhaps You Can Have Too Much of a Good Thing', forthcoming in Michael Lambek (ed.), *Ordinary Ethics: Anthropology,*

Evans-Pritchard makes quite clear that what 'witchcraft' explained for the Azande was not the occurrence of events or circumstances as such, but specifically their moral quality; if an event or circumstance were caused by witchcraft what this meant was that it was an act of human malevolence and therefore that someone, and someone other than the sufferer, was to blame for it. In addressing an oracle or a witch doctor and in attempting to identify who is bewitching him, an aggrieved Zande man was not seeking merely to identify a proximate cause. As in the famous case of the collapsing granary, he knew that already. (Termites ate through the supports.) What he was seeking was someone to hold to account.[4]

Laidlaw later contrasts the Azande's moral world to that of the Nuer (that other classic ethnographic case-study we owe to Evans-Pritchard), connecting it to their contrasting conceptions of the influence of supernatural forces, which, among other things, turn on differences in the prominence accorded to divination and witchcraft.[5] Certainly, there is no reason to assume that indigenous associations between divination and questions of morality are in any way uniform or, indeed, universal – they may be as varied as there are cases to describe. My point is just that if something that looks a lot like morality (and the allocation of blame is just one example of the kinds of phenomena that could be treated under this banner) can be an *indigenous* concern, as Laidlaw shows so clearly, this must raise questions that are analogous to the questions contributors to this volume have been raising with regard to the cosmology and ontology of divination. Furthermore, I want to argue, the fact that divination may (in certain contexts) raise questions about normativity *together* with the cosmological and ontological questions about truth, body, spirit and so on would also suggest that if normativity is at stake here at all, it may be so in a sense that rescinds the distinction between morality and cosmos.

In sketching these points out, I shall adopt the anthropological ploy of referring to a single ethnographic case – the one about which I know most, namely Ifá divination as it is practised in Cuba today. And since my point pertains to the connection between questions of cosmology/ontology and questions of ethics, I shall begin by drawing rather freely a parallel with my earlier work on Ifá, which focuses on the ontology of divinatory truth in particular.[6]

Language, and Action (New York: Fordham University Press). Cf. Max Gluckman, 'Moral Crises: Magical and Secular Solutions', in Max Gluckman (ed.), *The Allocation of Responsibility* (Manchester: Manchester University Press, 1972), pp. 1–50 and Mary Douglas, *Evans-Pritchard* (Brighton: Harvester, 1980).

4   Laidlaw, 'Agency and Responsibility', pp. 17–18.

5   Ibid., pp. 22–4.

6   For example, Martin Holbraad, 'Definitive Evidence, from Cuban Gods', in Matthew Engelke (ed.), *The Objects of Evidence: Anthropological Approaches to the Production of Knowledge* (Oxford: Royal Anthropological Institute of Great Britain and Ireland, 2009), pp. 89–104 (originally

Much in line with approaches taken by contributors to this book, my work on the notion of truth in Ifá divination is cast as a critique of approaches that reduce divinatory truth to questions of belief. In rudiment, the critique goes as follows. When scholars ask why practitioners might believe that divination is a good way of arriving at the truth, they must be assuming that divinations cannot be accepted as being true inherently. Indeed, the very fact that anthropologists have not traditionally balked at saying that most divinations – regarding witches, the influence of divinities and so on – are likely, actually, to be false shows that the putative 'verdicts' of divination are, to say the least, open to doubt. This, however, is analytically to put the cart before the horse. As far as practitioners of Ifá are concerned, the whole point of going to see a diviner in the first place is that his pronouncements, insofar as they are genuine, *must* be true. Divination, then, issues truths that have the peculiar characteristic of being beyond doubt. Certainly diviners (who in Ifá are called *babalawos*) may offer a false verdict, since, being 'imperfect humans', as one of my informants put it, they may make mistakes or even lie on occasion. But all this means, *ipso facto*, is that the putative verdict was not a genuine one. Genuine verdicts, practitioners of Ifá say, are ones in which Orula (the god of divination) speaks through the oracle, and the mark of Orula's words is, precisely, that they are true. Hence, from the practitioners' point of view, to wonder why people might 'believe' that divinatory verdicts are true is just to misunderstand what divination is – a misunderstanding equivalent to wondering why children in Britain 'believe' that 4 is a number, or, later, when they become of marrying age, why they 'believe' that bachelors are unmarried men.

I want to suggest that the same order of problem arises in relation to the moral character of divination – the observation that its verdicts are also, often, edicts. For one could imagine similarly 'reductive' questions being raised in this connection too. Why should practitioners of divination think that what oracles tell them is in any way morally compelling? How does the normative character of divination get 'constructed'? What is it that makes it so compelling to practitioners? Once again, just as with the question of belief, posing questions in this way presupposes that the pertinent puzzle is how the moral characteristics of divination come about. And again, this would involve the basic assumption that divination is not *inherently* moral or, in other words, that diviners' and their consultants' claims to morality – if such they are – are not to be taken at face value. Here, so to speak, is divination, and here is morality, and the job of the anthropological analyst is to work out through what mechanism the two are conjoined (for example through intersubjective negotiation, the dialogic character of the séance or what have you). Just as with the question of truth, I want to suggest the contrary, namely that Ifá divination is 'inherently' moral in the sense that moral obligation is constitutive to it: for a diviner's utterance to *be* genuinely divinatory is for it to *be* morally

published as a special issue of *Journal of the Royal Anthropological Society* 14, April 2008) and 'Ontography and Alterity: Defining Anthropological Truth', *Social Analysis* 53/2 (2009): 80–93.

compelling. Furthermore, the constitutive roles of truth and of moral force in divination are analytically interconnected: they are each other's corollaries.

Before sketching the argument, however, we may note a second worry with assuming that the interesting question is how the moral character of divination comes about, one that has to do with the implicit assumption that we might know what *counts* as morality in this context. To the contrary, the fact that as far as practitioners of Ifá are concerned the verdicts of the oracle carry moral force *by virtue* of being divinatory suggests that, if we are dealing with morality here at all, we are dealing with it in a sense that is different from any familiar understanding we may invoke as a starting point. Again, arguments I have made before about the issue of truth in divination may serve to clarify the kind of conceptual shift that is at stake here. If *babalawos'* verdicts are, for practitioners of Ifá, true by virtue of being divinatory, I have argued, then they cannot be true in any familiar sense. Hence, for example, a typical divinatory verdict such as 'your disease is owed to witchcraft' may appear to claim truth in the same sense as any ordinary statement of fact, such as, for example, 'your disease is due to high blood pressure'. (Indeed, anthropological analyses of divination that seek to explain why people believe in it rely on just such analogies.) The analogy, however, cannot hold, since ordinary statements of fact are inherently doubtful (the disease may or may not be due to high blood pressure, depending on the facts), whereas divinatory statements are not so, by definition. It follows that divinatory statements claim truth in some other sense.

While I shall explain what I think that sense to be presently, my point here is just that the reasons for being sceptical about the anthropological question 'what makes people ascribe moral force to divinations?' are identical, from the viewpoint of analytical strategy, to the reasons for being sceptical about the question 'what makes people ascribe truth to divinations?' In particular, if in the case of truth the analytical sticking point is the assumption that truth is a property of statements that represent facts, in the case of morality, as I propose to show, the analytical hurdle is the assumption that morality is a property of 'normative' statements, if by that we understand statements that prescribe a particular course of action in the face of alternative ones. So, to see the sense in which Ifá divination is inherently moral involves conceptualizing morality as something other than a matter of normative prescription.

Let us see, then, how these points fare with respect to the ethnography of Ifá practice. Why might one want to say, ethnographically, that Ifá divination is inherently moral? To make the claim plausible, the first step would be to get away from an image that has at times been propounded both by academic scholars of Ifá and by practitioners themselves in certain contexts,[7] which exalts the primordial

---

[7]   For example, in Cuba *babalawos* sometimes emphasize the 'ethical' content of Ifá practice not least when seeking to publicize their activities through official channels, and get recognition for them in a political context of state socialism. The title of a popular book by one of the more 'visible' *babalawos* in Cuba today captures it: *Ifá: Holy Word, Ethics*

'wisdom' of Ifá tradition by highlighting the ethical content of its mythology. As the longstanding literature on this profoundly magisterial form of divination shows, Ifá is based on a vast and highly complex corpus of myths, which in Cuba take the form of narratives known as *pataki* (among Yoruba-speakers in West Africa, where the Cuban practice originates, they take the form of verses, known as *ese*, but this kind of poetry has been lost in the translation of Ifá into Spanish by successive generations of Cuban *babalawos*). Much as with the mythologies of the Ancient Civilizations, this enchanting universe of stories has been something of an interpreter's paradise, with what Wande Abimbola, for example, branded the 'Ifa literary corpus'[8] being mined in the academic and exegetical literature for ethical significance that may act as an indicator of the universal dignity of 'Yoruba culture'.

From an ethnographic point of view, there are two related problems with this. First, while it is true that Ifá stories often take forms that could be compared, say, to Aesopian fables – a typical example would show a mythical personage getting into all sorts of trouble by failing to heed a particular divine prescription – only a very selective reading of the vast mythical corpus would yield anything resembling a set of moral precepts. In fact, much like in the ancient mythologies of Mesopotamia, Egypt or Greece, the divine personages that feature in Ifá myth – including the divinities themselves, who in Cuba are called *orichas* or *santos* – are just as likely to trick, steal or murder as they are to do good. *Babalawos*, who spend a life-time memorizing and studying these stories, readily explain this by emphasizing that what makes Ifá mythology so powerful is precisely that '*everything* is in it' (*todo está en Ifá*). Every conceivable form of action, be it honest or duplicitous, constructive or destructive, benign or malign, is to be found in some *patakín* or other, they say. Whatever is in the world, one *babalawo* I knew was fond of saying, is also in Ifá, since everything came from Ifá in the first place – a central tenet of Ifá cosmogony on which I cannot elaborate here. So one might say that, to the moralist, Ifá presents the same problem as Borges's map, which was so detailed that it ended up covering the area it was supposed to chart: if the search for Ifá morality involves identifying precepts that would recommend some forms of action over others, then it must be in vain, since Ifá mythology encompasses *all* forms of action.

This relates to a second ethnographic distortion involved in the search for an 'Ifá ethics', discussion of which takes us closer to what I think the moral character of Ifá divination is really about. And this is that if everything is in the stories of Ifá, as *babalawos* say, that is because their role is not to compose a 'literary corpus' but rather to act as a resource in the practice of divination. Let me explain. Ifá divination is based on a system of 256 divinatory configurations, which are called

---

of the Heart (Adrián de Souza Hernández, *Ifá: Santa Palabra, la Ética del Corazón* (La Habana: Ediciones Unión, 2003)); my translation.

   [8]   Wande Abimbola, *Ifa: An Exposition of Ifa Literary Corpus* (New York: Athelia Henrietta Press, 1997).

odu and are considered as divine entities in their own right. Each of the stories that *babalawos* learn (that is, the *patakines*) is associated with one of these *odu*. During divination, *babalawos* use a complicated technique involving consecrated nuts or a divining-chain to cast a series of *odu*, on the basis of which they are able to advise their clients. In parts of the séance the *babalawo* is required to recount a selection of the many stories associated with the *odu* that have been cast (those he considers most pertinent to the circumstances of the consultation), in order then to interpret their 'message' for the client. The role of this process of interpretation is demonstrably *not* to impart moral advice to clients. Rather, the *babalawo*'s task is, first, to use the myths in order to identify particular *concerns* that may be relevant to their client's circumstances (illness, love prospects, witchcraft, money issues and so on) and crucially, second, to prescribe appropriate *remedies* for them, which may involve particular magical cures, offerings or sacrifices to specific divinities, or other ceremonies, including steps towards the initiation of the client him or herself.

The diagnostic and remedial role of divination is, of course, well discussed in the anthropological literature and, as I noted earlier, features prominently in the chapters of this book too. What is not explored, however, is the sense of obligation that diagnosis and remedy impose on clients. In Cuba practitioners talk of this in the language of 'obedience'. 'It's true', a *babalawo* friend once told me, 'my job is to give people advice (*aconsejar*). But let them watch out if they don't follow it! You may come to me for advice as a friend, and I may tell you what I think but then it's up to you. But when you come to me to ask Orula – watch out!' Ignoring the advice given during a séance – choosing not to follow it – is, practitioners often say, 'to fall into disobedience' (*caer en la desobedencia*), and one does that at one's peril. Indeed, much like the myths of Ifá themselves, which are replete with illustrations of the horrible things that can happen when one fails, say, to perform a sacrifice ordained by Orula, the stories and gossip practitioners of Ifá exchange with each other in daily life are full of tales of the kind of calamity that Orula and other *orichas* bring to consultants who failed to heed a divinatory edict – a man who went to prison for failing to carry out a ceremony for Ochosi, the god of hunting; a woman who lost a child for failing to get initiated as a daughter of Ochún, the goddess of love; a man whose cancer relapsed for failing to complete a promise to San Lázaro, protector from disease.

A lot more ethnographic flesh could be added here, particularly to show how this sense of obligation allows the oracle of Ifá to act effectively as the prime regulator of the organization of worship itself, since the crucial matter of who gets initiated, and in what capacity, is itself ordained by divinatory means in Cuba.[9] However, let me cut to the chase of my argument on morality and obligation. The key issue, I suggest, has to do with the question of choice. Consider the comparison my *babalawo* friend made between advice given by a friend and advice given by Orula through divination. Suppose a friend tells you, 'you look sick; you need to

---

[9]   Martin Holbraad, Relationships in Motion: Oracular Recruitment in Cuban Ifá Cults, *Systèmes de Pensée en Afrique Noire* 18 (2008): 219–64.

see a doctor'. As the *babalawo* pointed out, in such a case it is up to you to choose whether you follow your friend's advice or not. Indeed, the very notion of advice, in this context, presupposes the possibility of choice: it is precisely because you have the option either to go or not to go to the doctor that your friend deems it appropriate to advise that you do. Now suppose that, basing himself on an *odu* cast for you during a séance, a *babalawo* tells you (as he might) that *Orula* says you are sick and that in order to be cured you need to perform a sacrifice to a particular *oricha* – say Changó, the virile god of thunder. It would seem, once again, that whatever obligation Orula's prescription places on you presupposes that you are free to choose whether to heed it, that is, you can choose not do the sacrifice he demands. Indeed, as illustrated by the stories about the calamities that befall those who choose to disobey the oracle, people do often fail to heed the oracle's prescriptions.

However (and this is the crux of my argument), such an analogy between ordinary imperatives voiced by a friend and the divinatory ones given by Orula is misconstrued. For while whatever consequences might flow from failing to follow a friend's advice are contingent, the calamities that befall those who disobey Orula are *necessary*. As far as practitioners of Ifá are concerned, and as their myths emphasize time and again, disobedience does not merely court divine wrath: it implies it, as it were, by metaphysical principle. And this crucial point pertains directly to the question of choice. What we are dealing with here, I suggest, is what classicists call 'tragic irony'. Like heroes in a Greek play, consultants may *think* that they have the option to ignore the edicts *babalawos* give them in divination. But what the stories of the calamities that necessarily follow such a choice show is precisely that the edicts of Orula *cannot be ignored*. You may think that you are free to do so, but in fact you are not – divinatory obligation will always catch up on you in the end, so the options you thought you had open to you were in fact always closed, by divine necessity.

So this is why the obligations that Ifá divination places on people cannot be characterized as 'normative', if by that we mean a moral force that regulates people's choices – do this, rather than that. The question, then, is how one might characterize divinatory obligation without appealing to notions of choice. Here I shall merely state what I think the answer is, and make a single point in its favour. The key premise on which normative conceptions of morality turn, I would argue, is that moral obligations are *external* to the moral agents upon which they operate. The normative realm (comprising injunctions such as 'thou shalt not kill' and so on) is, in other words, ontologically distinct from the agents whose choices it purports to prescribe. In the social sciences, perhaps the most familiar rendition of this assumption about normativity is that of Durkheim: the moral realm, society, is ontologically distinct from the individuals whose behaviour it regulates through 'socialization'. So what if one were to make sense of divinatory obligation by discarding just this assumption? What if one were to propose that the injunctions of the oracles were not external to the consultants, but rather internal – that is, internal in the philosophical sense that the very definition of the consultants (of what they are, ontologically) would depend on the oracle's pronouncements, in the same way as the definition of 4 depends on the idea of 'number' or the definition of 'bachelor' depends on the ideas of 'man' and 'unmarried'? On such a view, when an oracle tells you that you are ill and that therefore you need to do a sacrifice to Changó, it is not making a statement 'about' you and what you 'should' (given a choice) do. Rather, it is transforming who you are, turning you from a healthy person who has no need of Changó into a sick one who does. To fail to heed what the oracle says, then, is effectively to act against one's nature, that is, to act as if one were something other than one is, or, better, other than what the oracle has turned one into.

Clearly, the idea that Ifá divination induces obligations by interfering not with consultants' choices but with the consultants themselves – altering their ontological constitution – would need to be defended on more fronts than I can for purposes of this Afterword. I would, however, make a single and in my view important point in its favour, namely that it is analytically parsimonious. I noted earlier that the problem of divinatory morality is formally analogous to the more familiar problem of divinatory truth. Recall that the problem there was that practitioners are adamant that what makes divinatory pronouncements so special is not just that that they are true, but that they are indubitably so, and this implies that such pronouncements cannot be understood as representations of facts, since such representations are inherently open to doubt. Taking divinatory pronouncements as definitions that transform people (rather than as statements of facts about them) gets us out of this problem. Thus construed, divinations are true, precisely, *by definition* (since they just *are* definitions), and are therefore indeed indubitable, much like analytical truths such as 'bachelors are unmarried men'. In other words, the analytical shift that I am proposing renders the analysis of morality and of truth in divination as a single and coherent project – one that I suggest is worth pursuing.

Index